EPISTEMOLOGY

Other interview books from Automatic Press ♦ VIP

Formal Philosophy
edited by Vincent F. Hendricks & John Symons
November 2005

Masses of Formal Philosophy
edited by Vincent F. Hendricks & John Symons
October 2006

Political Questions: 5 Questions for Political Philosophers
edited by Morten Ebbe Juul Nielsen
December 2006

Philosophy of Technology: 5 Questions
edited by Jan-Kyrre Berg Olsen & Evan Selinger
February 2007

Game Theory: 5 Questions
edited by Vincent F. Hendricks & Pelle Guldborg Hansen
April 2007

Legal Philosophy: 5 Questions
edited by Morten Ebbe Juul Nielsen
October 2007

Philosophy of Mathematics: 5 Questions
edited by Vincent F. Hendricks & Hannes Leitgeb
January 2008

Philosophy of Computing and Information: 5 Questions
edited by Luciano Floridi
Sepetmber 2008

Philosophy of the Social Sciences: 5 Questions
edited by Diego Ríos & Christoph Schmidt-Petri
September 2008

Complexity: 5 Questions
edited by Carlos Gershenson
September 2008

Probability and Statistics: 5 Questions
edited by Alan Hájek & Vincent F. Hendricks
November 2008

See all published and forthcoming books in the 5 Questions series at
www.vince-inc.com/automatic.html

EPISTEMOLOGY
5 QUESTIONS

edited by

Vincent F. Hendricks
Duncan Pritchard

Automatic Press ♦ $\frac{V}{I}$P

Automatic Press ♦ V|P

Information on this title: www.vince-inc.com/automatic.html

© Automatic Press / VIP 2008

This publication is in copyright. Subject to statuary exception and to the provisions of relevant collective licensing agreements, no reproduction of any part may take place without the written permission of the publisher.

First published 2008

Printed in the United States of America and the United Kingdom

ISBN-10   87-92130-07-0   paperback
ISBN-13   978-87-92130-07-5   paperback

The publisher has no responsibilities for the persistence or accuracy of URLs for external or third party Internet Web sites referred to in this publication and does not guarantee that any content on such Web sites is, or will remain, accurate or appropriate.

Typeset in $\LaTeX 2_\varepsilon$
Photo (White Sands / New Mexico, 2008) and graphic design by Vincent F. Hendricks

Contents

Preface   iii

Acknowledgements   v

1   Horacio Arló-Costa   1

2   Sergei Artemov   11

3   Alexandru Baltag   21

4   Johan van Benthem   39

5   Luc Bovens   47

6   Lorraine Code   63

7   Fred Dretske   79

8   Pascal Engel   87

9   Robert J. Fogelin   95

10   Richard Fumerton   105

11   Clark Glymour   117

12   Alvin I. Goldman   121

13   Alan Hájek   139

14   Joseph Y. Halpern   155

15   Sven Ove Hansson   167

16   Jaakko Hintikka   179

17   Wiebe van der Hoek   185

18 Kevin T. Kelly	191
19 Hilary Kornblith	211
20 Martin Kusch	217
21 Jonathan L. Kvanvig	231
22 Isaac Levi	241
23 Rohit Parikh	257
24 John L. Pollock	267
25 Krister Segerberg	283
26 Ernest Sosa	305
27 Wolfgang Spohn	311
28 Timothy Williamson	323
29 Linda Zagzebski	335
About the Editors	343
About Epistemology: 5 Questions	345
Index	347

Preface

Epistemology: 5 Questions is a collection of interviews with some of the most influential epistemologists of the last decades. We hear their views on epistemology; its aim, scope, use, broader intellectual environment, the future direction of epistemology and how the work of the interviewees fits in these respects.

◆

Epistemology is thriving without any advertising and thus the idea was not to produce a bill-board for epistemology along the highways of science and buildings of academia. The idea was rather to produce a forum in which the giants of the field could speak their minds freely without the standard constraints of a scientific paper imposed. Posing five open and relatively broad questions turned out to be the perfect format for this. Besides fascinating intellectual biographies, career recaps and racy memoirs, the contributions – either in the form of direct answers to the questions or as complete essays based on them – offer interesting new conjectures, pointers to work overlooked, and methodological reflections on epistemology.

Given the format of this collection the purpose is not to articulate or push any particular agenda for epistemology save for perhaps two (inter-)related exceptions: In recent years mainstream and formal approaches to epistemology have begun to converge. *Epistemology: 5 Questions* is a witness to this effect and may hopefully serve as a fulcrum for the continuation of this fruitful interaction. Epistemology is also going largely interdisciplinary these days, and the spread of distinguished scholars invited to contribute to this volume mirrors this other fruitful tendency.

The responses to the five questions are self-contained, independently readable and no overarching view of the nature of epistemology is lurking in the wings. The ambition is much more modest; to initialize the discussion as to how epistemologists understand their own enterprise and why these luminaries decide to make epistemology central to their work. In addition to intellectual biographies the book does also have some interesting, illuminating and most importantly *instructive* stories to tell about the methodology of epistemology and its wide range of interdisciplinary consequences.

Vincent F. Hendricks & Duncan Pritchard
Copenhagen and Edinburgh
September 2008

Acknowledgements

We are particularly grateful to the contributors for devoting time to writing such erudite, enlightening and often thought-provoking interviews and grateful to the philosophical community in general for showing interest in this project. In addition we would like to express our gratitude to Claus Festersen and Rasmus Rendsvig when encountering LaTeX-related problems and to our publisher **Automatic Press ♦ $\frac{V}{I}$ P**, in particular senior publishing editor V.J. Menshy, for continuing to take on these 'rather unusual academic' projects.

Vincent F. Hendricks & Duncan Pritchard
Copenhagen and Edinburgh
September 2008

1
Horacio Arló-Costa

Associate Professor of Philosophy

Carnegie Mellon University, USA

Why were you initially drawn to epistemology (and what keeps you interested)?

I became seriously interested in epistemological issues in 1989 as I completed my master's thesis. My thesis work focused on formal models for the notion of belief revision, a topic mainstream epistemologists at the time only treated marginally. My advisor was Carlos Alchourrón who at the time worked with Peter Gärdernfors and David Makinson on a theory of belief change that became known as AGM theory. Although many philosophers had considered the problem of belief change before (e.g., Isaac Levi, Bas van Fraassen, Richard Jeffrey, and William Harper), AGM succeeded to produce the first axiomatization for an operator of belief change. Their approach afforded a clearer mathematical treatment of some of the central notions of belief change. This, in turn, attracted the attention of various researchers from communities outside philosophy (e.g., Artificial Intelligence, Mathematical Psychology, Economics, etc.).

Back then Bayesian epistemologists approached the main issues in epistemology with different tools but with a similar stance that was basically dismissive of a form of doing epistemology Bas van Fraassen called *defensive epistemology*:

> What I hope for is some reconciliation of the diverse intuitions of Bayesians and traditionalists, within a rather liberal probabilism. The old we might call defensive epistemology, for it concentrates on justification, warrant for, and defense of one's beliefs. The whole burden of rationality has shifted from justification of our opinion to the rationality of change of opinion. (Laws and Symmetry. Oxford: Oxford University Press, 1989).

The theoretical framework of AGM is in a way more flexible than the framework in which van Frassen developed his liberal probablism. It employs logical tools to represent belief and change of belief and therefore is not committed to the strictures of the Bayesian credo. Yet the theoretical framework of AGM has many of the same applications that Bayesians had considered, such as analyses of laws and conditionals, of the notion of explanation and cause, etc. In practice, many applications of the AGM framework tried to show by example that it was possible to develop a Bayesian epistemology free of numbers.

Still, the AGM theory has many limitations. Some of its axioms have been controversial (especially concerning the notion of contraction) and it lacks the expressive power to represent iterated changes of belief and to understand important notions like induction. The work in my PhD thesis, (completed at Columbia under the direction of Isaac Levi) addresses many of these problems.

Columbia was then (and is today) a repository of a rich Pragmatist tradition that influenced some of its most distinguished philosophers (Levi and Morgenbesser are salient examples), and this tradition, in turn, deeply influenced the work in my PhD thesis. The foci of my thesis are notions of supposition used in the analysis of conditionals. In my thesis I study in particular a purely synchronic notion of belief change and use it to develop epistemic models for conditionals and non-monotonic notions of consequence. Philosophically the idea was to develop an epistemic alternative to the possible worlds semantics for conditionals first proposed by Robert Stalnaker, Rich Thomason and David Lewis, among others.

In a way I continue to be motivated by many of these problems. Some of the issues that keep me interested are, on the one hand, relatively tractable questions that can be formulated in the context of formal models of belief, knowledge and belief change; and on the other hand, the deeper epistemological questions at the root of these local questions. Examples are the problem of induction, the problem of logical omniscience, and the nature of bounded rationality.

What do you see as being your main contributions to epistemology?

My main contributions have focused on various areas of formal epistemology.

a. *Bayesian epistemology*: There is a fundamental issue concerned with the relation between Bayesian and traditional epistemology: is it possible to take probability as the only epistemological primitive and derive the main traditional notions of epistemology (such as belief, belief revision, and conditionals) from this unique primitive? When the notion of probability is the standard monadic notion of probability this is impossible due to the so-called paradox of the lottery. But when the basic notion is primitive conditional probability it is possible to derive belief and belief revision from this sole probabilistic primitive. Bas van Fraassen first proposed the basic idea for this reduction (following previous insights by De Finetti). In a series of papers I have revised and extended this initial proposal. One of the main extensions (done in collaboration with Rohit Parikh) extracts conditionals out of primitive conditional probability. The model makes clear that the basic notion of probability must be finitely additive, indicating that the notion of conditional probability that is philosophically relevant is akin to the one proposed by De Finetti (rather than the one derived from the work of Kolmogorov).

b. *Belief revision*: What is the axiom system that completely characterizes a notion of contraction constrained by the principle of *cognitive economy*, which demands that loss of informational value be kept to a minimum. Recently Isaac Levi and I have answered this question in a joint paper. This provides the first completeness result for a decision-theoretic notion of belief contraction in the literature. Most work in belief revision assumes that selection functions used in models of belief change are *relational*, i.e. that there is some underlying binary relation—whether over all sentences, sets of sentences, worlds, sets of worlds, models, or sets of models— according to which a selection function picks the 'best' elements from its arguments. In the context of rational choice this assumption appears as the requirement that selection functions must be *rationalizable*. If the epistemic values of an agent are indeterminate, this assumption needs to be weakened. The agent in this case might face a *set of orderings* of feasible options. In this case it makes sense to select undominated options (maximization). In recent articles I have axiomatized a notion of *liberal contraction* along these lines. More generally, there are reasons to doubt the requirement of rationalizability in the theory of rational choice. Amartya Sen has presented convincing arguments articulating these doubts. In recent papers in collaboration with Paul Pedersen I study how a phenomenon called menu dependence arises in the area of belief change, threatening some of the central AGM axioms. We have explored how to accommodate the possibility of menu dependence in belief revision theory.

c. *Bounded rationality*: According to Herb Simon the term 'bounded rationality' is used to designate rational choice as it takes into account the cognitive limitations of the decision-maker—limitations of both knowledge and computational capacity. But recent work by Gerd Gigerenzer and his associates has focused on 'fast and frugal' methods that, when adapted to the environment, are accurate in spite of failing rationality conditions such as transitivity. Still it is possible to construct a theory of choice functions for algorithms of this kind. Paul Pedersen and I have recently identified constraints on choice conditions which completely characterize an algorithm called Take the Best. This is a first step towards developing a descriptively accurate theory of choice functions. The sole function of this theory is not to impose rationality constraints on choice but to faithfully register patterns of choice permitted by the bounded algorithm. The theory that thus arises still retains some of the abstract conditions of the normative theory of rational choice but the interpretation of these principles is different in the context of the descriptive theory. The conditions reflect regularities of choice functions that correspond to the algorithm, which, in turn, is taken as an epistemological primitive (selected in terms of its psychological plausibility and its cognitive virtues—like its accuracy).

d. *The problem of logical omniscience*: Most well-known epistemic logics suffer from the problem of logical omniscience. For example, they impose axioms requiring that all tautologies must be known or axioms demanding that proposition A is known and proposition B is known just in case the conjunction of these two propositions is known. Kripkean semantics presupposes these axioms, so if one wants to study logics for which some of these axioms fail, one has to adopt a different semantics. One possible alternative is so-called neighborhood semantics, first proposed (independently) by

Dana Scott and Richard Montague in the 1960s. When I first considered this option in 2002 I noticed that epistemic applications have never been considered and that almost nothing was known about first order neighborhood semantics, in spite of the fact that the most interesting philosophical applications required the expressivity of quantifiers (for example, the Barcan formula encodes the lottery paradox when the modality is an operator of high probability). So, in a series of articles (some of which were written in collaboration with Eric Pacuit), I characterized all first order classical modal logics in terms of an extension of neighborhood semantics (general first order frames) and I considered various salient applications. One of them is the logic of high probability and non-adjunctive logics more in general. Also Rohit Parikh and I showed in a recent note that neighborhood semantics can be used to formalize precisely and clarify conceptually the logic of knowledge proposed by Robert Nozick.

e. *Paradoxes of rationality.* The received view of rationality encoded in some of the most salient theories of choice (like Savage's theory) has been brought to doubt by well-known paradoxes. Daniel Ellsberg offered a particularly compelling one. In 2005 Jeff Helzner (Columbia University) and I initiated a research program whose main target is the analysis (empirical and theoretical) of decision situations under indeterminacy of the sort that appear in the Ellsberg scenario. Part of his research agenda focuses on testing experimentally the psychological theories intended to explain non-Bayesian behavior via the postulation of psychological effects; and in comparing the explanatory power of some of the normative theories that intend to rationalize non-Bayesian behavior. We have reported so far some interesting empirical results indicating the inadequacy of some of the most influential descriptive theories of uncertain choice. Ellsberg's own initial normative intuitions seem better equipped to interpret non-Bayesian behavior.

f. *Epistemic models for conditionals and non-monotonic notions of consequence.* In my PhD thesis and a series of companion papers I have developed an epistemic semantics for conditionals and applied it to characterize some of the existing notions of non-monotonic consequence proposed by computer scientists. F.P. Ramsey first proposed the central ideas of the semantics. Then Peter Gärdenfors showed how to connect Ramsey's ideas with theories of belief revision. Finally, Isaac Levi provided additional insights to circumvent a well know impossibility result proved by Gärdenfors in the 1980s. I extended the semantics to iteration and isolated axioms that completely characterize well-known logics of conditionals. The semantics remains as one of the main epistemic alternatives to interpret conditionals (together with probabilistic models).

What do you think is the proper role of epistemology in relation to other areas of philosophy and other academic disciplines?

Epistemology is naturally related to other areas of philosophy. In the case of formal epistemology it is usually seen either as a branch of philosophical logic or as intimately related to philosophical theories of confirmation (and therefore connected with various sub-areas of philosophy of science) or as related to rational choice (and therefore connected with various sub-areas of the theory of games and decisions). But epistemic insights might be crucial as well when it comes to provide semantics for natural language (see point f of the previous question). More generally, perhaps it can be said that today epistemology occupies the prominent role that philosophy of language had in analytical philosophy thirty years ago.

Of course, formal epistemology is naturally connected to other academic disciplines. During the 1980s and 1990s a great deal of formal epistemology was directly done in computer science, specifically in AI. Some interdisciplinary conferences such as TARK still reflect the strong links between AI and formal epistemology. More recently there also has been a strong link with theoretical and experimental economics. For example, the program (initiated by Robert Aumann) concerned with providing epistemic foundations for solution concepts in games made possible the exact logical analysis of the notion of common knowledge (pioneered by David Lewis, among others). Finally, there is also a natural connection with some of the work in psychology. For example, the work of psychologists such as Gerd Gigerenzer (bounded rationality), Daniel Osherson (formal learning theory, Bayesian theory, behavioral decision theory), Jonathan Baron (behavioral decision theory) and Daniel Kahneman (heuristics and biases, bounded rationality), just to mention a few salient names, is obviously relevant to many aspects of epistemology, both formal and traditional.

What do you consider to be the most neglected topics and/or contributions in contemporary epistemology?

Possible worlds semantics has had an undeniable impact in contemporary epistemology (as well as in metaphysics and in many other areas of philosophy and the cognitive sciences). And a particular form of understanding the modalities, deriving from seminal work by Saul Kripke, Jaakko Hintikka, Ruth Barcan Marcus and others, has been couched in possible worlds semantics. The so-called normal family of modal logics tends to occupy a central role both in purely formal work and in applications.

But neither possible worlds semantics nor the relational understanding of the modalities are necessarily the right tools for many applications in epistemology. For example, one of the effects of focusing on normal modal logics is the so-called problem of logical omniscience. There are, nevertheless, alternatives to the relational approach within the possible worlds semantics and there are alternatives to possible world semantics. But to some extent these alternatives have been neglected in contemporary work. An example of a non-relational account of modalities can be set forth within the neighborhood semantics initially proposed by Dana Scott and Richard Montague in the 1960s. I have argued that this semantic approach is particularly useful for the analysis of the epistemic modalities, but many interesting issues remain unexplored in this area.

And, of course, there are semantic alternatives to possible world semantics. One can count epistemic approaches (of the sort used in the semantics of conditionals), probabilistic approaches, categorical approaches, and algebraic approaches. Again, these accounts remain relatively unexplored. They have been neglected in contemporary literature, which has been heavily influenced by the modal realism implicit in possible worlds accounts.

Another area in which one can identify topics and research programs that have been neglected is the contemporary debate about theories of rationality, especially bounded rationality. During the previous twenty years or so the decision sciences have changed profoundly. Behavioral decision theory and game theory have flourished and to some extent a theory of bounded rationality has been developed. In a way the seminal ideas of my late colleague Herb Simon have finally entered the mainstream in theoretical economics, computer science, etc. This leads to a new manner of understanding human action, which integrates both experimental techniques and abstract formal modeling. This revolution in the decision sciences has been absorbed slowly and defectively by mainstream philosophy. It is unclear why these areas have been relatively neglected. One might think that philosophers have been reluctant to engage in empirical work, for example. But this cannot be the explanation. After all, in recent years we have seen the development of an interesting sub-area of philosophy called experimental philosophy, which does appeal to empirical research. But experimental philosophy seems mainly focused on testing empirically the intuitions of analytic philosophers in areas like moral theory.

Perhaps the failure to absorb the recent work in the decision sciences can be attributed to a certain lack of academic contact between the decision sciences and philosophy. Not many philosophy departments teach courses on rational choice, for example, or game theory, and when they do so, they tend to focus on analytic results rather than experimental techniques or simulations. Carnegie Mellon University is perhaps one of the few places where a PhD student in philosophy can be exposed to the rich and diverse corpus of work in the contemporary decision sciences (Irvine (HPS), Columbia and LSE are other places).

Notice that being attentive to these developments in the decision sciences does not mean that one must accept some form of naturalism or some variant of the Quinean program in naturalized epistemology. One can retain a normative stance in theories of rationality. But at the same time one can focus on normative theories capable of accommodating actual behavior. Or one can focus on bounded methods that when adapted are accurate and approximate normative standards.

We should mention finally the sophisticated view of rationality that Amartya Sen has developed in recent years. Sen's work has questioned some of the central axioms of the traditional theories of rationality, like the axiom of ordering; and he has done this by focusing on a variety of important phenomena like the role of external social norms in choice. His work presents a more inclusive and rich view of rationality that has not been sufficiently understood or studied by mainstream epistemologists (or even by formal epistemologists).

Sen's work has an interdisciplinary character. It belongs to the interface between economics and philosophy. A few philosophers have tackled some of these issues as well. Isaac Levi, for example, has also developed a sophisticated view of rationality that questions as well central assumptions of the theory of rationality, like the ordering axiom, although his account is quite different from the one proposed by Sen in the first part of this recent *Rationality and Freedom*. Much of the recent philosophical work in theories of rationality has neglected these important developments by focusing on other issues like the notions of intentionality and planning. These issues are, of course, fascinating, but their study seems to depend on extending a basic theory of rationality. And it is this basic notion of rationality that has been questioned by the work of Sen and Levi, among others.

What do you think the future of epistemology will (or should) hold?

In recent years we have witnessed the resurgence of an area of research called formal epistemology. In a way the selection of contributors to this volume (including researchers in computer science and the social sciences) is evidence of this interest.

To a great extent the immediate future of epistemology depends on the way in which formal epistemology interacts with traditional epistemology. They could grow independently of each other, or they can be integrated into a new and vibrant sub-area of philosophy.

Formal epistemology has already been integrated with traditional epistemology in the work of many of the philosophers who have contributed to this volume. For many of the most senior contributors to this volume (Jaakko Hintikka, Isaac Levi, etc.), and for other (less senior) researchers (like Wolfgang Spohn, John Pollock, Timothy Williamson, etc.), the use of formal methods to develop their philosophical systems was a natural, almost unavoidable, choice. Three or more decades ago formal methods were widely known and used by professional philosophers in general. But to some extent the general interest in these formal approaches faded away in recent years. Entire research programs were abandoned or remained inactive for decades. So, it is interesting to see how some discussions have reappeared in philosophy after a hiatus of more than forty years (like the revival of the Carnapian program for inductive logic).

Today talk of formal epistemology as a new discipline is in a way misleading. By doing formal epistemology today in philosophy departments we are in a way restoring a research tradition that in recent years was more popular outside of philosophy than inside philosophy (in AI, cognitive science, the decision sciences and in some interdisciplinary programs like Carnegie Mellon, HPS Pittsburgh or Irvine, Caltech, etc.). I hope that this tradition will return to philosophy completely in the near future. This will require a reform of the curriculum in most philosophy departments in the USA. In other words, this will require making available to philosophers in general the necessary formal tools needed to do creative work in this area.

2
Sergei Artemov

Distinguished Professor
The Graduate Center of the City University of New York, USA

Why were you initially drawn to epistemology (and what keeps you interested)?

My primary academic interest has always been in logic and constructive reasoning. This determined the direction of my basic university training: mathematics and mathematical logic at Moscow University under Andrei Andreevich Markov (the founder of Russian constructivism) and Andrei Nikolaevich Kolmogorov, a great mathematician who made fundamental contributions to many fields ranging from logic and complexity to probability and the theory of turbulence. Within mathematical logic, my key interests were of an epistemic nature, as represented by proof theory. This, of course, included Gödel's incompleteness theorem which struck me as a universal law of reasoning, its reach extending far beyond the scope of formal mathematics.

In 1979–1991, my research focus was provability logic, initiated by Gödel in a short note [18]. I worked all those years under the assumption that provability logic, in which the modalized assertion $\Box F$ is interpreted as the Gödelian sentence

$$F \text{ is provable in a given formal theory,} \qquad (2.1)$$

was the right model for Provability and for human reasoning in general.

In 1991, I came to realize that the true theory of Provability should include the calculus of individual proofs anticipated by Kolmogorov, Gödel, and Heyting, in addition to the modal logic of the provability predicate (2.1). Provability logic is capable of formalizing Gödel's incompleteness theorem but ignores individual proofs, the core element of the Brouwer-Heyting-Kolmogorov semantics of explicit proofs for intuitionistic logic and the Curry-Howard isomorphism – the key links between mathematical provability and other areas. Due to the well-known distortion of existential quantifiers in first-order theories (a.k.a. the $\exists$-*sickness* of first-order logic), the provability predicate (2.1) does not model the very notion of mathematical provability in a satisfactory manner. For example, the basic *reflexivity* principle of mathematical provability,

if F is provable, then F is true,

which Gödel included in his list of basic provability principles in [18], fails in provability logic (cf. [3] for a detailed discussion).

The Logic of Proofs LP was developed and announced at seminars in Amsterdam and Münster by the end of 1994. The first publication on the complete system of the logic of proofs was a technical report [2] of the Mathematical Sciences Institute of Cornell University, of which I was a member from 1994–1998. That paper included the completeness theorem with respect to the intended provability interpretation and the realization theorem which revealed that Gödel's provability modal logic S4 was sound and complete with respect to the natural semantics of explicit mathematical proofs. Thus, the old questions regarding the provability semantics of S4 and intuitionistic logic were resolved along the lines of Gödel's approach ([18, 19]) via the modal logic S4 and the Logic of Proofs LP. The master paper on the logic of proofs, [3] appeared six years later. Note that despite its suggestive title, [1] **did not** introduce the full logic of proofs.

From its very inception in 1991, it was clear that this project would extend well beyond the original scope of mathematical proofs. In particular, the epistemic significance of this approach has been discussed in [33]. Mathematical proofs are specific kinds of justifications, and a logic of proofs can suggest the means of building a much more general justification logic which could meet some needs of epistemology. In particular, the Logic of Proofs LP may be regarded as a sufficient system of justifications for the basic epistemic logic S4.

The next natural tasks were to find an epistemic semantics for the logic of proofs and to extend this approach to other epistemic modal logics. The paper [6] introduced an arithmetically sound version of an explicit proof system corresponding to another major epistemic modal logic S5. By that time, it became clear that in order to build a broad logical theory of justification, we had to reach beyond the limits of the semantics of mathematical proofs, and that a Kripke-style epistemic semantics for LP-like systems was badly needed. I announced the problem of finding a Kripke-style semantics for the logic of proofs at large; in particular, it was listed as number one on my website's list of open problems in 2003.

The solution came from Mel Fitting, who in [15, 16] offered an elegant and natural extension of Kripke semantics covering the Logic of Proofs LP. Fitting semantics may be regarded as the next step after awareness models by Fagin and Halpern [13]: in Fitting models, the awareness function reflects the structure of justification terms and enjoys natural closure properties. The name for this enriched awareness function in Fitting semantics is the *admissible evidence function*. Fitting semantics also absorbs an earlier Mrktychev semantics [27] for LP in which all the weight has been carried by the admissible evidence function and the Kripke structure collapses to a singleton. Since then, Fitting semantics and its natural modifications (cf. [4]) have become the standard epistemic semantics for justification logic.

The first paper which introduced justifications into an existing epistemic modal logic was a technical report [8] which prompted follow-up publications [4, 9, 10]. A full-scale logical treatment of epistemic justifications was performed in [5] in which a variety of justification logic systems were introduced and supplied with Fitting-style epistemic semantics.

Note, that within the traditional Hintikka-style modal approach to knowledge [23],

$$F \text{ is known} \quad \sim \quad F \text{ holds in all possible situations.} \quad (2.2)$$

This approach led to a rich theory and applications (cf. [14, 26]), but it has its limitations. First, it does not include justifications, which, since Plato, have been in the epicenter of epistemic discussions, thus leaving a gap between formal and mainstream epistemology and limiting the scope of the former. Second, it smuggles the *logical omniscience* defect into formal epistemology [12, 13, 24, 28, 30]. Besides, (2.2) may be rather counterintuitive: it is easy to imagine facts that hold in all possible situations, e.g., true mathematical facts (as suggested by Mel Fitting) which nevertheless remain unknown to the agent due to lack of evidence (proof, justification, awareness, etc.).

In [5], a general correspondence theorem stated that behind each major modal logic of knowledge or belief, there is a robust adequate system of justifications. This renders a new, evidence-based foundation for epistemic logic according to which

$$F \text{ is known} \quad \sim \quad F \text{ has an adequate justification.} \quad (2.3)$$

The correspondence theorem states that though the language of explicit justifications is more expressive than the modal epistemic language, (2.3) **validates all epistemic tautologies in the old modal language**, hence providing them with a natural justification semantics. Semantics (2.3) **enriches** (2.2) with an evidence apparatus while confirming major epistemic modal logics.

In [5], justification logic has been used to formalize and analyze the paradigmatic Gettier examples [17] and other epistemic scenarios, and has contributed to the studies of the well-known *Knowledge vs. Justified True Belief* problem (cf. [11, 20, 25, 29, 32] and many others).

What do you see as being your main contributions to epistemology?

A. Introducing justifications into formal epistemology. I argue that justifications have structure which can be formalized and studied by logical methods, introduce basic logical principles for justifications, and relate them to mainstream epistemology, in which the notion of justification has been the focus of attention since Plato.

B. The correspondence theorem, which states that behind each major epistemic modal logic, there is an adequate system of justifications. This provides an evidence-based semantics for epistemic modal logic.

C. Offering a new theoretical approach ([7]), based on proof complexity, for treating the *logical omniscience* of modal epistemic logic. Justification logic provides a natural means of escaping logical omniscience by keeping track of the size of evidence terms.

What do you think is the proper role of epistemology in relation to other areas of philosophy and other academic disciplines?

Like many other foundational disciplines, epistemology is ubiquitous, though not always properly acknowledged. Let us briefly cite some examples.

In areas such as Computer Science, Artificial Intelligence, Cryptography, etc., the logic of knowledge and belief, the formal realization of epistemology, is a key component (cf. [14, 26]).

In Mathematics, the foundational dispute between classical and intuitionistic traditions is of an intrinsically epistemic character: classical mathematical truth is omniscient and manifests itself, e.g., via the law of excluded middle, whereas intuitionistic truth is provability, hence the law of excluded middle is not valid.

Here is another, more specific example from Mathematics. It seems counterintuitive to accept as computable the function

$$f(n) = \begin{cases} 0, & \text{if the Riemann Hypothesis holds} \\ 1, & \text{otherwise,} \end{cases}$$

since there is no visible way to compute even $f(0)$. Nevertheless, classical recursion theory accepts f as computable. I would like to think that it is possible to develop a kind of epistemic computability theory which combines both classical computability theory and proof theory to provide a more adequate mathematical theory of Computability, within which f will not be accepted as an ordinary computable function.

Classical game theory sometimes silently makes strong assumptions concerning the epistemic states of agents. For example, in Solomon's Dilemma of dividing a baby, it is tacitly assumed that Solomon's wisdom is far superior to that of the child's bogus mother, otherwise she would know how to respond in order to foil Solomon's tactic. There is a whole new emerging area called epistemic game theory which studies the strategies of players, taking into account their epistemic states. This is yet another exciting field of application for epistemology. Since the natural game theoretical semantics of justification logic interprets justifications as strategies [31], we could imagine that justification logic rather than the traditional epistemic modal logic would provide an adequate logical foundation for such a theory.

In many respects, the Law makes fundamental use of epistemic notions such as belief, knowledge, and evidence and looks to be a promising avenue of application for epistemology.

Yet another common situation in which the evidence-based approach might be relevant and useful: When an agent communicates with an unreliable source of data (think Internet), it is often not reasonable to treat answers obtained there as knowledge. On the other hand, the Internet often provides checkable references and links which can be treated as pieces of evidence and with proper verification, can lead to knowledge. In this situation, it seems that the data obtained have the natural format

$$t \text{ is a piece of evidence supporting } F,$$

and an appropriate language with the capacity to handle justifications might be a useful epistemic model here.

What do you consider to be the most neglected topics and/or contributions in contemporary epistemology?

I would rather limit my observations to formal epistemology, in which the notion of justification has rather inexplicably been neglected, taking into account the central role played by justifications in mainstream epistemology and applications. Even now, when justification logic is on the table and apparently working in many directions, there is still discussion as to whether or not justifications are objects worth studying. This situation contrasts sharply with mathematical knowledge in which justifications, i.e., formalizable proofs, are first-class citizens and have a special designated area, proof theory. It is also fair to compare epistemology with game theory, in which justification-type objects, namely strategies, have been studied from the very moment of its inception in the 1950s.

In a broader context, the quest for a theory of justification in epistemology may be regarded as part of the tradition to capture the dynamics of information and reasoning [21, 22].

What do you think the future of epistemology will (or should) hold?

Given successful and timely foundational improvements, the development of exact methods which include justifications, and ultimately extending itself to other areas, the future of epistemology should be bright indeed.

Acknowledgements

I am very grateful to Elena Nogina, whose advice helped me with this paper. Many thanks to Karen Kletter for editing this text.

2.1 REFERENCES

[1] S. Artemov. Logic of proofs. *Annals of Pure and Applied Logic*, 67(1):29–59, 1994.

[2] S. Artemov. Operational modal logic. Technical Report MSI 95-29, Cornell University, 1995.

[3] S. Artemov. Explicit provability and constructive semantics. *Bulletin of Symbolic Logic*, 7(1):1–36, 2001.

[4] S. Artemov. Justified common knowledge. *Theoretical Computer Science*, 357(1-3):4–22, 2006.

[5] S. Artemov. Justification logic. Technical Report TR-2007018, CUNY Ph.D. Program in Computer Science, 2007. To appear in the Review of Symbolic Logic.

[6] S. Artemov, E. Kazakov, and D. Shapiro. Epistemic logic with justifications. Technical Report CFIS 99-12, Cornell University, 1999.

[7] S. Artemov and R. Kuznets. Logical omniscience via proof complexity. In *Computer Science Logic 2006*, volume 4207, pages 135–149. Springer Lecture Notes in Computer Science, 2006.

[8] S. Artemov and E. Nogina. Logic of knowledge with justifications from the provability perspective. Technical Report TR-2004011, CUNY Ph.D. Program in Computer Science, 2004.

[9] S. Artemov and E. Nogina. On epistemic logic with justification. In R. van der Meyden, editor, *Theoretical Aspects of Rationality and Knowledge. Proceedings of the Tenth Conference (TARK 2005), June 10-12, 2005, Singapore.*, pages 279–294. National University of Singapore, 2005.

[10] S. Artemov and E. Nogina. Introducing justification into epistemic logic. *Journal of Logic and Computation*, 15(6):1059–1073, 2005.

[11] F. Dretske. Conclusive reasons. *Australasian Journal of Philosophy*, 49:1–22, 1971.

[12] R. Fagin and J. Halpern. Belief, awareness, and limited reasoning: Preliminary report. In *Proceedings of the Ninth International Joint Conference on Artificial Intelligence (IJCAI-85)*, pages 491–501, 1985.

[13] R. Fagin and J. Halpern. Belief, awareness, and limited reasoning. *Artificial Intelligence*, 34(1):39–76, 1988.

[14] R. Fagin, J. Halpern, Y. Moses, and M. Vardi. *Reasoning About Knowledge*. MIT Press, 1995.

[15] M. Fitting. A semantics for the logic of proofs. Technical Report TR-2003012, CUNY Ph.D. Program in Computer Science, 2003.

[16] M. Fitting. The logic of proofs, semantically. *Annals of Pure and Applied Logic*, 132(1):1–25, 2005.

[17] E. Gettier. Is Justified True Belief Knowledge? *Analysis*, 23:121–123, 1963.

[18] K. Gödel. Eine Interpretation des intuitionistischen Aussagenkalkuls. *Ergebnisse Math. Kolloq.*, 4:39–40, 1933. English translation in: S. Feferman et al., editors, *Kurt Gödel Collected Works, Vol. 1*, pages 301–303. Oxford University Press, Oxford, Clarendon Press, New York, 1986.

[19] K. Gödel. Vortrag bei Zilsel, 1938. In S. Feferman, editor, *Kurt Gödel Collected Works. Volume III*, pages 86–113. Oxford University Press, 1995.

[20] A. Goldman. A causal theory of knowing. *The Journal of Philosophy*, 64:335–372, 1967.

[21] V.F. Hendricks. Active Agents. *Journal of Logic, Language and Information*, 12(4):469–495, 2003.

[22] V.F. Hendricks. *Mainstream and Formal Epistemology*. New York: Cambridge University Press, 2005.

[23] J. Hintikka. *Knowledge and Belief*. Cornell University Press, Ithaca, 1962.

[24] J. Hintikka. Impossible possible worlds vindicated. *Journal of Philosophical Logic*, 4:475–484, 1975.

[25] K. Lehrer and T. Paxson. Knowledge: undefeated justified true belief. *The Journal of Philosophy*, 66:1–22, 1969.

[26] J.-J. Ch. Meyer and W. van der Hoek. *Epistemic Logic for AI and Computer Science*. Cambridge, 1995.

[27] A. Mkrtychev. Models for the logic of proofs. In S. Adian and A. Nerode, editors, *Logical Foundations of Computer Science '97, Yaroslavl'*, volume 1234 of *Lecture Notes in Computer Science*, pages 266–275. Springer, 1997.

[28] Y. Moses. Resource-bounded knowledge. In M. Vardi, editor, *Proceedings of the Second Conference on Theoretical Aspects of Reasoning about Knowledge, March 7–9, 1988, Pacific Grove, California*, pages 261–276. Morgan Kaufmann Pbl., 1988.

[29] R. Nozick. *Philosophical Explanations*. Harvard University Press, 1981.

[30] R. Parikh. Knowledge and the problem of logical omniscience. In Z. Ras and M. Zemankova, editors, *ISMIS-87 (International Symposium on Methodology for Intellectual Systems)*, pages 432–439. North-Holland, 1987.

[31] B. Renne. Propositional games with explicit strategies. *Electronic Notes in Theoretical Computer Science*, 165(22):133–144, 2006. Proceedings of the 13th Workshop on Logic, Language, Information and Computation (WoLLIC 2006), Logic, Language, Information and Computation 2006.

[32] R.C. Stalnaker. Knowledge, Belief and Counterfactual Reasoning in Games. *Economics and Philosophy*, 12:133–163, 1996.

[33] J. van Benthem. Reflections on epistemic logic. *Logique & Analyse*, 133-134:5–14, 1993.

3
Alexandru Baltag

Associate Professor of Computer Science
University of Oxford, UK

Why were you initially drawn to epistemology (and what keeps you interested)?

I grew up in a post-modern Utopia. To me, as to all its inhabitants, in their rare moments of solitary reflection, it may have seemed more like a negative utopia (or, to use the correct technical term, a "Dystopia"). But I use the positive term to stress both the original, generous intentionality underlying a project that encompassed a third of the world, and its always-present, seductive public narrative, its almost irresistible "ideology". I think that an integral part of the utopian impulse, or at least a definitory feature of what I call a "post-modern Utopia", is the attempt to erase the very distinction between privately felt limitations, miseries and doubts and the public discourse of unlimited happiness and unlimited freedom. Indeed, in Communist Romania, the distinction between experienced reality and ideological fiction was commonly treated as an irrelevant detail. Even to insist (in public) on the existence of such a distinction would have been an unimaginable act of open rebellion, one fit only for anti-social hooligans, and not for serious, intelligent, socially responsible people. "Truth" was not a primitive notion, but a defined one: defined by the officially approved ideological narrative. Ideology was the fundamental concept, the most potent "reality" one could possibly encounter. The rest of reality was derived from ideology, and it was "real" only to the degree that it agreed with it.

The official narrative may have seemed rudimentary and primitive at a first sight, but it had multiple layers of increasing degrees of sophistication. Behind the brutality of the Policeman (called "militia-man", since he embodied the Will of the People), the flat, ever-repetitive mantras of the political Leader and the disgustingly submissive Odes addressed to him by the whole nation (odes that I was taught to proudly sing from early childhood, I still remember all the verses and sometimes I find myself singing them silently in the morning), behind this rather boring first layer, there were other, deeper layers, that I encountered only in high-school and college: the optimistic, compassionate, progressive social theory of the Marxist-Leninist Sociologist, the all-explaining, universal narrative of the materialist Historian, the rational, mechanistic understanding of the market by the Marxist Economist, and above all the others (venerated as the original source and ultimate justification of everything else in the world in which I was living) the intricate, apparently inescapable logic of the Dialectical Philosopher. The layers were so many and so deeply embedded with each other, the overall narrative was so powerful, its web was so finely weaved and all-encompassing that resisting it seemed like a foolish and deviant intellectual mis-adventure. Opposing it by contrasting it with one's own personally experienced "reality" was futile, while opposing it by spotting its internal inconsistencies was stupid: first, there was no space left in the net for any form of living, irreducible "truth", personal experience or private access to reality; as "everybody knew", truth was by definition a social-political construction, determined by history, social class etc. Second, contradictions and inconsistencies were not to be avoided, since they constituted the very essence of progress, movement, evolution. Believing in the existence of an irreducible, privately accessible truth beyond any social and political determinism was a "bourgeois" prejudice, betraying one's insufficient level of class consciousness. Believing that internal contradictions might constitute proof of the falsity of a theory was a simple-minded, "naive", un-enlightened assumption, betraying one's dogmatic, un-reformed, "pre-dialectic" way of thinking. Such antique, misguided notions have long ago been shattered by the founding fathers of Dialectical Materialism.

To sum up: together with millions of others, I had the rare historical privilege of living in Utopia. I didn't have to read about the "Brain-in-the-Vat" thought experiment or to watch the "Matrix" movie: I *was* a brain in the vat, nicely ensconced in a social-political-ideological matrix, regularly fed with intoxicating dozes of "reality", as defined by my society (guided of course by its most enlightened and progressive force, the Party). The small glitches in the program (inconsistencies in the socially defined reality, or inconsistencies between it and some of my private experiences) were easily dismissed as irrelevant noise. Descartes' evil demon (or deceiving God) had a name: society, as lead by the Party.

So I was directly confronted, as were all the other people born under the regime of Scientific Socialism, with the prototypical epistemological problem, in its sharpest form: how could I access the truth, when all the paths leading to it have been blocked, lost or hidden? What was the way to get out of the Matrix?

There were a number of clues. I already mentioned the internal logical inconsistencies, and the discrepancy between the public discourse and the private experience (and private discourse). In public, everybody I ever knew agreed on what's real, what's good and what's valuable. In private, people seemed to disagree, both with the public truth and with each other. My father's privately communicated opinion about what would be the best possible career for me was in obvious disagreement with the public discourse: he seemed genuinely shocked when I came home, full of proletarian enthusiasm, and told him my textbook-inspired idea of becoming a tractor-driver (that most romantic of the Communist heroes!). My mother also disagreed with my textbook on what's the best career, but then she disagreed on this with my father as well! In addition to all these semi-private disagreements, there was some powerful, but truly and absolutely private force (let's call it Logic) that seemed to inhabit my mind. This reactionary force made me unhappy when faced with any obvious, blatant inconsistencies. Despite the society's (and, most importantly, my teachers') happy submission to "dialectics", my unreformed mind seemed constructed to stubbornly look for coherence; it appeared to be offended by contradictions, and whenever faced with one it instinctively and dogmatically tended to try to eliminate one of the alternatives as un-true! As I approached puberty, it got even worse: there were now other secret, fully private forces, inhabiting my mind by day and my dreams by night, forces that disagreed with all of the above (society, my parents, Logic) and were making me dream instead of impossible, unspeakable, shameful and in general totally politically incorrect things!

So these, I think, were the first epistemological lessons I learned by living in a closed, centrally programmed society: to pay attention to the small glitches in the program, and to regard them as potentially more truth-revealing than the Monster-program, the all-encompassing narrative that was dominating my world. In particular, I learned to be somewhat skeptical of public truths, and to give at least some credit to humble un-social experiences, such as private and semi-private communication, as well as to my inner feelings and tendencies, such as Logic, introspection, and yes, even dreaming. My parents (both poets) have taken this last path, which became their own answer to what my father (following Mircea Eliade, a Romanian-originated historian of religions) called "the terror of History": dreaming, sublimated into Art, poetry and mystical practice, was their solution. A path that has always been of great appeal to me, and on which I sometimes shyly tip-toed, but which I never fully took.

In due time, I discovered my own escape path: Mathematics. The Party couldn't really eliminate classical logic and mathematical education, since the tractors, tanks, planes and factories still had somehow to be designated in a non-dialectical fashion. As soon as I felt its charm (after an early repugnance induced by bad teaching and by being forced to memorize the multiplication table), Mathematics seemed to me like the perfect, ideal antidote to Dialectical materialism, the anti-Utopia. Or better put (since by now I was more or less aware that our social Utopia was a fake one), Mathematics appeared to me, as it must have appeared before to Plato and Cantor, as the "true", authentic Utopia: the promised land, the country of freedom, which my mind was absolutely free to explore and construct, its liberty being limited only by its own innate horror of contradictions.

So at the age of 13 (when I suddenly fell in love with the beauty of infinite series and I tried to prove the irrationality of Euler's constant), I decided to live forever in that enchanted land: I became a "mathematician". Well, in a sense, from then on I never turned back (although I did look back) . I still tend to think of Mathematics in a "naively realist" manner (despite being aware of so many philosophical objections to this view): an almost physical world, in which one's logical alter-ego can escape the incoherent mess of our daily life, and instead freely and blissfully roam in a logical paradise, hiking on narrow trails towards its snow-covered peaks, building tunnels through its mountains and building boats and bridges to cross its rivers. Despite the hardships and obstacles encountered on the way, it was and still is a true land of the free. There is only one rule, and that rule comes from inside me: be consistent. All those hardships and obstacles are inherent in this inner rule, and they are the price for stepping into that perfect land. A price that is worth paying: absolute freedom and blissful happiness await inside.

I suspect that most mathematicians tend to think of it this way, at least in their more spontaneous and less philosophical moments. But there are of course other moments as well: the times when they cannot escape noticing the other glitches in the program. The mathematical Utopia may well be the only internally consistent one. But there are still discrepancies between its smooth logical perfection and the other forces assaulting us in this sub-lunar world: the external ones (society again, but also family and friends) as well as the internal ones (our impossible dreams, our not-always-correct-or-well-justified, but usually pleasant-and-useful-and-uplifting beliefs).

I think I did live for a while in the mathematical Utopia: the social-political reality was so intolerable, its totalitarian hold over personal lives was so strong, and my ideal refuge was so hardly-won and fragile, that I chose (like many other intellectuals) to disregard those other glitches and live in my freshly discovered land of the free. As a side-effect, I tended to apply the ideal, black-and-white rules of my logical world to the few personal relationships I did have: I tended to accept my parents, family and close friends in totality, as truthful witnesses of reality, and neglect their disagreements, while rejecting or suspending judgment on larger social truths. I also tended to apply the same rules to my lovers, accepting them as reliable sources of truthful information, with the predictable disastrous consequences. A typical mathematician's mistake, one could say. Or maybe just a typical lover's mistake.

But the social world and its public "truths" changed and collapsed in the meantime. I was a freshly-married 22-year old when Communism was overthrown in Romania, apparently as a result of a victorious popular revolution, in which about 1000 young people died. As many others, I was suddenly awaken from my private bliss by the sight of innocent blood on the pavement: I was in the army at the time (doing my short military service), and so I was being drilled and psychologically prepared to repress the "fascist terrorists", among which (I knew) there were my father, my brother and my wife. One was forced to choose an action, and non-acting (or acting only in the ideal world of Mathematics and Logic) was no longer a choice. One could not afford anymore to simply disregard all public truths, since this was now tantamount to complicity. I saw a young poet (a friend of my father) leading the revolution, live on TV. Or was he? For a very short while, I was hypnotized by a new centrally-issued narrative: the story of the people spontaneously and successfully rising against oppression, and freely installing a new, democratic order. But there were obvious glitches in this new program: too many inconsistencies, too many shadows, too many secrets. I owed it to my own rationality to try to get to the bottom of this, to try to find an "authentic" version of the public truth. After getting out of the army, I decided to give up Mathematics for a while and became a journalist, working for a newly independent journal. I was reviewing and commenting on freshly appeared texts by dissidents and opponents of totalitarianism: theoretical texts on politics, civil society and non-violent resistance, as well as prison memoirs. Together with my journalist colleagues, my friends and my wife, I was at all the demonstrations, all the riots, all the great violent clashes that troubled Romanian society in its first few years of fragile, unstable freedom.

The public truth that me and other young Romanians were looking for in those years has proved elusive. If I got anything of epistemological value from these experiences, it's about how easy it is to sell desirable appearances and self-fulfilling illusions to people who are starved for truth and meaning, provided that you pack them in a fresh, brightly looking envelope. Sadly and repeatedly, I learned my lesson: things in society are almost never what they appeared to be. The freedom fighters and the idealistic heroes were too often discovered to have been in the pay of the Secret Service. Ceausescu's criminal, supposedly brainwashed sharpshooters, who terrorized a nation by shooting in the crowds at night, suddenly vanished or were released for lack of evidence. The innocent protesters too often committed crimes themselves, all with good intentions, of course; but then wasn't the old order also built on the best, most progressive intentions? The "common people" were too often cowards, and too often chose to believe whatever was the safest thing for them to believe, and chose to hate whoever it was safest for them to hate. And the newly free, democratic government turned out to be a conspiratorial group of low-level crooks and former high-level Communist officials, united only by their willingness to use the violence and the misery suffered by a whole society as a smokescreen for their coup.

Not much to learn from so much blood. So I decided to go back to mathematics, and to another society: I went to pursue a PhD in Mathematical Logic in the US. But by now logic was not my only interest. Secretly, I was still hoping to find some type of "public truth": one built bottom-up by the free association and merging of millions of private truths, instead of the top-down public truth imposed on individuals by the official representatives of the society (the philosophers, the Party and the other enlightened forces and leaders). I became interested in the constitutional mechanisms that make possible an open society and a transparent governance; in those inbuilt safeguards that warrant the public's access to correct information while still protecting each individual's private truths, beliefs and interests; but also in the "logic of the market", which somehow always succeeds to find the best possible way to merge those private interests towards achieving the common good. Or does it?

Five years of living in Western openness and one messy, lying-induced divorce later, my trust in the truth-bearing qualities of both market-driven publicity and of private friendship and love was by now somewhat diminished. To put it mildly. I was slowly realizing that, deep down, beyond the huge contrasts in their quality of life, their public narratives and their inhabitants' personal feelings of happiness, the two worlds I've been living in were not after all so dissimilar in their relationship to the truth. The same ambiguities, opaqueness and dissimulation that blocked my access to private and public truth in Romania, the same onion-like layers of deeper and subtler, but in fact still fake, "truths", the same inescapable game of appearances seemed to be active, at a different level, in the free world. The difference, although immense, essential and life-changing, was still one of degree rather than a qualitative one. (But then ... the old Marxist philosopher is right, of course: "quantitative accumulations eventually lead to a qualitative leap". This is maybe the best argument one can find against closed Marxist societies and cheating partners: all governments, all media and all lovers may indeed be lying to some extent; but the exact extent may in the end be what makes all the difference between a true democracy and the "popular democracies", or between a true love relationship and a fake one.)

Well, call me paranoid. But after first-hand experiencing a brutal conspiracy-in-power and learning its sophisticated justifications (publicly uttered by virtually every intellectual in my country), it was much harder now for me than for my American friends to automatically dismiss all conspiracy theories and to always maintain my complete faith in the essential accuracy of free media and the blessings of democracy. At the very least, I needed some convincing logical argument. One that could preferably be formalized in a logical language, and thus inherit some of the accuracy and reliability of my old standard of veracity: mathematics.

So that's the story of how I first got to be interested, and why I stayed interested, in epistemological issues, and in particular in the logical formalization of epistemic issues. The story also explains why I am especially interested in various new extensions of the old "formal epistemology", meant to capture some of those subtler shades of truth and softer forms of "knowledge" that are usually investigated in the so-called "mainstream epistemology" (i.e. the informal variety).

What do you see as being your main contributions to epistemology?

I don't feel that my work has had any significant impact on mainstream epistemology to date. But one could look at my (very few) contributions to formal epistemic logic with an eye towards their potential epistemological significance (and hope against hope that this potential will eventually be recognized by mainstream epistemologists ...).

Among these contributions, the most influential was the notion of "epistemic action models", first proposed in my joint 1998 paper with Larry Moss and Slawomir Solecki, later developed into the notion of "epistemic programs" in my 2004 *Synthese* paper with Larry Moss, rebaptized "epistemic event models" by Johan van Benthem and his collaborators and generalized by them and other authors in various ways. This so-called "BMS approach" was widely adopted and became something like the standard paradigm in the new field of Dynamic Epistemic Logic. The basic idea of this formalism is very simple: treat and model "epistemic events" in a similar way to the usual treatment of "epistemic states". This yields a *separation of epistemological issues into two kinds of epistemics:* "static epistemics", dealing with possible worlds and epistemic possibility relations between them (or plausibility relations, or comparative similarity relations, or probabilistic measures over them); and "dynamic epistemics", dealing with possible events and possibility relations (or plausibility, probability etc.) between events. Of course, these two types are not always independent, but are typically related via an event's "preconditions", giving the event's conditions of possibility (or probability). These models allow one to represent the "appearance" of the actual (currently happening) event to various agents, similarly to the way in which the actual world may "appear" differently to different observers. Dynamic features of an event (e.g. *publicity*, as in "public announcements") are captured in an event model in a similar way to how static features (e.g. *common knowledge of the real world*) were captured in static models: for instance, publicity or common knowledge correspond semantically to *identity* between the real event or world and the apparent one, while various forms of privacy, ignorance, illusions or deceit correspond to more complex relations between reality and appearance. In effect, event models and the notion of appearance of an event were steps towards extending the scope of (epistemic) logic beyond the traditional realm of *inferences* and *introspection* to other "sources" of knowledge, such as *observation, communication* and *persuasion*. One can say that the main feature of this approach is that it makes explicit the "triggers" of belief change, the specific epistemic/doxastic events that are the primary sources, as well as the possible defeaters, of justified belief. One of the possible "lessons" that mainstream epistemology might extract from this work is the *importance of dynamic epistemics*: only by *taking seriously "epistemic events", as primitive logical notions,* at least as fundamental and as basic as the notion of "epistemic states", one can correctly understand and classify the various different types of "knowledge" and other related doxastic attitudes. The idea is that *"static" epistemic notions and properties are best characterized in terms of their potential dynamics*, in the same way that Felix Klein's 1872 Erlangen Program aimed at characterizing static geometrical structures and concepts in terms of their groups of transformations. (As we know, this idea was so successful that was later generalized to the whole of mathematics in the form of Category Theory, where the mathematical "objects" are less fundamental than, and completely characterizable by, their "morphisms".)

In Dynamic Epistemic Logic, the actual dynamics of information is *generated,* and thus "explained" (rather than simply described), by letting epistemic event models "act" over the epistemic state models, to produce new state models: new "possible worlds". Indeed, it has been noticed early in the development of Dynamic Epistemic Logic that no given situation (modeled as a *set* of possible worlds) is rich enough to represent in one blow the results of all possible epistemic events. (Only an unbounded proper class, such as the union of all possible Kripke models, could do it.) Hence, the effect of a non-public epistemic event is on the one hand to *eliminate* some possible worlds (since new information is *learned*), while on the other hand *multiplying* the possibilities (since *new uncertainty* is introduced by the event itself): this is the essence of the so-called "product update", proposed in my 1998 and 2004 papers, as a mechanism for combining state models and event models. So another potentially useful "lesson" of this work for mainstream epistemology is that *(unlike inference and introspection) communication and observation may create new epistemic possibilities*, going beyond the epistemic limits of any given, circumscribed situation.

The product update operation has been adapted and generalized by various authors to various different contexts and models of knowledge and belief. In particular, a natural *probabilistic* version was proposed by Barteld Kooi, and later refined by van Benthem, Gerbrandy and Kooi, and similar versions for updating *ordinal degrees of belief* (modeled as ordinal plausibility functions in the sense of Spohn) were proposed by Guillaume Aucher and Hans van Ditmarsch. In my own recent work with Sonja Smets, I proposed an asymmetric (lexicographic) version of product update (giving "priority" to the "new" information represented by the epistemic events over the "old" information represented by epistemic states, hence the name *Priority Update*), in order to incorporate ideas from Belief Revision into dynamic epistemic logic. We later realized that Priority Update is exactly the appropriate dynamics for the type of "soft" epistemics described by the so-called "defeasibility theory of knowledge" proposed by Lehrer, Klein and other mainstream epistemologists, while the usual Product Update is the dynamics governing "hard" (absolutely un-revisable) knowledge.

This lead us to a general "Erlangen Program for Epistemology", developed in my recent (not yet published) joint work with Johan van Benthem and Sonja Smets: classifying and characterizing the *range of possible different types and levels of "knowledge" and other closely related "doxastic attitudes"*, in terms of their *informational-logical dynamics*. Instead of taking a partisan view and proposing a concept or another as "the true" concept of knowledge and/or finding counterexamples against all the other such concepts (as many important epistemologists have done in the past), we adopt the logician's usual eclectic-pragmatic attitude, based on logical pluralism: we see our task to be one of "mapping the epistemic territory", using Dynamic Epistemic Logic as our compass. Each type of knowledge or doxastic attitude (including many of the concepts proposed by mainstream epistemologists, such as Lehrer's defeasibility theory, Nozick's counterfactual account based on truth-tracking, Dretske's causal-informational account, Williamson's safety etc.) is characterized by a different informational dynamics, captured logically in the form of causal-modal laws known as "Reduction Laws". These could be called the "fundamental equations of Dynamic Epistemology", and can be used to predict the effects of any specific doxastic event upon a specific doxastic attitude. Moreover, the formalization of the various concepts of knowledge within Dynamic Epistemic Logic reveals a number of subtle points and distinctions, that lead to interesting new variations of these concepts, as well as to new conceptions of knowledge. For instance, after investigating (in the spirit of the Erlangen Program) the class of doxastic transformations that leave invariant a given concept, one can turn the tables around and *define* that concept as a *fixed point* of that class of transformations. So "knowledge" of some specific type is understood as the fixed point of a corresponding type of epistemic events: you can be said to already "know" something if the epistemic situation would remain unchanged if you learned that something was the case. The intuition is that "knowing P" is what makes superfluous the action of "learning P". Though in principle very simple and intuitively appealing, this is as far as I know an original epistemological conception.

The view proposed in this latest work is that an approach based on Dynamic Epistemic Logic is not only "dynamic", but also inherently "social". By taking *epistemic interactions* as the basis for Epistemology, our account is obviously social, in the sense of involving multiple agents engaged in interaction. But its social (or more generally, what I call below its "higher-level") character goes deeper than this, covering the epistemology of groups, fictional agents (including ideal, perfect agents having normative value) and other "super-agents". At this juncture, Epistemology meets with Social Choice Theory and Political Science, addressing questions such as: how do the (sometimes contradictory) beliefs of individual agents combine into an emergent "belief of the group"? Is there a proper, correct way to do this, an ideal "epistemic voting procedure", an "epistemic norm" or even an idealized "epistemic role model" for the group, and if so then what is the function played by such ideal agents in the reasoning of the actual members of the group? How (by what concrete strategy involving actions such as communication, deliberation, persuasion, manipulation or diktat) can such potential group beliefs be "realized" as actual beliefs among the group? (Based on my unfortunate "Utopian" experience with social "truths" imposed top-down on the individuals, I am of course more interested in how a doxastic consensus might emerge in a bottom-up manner from the natural dynamics of a group of free agents.)

In fact, our formalism suggests that the dynamic and the social aspects are two sides of the same coin. As noticed by van Benthem, the above-mentioned update operations (the product update, the lexicographic update etc.) can be recognized as instances of "preference merge" operations, as explored in Social Choice Theory (to explain how and if the individual preferences can be merged into a group preference). This seems to suggest that *a single agent's information update or belief revision* after some new observation *can be thought of as* a form of "virtual interaction", an instance of *a two-agent belief merge* (between the "old" beliefs before the observation, and the "current" beliefs about the on-going observation). So social epistemology is essential even when dealing with a single isolated subject, having no real interactions with other agents.

I could mention here some other contributions of relevance to epistemology: my work on *the logic of "learnability" and "knowability"* (joint work with Balbiani, van Ditmarsch, Herzig, Hoshi and de Lima) and its relation to Fitch's paradox; my joint work with Smets on the use of Dynamic Epistemic Logic for understanding *quantum information flow* as a non-classical form of logical dynamics, characterized by the fact that all epistemic actions have ontic side-effects, including non-local ones; and my work (with Sonja Smets and Jonathan Zvesper, as well as with my student Dan Mihalache) on the epistemic presuppositions underlying Game-Theoretic solution concepts, such as backward induction. The main idea in this last piece of work is that the paradoxes and misunderstandings surrounding the backward induction solution (e.g. the famous debate between Stalnaker and Aumann) arise from an inherent tension between the usual game-theoretic assumption of "common knowledge of rationality" (as proposed by Aumann) and another implicit assumption underlying all strategic and counterfactual reasoning in Game Theory: namely, the players' freedom of choice, their ever-present liberty of choosing any moves (including ones that deviate from their own plan of action), and thus the possibility of making "mistakes". From an epistemological point of view, this last assumption boils down to the assertion that (in systems involving free agents) *the future is epistemically open: nobody can have any "hard information" about the players' future freely-chosen actions (*although of course one may possess hard information about other features of the future, such as the ones predicted by natural laws). We take this as an essential epistemic property of any system that includes "true" (free) subjects. Since (substantive) rationality is a constraint on players' future behavior, this means that "common knowledge of rationality" is an untenable postulate, as long as we take "knowledge" (as Aumann does) in its "hard" sense, to mean *"irrevocable" (absolutely certain and un-revisable)* knowledge. By either weakening the notion of rationality or adopting "softer" notions of knowledge (such as defeasible knowledge etc.) to accommodate the future's epistemic openness, we obtain various weaker versions of Aumann's postulate, some that imply the backward induction solution and some that don't.

What do you think is the proper role of epistemology in relation to other areas of philosophy and other academic disciplines?

There are at least two dual roles that epistemology can play in relation to sciences (roles that I could call "active" and "passive"), each having two aspects (let's call them "foundational" and "seminal").

On the one hand, epistemology can and should (and *did*) *actively contribute* to sciences. The first and most obvious aspect of this active role is *foundational*, when an epistemological analysis is applied to already existing scientific theories, in order to gain a better understanding of their underlying postulates in relation to their epistemic sources (empirical evidence, induction, logical or probabilistic inference, or even abstract insights of a purely "aesthetic" nature). This is not a sterile exercise, but maybe the most practical and useful of its roles: by elucidating, systematizing and clarifying the epistemic foundations of scientific theories that are already in use, epistemology makes a significant contribution to scientific practices, to the way in which these existing theories are understood, applied and taught by scientists. The second active aspect is *seminal*: by uncovering new epistemic possibilities that have not yet been explored by sciences, epistemology can act as a source of new frameworks and alternative postulates for sciences. An example in this sense is formal epistemology itself: the first formal-logical approaches to knowledge, belief and belief revision were proposed by philosophers, and they were later taken on, developed, investigated and applied by Computer Scientists. (Unfortunately, this evolution actually arrived now at a point in which the new work and the interesting contributions to formal epistemology are done almost exclusively by logicians working in Computer Science, while most philosophers seem to have lost all interest in the topic. One can only hope this tendency might reverse itself in the future, maybe in a reverse influence, from Computer Science back to mainstream epistemology.)

This leads me to the second, "passive", role of epistemology, as a "receiver" of ideas, insights, frameworks, methods and results from the sciences. While philosophers may understandably be reluctant to admit this, I think that the history of philosophy is full of examples illustrating the contributions to epistemology made by the sciences. One could even say that this influence was fundamental and formative: it would be hard to understand Plato's epistemology without being aware of the development of Greek geometry and most importantly the Greek invention of mathematical proofs; similarly, Aristotle's epistemology makes sense only in the view of the Greek development of empirical sciences, and in particular botany, zoology and geography; Kant's epistemology is clearly and profoundly influenced by the rise of Newtonian mechanics, and so on. It might not always be the case that philosophy keeps pace with scientific advances, but when it ignores them, it does it at its own peril. For instance, I argue below in my next answer that today's epistemology did not yet catch up with the latest relevant evolutions in Logic and Theoretical Computer Science. I regard this as a most unfortunate limitation of mainstream epistemology in its current incarnation.

What do you consider to be the most neglected topics and/or contributions in contemporary epistemology?

One of the neglected topics is what I mentioned above (in connection to my own work with van Benthem and Smets) as *higher-level epistemology:* this covers both *social (inter-subjective)* epistemology, and *emergent ("super-subjective")* epistemology. In other words, this concerns the knowledge acquired by *interacting* agents, but also the "knowledge" that can be ascribed to groups, networks, cultures, memes, gods (and God), and other such *emergent "super-agents"*. While the uses of epistemic logic in Artificial Intelligence, Computer Science and Economics were from the beginning emphatically "multi-agent", mainstream epistemology has by and large confined its investigations to the epistemics of a single knowing subject, considered in isolation from other subjects. This isolation is of course not complete, the other subjects being part of the reality that forms the "object" of one's knowledge, and communication being after all one of the main "sources" of knowledge. But overall the central relationship in mainstream epistemology is still the subject-object one (not the inter-subjective, nor the super-subjective). To use Martin Buber's famous phrasing, most of mainstream epistemology seems stuck in a simple "I - it" relation, refusing to open itself up to the warmth and the complexity of an "I - you" or an "I - Thou" relation. But rationality, learning and subjectivity are higher-level social notions: an intelligent agent becomes a knowing subject only in interaction with her peers, her team, her opponents, her role models, her demons and her gods. At least from her perspective, these all are epistemic agents (be they real or fictional), who may come to "know" her and to influence her own knowledge. In my view, the problem of finding good conceptual frameworks for the epistemics of groups, societies, sportive teams, artistic and religious movements, cultural icons, literary characters, mythical heroes etc., is central for understanding the epistemics of even one true "subject". As already mentioned, my recent joint work touches on this topic, and there are other logical formalisms of great relevance in this context, such as the ones arising from the "Social Software" school of Rohit Parikh. But this is just the tip of the iceberg. I suppose that a complete epistemological approach to this problem would have to use insights and frameworks borrowed, not only from Computer Science, Sociology and Political Science, but also from Economics (Game Theory), Cognitive Science and Psychology, and maybe even from Literary Criticism and Philosophy of Religions.

Another neglected topic is the *computational and information-processing* aspects of epistemology, and more generally its *relation to Theoretical Computer Science (* for which the old name "Informatics" might be more appropriate in this context). In this sense, I can list among the "most neglected contributions" the body of (epistemo-)logical work done by Computer Scientists (and logicians inspired by insights from Computer Science). I mention in particular the sophisticated new understanding of some of the main qualitative features of the concepts of "information", "computation", "process", "interaction", "epistemic event", "communication", "observation", "observational equivalence", "computational resource", "evidence", and "(bi)simulation", as investigated in areas such as Process Algebra, Temporal Logic, Domain Theory, Epistemic-Dynamic Logic, Game Semantics, Linear Logic,

Justification Logic etc. As I already mentioned, it seems to me that mainstream epistemology did not yet catch up with these evolutions. I have heard philosophers saying that Logic is of no use to contemporary epistemology and philosophy of science simply because Logic is supposedly "static" and confined to the investigation of the "hard", narrow "inference base" of our knowledge (while contemporary epistemology is mainly concerned with the non-inference sources of knowledge and its "soft", dynamical and counterfactual aspects, such as defeasibility, sensitivity and safety). Such remarks only show the ignorance of their authors, who seem unaware of the main logical trends in Theoretical Computer Science in the last twenty years, and in particular the *dynamic* turn in Logic and the flourishing of logics of *communication, observation, interaction and resources*. This ignorance can only be counterproductive, depriving mainstream epistemology and philosophy of science of access to some of the newest and most profound formal clarifications into the various meanings of notions such as "dynamics", "process" and "simulation". As a consequence, the un-reflective, un-analyzed, pre-logical use of such concepts in contemporary epistemological discourse can sometimes give a theoretical computer scientist an impression of quaint obsoleteness, as if most (though not all) contemporary epistemologists continue to live in the good old 1950's, when "Logic" meant First-Order Logic, "computers" were huge isolated mainframes engaged in solitary calculations, and the only models for computation were Turing machines. No concurrency, no communication, no distributed or mobile computation, no networks, no Internet, no dynamic logic, no process calculi, no game semantics, no resource-sensitive logics!

What do you think the future of epistemology will (or should) hold?

The future, oh ... Well, I think I already answered both versions of this question, either implicitly or explicitly. My hopes about what the future *should* hold are obviously informing all my previous answers. When I mentioned the philosophical "monsters" of the past and their truly monstrous political, personal and epistemic consequences, I implicitly expressed my hope that that past will not be repeated, but instead will be better understood by a better Epistemology, one that is in the same time more coherent logically, more informed by real science (as opposed to pseudo-scientific "isms") and more "humane", i.e. more respectful of the needs of individuals, communities and ecologies. When mentioning the few potentially useful contributions contained in my own work and sketching an Erlangen Program for epistemology, I could not help but hope (as is human nature) that these contributions will come to be more recognized, that this program will actually be pursued by both formal and mainstream epistemologists, and that this will prove to be a fruitful approach to the nature of knowledge. When mentioning the "proper role" of epistemology in relation to sciences, I was implicitly hoping that epistemology will continue to play this role, even more than it does today. Finally, when I mentioned some topics as being "the most neglected", I was expressing my hope that this neglect will soon stop and that those topics will be more thoroughly addressed.

As for what the future *will* hold, I can only reiterate the conclusions of my work on the epistemics of Game Theory: *in a community of free agents, the future is epistemically open*, in a fundamental sense. Since last that I checked epistemologists were free agents (as much as I could tell), continuously interacting with many other free agents (including governments, markets and religions), they form an essentially open system. The most one can do is to extrapolate from the current trends. But this is as futile an attempt as trying to predict the market: the current trends can always be interrupted, and to an extent one should in fact hope they will be interrupted (in order for what the future "should" hold to ever have a chance to happen). Beyond all this, of course, what the future will actually hold might go in a completely new and unknowable direction, leaving behind all the current trends, all our hopes and our predictions, as so many dead leaves lying on the ground in the glorious autumn sun.

4

Johan van Benthem

Professor

University of Amsterdam, The Netherlands

Stanford University, USA

Why were you initially drawn to epistemology (and what keeps you interested)?

There was no dedicated course on epistemology, when I became a philosophy student in Amsterdam. But our diet was diverse, since the active students of my generation supplemented their education by reading from the sea of wonderful publications that were available cheaply in broad public series like the Dutch 'Prisma Reeks', the German 'Hochschultaschenbücher', or English language pocket-books. Many of my long-standing interests were picked up in that way – why just follow the menu choices of your teachers in their courses? – and epistemology is no exception. For a few guilders, I bought Roderick Chisholm's *Theory of Knowledge*, translated into Dutch by a senior fellow student, Herman Slangen, who had been to the promised land of the United States (very rare in those days) on a Harkness Fellowship. I read the first few pages about Plato's discussion of knowledge as distinct from true belief in the *Theaitetus*, and from then on could not stop. As it happened, I had read parts of that dialogue in our classical Gymnasium, but my only memories were of Greek grammar training, where syntax took precedence over semantics. Now I saw how philosophers in Antiquity were live teachers and discussion partners today. Reading on, even though I had come to study logic, what intrigued me at once was the curious relationship between logic and epistemology. Clearly, Chisholm discussed deep and significant questions about the nature of knowledge and evidence – which my cherished logic books might have dealt with, but did not – and moreover, though his presentation contained no formulas and theorems, it was obviously rigorous, convincing and insightful. Later on I would find the same virtues in analytical philosophers like Gilbert Ryle, and many others. Even so, I remained a logician at heart, and thus resonated eventually with philosophers like Peter Geach, Jaakko Hintikka, or Paul Lorenzen, who each in their own way managed to combine logical techniques with philosophical issues.

Ever since those student days, two things have been on my mind. One is an interest in topics like knowledge, information, belief, or learning, which live at the interface of epistemology and logic. They seem crucial to serious intellectual endeavour, and yet it is amazing to see how little substantial consensus we have about them. The other thing is the issue of research style, and just when formal methods really add to our understanding of an issue: rather than symbolic mystery, and maybe hidden agenda change. There is a quote I remember from Aristotle that "It is the hallmark of an educated mind to treat a subject with no more than the rigour which is its due", and logic sometimes formalizes insight away. As it happens, the only Aristotle quote I can really find on the Internet is different: "It is the mark of an educated mind to be able to entertain a thought without accepting it." That seems very true, too. My sons sometimes complain that, after some 40 years of academic life and tending its delicate balance of community interests, I no longer know what I truly accept, and would not even recognize my own beliefs if I met them.

What keeps me interested in epistemology? Well, its fundamental questions remain as important and relevant as ever, and also, the interface with logic remains lively and surprising because of a 'friendly competition'. Logicians have new ideas and techniques to offer to philosophy (more on this below), when coming home from their travels to foreign countries like computer science or game theory. But philosophers continually manage to come up with surprising new ideas of their own. I find the post-Gettier sequence of new definitions of knowledge by Dretske, Nozick, and others fascinating in their fresh perspectives, and much more imaginative than what traditional epistemic logic has come up with. Reading the philosophical literature can be a treat.

What do you see as being your main contributions to epistemology?

All of my work in epistemology has arisen from reflection on how major epistemological themes play in logic. Writing with very broad strokes, I would say that I use the logical mind-set to look at epistemological issues in a new light, providing new answers, but maybe more often: new problems changing the agenda. And what enabled me to do that is the position of logic at the interface of many disciplines, allowing logicians to draw inspiration from many sides.

Some of this work is just asking questions by comparing fields and research programs, since so many natural contacts and confrontations fail to happen in the academic market place of ideas. In a 1992 lecture at TARK, the conference on "Reasoning about Rationality and Knowledge", started by a group of computer scientists, which placed epistemology at its proper interdisciplinary interface with computer science, economics, and linguistics, I gave the following example. 'Explicit' systems like epistemic logic analyze the meaning of knowledge on top of classical logic by introducing new modal operators, while intuitionistic logic, the oldest epistemologically flavoured formal system, is an 'implicit' approach, which 'loads' the interpretations of the standard logical constants themselves in epistemic terms. How are these two approaches to knowledge related? To me, this is still an unresolved issue, despite formal analogies at the level of the modal logic $S4$, and it may force us to rethink the very notion of information in logic.

My systematic work over the last decades has revolved around three main themes. The first strand is the importance of *information* as a crucial concept underlying knowledge, belief, and other cognitive attitudes. My publications from the 1980s and 1990s on modal and categorial logics of language and information structure (culminating in the book *Language in Action* from 1991) are a sustained attempt at understanding information at some abstract level that underlies all of its significant uses. I cannot say that this has been entirely successful, and there is no consensus on the basic laws of information even in logic. Therefore, my recent chapter with Maricarmen Martinez in the *Handbook of the Philosophy of Information* steps back, and brings to light three major intuitions that play across the field: *semantic-observational* in terms of ranges of options (as in Carnap's semantic information, or the possible worlds semantics of epistemic logic), *semantic-correlational* (as in Shannon's channel theory of information, or in situation theory), and *syntactic-inferential,* working on more fine-grained syntactic representations. The first two perspectives form a natural unity, and can be merged. The third perspective is more recalcitrant, high-lighted by the process of deduction and the notorious problem of 'logical omniscience'. But it really covers a wide range of processes of 'elucidation' that turn implicit information into explicit information: from steps of proof and computation to acts of memory and introspection. My current work is about ways of combining all three intuitions, and the processes that drive them. For instance, logical omniscience gets solved if we combine events of observation or communication with acts of 'realization' turning implicit into explicit knowledge. I see this unifying program as continuing classical issues in epistemology on the nature and sources of knowledge in logical terms. But, at the risk of offending some colleagues who claim to have 'solved it all', I see it as a goal still on the horizon, even within the restricted compass of logic.

The second strand is my work on *logical dynamics* since the 1990s, which is based on the distinction 'product' versus 'process', pointing out how logical theories should not just describe products of cognitive activities, such as proofs or sentences, but also these activities themselves. After all, a 'statement' is primarily something that we do, and 'argument' is something we engage in. I occasionally hear the same sentiments verbatim from philosophical colleagues, but then with 'epistemology' substituted for 'logic'. My book *Exploring Logical Dynamics* from 1996 develops a theory of this based on dynamic logics of processes developed in computer science. My work since then has focused on two research lines: *dynamic epistemic logics* of information update, knowledge change, and recently also belief revision, and *logics of games* which combine logical systems with ideas coming from game theory. Together, these systems show that informational activities can be treated on a par with their products, and that a dynamic stance throws new light on many traditional problems in epistemology. A concrete example is my analysis of the 'Fitch Paradox' of Verificationism in dynamic terms, where the issue shifts from somewhat defensive worries about, and patches for, the consistency of verificationist positions to an activist new theme: understanding the logic of *learning processes* which themselves involve epistemic statements in addition to purely factual ones. Another example is my recent work on dynamic logics for belief change, which brings this learning process squarely in line with standard logical systems, without any need for ad-hoc formalisms. Traditional mysteries like the (im-)possibilities surrounding the 'Ramsey Test' for conditionals as a guide to belief revision then dissolve in the light of logic. Finally, returning to my initial example, I would now think that the real issue in understanding intuitionism is a good grasp of the processes of discovery and definition which underlie that system in the first place—and in a recent paper, I show how this may involve a new notion of 'procedural information' in addition to the existing ones.

In combining information with dynamics, I have made a major turn to a third driving theme: away from single agents to *multi-agent interaction*. As a student, I thought that there was nothing grander and nobler than ignoring 'the others' (leaving them in Jean-Paul Sartre's Hell where they belong), and just think about the mind of one single agent, alone with the Universe. In line with 'interactive' and 'social' trends in epistemology, and simultaneous developments in other disciplines like computer science and linguistics, however, I have now come to think that understanding information flow between different sources and different agents is not a nuisance, but actually more essential than understanding 'one-dimensional projections' to single agents. Thus, with due respect for Plato, I now think the surplus of knowledge over belief is not to be found in further magical 'attunement' to reality, but in the powers that agents have for maintaining true belief as new information comes in, and criticisms by others have to be faced. I am currently engaged in a project with Alexandru Baltag and Sonja Smets of looking at the development of epistemology after Gettier, systematizing the innovative approaches proposed since by Dretske, Nozick, and others in terms of multi-agent information dynamics. We find that many things fall into place, while 'dynamic epistemic logic' suddenly acquires an importance that epistemic logic per se never had. Another instance of this multi-agent stance is recent work on acquiring and maintaining common knowledge, which turns out to have many surprising process structures beyond traditional epistemic logic. But I find my thinking turning in still more radical directions. Only last year, I wrote a paper on belief change and belief merge which gives an underpinning for existing revision policies in terms of *social choice* between inputs from different sources. Maybe we ourselves are in fact communities, and the idea of a rational agent as a 'society for observation and deliberation' exerts a strong attraction on me right now.

Eventually, I see this multi-agent perspective as a return to my initial Chisholm inspiration. Plato's "Dialogues" themselves are a social activity, and as such, as good a paradigm for logical theory and practice as agent-free mathematical proofs. And I would even say that the best standard of Plato's 'justification', or the modern notion of 'evidence', is how well it functions in contacts with *others*. How did philosophy, from these interactive beginnings, develop into what Popper once described as a cult of great philosophers preaching Sermons from the Mount? Why is philosophy one of the last disciplines where joint papers are considered somewhat odd? I hope the wheel will turn soon.

What do you think is the proper role of epistemology in relation to other areas of philosophy and other academic disciplines?

As I have often said (is repetition laudable consistency, or just old age?), I find traditional divisions into fields like logic, philosophy of science, epistemology, or philosophy of information a perhaps necessary, but also misleading nuisance. What counts is rather the natural development of *themes*, such as knowledge, information, and the processes which produce and transform these. One should just follow themes wherever they lead, without worrying about a visa for the next sub-field. For instance, much recent work with my students is about the notion of *preference*, its interaction with information flow, its dynamic changes under triggers like commands or suggestions, and its social structures with changing group preferences. That theme was not planned: it just happened naturally in the course of thinking about rational agency. Are we now suddenly leaving epistemology, trespassing on the philosophy of action or social philosophy? My mental map of my intellectual environment runs along with natural development of themes, and I wish more histories of ideas were written that deviate from the accepted 'subfields'. Given all that, I think epistemology is about major issues that are of importance across many disciplines, and it would be a pity if epistemologists chose to just talk to themselves, and at best some fictional further discussion partners like the Sceptic, Swampman, and the like. There are so much more interesting live communities to interact with!

What do you consider to be the most neglected topics and/or contributions in contemporary epistemology?

I have hated this question in every book in this wonderful Series, since any answer is bound to sound, and bound to *be*, arrogant. But if I were to mention something that strikes me, it would be the lack of contacts with other disciplines: logic for sure, but also other sciences of information, such as computer science (informatics), information theory, and so on. And also, I would think that the development of empirical fields like cognitive psychology and cognitive science might be more of a challenge. I am always amazed at the insulation techniques that philosophers use to keep their discourse free from externally refutable claims. The classical 'barrier thesis' of 'anti-psychologism' is a famous example, but the attitude is of all times. At a recent lecture, I heard a hour of wonderful presentation on information, knowledge, cognitive architecture, and rational agency – and (I should have brought a tape recorder) the frequency of expressions like "this is the common sense account of how we do it" was high. When I asked the speaker what precise claim (s)he was making, the answer was that philosophers had analyses of a subtlety unmatched in the crude minds of psychologists, scientists and so on. Maybe so, maybe probably so. But if so, why not go out, and show it?

One reason why I feel justified in preaching are the outreach efforts that I myself am engaged in, with Amsterdam's 'Institute for Logic, Language and Computation' and Stanford's 'Center for the Study of Language and Information' as long-standing bases. An epistemologically relevant example is the recent *Handbook of the Philosophy of Information*, edited with my colleague Pieter Adriaans, which brings together philosophers with mathematicians, physicists, linguists, psychologists, game theorists, and computer scientists. In preparing this handbook, I learnt a lot from my fellow editor. Trained as a continental philosopher going for the Large Questions about Knowability of the Universe, but wholly open to, and deeply conversant with ideas from mathematics, the natural and computational sciences, he disturbed my dogmatic slumbers about the analytical tradition in philosophy being the more science-friendly milieu.

What do you think the future of epistemology will (or should) hold?

It is a commonplace to say that epistemology has become more informal over the last decades, drifting apart from logic—even though (or precisely because?) many major epistemologists started out as logicians. I foresee new contacts between epistemology and logic, if only, because the philosophers are ahead of the logicians now in their rich new accounts of knowledge based on counterfactual tracking, evidence, and the like. Out of sheer intellectual curiosity, logicians are bound to start looking at these ideas, taking them further, and asking to be allowed to 'play'. More generally, the current trend toward 'Formal Epistemology' is natural, as it shores up informal discussions, tests proposed ideas to a greater extent than possible otherwise, inputs new ideas from elsewhere, and opens further potential interfaces with other disciplines. Even so, I do not foresee a return to the classical situation with logic as the 'most favoured trade partner'. We might all be better off if epistemology were the area where philosophy meets with a large array of formal disciplines: logic, information theory, probability theory, learning theory, complexity theory, and so on. What is the status of all these claims? As long as a university pays my salary, I am a professional optimist and wishful thinker, letting duty coincide with inclination: the preceding is both what I predict, and what I would dearly like to happen.

5
Luc Bovens

Professor

Department of Philosophy, Logic and Scientific Method

London School of Economics and Political Science, UK

Why were you initially drawn to epistemology (and what keeps you interested)?

Intellectual paths, like other paths in life, are somewhat of a *Rashomon*—there are many stories to be told, with no single one having a claim to the truth. The story below is a story that favours contingencies. I could have told the story so that every link in the chain was somewhat less haphazard. Yet my interest in epistemology comes mainly through thinking about chance—so telling the story in this way seems fitting.

As a graduate student in the University of Minnesota, I became interested in Rational Choice Theory and had the opportunity to work with Jon Elster while holding a fellowship at the University of Oslo. I was trying to write a dissertation entitled 'Reasons for Preferences' and was stuck for month after the first chapter. I had a background in the social sciences, but knew too little economics to continue on this route. So, I attended a series of graduate courses in microeconomics by Leonid Hurwicz. All this work did little to unthaw my dissertation, but it sparked my interest in formal methods and in philosophy of economics. The blowtorch came from an early article by Susan Hurley (*Mind*, 1985) on the relevance of Arrow's Theorem to moral theory, which nudged my dissertation work in the direction of moral epistemology. Preference change led to belief change and in the early 90s I wrote a few disparate papers on the dynamics of belief—so disparate that my Chair in the University of Colorado warned me that he saw little hope for tenure unless I could bring more unity to my research profile.

To make matters worse, my colleagues Graham Oddie and Steve Leeds introduced me to Bayesianism in philosophy of science in the mid 90s. The University of Colorado had a strong programme in probabilistic modelling at the time. So I lined up my bookcase with Sheldon Ross's books and pretended to be a student again in a series of courses in the mathematics department.

I was trying to scrape a living together to feed a family in those days. On a nine-month appointment and wages that would shock any beginning academic today, survival during the summer months always proved to be quite tenuous. The University of Colorado is one of the Big 12 schools—a football conference of schools in the south-central states of the US. To give the Big 12 some academic respectability, a summer fellowship scheme was put in place for collaborative work between the faculty of these institutions. In 1997, I was awarded a fellowship to do joint work with James Hawthorne at the University of Oklahoma. So the water and electricity did not get cut that summer—but more importantly, Jim and I had a most wonderful time thinking about Foley's work on the Lockean thesis and the preface- and the lottery-paradoxes.

Jim steered me toward the last chapter of Judea Pearl's *Probabilistic Reasoning in Intelligent Systems*, which is on the connection between logic and probability. I was actually more taken by the chapters on probabilistic networks and started reading avidly on the subject. My tenure file was in and I gave myself some time to play around. I actually think that I had a secret wish at the time to kiss philosophy goodbye and to do something real—oil prospecting with Bayesian Networks, or what have you.

But fate had it differently. I was on a vonHumboldt fellowship in the University of Konstanz in 1998–9 and attended a seminar led by Wolfgang Spohn. Erik J. Olsson was presenting a curious paper by Klein and Warfield (*Analysis* 1994) which features an argument against the coherence theory of justification. The argument was the following. Adopting additional beliefs sometimes increases the coherence of one's beliefs. But one's credence in a superset of propositions cannot be greater than one's credence in the original set. So how could the coherence of one's beliefs provide a justification for them? This struck me as a nice puzzle to analyse in terms of Conditional Independence Structures and Bayesian Networks. It was good fun and I think that we had something to say, but given my dreams about oil prospecting or what have you, something was deeply amiss. I could not face myself in the mirror knowing that I was thinking about an issue in the neighbourhood of Cartesian scepticism.

At the 1999 Conference of the European Conference for Analytical Philosophy, I tried to extend some of these ideas to experimentation and the use of unreliable instruments in philosophy of science, which seemed a bit more tangible than Cartesian demons. Stephan Hartmann had just taken up a position in the University of Konstanz and shared my interests in modelling and philosophy of science. We started thinking about how to represent standard problems in philosophy of science, such as the variety-of-evidence problem and the Duhem-Quine problem, in Bayesian Network models. Furthermore, we constructed a procedure to rank sets of propositions according to their relative coherence—that is, according to how well they fit together.

Wlodek Rabinowicz and I met in the University of Leipzig in 1999 at a conference with Margaret Gilbert on collective intentionality. We not only discussed what it means to go for a walk together, but actually went for a walk together through old Leipzig while Wlodek told me about some joint work with Philip Pettit on the discursive dilemma. We started exploring these ideas further which led to joint publications on the truth-tracking potential of premise-based and the conclusion-based voting in the discursive dilemma.

Wlodek and I knew that our curiosity seemed to be sparked by the same kind of things. Much of my later research started with two short newspaper clippings that we sent to each other. Wlodek was amused by the French response to a proposal by the Swedish delegation to set the weights of the various countries in the EU Council of ministers proportional to the square root of their population sizes. Chirac commented that he failed to see the political significance of the square root. I sent Wlodek a clipping about a curious hats-puzzle that was first formulated by Todd Ebert and was occupying computer scientists. Hats are distributed in the dark to a group of players and each person has an independent fifty-fifty chance of obtaining a white or a black hat. The light is turned on and one sees the colours of other people's hats, but not of one's own. The players are asked to simultaneously call the colour of their own hats. If at least one person correctly and nobody incorrectly does so, allowing for passes, then the group receives a prize. No communication is allowed except for a pre-play session of strategising. What strategy should the group adopt?

The first clipping led to a line of joint work on voting theory with Stephan Hartmann and Claus Beisbart, which I will address in more detail in my contribution to *Probability and Statistics: Five Questions*.

As to the second clipping, Wlodek responded with a variant of the puzzle that seemed to indicate that it was possible to make a Dutch Book against a group of players who were making independent decisions in the interest of the group. It only dawned on us much later that this is a strategic decision-making problem. A simple game-theoretical argument shows that rational players would actually evade the Dutch Book. At first, this seemed like a story of paradox gained and paradox lost. But *en route*, there were a wide array of lessons to be learned. The puzzle is relevant to Ramsey's analysis of credences as fair betting rates, to Dutch Book arguments for the Sleeping Beauty, to the Tragedy of the Commons (which I am currently exploring with Franz Dietrich, Maurice Koster and Ines Lindner), and to the strategic voting literature.

I received a Sofja Kovalevskaja award from the vonHumboldt foundation, which permitted me to set up the *Philosophy, Probability and Modelling* (PPM) research group in the University of Konstanz from 2002–5. Stephan Hartmann and I co-directed the group. There was a wonderful sense of synergy in the group and over the years we counted a total of 29 researchers and visiting fellows.

I am grateful to the many people with whom I have had the good fortune to work – many more than named above. I have learned a lot from every single one of them. Let me also mention Josh Snyder, who joined me one Spring in Boulder to learn some programming in *Mathematica*, Branden Fitelson, whose work has been an inspiration and to whom I have often turned for advice, and the various members and visitors to the Choice Group at the LSE. What I like about probabilistic models is that they often lead to surprising results. I think that that is also what attracts me to doing collaborative work. You never know beforehand what will happen when you hook up two or more cognitive systems, especially when they have been trained differently. And then it does make the journey less lonesome.

Why do I remain interested in epistemology? The short answer is that there are always interesting puzzles on the fringes of epistemology that bring a sparkle to my eye and then I can't keep from obsessing about them. I must disappoint you though—I don't feel that I have some grand project to complete or some puzzle to solve before I bid farewell to this earthly existence. In future work,

I would like to combine my interest in formal epistemology with my interest in policy research. I am presently doing work on asylum statistics in the European Union. Furthermore, I am always fascinated by issues in epidemiology and public health—but alas, text books have been sitting unopened on the shelf for too long.

What do you see as being your main contributions to epistemology?

In my early work I was most interested in the intersection of moral psychology and epistemology.

I thought it was curious that there was the following asymmetry between preferences and beliefs. We have no objection if a person tries to revise her preferences in the light of available opportunities, but trying to change one's beliefs at will on grounds of expediency meets with concerns of epistemic integrity. At least this is typically the case—there are admittedly some interesting cases that do no fit this pattern. Furthermore, moral attitudes seem to fall on the side of beliefs in this split. Why is this so? I showed that solutions by the usual suspects (Price, Davidson, Williams) were problematic, spelled out a taxonomy of atypical cases and tried my hand at solving the puzzle. (*Journal of Philosophy* 1992; *Philosophy and Phenomenological Research* 1995)

In response to Susan Hurley, I argued that it was an interpretation of Sen's Libertarian Paradox and not of Arrrow's Theorem that was problematic for moral epistemology. The idea is very simple. Suppose that moral choices rest on weighing multiple values and that certain background circumstances can make particular values weightier in our decision-making than others. Then we can invoke the structure of Sen's Libertarian Paradox to generate a moral dilemma, conceived of as a choice over a set that contains no best element. Let there be four actions $\{a, b, c, d\}$, precisely two relevant values V_1 and V_2, background circumstances for b and c so that V_1 is decisive over this pair, and background circumstances for a and d so that V_2 is decisive over that pair. Then all we need to do is to specify the actions so that $a \succ b \succ c \succ d$ on V_1 and $c \succ d \succ a \succ b$ on V_2 to generate a cycle $a \succ b \succ c \succ d \succ a$ in our all-things-considered judgment. This is a worrisome result for a value pluralist moral epistemology. (*Philosophical Studies* 1994)

I subsequently became interested in the future-tense variant of Moore's paradox, i.e. could it be meaningful to say "p, but I will believe that not-p". Inspired by the various counter examples to the principle of reflection, I tried to specify a diachronic constraint on rational belief that avoids these counter examples and that provides a taxonomy of the special circumstances under which it is meaningful to utter the future variant of the Moore sentence. (*Mind* 1995)

Jim Hawthorne and I explored the relationship between belief and credence through the preface- and the lottery-paradoxes. The Lockean thesis states that belief is credence above a threshold value—i.e. to believe that p is to assign a subjective probability to p above some threshold value. Now consider an agent who can tell us nothing about her credences or threshold values for beliefs. She can tell us only whether she believes certain propositions and whether she deems certain propositions equally plausible. Now by asking the right kind of questions, involving her doxastic states concerning winning lotteries of various shapes and sizes, we can represent this agent as an agent who has credences for propositions and a threshold value for belief. (*Mind* 1999)

Most of my work in Bayesian epistemology can really be summarised as addressing one question. What could it possibly mean to say that we have better reason to believe items of information that fit together well than items that do not? There seems to be something to this, but how can we give it a precise interpretation? First, Erik J. Olsson and I constructed several cases in which we are informed of two propositions by independent witnesses who are only partially reliable. Our prior credence that both propositions are true is kept fixed. We then varied the coherence of this information, i.e. how well the propositions fit together, in some straightforward manner. Conditional Independence Structures and Bayesian Networks made it possible to provide perspicuous interpretations of witness independence and partial reliability. And indeed, under certain interpretations, our posterior credence is an increasing function of the coherence of the information provided. (*Mind*, 2000) This same methodology also made it possible to take on the Klein and Warfield puzzle. If we receive a new item of information that makes previously disparate information look coherent, then it is quite plausible that our credence in the old plus the new information, *conditional on the old and new witness reports*, is indeed greater than our credence in the old information, *conditional on the old witness reports*. A simple detective story in Klein and Warfield style made this plain. (*Erkenntnis*, 2002)

But the challenge remained whether we could give a precise account of what it means for one story to be more coherent than another. I became wary of even the sufficiency condition for pairs of propositions that we had laid out in the *Mind* 2000 article, and before the article went into print I insisted on adding a *caveat*. The condition was fine to construct a quasi-ordering over information pairs *with the same joint priors*. Strengthening this condition into a proper coherence measure, as in as in David Glass (O'Neill and Sutcliffe [eds.]. *Artificial Intelligence and Cognitive Science*, 2002) or as is suggested in Olsson (*Journal of Philosophy*, 2002) seemed to open up too many counter-examples, as did other measures in the literature.

Stephan Hartmann and I tried a different tack in *Bayesian Epistemology* 2003. An analogy can be made to the measurement of equality in welfare economics in the style of Atkinson. One could ask—look, what is equality good for? Well if it's good for increasing total welfare, then we could compare levels of welfare in different societies with a fixed total income. Society A has an income distribution that is less unequal than the income distribution of society B, if it is the case that total welfare is greater in A than in B *for any strictly concave utility function of income*. This criterion yields a quasi-ordering for the relation '... being no less unequal than ...' Similarly, we asked—what is coherence good for? What it is good for is that it makes us more likely to believe the story that transpires upon being informed of its constituent items by partially reliable and independent witnesses. So let us assess the actual joint posterior probability after the information is in. Now suppose that the information would have come to us in *fully coherent* format—i.e. each witness would not have provided us with one single item of the story, but with the whole story. We assess what the joint posterior probability would have been under these idealised conditions. Now construct the ratio of the actual joint posterior probability over the joint posterior probability under conditions of full coherence. If this ratio for one information set exceeds the ratio for another set *no matter how we specify the degree of reliability of the witnesses*, then the former set is more coherent than the latter. This only yields a coherence quasi-ordering, but this is how we like things to be. For sets that remain unordered by this procedure, we also lack a clear intuitive judgment whether one set is more or less coherent than the other. There have been clever counter examples to this proposal. (Meijs and Douven, *Mind*, 2005) I am somewhat nervous, but there is some room to wriggle and I am not convinced that our wriggling has been unsatisfactory. (Bovens and Hartmann, *Mind*, 2005)

The coherence of the information obtained typically affects our views about the reliability of the source or sources and this in turn affects the credibility of the reports. We started tinkering with all kinds of puzzling issues in epistemology broadly construed by constructing models to cash out this simple intuitive idea. Bayesian Networks are a handy tool to construct models of information gathering from partially reliable sources. Here are some of the puzzles we addressed.

First, one could interpret the variety-of-evidence thesis to state that it is preferable to obtain test results from multiple independent sources rather than from a single source. But is this so? If we receive consistent test results from a single source, might this not boost our confidence in the reliability of the source so that n test results from a single source actually trump n test results from multiple sources, *ceteris paribus*? Depending on the values of the relevant variables, this may indeed be the case and this would be a counter-example to the variety-of-evidence thesis, so interpreted.

Second, there is the absolute-margin problem in the Condorcet Jury Theorem (CJT). Independent voters are asked to vote on a particular proposition. Given the outcome of the vote we update our credence that the proposition is true. The curious thing is that in the CJT voting model, our credence is exactly the same whether the vote came out 10 yes-votes versus 0 no-votes or 505 yes-votes versus 495-no votes. Only the absolute margin is what matters. But intuitively one would say that our credence would be greater after the former than after the latter vote. The voting profile tells us something about the reliability of the voters—the 10-person group seems to know something, whereas the 1000-person group seems to be guessing. A model that allows for dependency between the reliability levels of the voters confirms this intuition.

Third, there is the conjunction fallacy or the Linda problem. Subjects are provided with some description of a Linda who used to participate in various left-wing causes. They are then asked in some roundabout way whether they find it more likely that Linda is (i) a bank teller or (ii) a bank teller and active in the feminist movement. A fair number of subjects opt for the latter, which seems to be a blatant violation of the laws of probability. But is it? What if the subjects answered the question—how likely would you take (i) to be, *if you were so told by a single source*, and similarly for (ii). Now then it is not unreasonable for a subject to find (ii) more likely than (i). By providing the plausible information that Linda is active in the feminist movement, the source in (ii) establishes a reputation of being a reliable source—she seems to know Linda!—and this makes us favourably disposed towards the conjunction, whereas such an argument is not present for (i). For a plausible range of values of the model parameters this result holds and the subjects can avert the verdict of irrationality.

Here are two things I dislike in *Bayesian Epistemology* (2003). The first goes back to a comment by Josh Snyder. If witnesses, whom I previously took to be independent, provide me with coherent but highly implausible information, then I may revise my views, not about their reliability, but rather about their independence. Our models do not allow for this since the degree of dependency between the voters is exogenous to the model. This is a glaring shortcoming. Second, in our models, unreliable sources do not look at the world for information but are, rather, randomisers. This is highly unrealistic. Unreliable sources tend to be intentional liars or they latch onto the wrong thing in the world—but typically they do not randomise. Fixing these two issues is, in my opinion, a necessary condition for there being any chance of connecting our work to real-life empirical issues.

My walks in Leipzig with Wlodek Rabinowicz led to the following ideas about the discursive dilemma. Suppose that a board needs to decide on a complex issue—say whether to give tenure to a candidate and tenure should be awarded just in case the candidate is qualified both on teaching and research fronts. Now the Dean may ask the faculty to cast one vote and she will award tenure just in case a majority favours tenure. This is the conclusion-based procedure. Or the Dean may ask the faculty to vote on each issue and she will award tenure just in case there is a majority for each issue. This is the premise-based procedure. Which procedure is the best truth-tracker, i.e. is more likely to lead to tenure for all and only qualified candidates? It turns out that the answer is dependent on the values of the parameters. For smaller boards whose members are relatively poor at assessing candidates and for relatively low success rates, the conclusion-based procedure does better—otherwise the premise-based procedure does better. (*Synthese* 2006)

I turn to some more recent work. Todd Ebert's hats puzzle inspired Wlodek to construct the following hats puzzle. Distribute hats in a dark room to three players so that each person has a 50-50 chance of receiving a black or a white hat. Let (D) be the proposition that not all hats are of the same colour—i.e. that there are *different*-coloured hats. Clearly $P(D) = 3/4$. The bookie offers to sell one bet on D that pays 4 and costs 3. Let this be round one. The light is then turned on and the players can see the colours of the other players' hats, but not of their own hat. Whatever the distribution of hats, at least one person will see two hats of the same colour and for her, $P(D) = 1/2$. The bookie now offers to buy one bet on D that pays 4 and costs 2. Let this be round two. Players act strictly in the interest of the group as a whole and are fully rational. Since the bets are fair, each player would be willing to buy the bet in round one and at least one player is willing to sell the bet in round two. (If there are several people stepping forward, the bookie will randomly pick one of them.) If D holds, the bookie loses 1 in round one and gains 2 in round two—a net gain of 1. If D does not hold, the bookie gains 3 in round one and loses 2 in round two—a net gain of 1. So it seems that the bookie succeeded in making a Dutch Book against a group of fully rational players who are acting in the interest the group.

But is stepping forward to sell a bet in round two in case you see two hats of the same colour (i.e. in case your credence for D matches the odds) a rational strategy? Not quite. Suppose all players were to play this strategy. If D is true, so that the bookie would win the bet, then I am the only one who would be stepping forward. If D is false, so that the bookie would lose the bet, then all players would be stepping forward, but only one of them would get the bet. So unilateral deviation from the strategy of stepping forward when seeing two hats of the same colour may avoid a group loss but would not forego a group gain. Hence a profile with all players playing this strategy cannot be a Nash Equilibrium.

There are some interesting lessons to be learned from this (*Synthese*, forthcoming). I focus on two of them here.

This is an interesting case in which Ramsey's connection between credences and betting rates is broken. If each player were willing to step forward if her credence matched the offered rate, then, whether she would actually engage in the bet, would be dependent on the truth of the proposition betted on. Clearly, if the chance of engagement is lower when the bet is advantageous and greater when the bet is disadvantageous, then it is rational to insist on betting rates that are more advantageous than the betting rate that matches one's credence. (*Foundations of the Formal Sciences VI*, 2008)

There is another way to tell the story of the hats paradox. Seeing two hats of the same colour is a private signal that makes it more likely that D is false and seeing two hats of a different colour is a private signal that makes it certain that D is true. Should I act on my private signal, i.e. should I step forward to sell the bookie the bet just in case I see two hats of the same colour? Not quite, because if everyone were resolved to act on their private signals, then unilateral deviation from this profile would be advantageous. Now this description of the problem is reminiscent of the strategic-voting problem for juries (Fedderson and Pesendorfer, *American Political Science Review*, 1998)—which is a problem at the heart of social epistemology. Let a jury require unanimity for conviction and suppose jurors are asked to cast independent votes. They receive a private signal of guilt or of innocence. Should they vote on that signal, viz. cast a 'guilty'-vote on a private signal of guilt and cast an 'innocent'-vote on a private signal of innocence? A person receiving a signal of innocence might reason as follows. My vote only matters when all other voters vote guilty. In this case, if everyone voted on their private signals, there is massive evidence for guilt outweighing my private signal of innocence. So I really should vote innocent notwithstanding my private guilty signal—unilateral deviation from the strategy profile in which each person votes her private signal would be advantageous. With some qualifications, both problems can be shown to have the same structure and furthermore can be solved by means of the same optimisation techniques. One can then ask a question of mechanism design, viz. can we shift the threshold for a guilty verdict away from unanimity in order to assure that both the jurors will vote truthfully *and* that the expected utility of the vote will be maximal? It turns out that the answer is a qualified *not quite, but close.*

What do you think is the proper role of epistemology in relation to other areas of philosophy and other academic disciplines?

I have never taken a course on epistemology. I have never taught a course on epistemology. Frankly, aside from the classics in modern philosophy, I have never read a book cover to cover on epistemology, as it is conceived of, say, under the entry 'Epistemology' in the *Stanford Encyclopaedia of Philosophy*. I have always had a broad interest in analytical philosophy, but contemporary epistemology, in its unadulterated form, never engaged me much. I do enjoy working on the fringes though. Each time I tried to dive into the core in order to learn something that might benefit my work on the fringes, I didn't find much that is of help to the query at hand and was glad to be back at the fringes. But of course let a thousand flowers bloom. This is by no means a value judgment—just a statement about what does and does not make me tick. But it is difficult for me to assess the relation between epistemology proper and other areas of philosophy, since I only know it in some of its adulterated forms.

What about the coherence theory of justification—does *Bayesian Epistemology* not address the coherence theory of justification? Frankly, the coherence theory of justification was the inspiration, but our work has little to say about it. If there is a Cartesian demon, then the information that came to us did not come from independent sources. Furthermore, judgements about the coherence of a set of propositions are contingent on our knowledge of probabilistic information that needs to come from somewhere and that requires independent justification. What I found fascinating is the question of how the coherence of information affects our credence and our judgment about the reliability of the sources. But I am afraid that our work won't stem the laughter of a Cartesian Demon by one decibel.

Of course there are many fringes of epistemology. First, I have always enjoyed working on paradoxes of rationality. Second, social epistemology is a contested label, but I have an interest in how to form group judgments on the basis of a set of individual judgments—and this interest borders my interest in voting theory. And finally, I would very much like to do more work on the nature of scientific evidence—especially in the social sciences and in particular its relevance to policy making. That is an obligatory line as a courtesy to my employer. No seriously, there are so many interesting things under the sun and yet so little time.

As to paradoxes of rationality, I think that there is little hope of progress without interacting with formal disciplines. We need help from any corner we can get it from—logic, probability theory, decision theory, game theory, artificial intelligence. I don't think of philosophy as being called upon to do *foundational* work in any of these areas. That would be quite arrogant – as if philosophers have some special chip in their brains for thinking about the truly deep problems in these disciplines – problems that are somehow too deep for the practitioners themselves. I also don't think that philosophers are merely borrowing tools to solve problems that are internal to philosophy. Rather, closely related puzzles and paradoxes seem to raise their heads often independently within multiple disciplines and this is the mark of a good problem. At the same time, there is often insufficient interaction between the disciplines and different formal machinery can hamper the exchange of ideas. Nice examples are Piccione and Rubinstein's Absent-Minded Driver (*Games and Economic Behavior*, 1997) and Elga's Sleeping-Beauty problem (*Analysis*, 2000), or Rosenthal's Centipede (*Journal of Economic Theory*, 1981) and the Surprise Exam Paradox—as analysed aptly by Wright and Sudbury (*Australasian Journal of Philosophy*, 1977).

Judgment aggregation is just an inch away from social choice, voting theory and democratic theory. The existence of interest groups has always been a troubling feature in democratic theory. There are opinion leaders, bandwagon effects etc. In joint work with Claus Beisbart, we study these kinds of dependencies by means of various aspects of the methodology of Bayesian Networks. E.g. if Thomas duplicates Scalia's vote in the Supreme Court but not vice versa, then we can appeal to the Balke-Pearl theory of counterfactuals to measure their respective influence on the verdicts. Or probabilistic modelling and simulation techniques become important when we want to assess the effect of various voting procedures on the outcome of the vote—the more so if there are complex dependencies between the interests of the voters. At the same time, it is important to keep oneself informed about the actual challenges that are facing democratic decision-making bodies in the world today. (*European Union Politics,* 2005; *Social Choice and Welfare*, 2007; *Public Choice*, 2008)

As to scientific methodology, there has been substantial interaction between philosophy, computer science and the special sciences in the area of probabilistic causation and causal search. This has been a success story of interdisciplinary research involving philosophers, statisticians, probability theorists, and computer scientists. But I think that philosophers could be much more involved in assessing the nature of evidence in the special sciences—but let me leave that for the next question.

What do you consider to be the most neglected topics and/or contributions in contemporary epistemology?

Let me read this question in the following way—if the day had thirty-six hours, what are the sort of questions that I would want to get my hands on? Let me mention two topics that I think might be fruitful lines of research. There should be no surprise that these are not novel tricks to trip Cartesian demons.

I recently became interested in refugee policy. Attempts are made in the European Union to construct a more homogeneous policy in order to avoid asylum shopping. The textbook example is the low acceptance rate in Slovenia and the high acceptance rate in Sweden for Chechnyans. But how could one measure the degree of parity in the acceptance practices of the various EU countries? Now there is much to be said about this issue and this is not the place for it. But this led me to read Bartholomew *et. al.*'s text book *Analysis and Interpretation of Multivariate Data for Social Scientists* (2002) which I found fascinating. The overall question is how to represent and assess similarities between multiple items that bear more or less resemblance to one another in various respects. There is a wide range of interpretational questions and conceptual issues flagged that invite philosophical attention. It is quite natural for philosophers to be involved in causal modelling in statistics, considering their long-standing interest in causation, induction and counterfactuals. But similarly, they should take an interest in statistical techniques such as cluster analysis, multidimensional scaling, and latent class analysis, considering the affinity to the question that defines the theory of universals—viz. in virtue of what are two objects tokens of the same type? I suspect that some of the old debates in resemblance nominalism may even have a direct bearing on questions raised in this corner of statistics.

Let me return to the issue of the nature of evidence in the special sciences. Instead of rehashing the old Kuhnian mantras involving mention of the P-word every other line, an interesting line of research in social studies of science would be to critically assess the scientific methodology that underlies contested claims in the sciences. For example, there is contested work on race and clustering of human populations on the basis of genetic information. (Rosenberg *et.al.*, *Science*, 2002) There are interesting philosophical issues here concerning the choice of data and concerning statistical techniques to assess similarities in complex data sets. Or think of various public health campaigns. What sort of evidence is being used when the government puts forward recommendations for responsible alcohol consumption, decides to upgrade or downgrade various drugs? Philosophers have been engaged in such debates in fruitful ways, but my impression is that formally minded epistemologists and philosophers of science are wary of getting their hands dirty with empirical matters, whereas socially engaged philosophers consider opening up a book on scientific methodology – or heaven forbid, statistics – tantamount to sleeping with the enemy. Little is gained by such attitudes—we should get over this.

What do you think the future of epistemology will (or should) hold?

It should come as no surprise that I favour a type of epistemology that is contiguous with the sciences—in various ways and to various purposes. But I am not trying to stake out more turf. I equally encourage rereading the classics, thinking about warrant for religious belief, or proving a few more theorems in Belief Revision. In doing interdisciplinary work – despite all the lip service paid to it – one is too often on the receiving end in the turf wars. And what purpose is served by screaming the future is mine? Some philosophers will say that much of what they read above is just not philosophy. And some scientists will reject research proposals on grounds that the author is just not one of them—questions that are insufficiently empirical, not a fluent speaker of the local idiolect, and who is this bloke anyway? But of course, sometimes it all does work beautifully and that's what we live for.

6
Lorraine Code

Distinguished Research Professor

York University, Toronto, Canada

Why were you initially drawn to epistemology (and what keeps you interested)?

When I entered graduate school several years after completing a BA in philosophy, my intention was to study linguistics, to which end I audited a course on Noam Chomsky's *Cartesian Linguistics*. I had also, in the interim, been thinking along lines I came to recognize as Whorfian: as falling within the conceptual frame of the Sapir-Whorf hypothesis. Part of the impetus came from a year I spent as an exchange student in Germany. Living in another language brought me, daily, to observe how turns of phrase from the smallest to the most complex could attest to subtly different orientations to, and ways of knowing, the world. Although I would concede that it is logically possible to translate with notable accuracy between languages, it was continually apparent, trite as it sounds, that something is lost in translation. The semantic residues were intriguing. Even the smallest exchanges carry traces of epistemological and metaphysical differences between languages: even the contrast between "open the door" and "mach' die Tür auf!" reveals subtly different relations to everyday objects and human actions. More complex examples are easy to assemble. Some such differences are insignificant for knowing the world "well enough"; others have deeper philosophical and practical implications. But the face-off between Chomskyian linguistics with its focus on formal structures and consequent neglect of semantics, and Whorfian linguistic relativism where meaning and communication are central, posed questions about knowledge *with* a knowing/speaking subject that were more philosophical than "purely" linguistic. Consequently, I returned to philosophy.

"Language and Knowledge"[1] was my first (1980) publication in English.

Turning from linguistics to work toward a doctoral dissertation on theory of knowledge came from a combination of frustration and fascination: frustration with analytic philosophy of language and formal epistemology, which I saw as rough counterparts of formal linguistics, for losing sight of human endeavours to *be*, knowledgeably, in the world and make meaning of its puzzles and confusions; fascination with the sheer complexity of producing a cogent answer to Bertrand Russell's question "Is there any knowledge in the world which is so certain that no reasonable man could doubt it?", and the challenge of negotiating between relativism and absolutism which, in various guises, runs through my subsequent work.

Some of the fascination came from studying phenomenology and existentialism, where epistemology rarely figures as explicitly as in Anglo-American philosophy, and the challenge of scepticism does not loom so large: where "thrown-ness" into the world is a given, and ways of "being in the world" enact assumptions about knowledgeable relations to/with places, people, things, events—as in Martin Heidegger's "The Origin of the Work of Art", or "The Question Concerning Technology"; and Maurice Merleau-Ponty's *The Phenomenology of Perception*. I was frustrated by the compartmentalization effected by the analytic/continental divide, convinced that each mode of thought has much to offer the other—and found a certain (albeit tenuous) rapprochement in Ludwig Wittgenstein's *Philosophical Investigations*. His concentration on forms of life offered ways of achieving continuity across this divide and with the epistemological issues that captured my interest in classical philosophy. Such continuity was also evident in the little-known *Interpreting the Universe* by John Macmurray: a required text in my first undergraduate philosophy course. Central, for Macmurray, is the idea that people experience the world, both human and other-than-human, through "unity patterns" – mathematical, biological, and/or personal – which he parses not as distinct subject matters, but ways of thinking that shape an entire complex of approaches to experience. My current interest in philosophical *imaginaries* as they shape possibilities of knowing and being bears a distant resemblance to Macmurray's views

---

[1] Lorraine Code, "Language and Knowledge". *Word: Journal of the International Linguistics Association*, 31:3, 1980.

there and in *The Boundaries of Science* and *The Self as Agent*. These works, which I have not revisited for years, influenced my initial thinking about knowledge and subjectivity.

These thoughts came together in my MA thesis, "Three Philosophies of Language: Wittgenstein, Heidegger, and Merleau-Ponty", and took a turn, away from the substance but not the influence of phenomenology, in my doctoral dissertation, "Knowledge and Subjectivity", where I began to articulate a position that, with variations, I am still developing. It takes seriously the quest for certainty in knowledge and evinces a firm respect for objectivity while arguing that subjectivity contributes crucially, if differently through history, place, and circumstance, to objectivity, and thence to knowing as process and product. Analyses of its contributions are, I maintain, not merely sociological but epistemological. Questions about the politics of knowledge or about knowledge and gender had not then occurred to me in precisely those terms, but these questions as they animate and permeate many aspects of present-day professional philosophy keep me interested in a now-reconfigured "epistemological project".

What do you see as being your main contributions to epistemology?

My main contributions which, often implicitly, address the question "Whose knowledge are we talking about?" have been to move the idea(l) of *epistemic responsibility* to a central place in evaluating epistemic conduct; to urge a re-configured conception of "the knowing subject" that, in its abstract individualism and (masculine) gendered inflections, has governed post-positivist Anglo-American epistemology; and to propose ecological thinking as a renewing conceptual apparatus for theory of knowledge and wider areas of inquiry. These contributions interrogate received conceptions of epistemology's regulative functions and are thus often dismissed as not "properly" epistemological. Yet epistemology itself, I suggest, is a contestable concept, open to revision and rearticulation even within a constancy of commitments and issues. Thus I see my work as a form of immanent critique and reconstruction.

Epistemic responsibility is not my "own" idea: having encountered it in a 1978 article by Laurence Bonjour,[2] I sought to ex-

---

[2] Laurence Bonjour, "Can Empirical Knowledge Have a Foundation?" *American Philosophical Quarterly*, 15:1978, 1-14

plore its implications. Others have taken it in different directions, and virtue epistemology – toward which I gesture in *Epistemic Responsibility*[3] – has become a thriving industry. Yet my book remains something of a sleeper, on the periphery of this movement, for reasons about which I can only speculate. By contrast with more central texts, my book is allusive, neither firmly based in analytic epistemology nor univocally speaking its language; neither directed toward seeking necessary and sufficient conditions for virtuous epistemic conduct nor offering rules for its achievement. Its approach is to some extent phenomenological, if not explicitly so in the literature it engages, and thence has faced charges of being more descriptive than normative. It takes modalities of epistemic and moral subjectivity as integral to knowledge-making, -justifying, and -circulating, and hence as epistemologically significant; finds sources of knowledge in fiction; and situates itself at the intersections of Aristotelian ethics, Kantian-Piagetian theories of subjectivity, Wittgensteinian forms of life, and Foucauldian questions about knowledge and power. None of these "styles of reason" have claimed prominence in virtue epistemology, or in epistemology *simpliciter*.

A guiding idea, of quasi-Aristotelian origin, is that epistemic virtue – principles of responsible epistemic conduct – is/are learned *in media res*, by example, both positive and negative: by observing and learning from the conduct or misconduct of other practitioners in an epistemic community, and in deliberation with other knowers. Hence again, the analysis is both descriptive and normative. Equally central is the idea, indebted to Kant's creative synthesis of the imagination, that there are choices about how the world – human and other-than-human – can be known: knowledge does not simply imprint itself on universally replicable, receptive minds but people are creative in making knowledge from experience, and hence complex responsibilities attend and are invoked by/in any knowledge project, however small or large, and need to be evaluated. Responsibility, on this view, is multi-directional: to principles of knowing well; to "object(s)" or "subject(s)-as-object" of knowledge; to other members of epistemic communities. It is tempting, and often plausible, to exempt medium-sized material objects from these claims, but the "S knows that p" rubric that accords knowing such objects exemplary, even paradigmatic sta-

---

[3] Lorraine Code, *Epistemic Responsibility*. Hanover, NH: University Press of New England, 1987.

tus, assumes a common world of materiality and uniform access to it, which, as I elaborate in later work on the politics of knowledge, cannot be taken universally for granted.

The epistemic and moral individualism *Epistemic Responsibility* presupposes is deeply implausible: I have repudiated the simplistic doxastic voluntarism and the conceptions of subjectivity and agency on which it relies. But the core idea[l] of responsible/accountable epistemic conduct, reconstructed, continues to animate my work. It becomes more complex when the negative social-political implications of autonomous, abstract epistemic and moral-political agency are exposed. Hence, a form of *diagnostic-genealogical investigation*, exemplified in Genevieve Lloyd's now-classic text *The Man of Reason*,[4] often animates feminist and other post-colonial projects, whose goal is less to determine necessary and sufficient conditions for knowledge "in general" than to unmask hitherto "unthought" conditions that hold instituted social-epistemic imaginaries in place, with their emblematic figures and governing ideals of subjectivity, objectivity, and agency, even as they suppress, discredit, or silence other contenders. Feminist and other post-colonial Others have shown that the putative "knowing subject" is no neutral figure, no natural kind, but the presumptively male product of the dominant white western post-Enlightenment social-cultural imaginary, whose knowing and acting bear the mark of their maker, and whose effects have been exclusionary, imperialistic, and oppressive of "Other" would-be knowers and their claims to epistemic authority. Exposing the effects of abstract masculinity is again both descriptive and prescriptive, prompting scepticism about any suggestion that reason is alike in all *men*.

The working conception of subjectivity I advocate contests the hegemony of autonomy as a regulative epistemic-moral ideal, arguing that overblown ideas of the autonomy of (universal) reason, and of self-reliant epistemic and moral-political individualism exercise a humanly and socially harmful normative force. From a feminist and post-colonial position, the point must be argued with delicacy, because women and other Others have long been thwarted in attempts to claim the autonomy to which white, educated, affluent men have assumed entitlement. Hence autonomy has figured centrally, and aptly, in feminist agendas. Yet in its hy-

---

[4] Genevieve Lloyd, *The Man of Reason: 'Male' & 'Female' in Western Philosophy.* 2nd Edition. London: Routledge, [1984] 1993.

perbolic, all-or-nothing, instantiations autonomy invites critique. The abstract autonomous epistemic subject, like the autonomous moral agent, is neither credible nor worthy of emulation: his positioning as an exemplary knower and doer contributes to implausible ideals of knowing as a solitary, monologic project, discounting the divisions of intellectual labour in which knowledge more commonly is produced, and glossing over the power structures it tacitly enacts. The ideal is sustained by an epistemic and moral imaginary in which people are singly and separately responsible for "their own" being and doing, in ways that tell against taking into account how human beings are "produced, reproduced, deproduced"[5] in climates of uneven epistemic and moral-political credibility. Its abstraction from the materiality and affectivity of human lives limits its capacity to contribute well to responsible participation in epistemic and moral practices. My aim, in part, is to bring epistemology down to earth.

Contesting autonomy requires a radical revaluation of testimony as a source of knowledge. Concomitantly, it prepares the way for my proposal in *What Can She Know?*[6], that persons are essentially second persons. Both revisions move toward re-configuring knowledge-production as a collaborative, negotiative, interactive quest for the best possible explanation(s), while casting doubt on possibilities of single-handedly achieving (very much) knowledge so certain that no reasonable man – or woman – could doubt it. Epistemology moves away from its self-representation as an *a priori* normative project toward studying how and why people know, considering how they acquire and impart knowledge in the world as they find it, and engaging with multiple epistemic practices whose purposes are often articulated and realized in response to the complexities of the unexpected, the surprises of circumstance and sociality.

To charges that epistemology naturalized and, by extension, socialized reduces to merely descriptive, quasi-sociological analysis, I respond that even if, at the outset, inquiry is primarily descriptive, it will not be *purely* descriptive, for descriptions are rarely "pure". They are value-laden artefacts of location and choice: they begin (and end) within always-contestable theoretical presuppositions,

---

[5] The terms are from Judith Butler's essay "The Question of Social Transformation", in *Undoing Gender*. New York: Routledge, 2004.

[6] Lorraine Code, *What Can She Know? Feminist Theory and the Construction of Knowledge*. Ithaca, NY: Cornell University Press, 1991.

conjectures, and background assumptions. Good descriptions are not easily achieved and rarely definitive, final. Articulating intelligible, reasonably accurate descriptions and circulating them well are challenging tasks; in the public domain (at "street level", in Russell Hardin's terms[7]) they become catalysts of ongoing deliberation, contestation, negotiation, and action. If mainstream epistemology systematically mis-describes all but a select portion of cognitive activity, as I believe it often does, then better descriptions are crucial to understanding the place and the vagaries of epistemic practices in human lives, and to developing viable normative principles whose observation is within reach of human knowers. Hence the descriptive and normative aspects of epistemology are reciprocally constitutive.

Conceiving of persons as "second persons" eschews abstract individualism in favour of relational analyses of knowledge, subjectivity, and autonomy itself in its plausible articulations. It implies a mode of address to/of a specific (singular or plural) "you"; affirms the interactive nature of human subjectivity, from the dependence of infancy through the activities and projects of adulthood, and echoes Wittgenstein's pivotal observation, "knowledge is in the end based on acknowledgement."[8] Hence, it accords testimony a central location among sources of knowledge, contesting its third-place ranking in the old perception-memory-testimony triad where it is discounted as mere hearsay. In short, wholly self-sufficient knowing is an incoherent fiction; nor, from third-person spectator observations is it possible to know other people well enough to act well with or for them in the specificity of their circumstances. While such thoughts may seem not to translate well to the world of objects that has afforded standard examples for post-positivism, if the approximate, often ambiguous character of knowledgeable dealings with other people were granted exemplary status, some of the hubris that generates overblown claims to know, and the epistemic violence people do to one another and to the world around them could be countered. Such thoughts may sound naively idealistic, but epistemic humility is a worthwhile virtue for counteracting processes of riding roughshod over the

---

[7] See Russell Hardin, "Street-Level Epistemology and Democratic Participation". *The Journal of Political Philosophy*, 10:2, 2002, 212–229. Thanks to Greg Scherkoske for bringing this article to my attention.

[8] Ludwig Wittgenstein, *On Certainty*. Ed. G.E.M. Anscombe and G. H. von Wright, trans. Denis Paul and G.E.M. Anscombe. Oxford: Basil Blackwell, 1968, §378.

human and other-than-human-world that an excessive, putatively value-neutral yet frequently imperialistic scientificity in epistemology and actions based upon it, driven by an excessive veneration of abstract autonomy, have validated.

Questions about epistemic subjectivity may seem irrelevant to epistemology "proper" with its mission of determining necessary and sufficient conditions for knowledge and establishing *a priori*, normative justificatory principles. But subjectivity in its diverse situations, sensitivities, and commitments counts among conditions that make knowledge possible: empirical knowledge is, inherently, "situated knowledge".[9] Hence "situation", too, has to be taken into account in adjudicating, crediting or discrediting knowledge claims. While it may not *determine* the form and content of knowledge, it often plays a constitutive part in processes of inquiry and in its products. For this version of epistemology naturalized and socialized, epistemic practices are as open to evaluation as the knowledge they produce: the (traditional) context of discovery demands as careful critical scrutiny for the inclusions and exclusions it condones as do the principles and methods of justification.

In *Ecological Thinking*[10] – the book and the practice – these thoughts coalesce in an approach indebted to Quinean naturalized epistemology, yet enlisting ecological science as a "natural" epistemic practice, if not precisely as Quine positions cognitive science. By contrast with locating paradigmatic knowledge-seeking in the cognitive science laboratory, ecological thinking relocates inquiry "down on the ground" where knowledge is made, contested, circulated, in practices where the nature and conditions of the "ground," the situations and circumstances of knowers, their interactions, commitments, and negotiations, require critical scrutiny more fully engaged than isolated, discrete knowledge claims do. It evinces affinities to situated knowledges, elaborated to show that "situation" is not just a place *from which to know*, indifferently available to anyone who stands there, but is *a place to know* whose intricacies "shape"subjectivities and objects of knowledge; legitimate and/or disqualify knowledge projects; are constituted by and constitutive of instituted social imaginaries, with the rhetoric

---

[9]See Donna Haraway, "Situated Knowledges: The Science Question in Feminism and the Privilege of Partial Perspective", in *Simians, Cyborgs, and Women: The Reinvention of Nature.* New York: Routledge, 1991.

[10]Lorraine Code, *Ecological Thinking: The Politics of Epistemic Location.* New York: Oxford University Press, 2006.

that sustains them.[11]

Ecological thinking unsettles the social-epistemological imaginary of mastery and control that autonomous man in his spectator and instrumental incarnations has inhabited, promoting an *ecological* imaginary which draws its substance from the detail of, and interrelations among, elaborated examples, case studies, situated investigations and analogies from place to place, where older knowledge projects made do with attenuated one-liners and punctiform, monologic claims. It is an achieved epistemic stance, whose overriding interest is in imagining, articulating, endeavouring to enact principles of ideal cohabitation. Asking *who is* this faceless, incorporeal, infinitely mobile abstract Man who has populated western epistemology and moral-political theories, and *who* has *not* been there, ecological thinking departs from practices of according him (or her?) mere place-holder status. Paradoxically, place-holder status relegates *place* itself to an "unthought" of epistemology: universal Man is everywhere and nowhere in analyses marked by a principled indifference to place, for which knowledge prevails untouched by locational specificities and, leaving corporeal particularity behind, postulates impersonal necessary and sufficient conditions for knowledge "in general", in the name of an individual*ism* that fails to individuate.

Ecological thinking is "multi-disciplinary": it moves across modes of knowledge and domains of inquiry. Often, as in Rachel Carson's epistemic practice, which is exemplary in this regard, the complexity of each subject matter requires knowers to be multilingual and multiply literate. Such requirements are not those of neutral, infinitely replicable, dispassionate spectators.[12] Programmatically, ecological thinking enacts a thoughtful practice that moves laterally across epistemic terrains, with the goal of knowing people, places, circumstances, issues responsibly enough to act well, singly and collaboratively, while remaining wary of reductivism, prema-

---

[11] I owe the analysis of instituted (and instituting) imaginaries, which figures centrally in my current work, to Cornelius Castoriadis. See *inter alia* his "Radical imagination and the socially instituting imaginary". In Gillian Robinson and John Rundell, eds., *Rethinking Imagination: Culture and Creativity*. London: Routledge, 1994.

[12] Carson figures centrally in *Ecological Thinking*. Epistemological requirements such as these are variously enacted throughout the essays in Robert Figueroa and Sandra Harding, eds., *Science and Other Cultures: Issues in Philosophies of Science and Technology*. New York: Routledge, 2003; and in the case studies in Kristin Shrader-Frechette *Environmental Justice: Creating Equality, Reclaiming Democracy*. New York: Oxford University Press, 2002.

ture closure, and hasty assumptions about how knowledge made in one situation can translate into others. It is governed by a cluster of precautionary principles, yet sufficiently practicable to make a difference to people's relationships with one another and to/with the social-political-physical-material world. Acknowledging the partiality of their knowing, and cultivating a circumspect commitment to understanding its promises and dangers, ecological subjects are well placed to "own" and take responsibility for how and what they know.

What do you think is the proper role of epistemology in relation to other areas of philosophy and other academic disciplines?

Epistemology underpins and informs most areas of philosophy and other academic disciplines, but my interest is in its relation to moral and political philosophy. While it may not be named as such in disciplines other than philosophy, inquiry, almost without exception, is based in and/or derives from entrenched epistemological assumptions and expectations. Such claims hold across the physical, biological, and social sciences, and research in the humanities and the arts. Inquirers may find little purpose in critically interrogating the epistemological presuppositions that drive their endeavours, but these need to be exposed and evaluated; and inquiry is usually better, more responsible, for so doing. Epistemological principles and practices are frequently elaborated, refined, modified, rendered obsolete as discipline-specific research feeds into common knowledge; and common knowledge often appears incongruous with the precepts of academic epistemology, and may be unjustly denigrated in consequence. In short, knowledge producing practices and the epistemological principles that inform them develop in concert, with practitioners moving critically and self-critically among them; and responsible knowers will be open to such possibilities. Often, sedimented epistemological assumptions are destabilized when research projects expose their inadequacy: questionnaires, for example, based on assumptions about how human responses can best be categorized: approaches to events which fail to take salient features into account because of entrenched epistemic assumptions. Established research practices are frequently enhanced by incorporating variations on standard practice: the argument for participant observation in anthropology is one example, as are the introduction of a case-by-case method in ecological research, and critiques levelled against Evidence-Based Medicine, where one-size-fits-all assumptions obscure or conflate possibilities of knowing crucially relevant specificities.

Ethics is a case in point, continuous with my claims about the urgency of working to produce good descriptions. Common practice is to begin ethical deliberation from an assumption that situations, events, people are well enough known to allow ethical questions to be debated as though the knowledge informing their descriptions is firmly in place. Deliberation becomes a stand-alone endeavour where received ways of knowing, classifying, understanding people, policies, and events are taken as read. Such practices underestimate the extent to which ethics and epistemology are reciprocally informative, not only because knowing has ethical-political consequences and invokes responsibility requirements, but because debating how a situation should be judged, morally, presupposes that it is well enough known to make reasonable judgement possible. Thus, prior to the consciousness-raising movements of the mid-twentieth century, when people gradually learned to see hitherto invisible sexism, racism, and other matter-of-course stances that silently informed moral-political deliberation, the knowledge was not available to make good judgement possible. When coerced sexual intercourse in marriage did not count as "rape", this entrenched ignorance shaped moral-political responses to women's protests. Ossified epistemic assumptions had to be disrupted before women's imprecations could be acknowledged. Nor are such processes unidirectional: often the moral-political consequences of certain policies and actions animate reconstructions of the "knowledge" they have silently reenacted. Here as elsewhere, connections between knowledge and acknowledgement are especially pertinent, and conditions for granting or withholding acknowledgement have to be excavated from beneath the seemingly smooth surface of moral judgement.

What do you consider to be the most neglected topics and/or contributions in contemporary epistemology?

Most of the neglected topics derive from hegemonic conceptions of knowledge and subjectivity, according to which, more than three decades after feminist and post-colonial inquiry entered the epistemological domain, philosophers still pay insufficient attention to how knowledge is, in effect, a commodity of privilege. There are good historical reasons to seek the kind of universal enlightenment and rational self-governance that philosophers have sought as a route toward quelling rampant irrationality and chaos. Yet unequal distributions of epistemic authority and privilege, uneven conditions of acknowledgement and uptake that moved the authorized subject matter of epistemology toward presumptions of uniformity failed cultivate the openness that allows recognition of how knowing takes place, variably, across a by-no-means homogeneous "humanity". Hence, there are good present-day reasons to see in responsive and responsible situated knowing a resource for informed resistance to oppression.

Pertinent here is a neglect of advocacy and negotiation as epistemologically significant practices that can make knowledge possible or prevent its going through. These thoughts have to be elaborated with care, for the very idea of advocacy sounds alarm bells for epistemologists committed to preserving maximally value-neutral objectivity, untainted by special interests, political lobbying, or might overwhelming right. Post-positivist ideals manifest in an ongoing faith in something akin to an invisible hand at work in producing objective knowledge: an impartial knowledge-making process whose effects are apparent in impersonal claims to the effect that "science has proved", "the facts show", "it has been demonstrated". Such claims attest to a conviction that knowledge *as such* holds everywhere, for everyone: it neither requires nor tolerates advocacy. Yet inquiry into "situated knowledges" that works with intricate connections between knowledge and power, acknowledges epistemic interdependence, and takes seriously questions about *whose* knowledge "we" are talking about sits uneasily within an epistemic imaginary that – nostalgically – looks to a bygone ideal of the autonomous, replicable, impartial knower as the producer of objective, universally valid knowledge. That unease opens space for thinking about how such discredited practices as advocacy and negotiation, for all their dangers, could claim a respectable place in epistemology.

Advocacy is a vexed process for epistemologies of mastery with their adherence to the individualism of autonomous man and their imagery of knowledge claims as monologic pronouncements, uttered into a void. It is vexed, too, for feminists and other others who are rightly wary of (paternalistic) practices of speaking/knowing for others. Critiques tend to generalize from places where advocacy sacrifices objectivity in favour of vested interests; where its imagined proximity to the worst rhetorical excesses expands to encompass all practices falling under that label. But there are multiple modalities of advocacy. In their public epistemically-morally responsible modalities, advocacy practices endeavour to *get at* truths operating below the surface of the assumed self-transparency of evidence. Al Gore's "inconvenient truth" is one example. His is unashamedly an advocacy project, advocating for recognition of truths "inconvenient" because of major losses they entail, fundamental changes in ways of life they require: losses of taken-for-granted materialities that constitute those ways of life, for the affluent western world. Because of their widespread social-political "inconvenience", such truths require vigorous advocacy if they are to infiltrate and destabilize a social-epistemic imaginary where rhetorically-fuelled counter-advocacy devises strategies to gainsay them.

The "advocacy" I promote names the collaborative epistemic-moral-political practices evoked in Marilyn Frye's apt phrase "hearing each other into speech."[13] It need not be uni-directional, yet it can inform practices that support certain causes, undo patterns of silencing, intervene in an intransigent social order on behalf of or in concert with the epistemically disenfranchised, enlist expertise and sometime privilege for others less expert, less well positioned to claim acknowledgement. None of these thoughts will undo advocacy's negative implications or its dangers. Hence biologist Karen Messing, about whom I write in *Ecological Thinking* advocates for workers disenfranchised by material-institutional structures to the extent that they need help in speaking "for themselves": advocacy informed by biological knowledge whose credibility derives from Messing's credentials and social-professional positioning, yet is true to the specificities of their situations, and available for, negotiation, contestation, or acknowledgement Analogous examples can be adduced from advocacy for people so ill, old, or so disabled as to be unable to advocate for themselves. These too are fraught, fragile situations which require ethical-epistemic monitoring at every level. But they are vital to the very possibility of living well and ultimately to achieving more even distributions of human and environmental good. At their best, advocacy practices can be effective in claiming discursive space for "subjugated knowledges", putting such knowledge into circulation where - with informed negotiation - it can seek acknowledgement; working to promote emancipatory moral-political-ecological effects.

---

[13] Marilyn Frye, "The Possibility of Feminist Theory". In Ann Garry & Marilyn Pearsall, eds., *Women, Knowledge, and Reality: Explorations in Feminist Philosophy*. New York: Routledge, 1996, 38.

What do you think the future of epistemology will (or should) hold?

Since I am better able to wish than predict, my response is directed to what the future *should* hold, although the plausibility of my wishes, and reasons why they are more than merely fanciful, derive from how I read the state of epistemology today.

Interesting work in epistemology is taking place in naturalized and social epistemology projects that locate themselves close to ethical and political inquiry, and follow the lead of some feminist and other post-colonial scholarship which (in Joseph Rouse's words) "transcend... epistemology" by focussing on relationships or "intra-actions" between knowers and known. Because they conceive of "knowing" as populated and situated, thus as "more interactive than representational"[14] they are, Rouse suggests, no longer constrained to studying "the semantic content of knowledge or belief", but committed to engaging with epistemic practices as participatory, open to social-political criticism, and committed to a significant measure of reflexivity with respect both to process and to product.

Admittedly, reflexivity is itself a contestable concept. Post-modern, post-Freudian conceptions of subjectivity as no longer transparent to itself in the enlightenment sense render its achievement uncertain and its injunctions imperfectly realizable. But the effort is a worthy one nonetheless. Reflexivity, to the extent that it is possible, is no internal, self-examination on the part of a knower alone and face-to-face with his/her epistemic conscience. Prejudgements and biases, which it is a principal task of reflexivity to recognize and counteract, are not exclusively individual possessions - although they manifest in individual epistemic distortions and failures - but are carried and communicated, indeed ingested, within a going social-epistemic imaginary, and need to be addressed in discussion, conversation, forms of open address and debate. Its point is not to transcend epistemic locations to achieve a purely objective, bias-free and anti-relativist view from nowhere, but to develop critical and self-critical ways of achieving understanding, wisdom and knowledge, that could avoid the epistemic violence performed in the name of a universal truth that, more often than not, damages the "known" through misrepresentation, ignorance, reductionism, false universalization.

---

[14] Joseph Rouse, *How Scientific Practices Matter: Reclaiming Philosophical Naturalism*. Chicago: University of Chicago Press, 2002, pps. 146–159.

Issues of epistemic justice and injustice, epistemic violence, vulnerability, and ignorance are claiming a place in epistemological inquiry itself rather than being relegated to its margins. Miranda Fricker's work on testimonial and hermeneutic injustice is setting the stage for a range of epistemic inquiry,[15] as are projects of studying conditions that make ignorance possible and hold it in place.[16] These new directions are, if indirectly, consequent on the increased sophistication in naturalized and socialized epistemology, and on processes of softening the boundaries of epistemology itself, secularizing it in ways that bring it closer to the values, experiences, practices and goals of a rapidly changing, no longer even plausibly Eurocentered or androcentered world. Perhaps in the process, some version of epistemological relativism will begin to lose its sting, to be seen not as a careless or truth-denying stance, but as a way of judiciously, responsibly, avoiding the rigidity that has often been the mark of universal disembodied epistemology. I think epistemologists should avoid dreaming of a view from nowhere to attempt to determine how views from the various "somewheres" that differently constrain and enable human knowing can be understood and respected in the name of doing justice to diversity in the human and other-than-human world. Would such a project still be epistemology? Not in the traditional sense, but it could open ways to responsive and responsible reconstructions of the scope and limits of human knowing.

---

[15] Miranda Fricker, *Epistemic Injustice: Power and the Ethics of Knowing*: Oxford: Oxford University Press, 2007.

[16] See for example Shannon Sullivan and Nancy Tuana, eds., *Race and Epistemologies of Ignorance*. Albany, NY: State University of New York Press, 2007.

7

Fred Dretske

Professor
Duke University, USA

Why were you initially drawn to epistemology (and what keeps you interested)?

I began my career as a philosopher of science. My first major research project after taking my degree was on the topic—a hot topic in the early 60's–of the theory/observation distinction. People like Norwood Russell Hanson, Paul Feyerabend, and Thomas Kuhn were advancing what I thought were implausible claims about what scientists (and, by extension, everyone else) could and could not observe. These claims were often based on what I suspected was a faulty epistemology, a misunderstanding of how prior theoretical knowledge (or the lack of it) affected perception. I set out to write a book on this topic in 1965. By the time the book – *Seeing and Knowing* – was published (1969) I had ceased to think of myself as a philosopher of science. The book itself didn't contain much philosophy of science. I became then – and I remain to this day – captivated by epistemology. My interests broadened, of course, and I now think of myself as much a philosopher of mind as an epistemologist. My current interest, for example, straddles these two areas. I currently puzzle over whether and, if so, what (and how) we know about our own mind.

What keeps me interested in epistemology is, often enough, those aspects of it that relate to problems and developments in the philosophy of mind and cognitive science. I have, for instance, written on the topic of perception *without* awareness (Dretske 2006a), a possibility that would not have made much sense forty years ago. The existence of such puzzling phenomena (for a philosopher trying to develop a theory of perception) as split brains, blindsight, unilateral neglect, and extinction—all apparent examples of a subject getting visually transmitted information about an object without acknowledged awareness of that object–provide a wealth of fascinating data for rethinking and reformulating some traditional philosophical ideas about perception. I have also written (Dretske 2004 and forthcoming) on change blindness—the failure of subjects to detect or notice differences, often very prominent differences, when prevented (by suitable masks or distractions) from observing the change (the event) producing these differences. A conviction that these experimental results do not show what they are often alleged to show about conscious experience has nourished my continuing interest in this area.

What do you see as being your main contributions to epistemology?

Main contributions? Whether or not they've earned the kind of general acceptance that the word "contribution" connotes, the following are the ideas I have had a role in promoting and that I think deserve attention. They are both important and – I remain convinced – true.

(a) **Non-epistemic perception**: Perception of objects and events (I mean to exclude facts) is a genuine relation between perceiver and object (it requires both a perceiver and an object) that is independent of what a perceiver knows or believes about that object. It is something that young children and animals (with very little in the way of conceptual resources) can do as effortlessly and automatically as adult human beings. In this respect seeing a thimble is like touching a thimble. It is not an epistemological, not a conceptual, achievement.

(b) **Externalism**: In *Seeing and Knowing* (1969) I developed an externalist theory of perceptual knowledge (to be carefully distinguished—see (a)–from perception of objects and events) that I later (Dretske 1971, 1981) extended to all empirical knowledge. Seeing (and thereby knowing) that there are cookies in a jar is not a matter of having (or acquiring) good reasons, a justification, or evidence for thinking there are cookies there. It is simply a matter of getting oneself properly connected to the cookies in the jar. This connection I variously described as having a conclusive reason (1971) or information (1981) that there are cookies in the jar. I still think the subjunctive conditional I originally (1969) used to characterize this connection is constitutive of knowledge. Causation (e.g. Goldman 1967) clearly isn't enough. You must–as Nozick

(1983) later put it—*track* the fact you come to know about, and tracking a fact is more than being caused by it. Circumstances must somehow eliminate alternative possible causes.

(c) **Closure and Relevant Alternatives**: To see (hence, know) there are cookies in the jar, one need not (and obviously does not) *see* that they (the cookies) are not clever fakes. A clever fake, at least the ones the skeptic proposes, are – by definition, if you will – what one *cannot* identify by the means one normally uses to see whether there are cookies in the jar (a casual glance into the cookie jar). Nor can one see that (what one takes to be) the "cookies" are not just figments of one's own imagination. You can (if common sense is right) see that there are cookies in the jar, but you cannot (if the skeptic is right—and I think he is) see that you are not just dreaming of cookies. Not only is this fact (that one is not being deceived in undetectable ways) not something one sees to be so, it isn't clear how one could know (in some other way) that it is so. Such skeptical alternatives are deliberately formulated so as to be immune from exclusion on the basis of evidence or reasons. One is often told that such skeptical scenarios are not plausible. And so they aren't. That, though, isn't the issue. The question is: do you *know* them to be false? If you do, *how* do you know it? How do you know that *this* time isn't exceptional, a first-time exception to your (perhaps) unblemished record, a time in which you turn out, quite remarkably, to be wrong? Do you know it isn't? If so, how do you know it?

This familiar (to all epistemologists) line of skeptical questioning has convinced me that if skepticism is false, if we really can know (by seeing) that there are cookies in the jar, then this (that one isn't deceived by some extraordinary confluence of circumstances) must be a fact one doesn't have to know in order to know there are cookies in the jar. This, though, is simply the denial of closure. One does not have to know all things one knows to be implied by what one knows. I have never read a convincing account of exactly how we (always) *know* it (what we come to believe by perception) isn't all a fantasy despite the fact that philosophers – most of them anyway – embrace closure and, therefore, think we *must* know it isn't a fantasy in order to know such humble things as that there are cookies in the jar.

As far as I can tell, the currently most fashionable way of dealing with this problem – contextualism – is merely a way of embracing skepticism. The only way it manages to avoid skepticism is by making closure an epistemologically useless principle and, therefore, not worth saving. One knows there are cookies in the jar in ordinary, everyday, contexts because the possibility of dreams and elaborate deceptions is simply not relevant. Nonetheless, if one tries to use closure to "find out" something one knows to be implied by what one knows – that, for instance, they (the things one sees) are not merely carefully contrived fakes – then one automatically creates a new context in which skeptical possibilities become relevant. The result? Well, given the validity of closure, one no longer knows there are cookies in the jar. Not unless one knows (not just has a reason to believe, but *knows*) that a host of skeptical possibilities are false. So the attempt to use closure to find out one is not dreaming or being deceived in some way robs one of the very piece of knowledge that the use of closure requires. So one salvages closure by rendering it useless. The patient dies on the operating table.

What do you think is the proper role of epistemology in relation to other areas of philosophy and other academic disciplines?

Aside from its intrinsic interest – and I do believe there are questions in epistemology with enough intrinsic interest to justify efforts to answer them even if there are no practical benefits – I have always regarded epistemology as an important restraint on excesses elsewhere (particularly in metaphysics). If you don't have to worry about how something can be known, there is very little to restrain one's imagination about what is or can be. I give only one example of this – an example taken from an area in the philosophy of mind – but examples from other areas (ethics is an obvious case) are also available.

An objection made to certain externalist theories of the mind, theories that view the representational efforts of the brain as basically relational in nature (you get to think about water only by being properly related – perhaps causally or informationally – to actual water in your environment) is that such theories make introspective knowledge impossible. How can one know, by peering inwards (where, presumably, the thoughts are occurring), that one is thinking about water if the fact that one has thoughts about water is a relational fact about one, a fact about the way one is or was related to the stuff in one's environment? Isn't this like trying to find out whether one is married or wealthy by looking in a mirror?

This objection to metaphysical externalism (about the mind) uses a premise that is basically epistemological in character. The premise is that we *do* know, by some form of *self*-examination, by awareness of what is going on *inside*, that we are thinking about water rather than a martini. The only way to defend externalism, then, is either to do epistemology yourself or to have someone do it for you (always a risky business). One must somehow establish that externalism is consistent with introspective knowledge of the mind or, failing that, that we (contrary to longstanding tradition) simply don't have introspective knowledge of our own mind—either because we don't have such knowledge (skepticism) or because the knowledge is not actually acquired introspectively. One cannot do this kind of metaphysics without doing epistemology.

I also think epistemology is – or that it should be – an important adjunct to work in neuropsychology and cognitive science— especially areas devoted to the understanding and study of perception and consciousness. Scientific experiments are rightfully designed to side-step tricky philosophical issues, but when it comes time to say what the results of the experiments show about the mind, philosophy starts creeping in. A little familiarity with the mistakes philosophers have made over the past few hundred years would help scientists avoid recapitulating them.

What do you consider to be the most neglected topics and/or contributions in contemporary epistemology?

For a time I thought there was insufficient attention paid to the role of testimony: knowing P because so-and-so told you that P or you read that P in the newspaper. Since most of what we know we get from others (teachers, parents, friends, newscasters, etc.), there should, it seems, be a proportional amount of attention paid to the vagaries of this channel for receiving information about the world. I spent some time in (Dretske 1969) talking about this issue (under the topic of secondary epistemic perception), but I saw very little attention given to it until the earlier articles and 2001 book of T. Coady. I still think there are a lot of interesting problems in this area relating to perceptual relativity and theory-loaded observation that are still (today) entirely neglected.

Another area that I think is neglected (the work of Chris Peacocke is an exception) is the light that developmental studies in psychology can throw on epistemological problems. Putnam's famous argument against brain-in-a-vat skepticism (if we were brains in a vat, we couldn't even believe we had hands; so that isn't a way we could be mistaken about it) is an example of how this approach might lead to useful results. Perhaps if we better understood how children acquire concepts, we would better understand what it takes to correctly apply these concepts and, therefore, something about the possibilities of mistake and, therefore, the possibilities of knowledge.

What do you think the future of epistemology will (or should) hold?

Epistemologists don't have crystal balls and even if they had them, they would be professionally averse to using them. Philosophical interests (but not, let us hope, results and conclusions) are fad-driven, and although one can, if clever enough, create a fad, one cannot predict them. So I won't try. I could, of course, guess about how things *will* go or declare how they *should* go, but such efforts would tell the reader more about me than they would the future of epistemology. Maybe, though, that is the purpose of this question.

References

Coady, T. 2001 *Testimony: A Philosophical Study*. New York: Oxford University Press.

Dretske, F. 1969. *Seeing and Knowing*. Chicago, IL; University of Chicago Press.

Dretske, F. 1971. "Conclusive Reasons," *Australasian Journal of Philosophy*, 49, 1–22.

Dretske, F. 1981. *Knowledge and the Flow of Information*. Cambridge, MA; MIT Press/A Bradford Book.

Dretske, F. 2004. "Change Blindness," *Philosophical Studies*, 120: 1–18.

Dretske, F, 2005. "The Case Against Closure." In *Contemporary Debates in Epistemology*, Ernest Sosa and Matthias Steup, editors, Blackwell Publishers.

Dretske, F. 2006. "Perception without Awareness." In *Perceptual Experience*, edited by Tamar Gendler and John Hawthorne, Oxford University Press.

Dretske, F. forthcoming. "What Change Blindness Teaches About Consciousness," in *Philosophical Perspectives*, John Hawthorne, ed.

Goldman, A. 1967. "A Causal Theory of Knowing," *The Journal of Philosophy*, June 22, p. 361.

Nozick, R. 1981. *Philosophical Explanations*. Cambridge, MA; Harvard University Press.

8
Pascal Engel

Professor of Contemporary Philosophy
University of Geneva, Switzerland

Why were you initially drawn to epistemology (and what keeps you interested)?

I am a late comer in the field. When I was a student in Paris in the 1970s, historical epistemology was all the rage, and Michel Foucault's views about the history of social sciences were very influential. But his so-called "archeology of knowledge" did not deal with knowledge at all. It dealt with the "will to truth", and knowledge was considered as just what is believed by a community at a certain time and used as an instrument of power. No one ever asked about what knowledge is, and traditional epistemology was ignored. When I turned to analytic philosophy in reaction against these relativist views, my interest did not focus directly upon epistemology, since I thought, with Dummett, that philosophy of language had replaced epistemology in the position of first philosophy. The only epistemological questions that we met had to do with language understanding, and through the various elaborations of a neo-Fregean theory of sense. I actually came to epistemology only when I tried to understand how a Davidsonian theory of radical interpretation for language and for thought could work. It worked with a minimal notion of belief as holding-true of sentences, and with an holistic view of knowledge as coming out of the coherence between beliefs. I focused on the notion of belief, but found the alternative functionalist conception equally unsatisfactory. L.J. Cohen's *Essay on Belief and Acceptance* opened my eyes to the necessity of a different analysis of belief, and I convinced me that believing is a much more complex phenomenon than what current philosophy of mind and cognitive science said it was. I have been attracted by a layered conception of belief, according to which one should distinguish levels of believing: pure dispositional-functional belief, partial belief as degree of subjective probability, belief as assent to propositions or sentences, and belief as acceptance. There are, however, different notions of acceptance. On the one hand, acceptance has been caracterised, in particular by Stalnaker and Bratman, as a pragmatic notion distinct from belief: someone can accept that P without believing that P, for strategic, be epistemic (e.g hypothesizing, guessing or arguing for a reductio) or practical reasons, e.g professional ones. On the other hand the notion of acceptance had been used by Keith Lehrer in epistemology, in order to distinguish it from belief and to emphasise what Lehrer calls the "metamind" dimension of thought, which is for him one of the necessary conditions of knowledge. Trying to understand these various layers of belief, and their interrelations led me both to think about the distinction between practical and epistemic reasons for believing, about the ethics of belief, and about the issue of epistemic justification in general. My Davidsonian first self had led me to rely upon upon the Bayesian conception of belief, which I understood mostly from the Ramseyan point of view. I was then influenced by the work of Richard Jeffrey, Isaac Levi and of Bas Van Fraassen, which all have a strong pragmatist inspiration.

In spite of my attraction for the Bayesian conception of belief and evidence, I could not accept Bayesian bolchevism nor the anti-realism which was implicit in many of these views on the epistemology of belief. Moreover I had always thought that Davidson's answer to scepticism – according to which scepticism is spurious because we cannot but presuppose the massive truth of our beliefs in interpretation – was deeply insufficient. This led me to realise that the epistemology of belief cannot be conceived apart from the epistemology of knowledge, and that knowledge is not merely a form of rational belief. I now take knowledge, and not simply truth and high degree of subjective probability, to be the aim of belief. If one adopts this perspective, the shape of the layered conception of belief becomes different. Knowledge is much less pragmatically determined than belief, and states of acceptance have also to be defined in relation to knowledge.

What do you see as being your main contributions to epistemology?

It is not for me to evaluate what are my contributions to the field, but I can say what I think important. I take epistemology to be a normative discipline, and, I want to take this feature seriously. Like in ethics where there is a division between "normative ethics" and "meta-ethics"– epistemology can be divided into a normative part , which forms the core of the subject – the various conceptions of knowledge and of justification, the various answers to the sceptical problem – on the one hand , and a meta-epistemological part, which deals with the nature of epistemic norms in general, on the other hand. With respect to the former domain, I have argued for, like many others, a neo-Moorean response to scepticism, and defended what is sometimes called a form of "epistemic compatibilism"—the attempt to combine an externalist conception of knowledge, which I think along the lines of safety principles, with an internalist component. I do not, however, conceive the externalist component as involving a form of skill or credit to the agent along the lines of virtue epistemology, and I intend to stick to a form of (externalist) evidentialism. And I do not conceive the internalist component as involving internal access of the agent to his/her justificatory states.

With respect to the latter domain, meta-epistemology, I have tried to investigate the nature of the normative component in epistemology, especially with respect to the central concepts of belief, of truth and of knowledge, and in trying to understand the specific nature of epistemic reasons. One can conceive the normativity which is attached to the concept of knowledge along the line of a deontological conception of epistemic justification. Alternatively one can take it to be involved in the evaluation of the value of the agent as a knower, along the lines of virtue epistemology. Neither one of these views seems to me to capture the proper nature of epistemic norms. I take these to be constitutive of the concepts of belief and of knowledge, and have tried to spell out in what sense these involve a normative dimension. One first has to formulate the appropriate norms, before assessing how they can regulate our beliefs. The normative component is closely associated to the nature of our reasons for believing, but it should not be reduced to it. It consists in spelling out the basic requirements for a state to be a belief or a state knowledge. Virtue theoretic approaches tend, in my view, to locate within the requirements for knowledge what belongs rather, according to me, to the nature of inquiry. Pragmatists too tend to assimilate knowledge and inquiry. That seems to me wrong. In this sense, I feel more sympathy for classical evidentialism and for a kind of monism about epistemic value (truth and knowledge being the only values), and I mean to resist recent attempts at "expanding" epistemology in the direction of social determinants of knowledge and of features which reveal the contingency of the justificatory links. I am interested in confronting epistemology with its borders, but I think that we should preserve its core from extrinsic elements. For instance I do not think that epistemic states are subject to "pragmatic encroachment" in the sense that practical matters affect the nature of what we know, and of the evidence which is necessary for knowing. Or, for another example, I find it very important to investigate the social determinants of knowleddge, but I do not think that epistemology can be "social" through and through.

What do you think is the proper role of epistemology in relation to other areas of philosophy and other academic disciplines?

Although much of contemporary epistemology tends to become a very specialised field, occupied only with a limited set of problems and circumscribed to a certain kind of literature, it seems to me wrong to insulate it from other fields within philosophy. There are, for instance, a number of structural parallels between ethics and epistemology, between practical and theoretical reasoning, or between epistemology and the philosophy of action. Although it would be wrong to reduce any of these subjects to the other – epistemology is not a branch of ethics for instance, contrary to what a certain kind of ethics of belief tends to say- it is very interesting to investigate the parallels. In the ethics/ epistemology case, this has been done quite a lot during the last two decades, but there is still work to do. To take an example of a useful parallel, why is it that wishful thinking is wrong with respect to belief, but not with respect to action ? Can there be epistemic *akrasia* in the same sense as there is practical *akrasia*? Can we form a belief which we take at the same time as not grounded on enough evidence? It also seems to me fruitful to investigate the links between epistemology and metaphysics, philosophy of science and philosophy of language. In what sense, for instance, is the factivity of knowledge – knowledge is knowledge of facts – related to the familiar ontological doctrine that the world is made up of facts, and does the former imply the latter? What consequence does it have for the way we conceive scientific knowledge and scientific progress the idea that knowledge is not a species of justified true belief? Good epistemology, as well as good philosophy, must not be narrowly specialised. Much of contemporary work displays this kind of pluralism and of open ended structure of the problems of epistemology, but there is progress to be done in broadening the perspectives. For my part, I have always been interested in the problems of the philosophy of logic, and the issues about the justification of deduction, of the warrant for our logical inferences and of the normativity of logical rules or laws, have always seemed to me to be closely related to those of epistemology in general. The problems of how we can be warranted in our inferences cannot be completely different from those which we encounters with the warrant for our perceptual beliefs, for instance.

What do you consider to be the most neglected topics and/or contributions in contemporary epistemology?

Neglect is relative, and can go from the complete ignorance of a certain kind of problem or topic to a relative ignorance. I cannot find any instance of a complete ignorance, but some topics seem to me to merit to be moved from a B series status to front screen.

One neglected topic is that of the relationship between what one might call general epistemology – the core issues of the subject which I have called "normative" – and what one might can regional or special epistemology, the epistemology of a specific domain. I think that we should conceive the whole subject in a very systematic way, in the sense, that what is true about knowledge in general should also be true about, say, medical or historical knowledge. If one intends to resist the kind of epistemological relativism which reigns in many sectors of the history and of the sociology of science, one has to try to connect general and regional epistemologies. Very often abstract philosophy of science or methodology deals with issues which are at too much a distance from actual scientific practice (think for instance of logical theories of belief revision with respect to the kind of theories of scientific progress that historians of science give).

A specific topic which I find neglected and worth invastigating, although there are some publications on it (mostly by Edna Ullman Margalit) is the problem of trying to understand what a *presumption* is. Presuming that P is neither believing that P, nor accepting pragmatically that P, nor even a prediction. It is a kind of hypothesizing, but of a specific nature, which we have to understand together with other states of conjectural belief. When Stanley (Henry, not Jason) meets Livingstone, what does he presume? The Epicurians and the Stoics called *prolepseis* the principles that the mind contains originally and which are awakened by external objects in various occasions (see Leibniz, *New Essays*, Pref.). These have a relationship between the status of what we are entitled to believe, and with the issue of implicit knowledge.

Another issue which I find somewhat neglected is the epistemology of memory. There is work on this, but much less that on the epistemology of testimony. It gives rise to the same kind of issues about memory preservation, reliability and entitlement, as those which are the focus of the epistemology of testimony.

I think also that contemporary epistemologists would gain profit from looking at works of the past in their field. In that respect I have always found very illuminating reading writers like Antoine Arnauld (the best analytic philosopher of the XVIIth century) Claude Buffier (less well known than Reid), William Whewell (shadowed by Mill), Jacob Friedrich Fries (shadowed by Kant and Hegel), Augustin Cournot (shadowed by Auguste Comte), and C.S. Peirce. These examples also remind us that epistemology may be a much more systematic enterprise than it is usually conceived by contemporary epistemology in the analytic tradition.

What do you think the future of epistemology will (or should) hold?

I am not good at presuming, even less predicting ! If one looks at present concerns in epistemology, one can predict that some of today's most discussed topics – contextualism, social epistemology, and the self-predicted advent of the so-called experimental epistemology – will continue to attract attention, given the sociology of our discipline. But I predict also that most of these views will at one point or another meet the law of diminishing returns. Not that these investigations are not useful or interesting, but I have strong doubts that epistemology will become an experimental subject nor that epistemology can be social through and through. The core of the discipline is, and will remain, a *priori*.

One development which I can predict, and which I would welcome as well, would be an attempt at integrating the methods of epistemology. It would be good if evidence for epistemological views did not come simply from the examination of linguistic intuitions and from the construction of test cases. For instance the distinction between knowing-how and knowing-that cannot simply rest on linguistic evidence, but has also to rest on data from cognitive science.

I think also that there has been a tendency – which I attribute here to to a form of parochialism – to consider that epistemologists cannot be metaphysicians, because that are supposed to be concerned with the issue whether we know something and how we know it, rather than with what there is and the properties of reality. It is thus assumed that epistemologists are by definition anti-realists . Much of contemporary epistemology is realist, and it is continuous to ontology and metaphysics. Similarly, many metaphysians seems to believe that epistemology of a subject matter is somewhat a secondary and optional kind of investigation, which fundamental ontology can dispense with. But we need to do the epistemology of our metaphysics, and vice versa. So I predict that the field will tend to be understood as much broader and wide ranging than it appears.

9
Robert J. Fogelin

Professor of Philosophy
Dartmouth College, USA

Vincent F. Hendricks and Duncan Prichard have asked a number of epistemologists to respond to five questions concerning the status of epistemology. In all probability, I will be odd man out, for I have strong reservations concerning the viability of this field, not only in its traditional form but also in its recent manifestations.

Why were you initially drawn to epistemology (and what keeps you interested)?

I wasn't exactly drawn to epistemology, but rather stumbled into it. My doctoral dissertation presented an analysis of evaluative language. The leading idea was that evaluative statements in their various forms could be treated as statements concerning the warrant in behalf of a prescription. Roughly – *very roughly* – "S ought to do x" = "The prescription: *S, do x!* is warranted." Or – again *very roughly* – "x is good" = "The prescription: *Opt for x!* is warranted." This analysis seemed to solve a number of problems, for example how normative statements can be taken to be true or false but also (at least in some contexts) can carry prescriptive force. It did a number of other useful things as well, including dealing with past-tense evaluations (a problem for prescriptivism), and giving a straightforward accounts of the logical relationships among normative statements. I still think it is a pretty good way of understanding evaluative statements, but it never much caught on.

In any case, when I began my march toward tenure by transforming my dissertation into a book, I was struck by the idea that the claims I had made concerning deontic modalities seemed to have a parallel application to epistemic modalities. This yielded what I called a *warrant statement* analysis of epistemic claims.

In 1967, when *Evidence and Meaning* was published, the notion of a warrant was not widely used in epistemological discussions, though later it did get some play. Looking back, I now think that I had too idealized a notion of what a warrant is. In any case, this was my pathway into epistemology and I began teaching theory of knowledge on a regular basis. Over time I became more and more dissatisfied with the field, in part because of the influence of Richard Popkin, who got me to take Pyrrhonian skepticism seriously.

What do you see as being your main contributions to epistemology?

Whatever contributions I have made to epistemology are chiefly found in *Pyrrhonian Reflections on Knowledge and Justification* (1994), "Two Diagnoses of Skepticism" (1999), *The Tightrope of Reason* (2003), and the light-hearted "The Skeptics are Coming! The Skeptics are Coming!" (2004).

Pyrrhonian Reflections begins with an examination of problems concerning the analysis of epistemic judgments that are generated in one way by Gettier problems and by skeptical scenarios in another. Gettier problems first. In an effort to drive home the point I was trying to make in *Pyrrhonian Reflections* concerning Gettier examples, I will state it in as provocative way as possible. It is generally thought that Gettier examples present a fundamental – perhaps unanswerable – challenge to the tri-part analysis that knowledge is *justified true belief* whereas, in fact, they support it.

I'll begin with an elegant Gettier example due to Fred Dretske (1970). Jones and his daughter are standing before a corral seemingly occupied by a herd of zebras. In fact only one of these creatures is a zebra, all the rest are mules cleverly painted up to look like zebras. Jones points to one of the animals and says to his daughter, "That's a zebra." By happenstance, he points to the one animal in the corral that is a zebra. He believes it is a zebra, and he is right in this. Is he justified in believing this? We are expected to answer, "Yes." Does he know that it is a zebra? We are expected to answer, "No." Taken together, these two responses are supposed to show that knowledge – at least for cases of the kind under consideration – cannot be identified with justified true belief.

The diagnosis. This example, like all standard Gettier examples, depends on there being a fact that we *as readers* are apprised of but that Jones, from his standpoint, has no reason to suspect. In this case, the reader is told that all but one of the animals are mules painted up to look like zebras. The animal Jones pointed to was in plain sight; he knows what zebras look like; he does not confuse them with other animals; and so on. Thus he has done nothing *remiss* in identifying the animal as a zebra. It is in this way that he was justified in doing so. Still, we, as readers, know that the reason Jones relied on – that the animal he pointed to looked just like a zebra – did not justify his calling it one. That is why we are inclined to say "No" when asked whether Jones knew whether it was a zebra. Thus our refusal to grant that Jones knows that the animal he pointed to was a zebra actually *invokes* the notion that knowledge is justified true belief, and cannot be used as a reason for rejecting it.

Let me change the example in a way that will, I hope, produce a Gettier example to end all Gettier examples: Not only did the epistemic pranksters paint up the mules to look like zebras, they also painted the sole zebra to look just like a zebra. As before, Jones, by chance, points to the (now painted) zebra and tells his daughter that it is a zebra. But he does more than this. Violating the zoo's regulations, he reaches over the fence and pats the animal. Then, withdrawing his hand, he discovers that it is covered with paint. What would Jones think? Pretty clearly, he would recognize that there was funny-business going on at the zoo and that it is not a place where one can identify even a common animal in plain view just by looking at it. He will therefore recognize that his original identification of the animal he pointed to was not justified. In the situation, as he now recognizes it, identifying an animal as a zebra by just looking at it isn't good enough. An application of paint-remover is in order. Would Jones think that he was remiss in making his original identification? No, he would probably place total blame on the lunatics who ran around painting up animals to look like different animals or even painting up animals to look like themselves. Shouldn't he have taken precautions against the possibility of painted animals? Of course not.

In *Pyrrhonian Reflections* I expand on this last point by introducing the notion, borrowed from law, of *levels of scrutiny*. I might also have spoken of principles of *due care,* or *proper vigilance.* In the contemporary literature some epistemologists draw a contrast between two sorts of contexts: the *everyday* context and the *philosophical* context. Indexing justification to context, it is then claimed that the same judgment can be justified (or count as knowledge) in one context but not justified (or count as knowledge) in the other. This is not the contrast that I have in mind in speaking of levels of scrutiny, and I want to distance myself from it. As I use the notion, level of scrutiny is a feature of everyday methods of justification. What I am calling everyday contexts would include identifying animals in a zoo, but also sophisticated activities such as checking on the attribution of a painting to Leonardo, tracing its provenance, subjecting it to x-ray or chemical analysis, and so on. Discovering painted animals at the zoo increases the proper level of scrutiny for identifying animals in it, as does discovering that a painting under examination has passed through the hands of the art-dealer Joseph Duveen.

Learning how to operate at the proper level of scrutiny is part of commonsense training for making well-founded judgments. It is captured in a variety of commonsense sayings including, "Fool me once, shame on you; fool me twice, shame on me." In everyday life, fixing the proper level of scrutiny can be a delicate matter. Higher is not always better, because higher levels of scrutiny carry with them what we might call epistemic transaction costs. One can be too picky, that is, more demanding than the practical context demands. Being ultra-picky can completely stymie reasonable assessment of grounds.

Returning to Jones, it would be odd to say that he *ignored* the possibility that he was dealing with painted mules—that thought never entered his mind. Nor did he consider the possibility that what he took to be animals were actually holograms or that the experiences he was having were the product of neuroscientists manipulating his envatted brain with electric probes. Typically, the level of scrutiny is raised through encountering facts that we take as flags indicating that we should proceed with more than usual caution—check things that we do not normally check. Jones encountered no such flags until he patted the animal and found his hand covered with paint.

In the previous paragraph I (slyly) moved from discussing Gettier problems to considering skeptical scenarios—a second epistemological obsession. Both are related to levels of scrutiny, but in different ways. In Gettier problems, we, as spectators viewing the scene, are provided with a piece of information that triggers the need for a higher level of scrutiny than Jones (rightly) employed, given the information available to him. It is this mismatch in levels of scrutiny that – as far as I can see – lies at the heart of Gettier problems in all their various forms. Skeptical scenarios are related to levels of scrutiny in a different way. Normally we do not elevate the level of scrutiny unless something in the concrete context triggers our doing so. If, however, we are free to let our imagination roam without restraint, as many engaged in philosophy do, then there is no limit to the possibilities we can think up that will trigger a demand for a higher level of scrutiny. Normally we do not engage in such flights of fancy, and if we do, we do not take them seriously. But, as I remark in *Pyrrhonian Reflections,* "If we dwell on [remote possibilities], our level of scrutiny will rise, and we will find ourselves unwilling to claim to know many things that we usually accept as items of knowledge." (93) Later I add that "the theory of knowledge, as commonly pursued, has been an attempt to find ways of establishing knowledge claims from a perspective where the level of scrutiny has been heightened by reflection alone." (99) A central thesis of *Pyrrhonian Reflections* is that a theory of knowledge or a theory of justification pursued in the context of an unlimited range of possible defeaters will inevitably lead to radical skepticism.

Skeptical scenarios are generally thought to be philosophically important because of the profound challenges they present. But if we calm down, step back, we can see that nothing challenging or problematic is going on. In *On Certainty* Wittgenstein remarks:

> *OC,* 472. When a child learns a language it learns at the same time what is to be investigated and *what not.*
> (emphasis added)

An unfettered employment of the notion of levels of scrutiny effectively erases the *what-not* clause, and, for obvious reasons, a radical skepticism ensues.

For all that, skeptical scenarios are interesting. We can learn something from them about the normal operation of knowledge claims. In seeing how taking skeptical scenarios seriously undercuts all (or, with a nod to Descartes' "I think", almost all) claims to knowledge, we come to recognize, as Wittgenstein puts it, "how very specialized the use of 'I know' is" (*OC,* 11). I think that what Wittgenstein is getting at is this: Knowledge claims depend for their employment on largely stable surroundings, including a world that behaves in reasonably orderly ways, and a background of widely shared common knowledge concerning it. But isn't it grotesquely circular to cite common knowledge in giving an account of knowledge? No. Someone (perhaps a child) could possess a great deal of knowledge without commanding the concept of knowledge, just as someone (again a child) could learn the meaning of many expressions without commanding the concept of meaning. I do not think that the converse of either of these claims holds. In any case, teaching children the meaning of certain expressions does not begin with teaching them the meaning of "meaning." In a parallel fashion, imparting knowledge to children does not begin by explaining to them what knowledge is. Of course, nobody, as far as I know, would deny either of these claims taken *factually*. What is important is to recognize their conceptual significance. In the *Blue Book* Wittgenstein suggests that "meaning" is an odd-job word:

> "Meaning" is one of the words of which one may say that they have odd jobs in our language. It is these words which cause most philosophical troubles. Imagine some institution: most of its members have certain regular functions, functions which can easily be described, say, in the statutes of the institution. There are, on the other hand, some members who are employed for odd jobs, which nevertheless may be extremely important.–What causes most trouble in philosophy is that we are tempted to describe the use of important 'odd-job' words as though they were words with regular functions. (*BB* 43–4)

I think that "I know" and "S knows" are similarly odd-job expressions that come into play only later in the game when epistemic practices are in place. Neither *meaning* nor *knowledge* are fundamental notions.

A few years after *Pyrrhonian Reflections* appeared, David Lewis published "Elusive Knowledge" (1996), an article that presents ideas that, in many ways, parallel my reflections on levels of scrutiny. In the end, however, we draw fundamentally different morals from these reflections. The similarity between our approaches appears in passages of the following kind:

> Let your paranoid fantasies rip ... and soon you find that uneliminated possibilities are everywhere. Those possibilities of error are far-fetched, of course, but possibilities all the same. They bite into even our most everyday knowledge. (549)

Lewis draws the connection with epistemology in this way:

> Maybe epistemology is the culprit. Maybe this extraordinary pastime robs us of our knowledge. Maybe we

> do know a lot in daily life, but maybe when we look
> hard at our knowledge, it goes away. But only when
> we look at it harder than the sane ever do in daily life;
> only when we let our paranoid fantasies rip. (550)

I said essentially the same thing, but not with Lewis's inimitable gusto.

Though we start out the same, we part company quickly. My view is that skepticism is the inevitable consequence of raising levels of scrutiny in an unrestricted manner. Though Lewis never speaks of levels of scrutiny, it is clear that he would reject this diagnosis.

> But I myself cannot subscribe to this account ... because I question its starting point. I don't agree that the mark of knowledge is justification. (551)

Since it's the demand for justification that is causing the difficulty, "the link" Lewis tells us, "between knowledge and justification must be broken" (551).

Two things are worth noting. First, Lewis does not *fully* break the link between knowledge and justification. To his credit, Lewis attempts to specify, at least in a broad programmatic way, the rules that tell us which possibilities we may properly ignore and which not. In the process he introduces what he calls the Rule of Belief:

> A possibility that the subject believes to obtain is not properly ignored, whether or not he is right to so believe. Neither is one that he ought to believe to obtain – one that evidence and arguments justify him in believing – whether or not he does so believe. (555)

Later he remarks, "This is the only place where belief and justification enter into my story" (556). This amounts to saying that a person, given his own system of beliefs, will be remiss in ignoring a defeating possibility that he is committed to. No red-blooded externalist would make this concession to internalism.

Second, and more importantly, in his effort to protect knowledge from skeptical challenges, Lewis seems to have surrendered justification to the skeptic. This is an extraordinary concession, for whether we hold that knowledge amounts to justified true belief or not, we expect epistemology to give guidance in sorting out beliefs that are based on justified reasoning from those that are not.

That would be one way that epistemology might find application outside of philosophy—our next topic.

What do you think is the proper role of epistemology in relation to other areas of philosophy and other academic disciplines?

It should be clear that I am not a champion of most modern (including recent) epistemology. I do not know of any discipline that would be enriched through an introduction to Gettier problems or to skeptical scenarios. Beyond this, I cannot think of any discipline that would be enriched by employing the *methodology* characteristic of contemporary epistemology. I have in mind appeals to intuition, typically appeals to intuitions in dealing with exotic cases. It is not simply that intuitions are unreliable – which they probably are – but that the procedure involves the assumption that words have, if not an exact meaning, at least a reasonably exact core meaning. Invoking intuitions in exotic cases is a preferred method for teasing out this core meaning. In fact, many useful and unproblematic notions collapse under such pressure because the exotic examples under consideration are remote from the cases where the notion has its primary application. This is not a problem unique to epistemology. Think of the exotica that appear in discussions of personal identity (where we encounter people fusing with others, replicating themselves, minds exchanging bodies), ethical theory (with its veil of ignorance), metaphysics (with its twin earths, cosmic complements and possible worlds—near and far), philosophy of language (with its competing manuals of translation, equally good, but incompatible with one another.) Then there is *grue* and *bleen*—a class unto itself. As long as philosophy (epistemology included) is driven by the method of intuition, there is, I think, little chance that it will have an impact on other disciplines—or at least have any salutary impact.

What do you consider to be the most neglected topics and/or contributions in contemporary epistemology?

I'll take a bye on this one.

What do you think the future of epistemology will (or should) hold?

I have no idea what the future of epistemology will be like, but I can muse on what I think it should be like. First, pretty obviously, I think epistemologists should abandon the method of intuition as commonly practiced and replace it with an examination of the actual use of epistemic (and related) terms in productive standard contexts. This would involve revisiting the relevant works of Wittgenstein and J.L. Austin. Among other things, this would lead to an examination of the finer-grained terms of epistemic assessment. In "A Plea for Excuses," Austin remarks that the field of aesthetics would make more progress "if only we could forget for a while about the beautiful and get down instead to the dainty and the dumpy" (183). In the same way, it would be useful to forget about knowledge for a while and examine such terms of assessment as "picky," "pig-headed," and "off the wall." In a similar vein, it might be useful to set aside concern with "knowing that" for a while and reflect on sentences contain "knowing why" and "knowing how" as in "I know why the television isn't working and how to fix it." I do not think that this sentence contains a zeugma. It can also be useful to consider some common, but seemingly odd constructions, like "I think I know." Here two normally contrastive terms "think" and "know" are happily combined. In "Plea for Excuses" Austin refers to investigations of this kind as "linguistic phenomenology" (182). I think that epistemology would profit from a renewed interest in this now outdated way of dealing with philosophical problems

I also think that it is important not to concentrate solely or even primarily on the use of epistemic assessments as they occur in the context of linguistic exchanges. Taking over an idea from classical (not Rortian) pragmatism, these assessments should also be examined in the context of an ongoing inquiry. Among other things, this will bring into prominence how levels of scrutiny are exploited and constrained in concrete contexts of investigation. For example, it took a very long time for biologists to discover the cause of Legionnaires Disease. The procedures they routinely used were not turning up an answer. Because of the concrete problem they confronted, the level of scrutiny was significantly raised: Routines procedures that were normally taken for granted themselves became objects of scrutiny, then altered, and finally the problem was solved. Did they consider the possibility that their laboratory had been cursed by a deceiving spirit? Well maybe, but only as a joke.

Works Cited or Alluded To

Austin, J. L. 1979. *Philosophical Papers*. Edited by J. O. Urmson. and G. J. Warnock. 3rd ed. Oxford: Oxford University Press.

Dretske, Fred. 1970. "Epistemic Operators." *Journal of Philosophy* 67 (24):1007–1023.

Fogelin, Robert J. 1967. *Evidence and Meaning, International Library of Philosophy and Scientific Method*. London: Routledge and Kegan Paul.

⸺ 1994. *Pyrrhonian Reflections on Knowledge and Justification*. Oxford and New York: Oxford University Press.

⸺ 2003. "Two Diagnoses of Skepticism." In *The Skeptics: Contemporary Essays*, edited by S. Luper. Aldershot, England: Ashgage.

⸺ 2004. "The Skeptics are Coming! The Skeptics are Coming!" In *Pyrrhonian Skepticism*, edited by W. Sinnott-Armstrong. New York: Oxford University Press.

Gettier, Edmund L. 1963. "Is Justified True Belief Knowledge?" *Analysis* 26 (3): 144–46.

Lewis, David. 1996. "Elusive Knowledge." *Australasian Journal of Philosophy* 74 (4): 549–67.

Popkin, Richard Henry. 1980. *The High Road to Pyrrhonism*. San Diego, Calif.: Austin Hill Press.

Wittgenstein, Ludwig. 1969. *On Certainty*. Translated by G. E. M. Anscombe. Edited by G. E. M. Anscombe. and R. Rhees. Oxford: Basil Blackwell.

⸺ 1969. *The Blue and Brown Books*. Edited by R. Rhees. 2nd. ed. Oxford: Basil Blackwell.

10
Richard Fumerton
F. Wendell Miller Professor and Chair
University of Iowa, USA

Why were you initially drawn to epistemology (and what keeps you interested)?

My first philosophy course as an undergraduate was on the history of modern philosophy. I found the progression from Descartes's desperate attempt to secure commonsense empirical knowledge through knowledge of God, to Berkeley's optimistic effort to secure knowledge by reducing the content of empirical belief to propositions describing minds and their experiences, and ultimately to Hume's radical skepticism, fascinating. The questions these philosophers raised seemed simultaneously utterly bizarre, but at the same time, clear, precise, and compelling. The chasm between appearance and reality seemed both disturbing and inescapable. I have spent most of my career as an epistemologist thinking about these matters.

It sounds a bit trite, but I don't think any respectable philosopher can ignore epistemology. You can't make a claim in any field of philosophy without encountering a critic who will challenge you to provide reasons backing your claim. Whether you assert or deny the existence of universals, a dualism of mind and body, objective causal connections, or objective moral properties, you will be called upon to justify your philosophical position. And if you have a genuine philosophical temperament, you won't feel comfortable doing that unless you have thought long and hard about what constitutes having epistemic justification. There is simply no escaping epistemological issues when engaging in philosophical debate.

The field of epistemology is one of the most exciting in philosophy. It has undergone genuine revolutions in recent decades. Initially, through suggestive comments made by Quine, but particularly through the influential work of Alvin Goldman, externalist epistemologies have gained ascendancy. While I disagree strongly with this trend, I admire enormously the skill and sophistication with which these positions have been developed. I also enjoy what many take to be the uphill battle of defending very traditional forms of internalism in epistemology from the externalist insurgency. At the same time, I try to be as sympathetic as I can to the insights both camps offer the debate. The older I get, the more interested I am in trying to understand thoroughly the implications of various metaepistemological accounts of knowledge and justification for the ways in which the proponents of those accounts should think of traditional skeptical challenges.

When it comes to explaining my continued interest in the field of epistemology (and philosophy more generally), it is difficult to underestimate the role that teaching plays. While it is a cliché, I really do believe that teaching and research are intimately connected. It is not just the obvious fact that research informs teaching. It is also the fact that the task of explaining issues to students and answering the questions they ask informs research. And I don't just mean teaching at the graduate level. The truth is that one can "get away" with explanations to graduate students that simply won't wash with undergraduates. To discuss a philosophical issue with an undergraduate one must abandon much of the jargon behind which philosophers sometimes hide. In doing so, one can sometimes reach the painful conclusion that one never really did understand all that well a distinction the intelligibility of which one was presupposing for decades. While one often gets very similar questions from students over the years, the perspectives students bring to a philosophical issue often still surprise me. An undergraduate can ask a question that seems completely off the wall, but as I think about the question, sometimes days later, I occasionally suddenly see how thinking about things a certain way would allow one to make sense of the question. Such reflection often plants the seeds of future research.

What do you see as being your main contributions to epistemology?

I'll preface what I'm about to say with the observation that one's contributions to a field are best judged by others. While I am committed to the view that we have foundational knowledge of many of our own mental states, there are many kinds of self knowledge that is rather difficult to acquire. And one of the most difficult is the role one actually plays in furthering a field of knowledge.

Throughout my career I have been fascinated by the challenge of skepticism, and I have always tried to take that challenge seriously. I don't believe that one should dismiss skepticism at the outset and, essentially, adopt whatever modifications to one's view are necessary in order to avoid a skeptical conclusion. For years I have argued that there is a kind of epistemic justification that is of a special interest to philosophers trying to satisfy their intellectual curiosity in such a way that they get assurance of truth. I have never been opposed to recognizing derivative concepts of justification that fall short of the philosopher's epistemic ideal, but I have argued that one can't even develop plausible accounts of degenerate epistemic justification without understanding the way in which that sort of justification falls short of an ideal ("Achieving Epistemic Ascent").

In books and papers I have argued strenuously for what I take to be a very traditional, but now very unfashionable, form of foundationalism. That foundationalism defines noninferential justification relying on the sui generis concept of direct acquaintance. In short, I have argued that there is noninferential justification for S to believe P when S is directly acquainted with the fact that P (or a fact very similar to P), while S is simultaneously directly acquainted with the thought that P and a correspondence between that thought and the fact that P (or at least a relation very much like correspondence between the thought that P and a fact very similar to P.) We are not directly acquainted with facts about the physical world, the past, or other minds. Despite what most epistemologists think today, the radical empiricists were right in arguing that noninferential empirical knowledge is confined to propositions describing the contents of one's mind. Any justification we have for accepting propositions describing the physical world, other minds, the past, or the future are justified, if at all, only inferentially. To get inferential justification of the sort that gives one intellectual assurance, one must intellectually "see" the connection between one's premises and the conclusion they justify. To avoid a vicious regress, and with it a radical skepticism, there must be probabilistic connections between foundationally knowable premises and inferentially justified propositions that can be known a priori. In short, to avoid skepticism an "inferential internalist" must embrace the Keynesian notion that there are synthetic necessary truths describing quasi-logical probabilistic connections knowable a priori (See among others *Metaepistemology and Skepticism*, and "Epistemic Probability"). It may be that it is an illusion to suppose that such truths exist, but if that is so the philosopher will be frustrated in the search for intellectually satisfying epistemic justification.

While I have a number of strong and controversial positions, I am almost as interested in uncovering the implications of views as I am in arguing for any particular conclusion. That's a good part of what I tried to do in *Metaepistemology and Skepticism*. The primary argument against externalism is, I have argued, the very ease with which the view allows one to justify not only ordinary beliefs, but the belief that one has epistemic justification. If now familiar externalist accounts of epistemic justification were correct, then on the assumption that most of the ways we form beliefs are reliable (more generally are caused in the way we think they are), we can get reliably formed beliefs that our beliefs are reliably formed through straightforward "track record" arguments. But even some externalists are unwilling to follow through with the implications of their view and get cold feet when it comes to endorsing such means of acquiring justified belief about justified belief. When they come to that realization they must rethink their metaepistemological commitments.

Quite apart from any positions I have argued for, I like to think that I write in such a way that whether philosophers agree or disagree with me, they'll know precisely what I'm saying and why I am saying it. I will always be grateful for the education I received as a graduate student at Brown. Chisholm, Sosa, and the rest of the Brown faculty taught their graduate students how to write and think philosophically. Frankly, I find a disturbing trend in some contemporary philosophy towards obscurity masquerading as depth. Right or wrong, I try to be guided by nothing other than an attempt to follow as clearly as I can the logic of a position wherever it leads me. Fashions in philosophy come and go. It is always a mistake to try to conform one's views to the trends of the moment. More than anything else I have tried to keep alive not only currently unfashionable forms of foundationalism, but a way of doing philosophy itself.

What do you think is the proper role of epistemology in relation to other areas of philosophy and other academic disciplines?

I suggested above that there is no avoiding epistemology. Assertion without evidence is philosophical uninteresting. To answer challenges to the justification one offers or presupposes when employing premises in arguing for conclusions, one must *understand* epistemic justification—one must do epistemology. One can't look at contemporary philosophical debates in the philosophy of mind or in ethics without realizing the importance of epistemology. From Descartes to Jackson, *knowledge* arguments have occupied centre stage in arguments for dualism. Recently arguments for and against externalism about mental content have focused on alleged claims about the nature of introspective knowledge of mental states. One can't assess such arguments without delving into the nature of introspective knowledge (See, for example, "Introspection and Iternalism" and "Direct Realism, Introspection, and Cognitive Science"). Arguments for and against moral realism often appeal explicitly or implicitly to fundamental epistemic principles about sources of knowledge and evidence.

One ignores epistemology at one's philosophical peril. Perhaps nowhere has this been more evident than in the history of philosophy of science. For decades, philosophers of science argued about whether or not there is a defensible way to make a distinction between observational statements and theoretical statements. But a cursory examination of the debate suggests to me that the vast majority of philosophers suffered from a kind of epistemological illiteracy. Their candidates for observational truths were truths about breadbox-sized physical objects. And, unsurprisingly, philosophers with that presupposition came to the correct conclusion that claims about such objects are just as "theory laden" as claims about electrons and quarks. But the conclusion that *every* claim is theory laden involves a huge leap from the premise that truths about the external world are theory laden. The controversy in the philosophy of science was always really just the old controversy between foundationalism and coherentism, and one is never going to find *plausible* candidates for foundational knowledge thinking about truths about instrument readings. But the claim I just made is, of course, controversial, and to evaluate it properly one needs a background in epistemology.

If one brings a foundationalist epistemology to issues in the philosophy of science, one will need to reach conclusions about the ways in which can legitimately move from those foundations to justified belief in other propositions. The heart of the old controversy between realist and anti-realist conceptions of postulated theoretical entities in science often explicitly centered on alleged epistemological problems encountered by the realist. When verificationism was still riding high, the reductionists, instrumentalists, and fictionalists would often attempt to translate those alleged epistemological difficulties into challenges as to the very intelligibility of theoretical claims realistically understood. Again, to evaluate the epistemological charge that realism encounters skepticism one must come to grips with fundamental epistemological controversies concerning the legitimacy of various sorts of non-deductive reasoning. Are we restricted to inductive reasoning, or should we recognize an independent and equally fundamental reasoning to the best explanation ("Induction and Reasoning to the Best Explanation" and "Skepticism and Reasoning to the Best Explanation")? Are both just samples of indefinitely many other perfectly legitimate forms of reasoning? These are questions lying at the heart of epistemology.

In value theory, epistemic concepts again often have a critical role to play in our attempt to understand fundamental concepts of morality and rationality. Consequentialism is, of course, a very controversial approach to understanding claims about we ought to do. But almost all ethical philosopher recognize that consequences are at least partially relevant to the morality/rationality of actions. Once we concede the relevance of consequences, however, we need to decide whether it is actual, probable, or possible consequences that determine, entirely or partially, what one ought to do. In *Reason and Morality*, I've argued that the most plausible approach emphasizes possible consequences, but where the probability of the possible consequences must, of course, be taken into account. This in turn raises a question about how to understand the relevant probabilities. I've also argued that they should be understood as *epistemic* probabilities relative to the evidential position of the actor. If that's right, then there is a clear sense in which our understanding of one fundamental concept in theories of morality and rational action is actually parasitic upon our understanding of a fundamental concept in epistemology. This conclusion has significant implications. Some philosophers have tried to model our understanding of epistemic concepts on other normative concepts, in particular, the concept of what one morally ought to do. The difference between various "ought"s, the argument goes, is a difference concerning the relevant goals in terms of which we assess means. But if what I said above is correct, this approach is fundamentally flawed. What makes actions morally or rationally correct is not the actual means to achieve an end, but facts about the *epistemic* probability with which relevant consequences will occur. Once one realizes this, one should realize that attempting to apply this model to the epistemic "ought" will encounter hopeless circularity (see "Epistemic Justification and Normativity").

In suggesting that epistemology has a fundamental place in philosophy, I don't want to disparage the importance of other fields of philosophy. I would advise strongly against too much specialization in philosophy. It is folly, for example, to try to say much about epistemological problems of perception without thinking long and hard about the *metaphysics* of perception. While the strongest forms of verificationism have been decisively refuted, it remains true that one can only understand the way in which experience might confirm claims about the physical world if one thoroughly understands the *content* of claims about the physical world. In *Metaphysical and Epistemological Problems of Perception*, I argued that there are conceptual connections between thought about physical objects and thought about sensations. Berkeley was right to attack the primary/secondary quality, but the moral to draw is that one should treat all ascriptions of properties to physical objects as ascriptions of secondary properties. Our understanding of the external world is achieved through understanding of existential claims about the causes of patterns of sensation, where we have no idea of the intrinsic character of the causes that take the value of the variable.

It seems equally obvious to me that one can't engage epistemological issues without turning to deeper metaphysical issues concerning truth—issues that in turn connect to very traditional metaphysical problems concerning the nature of thought and the ultimate constituents of reality. On the view I defend, for example, noninferential knowledge involves both direct acquaintance with facts and a relation of correspondence between thought and facts. The ultimate rationale for the proposal involves presuppositions about the nature of truth—that thought is the primary bearer of truth value, that there is the ontological category of fact, and that there such a thing as correspondence between thought and fact. All of these claims are exceedingly controversial. Many contemporary philosophers reject the correspondence theory of truth with all of its various ontological commitments. Some claim that talk about facts is just shorthand for talk of truth. If that were correct, then it would be an almost comical mistake to think of facts as truth *makers*. But if we commit ourselves to a robust ontological conception of fact, we owe an account of what the constituents of facts are. That's the kind of question that leads to ontological controversies concerning the existence and nature of properties and the objects that exemplify them. The debates concerning the nature of thought are equally important and equally difficult. Thought is a representation of reality and one of the most fundamental questions in the philosophy of mind (and philosophy of language) concerns the nature of representation.

Because I see all these connections between epistemology and other philosophical fields, my research has never been confined to epistemology narrowly conceived. In *Realism and the Correspondence Theory of Truth*, I try get as clear as I can about the metaphysical presuppositions I bring to my epistemological work, presuppositions touched upon in early books like *Metaphysical and Epistemological Problems of Perception*, and *Metaepistemology and Skepticism*.

While I discourage a narrow focus on epistemology, I have a quite different view about the connection between philosophy and other academic disciplines. I am deeply suspicious about attempts to find intersections between philosophical epistemology and the natural sciences. I can't think of a single fundamental epistemological debate in philosophy, for example, that will be furthered by the discoveries of cognitive science. But then I have argued elsewhere for the decidedly controversial view that there are no fundamental philosophical issues in any field of philosophy that are settled, or even furthered significantly by scientific investigation ("A Priori Philosophy After an A Posteriori Turn," and "Render Unto Philosophy that which is Philosophy's"). This claim might seem extreme, almost absurd. I can soften it slightly by stressing that my assertion about the autonomy of philosophy is an epistemic claim. I am not denying that there are *causal* connections between empirical discoveries and thought about philosophical issues. It is probably no accident that the modern philosopher's great interest in the distinction between appearance and reality coincided with the rather surprising discovery that the properties of macro-objects seem to simply disappear as one gains new ways of accessing the microworld. And I should also probably candidly admit that my defense of armchair philosophy against the intrusions of science might come perilously close to a stipulative definition of philosophy. It does follow from my understanding of philosophy that a field like applied ethics, or even, perhaps, applied epistemology is only derivatively philosophical. Applied ethics, for example, is only philosophical insofar as there is a philosophical theory that is implicit in an attempt to find applications of the theory.

What do you consider to be the most neglected topics and/or contributions in contemporary epistemology?

Epistemological problems connected with memory are far more fundamental than epistemological problems associated with perception, other minds, the future, or the postulation of theoretical entities in physics. But memory has received, comparatively, far less attention. John Stuart Mill seems simply to abandon temporarily his otherwise stalwart defense of radical empiricism when it comes to knowledge of the past (See my *Mill*). C.I. Lewis has a brief discussion of the problem in *An Analysis of Knowledge and Valuation*, but doesn't seem to have any positive suggestion as to how to solve it. For the most part, however, discussion of the problem is conspicuous by its absence. And this is surprising given that other modes of reasoning can't get started without knowledge, or at least, justified belief about the past. Even the premises of deductively valid reasoning are hostage to memory unless the entire reasoning process takes place in a "specious present." Enumerative inductive reasoning requires justified belief in premises describing past correlations between properties if it is to generate justified belief in conclusions that project such correlations into the future or the unexamined present or past. So if one doesn't have a satisfactory account of how we can acquire knowledge or justified belief about the past, we are staring squarely at skepticism. To be sure, there is increased empirical investigation into the nature of memory, but that doesn't do much for those of us committed to an internalist approach to epistemology.

I don't know that I have much to say about neglected contributions. I would suggest that it is generally a bit frightening to speculate about how and why the cannon becomes what it is. I'm convinced that there is an enormous amount of sheer chance concerning what philosophical writing becomes well-known and what remains essentially lost on the dusty bookshelves of libraries. If one searches the stacks of old journals. one can't help but be impressed by the many original, thoughtful, clear, well-argued papers published by people whose work is virtually unknown. I have no particular confidence that the best philosophy somehow survives the test of time. Often a paper happens to be discussed by a critic, whose work gets discussed by two others, whose work then gets discussed by a few more until the original piece is now anthologized everywhere. So I've got my own favorite philosophers that haven't made the pantheon, many of whom are, I think, much better philosophers than others who have gained much more fame and whose work has achieved much more attention. But they are too numerous to list, and I don't want to offend anyone by leaving his or her contributions out of the discussion.

What do you think the future of epistemology will (or should) hold?

Well I worry a bit that I'm becoming one of those grouchy old men who complain incessantly about the present and have nothing but dark pessimism concerning the future. As I indicated above, I am particularly worried about the attempt by some philosophers to find a partnership between philosophy and science. I worry that the preoccupation, almost obsession, with science can destroy philosophy as an autonomous field of study. Worse still, I worry that the field will lose interest in the fundamental epistemological questions that have preoccupied philosophers for thousands of years. But the truth is that philosophical fashions come and go. My guess is that the questions and views that so fascinate me will return before long to centre stage. When I wrote my first book in the early 1980's one referee of the manuscript was "shocked" to find someone still talking about direct acquaintance as if it were a philosophically respectable concept. My views haven't changed all that much over the years, but my impression is that all sorts of philosophers, particularly younger epistemologists, are becoming interested in more traditional epistemology all over again. I suspect that internalism (both in epistemology, and in the philosophy of mind) will make a serious comeback. But this is a question in applied epistemology. As anyone who inspects my financial retirement portfolio will quickly discover, I am really not very good at making predictions.

References

(beginning with most recent)

Mill, with Wendy Donner (Mill's Logic, Metaphysics and Epistemology), Blackwell Publishing, forthcoming.

Realism and The Correspondence Theory of Truth. Boston: Rowman and Littlefield, 2002.

Metaepistemology and Skepticism. Boston: Rowman and Littlefield, 1996, 234 pages.

Reason and Morality: A Defense of the Egocentric Perspective. Ithaca, N.Y:Cornell University Press, 1990, 247 pages.

Metaphysical and Epistemological Problems of Perception. Lincoln and London: University of Nebraska Press, 1985, 211 pages.

Articles

"Render Unto Philosophy that which is Philosophy's." *Midwest Studies in Philosophy*, XXXI, 2007, 56–67.

"Direct Realism, Introspection, and Cognitive Science," *Philosophy and Phenomenological Research*, Vol. LXXIII, No. 3, November, 2006, 680–95.

"Epistemic Probability," *Philosophical Issues*, Vol. 14, 2004, 149–64.

"Achieving Epistemic Ascent," in *Sosa and his Critics*, Blackwell, 2004, 72–85.

"Introspection and Internalism" *New Essays on Semantic Externalism, and Self-Knowledge*, ed. Susana Nuccetelli. MIT Press, 2003, 257–76.

"Epistemic Justification and Normativity," in *Knowledge, Truth, and Duty: Essays on Epistemic Justification, Responsibility and Virtue*, ed. Matthias Steup. Oxford University Press, 2001, 49–61, reprinted in *Arguing About Knowledge*, eds. Pritchard and Neta (forthcoming).

"A Priori Philosophy after an A Posteriori Turn," in *Midwest Studies in Philosophy*, XXIII, 1999, 21–33.

"Skepticism and Reasoning to the Best Explanation" in *Philosophical Topics*, ed. by Enrique Villanueva, 1992.

"Induction and Reasoning to the Best Explanation," *Philosophy of Science*, December, 1980, 589–600.

11

Clark Glymour

Alumni University Professor of Philosophy
Carnegie Mellon University, USA

Why were you initially drawn to epistemology (and what keeps you interested)?

Call me Meno. I know just the moment. I was five. My grandmother, always wearing a long gray coat, summer and winter, and carrying a small black money purse, took me about Los Angeles by streetcar. Since my grandmother treated money so carefully it occurred to me that money, which I had never been permitted to touch, might be the best thing in the world. One day I crept into my parents' bedroom and stole a dollar bill. Taking it to my room, I looked it over from all sides, smelled it, ran my hands over it. Just paper—*this* couldn't be the best thing in the world. (To my credit, I returned the dollar.) So I thought I would look for other candidates for the best thing in the world, but then it occurred to me—if I found the best thing in the world, how would I know I had found it?

And then there was the little green man and the Rag Man. The friendly little green man lived in the tiny box house my father made and put on a shelf above the kitchen table, where my father and I would sometimes sit together to listen to Joe Louis' boxing matches. The Rag Man came down the street once a month in a wagon pulled by a horse, knocking on doors to ask for rags. My father assured me the little green man lived in the tiny house, and my mother assured me the Rag Man would carry away bad children. I did not think I believed either of them, but I kept looking for the little green man and I kept hiding whenever the Rag Man came to our street. That made me wonder what it is to believe something.

Despite my childish skepticism, I was pretty sure I was on to the best thing in the world in Junior High School, walking Jane

Trent home each day with my hand under her coat. This led in
high school to another epistemological concern. When I was 16
or so I spent a lot of time thinking about specific cases of the
problem of other minds: what do girls think, and in particular
what did Rettie Jane, then the subject (or object, however that
works) of my aspirations think when she said she was "washing
her hair"? I had no clue. So many hypotheses, so little evidence.
For a while I held the Butte high school record for most refused
dates. It occurred to me that some problems are underdetermined
and the best one can do is to make very general assumptions from
which experience can then lead to discoveries, discoveries that
will be true if the assumptions are. Knowledge is provisional, but
some provisions are indispensable. That girls, and in particular,
Rettie Jane, had perceptual experiences and beliefs and categories
pretty much like mine seemed a necessary assumption if I were to
have any real moral relations with them (I was interested mostly
in immoral relations, but morally arrived at), that they shared
everyday desires like mine, but maybe not my specific desires. This
led to my recognition of the importance of causal premises in the
assessment of hypotheses: discounting the boasts of some of my
buddies, I considered the hypothesis that females as a general rule
do not enjoy sex, but this seemed clearly refuted by the abundance
of people on the planet. Which of course led immediately to the
conclusion that the problem was my hair, but what alteration was
needed–waterfall and duck-ass, or Peter Gunn brushcut? I digress.

What do you see as being your main contributions to epistemology?

Creating the Philosophy Department at Carnegie Mellon.

What do you think is the proper role of epistemology in relation to other areas of philosophy and other academic disciplines?

In *The Dynamics of Reason*, Michael Friedman states my view
more eloquently than I can.

> Science, if it is to continue to progress through revolutions ... needs a source of new ideas, alternative programs, and expanded possibilities that is not itself scientific in some sense—that does not, as do the

sciences themselves, operate within a generally agreed
upon framework of taken for granted rules. For what is
needed ... is precisely the creation and stimulation of
new frameworks or paradigms, together with what we
might call meta-frameworks or meta-paradigms—new
conceptions of what a coherent rational understanding
of nature might amount to—capable of motivating and
sustaining the revolutionary transition to a new first-
level or scientific paradigm. Philosophy, throughout its
close association with the sciences, has functioned in
precisely this way.

What do you consider to be the most neglected topics and/or contributions in contemporary epistemology?

What can be learned under what computational bounds and with what assumptions, by what learning and inference strategies on what computational architectures, from what kinds of data? Contributions of these kinds can be found all over in various guises, but in philosophy they tend to be very localized efforts rather than, as they ought to be, the cynosure of contemporary epistemology.

What do you think the future of epistemology will (or should) hold?

I have said above what I think it should be. The rest of the question asks for a prediction. The present and past are prelude.

I am reminded of an event from some years past. The late Laurence Rockefeller, a benign benefactor of the Princeton Philosophy Department, once came to campus to announce optimistically that a great religious revival was about to sweep America, and he wanted the graduate students to tell him what philosophers were going to do when the great day arrived. Stumped, or too intimidated to object, they sat silent until a particularly resourceful student – Carolyn Magid, as I recall – told him that when the great religious revolution arrived, philosophers would surely analyze the concepts involved. Indeed. The faculty were relieved.

Michael. Friedman's book does not mention a single 20th century example of his vision for philosophy, not one. There are some—the elaboration and application of the idea of logical form, the foundations of decision theory, the theory of computable learning; near the middle of the twentieth century philosophical logic, part epistemology, formed the content of early attempts at machine learning. I could go on, but not far. My prediction is that epistemology will continue for a while to consist mostly of analyses of contrived puzzles disconnected from any practice (Sleeping Beauties, for example), and Bayesian "reconstructions" that exploit subtle logical relations they do not elucidate. I regard all of this as a waste of the time of good minds, but it is far from the worst that is and could be. The worst of mainstream epistemology requires parody rather than commentary, the talents of Tom Lehrer, which I do not share and which the present venue in any case does not allow. So, a device: *The New Yorker* runs an end-page column with cartoons for which captions are solicited, and candidate captions offered for vote. Quotations will have to do in place of cartoons; I solicit your captions and offer mine in italics. It seems sufficient to consider passages, taken very much not out of context, from three contributors to this volume.

> "... the potential of an ecologically modeled epistemology to disrupt a hegemonic social imaginary of domination and control. Ecological naturalism interrogates the instrumental rationality, abstract individualism, reductivism, and exploitation of people and places that scientistic epistemologies underwrite, to promote a social-political imaginary sensitive to human and geographical diversity, respectful of the natural world, and responsible in its democratic epistemic practices."

> —*C'mon, baby, just tell me that you hate me.*

"If I have reason to believe that someone else believes p, I have at least a weak reason to believe p myself."

> —*Sakes alive, I have reason to believe $2 + 2$ is five.*

"... all human beings will be saved and will enjoy everlasting life with Christ."

> —*Quantifying in may be no sin*
> *But is it quite logical*
> *That the epistemological*
> *Should turn eschatological?*

12
Alvin I. Goldman

Board of Governors Professor of Philosophy
Rutgers – The State University of New Jersey, USA

Five Questions Answered: My Epistemological Projects

How I Was Drawn to Epistemology

I studied epistemology as an undergraduate with Ernest Nagel (at Columbia) and as a graduate student with Roderick Chisholm (at Princeton, where Chisholm visited). It wasn't my first consuming interest in philosophy, however, and I wrote my dissertation on action theory (later published as *A Theory of Human Action*, 1970). In my third year of teaching, at the University of Michigan, I was asked to give a class on epistemology, and during that course I developed the causal theory of knowing ("A Causal Theory of Knowing," 1967).

Causal questions in epistemology, in that era, were largely taboo. Phenomenalism and its alternatives were more familiar issues on the table. A characteristic dichotomy of the period had been formulated by Reichenbach (1938), who distinguished questions of "justification" from questions of "discovery" (the genesis of hypotheses and beliefs). Epistemology was confined to questions of justification. Nonetheless, a few causal shoots were peeking out of the epistemological soil. H.P. Grice published his "Causal Theory of Perception" in 1961, and Martin and Deutscher published a causal approach to memory in 1966. A similar foray into the analysis of knowledge struck me as promising. The Gettier problem had recently invaded the scene, and everyone was obsessed by it. Could a causal theory provide a solution to Gettier's problem?

I made such an attempt and the *Journal of Philosophy* took the plunge.

My causal theory proposed that a true belief qualifies as knowledge in case there is a causal chain of an appropriate kind (or a pair of chains with a shared link) that connects the belief with its truth-maker. Chains containing inferences had to satisfy additional constraints involving warrant, etc. The details of the proposal undoubtedly had problems, but everyone recognized its novelty and some people approved of its adventurousness. Quine seemed to find it congenial when we exchanged a few papers during a sabbatical visit to Harvard in 1970–71. This wasn't surprising, given certain themes in his "Epistemology Naturalized" (1969). The causal theory neither rejected conceptual analysis nor advocated a systematic psychologization of epistemology; but it could be seen, nonetheless, as a specimen of epistemological naturalism. Appearing two years before "Epistemology Naturalized," it might be considered the earliest statement of one species of epistemological naturalism, an attempt to analyze the central epistemic concept of knowledge in naturalistic terms.

Problems in the formulation of the causal theory posed the question of which elements should be retained and which should be modified. In "Discrimination and Perceptual Knowledge" (1976) I abandoned the idea that a causal linkage between a belief and a truth-maker is necessary for knowing (even necessary for empirical knowing, as originally proposed). In addition, it was essential for a revised causal condition to be more specific. The 1967 paper said that the pertinent causal chains must be "appropriate," but no criterion of appropriateness was supplied. "Discrimination and Perceptual Knowledge" proposed the requirement that a knower of p must use discriminative capacities to exclude all relevant alternatives to p. Failure to exclude relevant alternatives was illustrated with the fake-barn example, which originated with Carl Ginet.[1] All of these themes, in the midst of similar ones being developed by others in that period, made for a lively epistemological scene, perhaps the liveliest in generations.

---

[1] Regrettably, I neglected to credit Ginet in my 1976 paper. The relevant alternatives idea was introduced by Fred Dretske in his "Epistemic Operators" (1970). Although he also advanced a modal account of knowing in "Conclusive Reasons" (1971), he did not at first incorporate the relevant alternatives notion into his modalized approach to knowledge. As far as I know, "Discrimination and Perceptual Knowledge" was the first such attempt.

Main Contributions to Epistemology

The causal theory of knowing and the no-relevant-alternatives analysis of perceptual knowledge were my first two contributions to epistemology. The third principal contribution came three years later, in "What Is Justified Belief?" (1979), where I formulated a reliable-process approach to justified belief. In simplified form the theory says that a belief is justified if and only if it is caused by a reliable belief-forming process, a psychological process with the property that most of its belief outputs are true. Three important implications of this theory are, first, that justifiedness is a function of how a belief is caused; second, it's a function of the reliability of the causal process(es) used; and third, it's a function of the subject's psychological history. The third implication stands in contrast to traditional foundationalism and coherentism, which hold that only states obtaining at the time of the target belief are relevant to its justificational status.

Five main objections to process reliabilism have dominated the debate over it. First, it is argued that reliability isn't necessary for justifiedness (e.g., the New Evil-Demon problem). Second, it's argued that reliability isn't sufficient for justifiedness (e.g., the clairvoyance and Truetemp examples). Third, it is claimed that the generality problem (a problem I raised myself in "What Is Justified Belief?") leaves it indeterminate what reliability a token belief-forming process has. Fourth is the value-of-knowledge (or "swamping") problem and fifth is the "easy knowledge" problem. Instead of reviewing the many rejoinders and modifications of reliabilism that have been offered to meet these challenges, I refer the reader to two recent reviews of this literature that trace the ongoing debate in some detail, viz., (Goldman, 2008a) and (Goldman, forthcoming a). I think it is fair to say that none of these objections has definitively refuted the core idea of process reliabilism. Perhaps process reliabilism can assume its strongest form if it is augmented with a few elements borrowed from a different theory, evidentialism, as suggested by Juan Comesana (forthcoming).

"What Is Justified Belief?" did not explicitly classify process reliabilism as a form of externalism. The internalism-externalism contrast had not yet gained a firm foothold, especially as applied to justification. The term "externalism" was introduced by D.M. Armstrong (1973) in connection with theories of knowledge. Laurence BonJour (1980) grouped work by Armstrong, Dretske, Alston and myself as specimens of externalism, which he then rejected. BonJour's paper appeared in a volume of *Midwest Studies in Philosophy* that also contained a paper of mine, "The Internalist Conception of Justification" (1980), which posed problems for internalism. According to Hilary Kornblith (2001: 2–3) these two papers inaugurated the current use of the terms 'externalism' and 'internalism,' applying the contrast to theories of justification rather than knowledge. Much later I published a more systematic critique of internalism, "Internalism Exposed" (1999a). A forthcoming paper, "Internalism, Externalism, and the Architecture of Justification" (unpublished), extends this effort to show the superiority of externalism over internalism. These three papers might jointly be considered my fourth principal contribution to epistemology, i.e., defending externalism over internalism in the theory of justification.

My critiques of internalism (especially the more recent ones) focus partly on the unclarity of, or inadequate motivation for, the "direct" accessibility requirement traditionally associated with internalism. Restrictive interpretations of direct accessibility run the risk of skeptical consequences: beliefs widely assumed to be justified would turn out to be unjustified. Some of the critiques also show that important types of justification-makers – e.g., support facts holding between propositions, and facts about the subject's prior states – would not qualify as justifiers under internalism. A satisfactory story of justification, however, must acknowledge such justifiers. Finally, only externalism offers an adequate framework or standard for the rightness of justificational rules that is needed for a full account of epistemic justifiedness.

A fifth principal contribution is the case I have advanced for a moderate naturalization of epistemology, a case made at length in *Epistemology and Cognition* (1986).[2] In contrast to Quine (1969), whose revamped epistemology would be a "chapter of psychology," I argued for a conception of (individual) epistemology that would have two parts. The first part would analyze epistemic concepts like knowledge, justification, or rationality to distill evaluative criteria or standards by which cognitive activities could be assessed. The second part would seek to identify the mental operations available to human cognizers and assess their respective qualities under the previously identified standards. This part would require empirical investigation to ascertain the pertinent properties of the relevant operations. In "Epistemology Natural-

---

[2] This case is additional to the less ambitious form of naturalization represented by "A Causal Theory of Knowing."

ized," Quine seemed to envision a purely descriptive task for epistemology, whereas *Epistemology and Cognition* endorsed the traditional notion that epistemology is evaluative or normative. My break with tradition was the insistence that empirically determined facts are needed to specify appropriate norms (norms governing cognitive processes), which cannot be done satisfactorily from the armchair.

Several additional topics I have tackled are amplifications or applications of epistemological naturalism. One of these is the viability of a priori warrant under a program of naturalistic epistemology. Some naturalizers want to get rid of the a priori altogether. By contrast, I think that a priori warrant can co-exist with naturalism (Goldman, 1999b). That some theses of epistemology require empirical justification doesn't entail that *all* justification is empirical. It is compatible with *some* sources of warrant being a priori. On a cognitive process approach to warrant, the crucial question is whether any psychological/computational processes (or sequences thereof) deserve to be considered a priori. Why shouldn't some (or all) processes of reasoning and mathematical calculation qualify as a priori, as long as they are devoid of elements of perceptual or quasi-perceptual cognition? Of course, a naturalist will probably want to distance herself from many traditional doctrines associated with the a priori, for example, infallibility, certainty, and rational unrevisability (incorrigibility). But grounds for separating the a priori from these features have already been laid by BonJour (1998) and Casullo (2003). So naturalists should feel comfortable endorsing the integrity of a weak kind of a priori warrant.

A second topic in this group is the use of intuitions in philosophical methodology (Goldman and Pust, 1998; Goldman, 2007). I myself employ this methodology, but how is it compatible with naturalism? Doesn't intuition smack of rational insight, ostensibly the antithesis of naturalism? So what is my story about intuitions and their role in philosophy? Skepticism about the evidential value of intuitions can arise from several sources. First, garden-variety intuitions are surely quite fallible, so why not philosophical intuitions? Second, there is no way to calibrate our intuitions (Cummins, 1998), and if a method's reliability cannot be calibrated (independently verified), surely it doesn't have epistemic merit. Third, experimental philosophers have identified interpersonal (and intercultural) conflicts in epistemological intuitions (Weinberg, Nichols, and Stich, 2001). Such conflicts seem to imply the unreliability of intuition; so why should philosophers trust them?

To answer the first challenge, different types of intuitions need to be distinguished. Philosophers are mainly interested in classification intuitions, in which a subject classifies or declines to classify a specified state of affairs in terms of a proffered predicate or concept (e.g., 'knows'). This class of intuitions may be more reliable than mere intuitional "hunches." Second, there is a general problem with respect to basic epistemic sources (e.g., perception or memory) that their reliability cannot be independently, i.e., non-circularly, corroborated. Thus, to insist on this requirement for the integrity of an epistemic source is to pave the way to skepticism. Third, whether the fact of intuitional diversity is a problem depends on what an intuition is supposed to be evidence *for*; it is not necessarily a problem for every construal of the "target" of philosophical intuitional methodology. It would indeed be a problem if intuitions were supposed to be evidence for the constitution of Platonic forms, natural kinds, or Fregean concepts. But if we take them to be evidence for concepts in the personal, psychological sense of 'concepts', then diversity is not necessarily a problem. Different intuitions may simply reflect (slightly) different concepts, or slightly different parameter settings associated with a concept. That is what I propose – although a full defense of this approach needs more space than is available here (see Goldman, 2007). Notice that intuitional methodology should not be assimilated to a priori methodology. A subject's "direct" knowledge that he is having a certain classification intuition ("This scenario does not exemplify knowledge") derives from introspection, not an a priori process, I would contend. Moreover, the process of concept application by which a personal concept (a non-conscious structure of some yet-to-be-determined type) generates an intuitional judgment is also not a plausible example of an a priori process. It more closely resembles memory retrieval, which shouldn't be assimilated to the a priori. Finally, I do not view the "experimental" investigation of intuitions as a wholly distinct project from classical philosophical methodology. Rather, it is a more controlled and sophisticated technique of posing questions to informants that can ultimately be more illuminating and more probative about their concepts than the traditional, comparatively casual way of eliciting intuitive judgments.

A third topic in this territory is an application of naturalistic epistemology: examining a putative cognitive process – introspection – to determine whether it is real and, if so, whether it is reliable. This inquiry should be pursued with the help of scientific psychology. Many psychologists have adduced experimental evidence that purportedly undercuts either the existence or reliability of introspection. Several have argued that so-called introspective reports really rely on an inferential or speculative operation of "confabulation." Evidence for this hypothesis cannot be ignored, although in various places I argue against it (Goldman, 2004; Goldman, 2006a: 231-234). It is much trickier to assess evidence for introspection's reliability. Two bodies of evidence that suggest limited reliability concern change blindness and inattentional blindness. Many studies have established that even if one 'sees' a certain scene, one can easily miss events or dimensions of the scene if one doesn't attend to them. For example, perceivers who were asked to watch a videotape of a basketball game and count the number of times one team took possession of the ball failed to notice a person in a gorilla suit stroll onto the center of the court and do a little jig. Asked whether they had seen this event, subjects would respond 'no'. Yet, assuming the perception of the event was conscious, this might be considered a false introspection. Thus, introspection's reliability may have to be restricted to *attended* conscious events. There are additional sub-fields of consciousness in which introspection is of doubtful reliability. Very brief conscious episodes, for example, do not admit of reliable introspection. Thus, if an epistemologist wants to certify introspection as a sound epistemic source (and if reliability is necessary for soundness), its range might have to be confined to suitably selected sectors of conscious phenomena and propositional contents. This cannot readily be accomplished from the armchair (Goldman, 2004).

A sixth category of contribution is the area of social epistemology. Epistemology has traditionally been highly individualistic, its emblematic protagonist being the solitary Cartesian inquirer embarked on a quest for knowledge from a position of solipsism of the moment. Epistemologies centered on the individual knower have dominated philosophy of science as well as mainstream epistemology. This perspective began to be challenged in the 1960s with the publication of Thomas Kuhn's *Structure of Scientific Revolutions* (1962) and the growth of social constructivism and science and technology studies. Much of this work was antagonistic to epistemology insofar as it repudiated objective conceptions of truth or rationality on which traditional epistemology and philosophy of science rested. The nihilistic flavor of much of this work was reflected in Richard Rorty's (1979) announcement that epistemology was dead and should be replaced by the "conversation of mankind." In the mid-1970s, I started to hatch ideas for a conception of social epistemology more closely continuous with traditional epistemology, taking notions like truth and reliability to be as applicable to social epistemology as they are to individual epistemology. This led to a series of papers in the 1980s and 1990s providing a general conception of social epistemology (Goldman, 1987) and specific exemplifications of this conception (Goldman, 1991, 1994; Goldman and Cox, 1996; Talbott and Goldman, 1998). All of this material, plus much else, was brought together in a unified treatment in *Knowledge in a Social World* (1999c).

Epistemology needs a social branch not because cultural diversity implies epistemic relativism but because what other people think and say influences our own beliefs – for good or ill. The social branch of epistemology should investigate the interpersonal interactions and institutional structures that influence what information is acquired and who acquires it, as well as what ignorance, errors, and deceptions are sustained through social systems. *Knowledge in a Social World* lays out a "veritistic" (truth-oriented) framework for social epistemology. A weak sense of 'knowledge' is introduced (later defended more fully in Goldman and Olsson, 2009), in which knowledge is simply true belief. Degrees of knowledge are degrees of credence attached to a true proposition. Veritistic social epistemology is an enterprise that examines a wide array of social practices with an eye to their veritistic consequences, i.e., the ways they influence the veritistic profiles of people whose opinions are affected by those practices. Social practice π is veritistically superior to an alternative social practice π' just in case π would produce a higher mean veritistic outcome than π' would produce. (Although *Knowledge in a Social World* focused on veritistic desiderata, I welcome other versions of social epistemology focused on knowledge in the strong sense or justification. In a later article on the problem of choosing among experts, for example, I explicitly focus on justification; see Goldman, 2001.)

Epistemology, Other Academic Disciplines, and Other Areas of Philosophy

Our discussion of epistemological naturalism in section 2 identifies one important set of links between epistemology and other academic disciplines. In this section I concentrate on a different such set of links, a set of links that would naturally arise from the tentacles of social epistemology stretching into law, social sciences, and (other) humanities.

Let me illustrate how these linkages or intersections arise in the area of legal evidence. Legal adjudication systems aim (at least in part) to secure accurate judgments about material facts arising in a legal dispute. Judgments are rendered on the basis of evidence presented at trial, and trials are conducted in accordance with procedures that govern the admission of evidence at trial. At the federal level of the American system such procedures are specified by the Federal Rules of Evidence. These rules, which are amended from time to time, are the subject of intense evaluation by legal scholars, who assess their merits, including their veritistic merits. The veritistic kind of analysis falls clearly into the province of veritistic social epistemology – social because what the legal system institutes are social practices, and epistemological because these practices are and should be evaluated (at least in part) by their tendency to generate judgments with relatively high or low error rates.

Rule 402 of the Federal Rules of Evidence (FRE) says that all relevant evidence is admissible except as otherwise provided by authoritative declarations, including other rules of FRE. Rule 403 says that "evidence may be excluded if its probative value is substantially outweighed by the danger of unfair prejudice, confusion of the issues, or misleading the jury". Thus, judges are allowed to exclude relevant evidence if they think that certain evidence is likely to prejudice or mislead jurors; and certain categories of evidence are specifically excluded because the legal system regards these outcomes as serious risks. The question is whether this "paternalistic" stance is good or bad from a veritistic point of view. One legal epistemologist who addresses this issue, Larry Laudan (2006), argues in the negative. Laudan holds that "the only factor that should determine the admissibility or inadmissibility of a bit of evidence is its relevance to the hypothesis that a crime occurred and that the defendant committed it." (2006: 25). This argument is based on veritistic considerations, or at least epistemic ones. Here is a philosopher-epistemologist working in what I would call social epistemology. Similar ideas could have been expressed by a legal scholar at a law school. Such scholars are concerned with issues of law and probability in much the same spirit (at least some of them, some of the time) as philosophical epistemologists (see issue 5.3 of the journal *Episteme, A Journal of Social Epistemol-*

ogy, devoted to legal evidence). At a higher level of abstraction, theorists of legal adjudication systems can debate the veritistic superiority of two differently structured traditions of legal adjudication: the common law system (a so-called "adversarial" system) and the civil law system (a so-called "inquisitorial" system). For a review of considerations on both sides, see *Knowledge in a Social World*, chap. 9.

Another major interface for social epistemology is between it and political theory, whose practitioners are housed sometimes in philosophy and sometimes in political science departments. One connection between social epistemology and political theory is through the theory of democracy, especially epistemic approaches to democracy. According to the epistemic approach, a principal virtue of democracy is its ability (compared to other political systems) to help the body politic adopt courses of action based on accurate factual judgments. For example, do the anti-pollution laws it adopts actually succeed in reducing pollution to acceptable levels at acceptable costs? The Condorcet Jury Theorem (Condorcet 1995 [1785]) is the first example of an epistemic democracy thesis. This theorem states that if voters vote independently of one another and each has a greater than 50% probability of being right, then, as the number of voters approaches infinity, the probability that the majority vote will yield the right answer approaches 1 (and it approaches 1 rapidly even with modest numbers of voters). Ways in which democracy can be conducive to problem solving, and problems in the relationship between knowledge and democracy, are explored by such contemporary writers as Elizabeth Anderson (2006), David Estlund (2008), Cass Sunstein (2003, 2006), and Philip Kitcher (2008). I have argued, in a slightly different vein, that majoritarian voting per se doesn't promote democratic ends unless voters are sufficiently well informed (Goldman, 1999c: chap. 10). There is a special kind of knowledge, which I dub "core voter knowledge," that each voter should possess. This is knowledge (true belief) about which of the candidates in an election, if elected, would produce the best outcomes as judged by a voter's own criteria or preferences. Democratic ends (suitably specified) are more likely to be attained the more voters in the electorate know the correct answers to their respective core voter questions. An important epistemic task for democracies, therefore, is to foster electioneering practices that promote core voter knowledge (which isn't necessarily in the interest of candidates or their supporters).

Unlike mainstream epistemology, social epistemology acknowledges the reality of corporate, or collective, agents that make factual judgments. A question for social epistemology and political theory is how collective judgments should be based on the judgments of their members. Majority voting is one obvious answer, but Christian List and Philip Pettit show that this encounters problems—very intriguing problems. List and Pettit (2002) have proved a certain impossibility theorem, i.e., that there is no possible aggregation procedure that starts from member judgments that obey a rationality constraint and generates collective judgments that also satisfy the rationality constraint plus three further natural conditions. This suggests a rationality problem at the level of collective doxastic agents that doesn't obtain at the level of individual doxastic agents, posing a variety of intriguing questions for both political theory and social epistemology (see List, 2005; List and Pettit, forthcoming).

Economics is a third academic field that promises significant alliances with social epistemology. One example is economics-inspired modeling of science. Philip Kitcher (1990, 1993: chap. 8) analyzes scientific research choices by representing scientists as entrepreneurs who make cost-effective choices. I have teamed up with a statistician, Moshe Shaked, to prove some Bayesian theorems that enable us to analyze experimentation choices by scientists as a function of expected "credit" from their peers, an economics-inspired approach (Goldman and Shaked, 1991). Separately, I have teamed up with an economist, James Cox, to criticize the historically popular claim that freedom of speech can be viewed as a market mechanism for speech that maximizes truth acquisition (Goldman and Cox, 1996; Goldman, 1999c: chap. 7). We deny that this follows from economic theory. Another example of economic modeling for social-epistemic ends has been executed by an economist, Roger Koppl, and colleagues who analyze the relationship between courts and forensic laboratories in game-theoretic terms, contending that serious problems about the accuracy of forensic evidence are traceable to the "monopoly" position of forensic labs (Koppl et al., 2008).

Three other fields that interface with social epistemology are information science, journalism, and education. The digital revolution has innumerable dimensions that invite social-epistemological contributions. One such dimension is the advent of large-scale collaborative projects of which Wikipedia is the most prominent example. Despite its popularity, Wikipedia does not receive high grades (in veritistic terms) by some critics. How should it be assessed in social-epistemological terms, and what changes in methodology might improve the product? A balanced analysis is provided by a philosopher/information scientist, Don Fallis (2008; forthcoming). The digital revolution is also producing a revolution in the journalism industry. With print media gradually being displaced by electronic media, the blogosphere is displacing traditional methods for disseminating and consuming the news. What are the veritistic consequences of this? I present some reflections on this salient public issue, responding in part to a market-oriented analysis by Richard Posner (Goldman, 2008b). The philosophy of education is a much-neglected area of philosophy that ought to be infused with epistemological perspectives. One of the few epistemology-based treatments is by Harvey Siegel (1997). I have also offered social-epistemological perspectives on educational theory generally (Goldman, 1995; Goldman, 1999c: chap. 11) and on whether to teach intelligent design (2006b).

This section has highlighted interdisciplinary connections involving the social aspects of epistemology. However, I do not mean to neglect interdisciplinary connections involving other parts of epistemology. The interface between epistemology and linguistics, for example, is a thriving enterprise that has already illuminated epistemological theory and promises more illumination. This is well known, however, and my endorsement is hardly needed. I don't mean to suggest by omission that I question or undervalue its contribution.

Neglected Topics in Contemporary Epistemology

I view epistemology, at the present time, as an enormously thriving and multifaceted enterprise, as it should be. Nothing leaps to mind as an egregiously neglected topic or contribution. Five years ago I might have answered differently, particularly with my special interest in social epistemology. But social epistemology has now begun to flourish. Two special topics in social epistemology (testimony and peer disagreement) are among the hottest topics in epistemology generally. Several monographs have been produced, and at least two full volumes of papers are scheduled for publication (Pritchard, forthcoming; Goldman and Whitcomb, forthcoming), together with half of a forthcoming volume of *Oxford Studies in Epistemology*. The journal *Episteme, A Journal of Social Epistemology* (which I edit) is in its fifth year of publication at this writing. Epistemology reference works increasingly feature lengthy entries on social epistemology. And a major European consortium, centered in Copenhagen and Edinburgh, plans to establish a center for social epistemology. Of course, other epistemological projects not headlined here – e.g., virtue epistemology and formal epistemology – are also thriving.

The Future of Epistemology

Naturally, I think that the epistemological topics reviewed here should be prominent parts of epistemology's future. Fortunately, my crystal ball assures me that they *are* in epistemology's future. (Now the only question is whether this crystal ball's assurance is good evidence.)

References

Anderson, Elizabeth (2006). "The Epistemology of Democracy," *Episteme, A Journal of Social Epistemology* 3: 8–22.

Armstrong, D. M. (1973). *Belief, Truth, and Knowledge.* Cambridge: Cambridge University Press.

BonJour, Laurence (1980). "Externalist Theories of Empirical Knowledge," in P. French, T. Uehling, and H. Wettstein (eds.), *Midwest Studies in Philosophy*, vol. 5, *Studies in Epistemology*. Minneapolis: University of Minnesota Press.

──────────── (1998). *In Defense of Pure Reason.* Cambridge: Cambridge University Press.

Casullo, Albert (2003). *A Priori Justification.* New York: Oxford University Press.

Comesana, Juan (forthcoming). "Evidentialist Reliabilism," *Nous.*

Condorcet, Marquis de (1995). "An Essay on the Application of Analysis to the Probability of Decisions Rendered by a Plurality of Votes," in I. McLean and A. Urken (eds. and trans.), *Classics of Social Choice*. Ann Arbor: University of Michigan Press.

Cummins, Robert (1998). "Reflection on Reflective Equilibrium," in M. DePaul and W. Ramsey (eds.), *Rethinking Intuition: The Psychology of Intuition and Its Role in Philosophical Inquiry*. Lanham, MD: Rowman and Littlefield.

Dretske, Fred (1970). "Epistemic Operators," *Journal of Philosophy* 67: 1007–1023.

_____ (1971). "Conclusive Reasons," *Australasian Journal of Philosophy* 49: 1–22.

Estlund, David (2008). *Democratic Authority: A Philosophical Framework.* Princeton: Princeton University Press.

Fallis, Don (2008). "Toward an Epistemology of *Wikipedia*," *Journal of the American Society for Information Science and Technology.*

Fallis, Don (forthcoming). "Wikipistemology," in A. I. Goldman and D. Whitcomb (eds.), *Readings in Social Epistemology.* New York: Oxford University Press.

Goldman, Alvin I. (1967). "A Causal Theory of Knowing," *Journal of Philosophy* 64: 357–372.

_____ (1970). *A Theory of Human Action.* Englewood-Cliffs, NJ: Prentice-Hall.

_____ (1976). "Discrimination and Perceptual Knowledge," *Journal of Philosophy* 73: 771–791.

_____ (1979). "What Is Justified Belief?" in G. Pappas (ed.), *Justification and Knowledge* (pp. 1-23). Dordrecht: Reidel.

_____ (1980). "The Internalist Conception of Justification," in P. French, T. Uehling, and H. Wettstein (eds.), *Midwest Studies in Philosophy*, vol. 5, *Studies in Epistemology.* Minneapolis: University of Minnesotal Press.

_____ (1986). *Epistemology and Cognition.* Cambridge, MA: Harvard University Press.

_____ (1987). "Foundations of Social Epistemics," *Synthese* 73: 109–144.

_____ (1991). "Epistemic Paternalism: Communication Control in Law and Society," *Journal of Philosophy* 88: 113–131.

_____ (1994). "Argumentation and Social Epistemology," *Journal of Philosophy* 91: 27–49.

_____ (1995). "Education and Social Epistemology," in A. Neiman (ed.), *Philosophy of Education 1995.* Urbana, IL: Philosophy of Education Society.

_____ (1999a). "Internalism Exposed," *Journal of Philosophy* 96: 271–293.

_____ (1999b). "A Priori Warrant and Naturalistic Epistemology," in J. Tomberlin (ed.), *Philosophical Perspectives*, 13, *Epistemology*. Malden, MA: Blackwell Publishers.

_____ (1999c). *Knowledge in a Social World*. Oxford: Oxford University Press.

_____ (2001). "Experts: Which Ones Should You Trust?" *Philosophy and Phenomenological Research* 63: 85–109. Reprinted in A. I. Goldman (2002). *Pathways to Knowledge, Private and Public*. New York: Oxford University Press.

_____ (2004). "Epistemology and the Evidential Status of Introspective Reports," *Journal of Consciousness Studies* 11(7–8): 1–16.

_____ (2006a). *Simulating Minds: The Philosophy, Psychology, and Neuroscience of Mindreading*. New York: Oxford University Press.

_____ (2006b). "Social Epistemology, Theory of Evidence, and Intelligent Design: Deciding What to Teach," *The Southern Journal of Philosophy*, Supplement, 44: 1–22.

_____ (2007). "Philosophical Intuitions: Their Target, Their Source, and Their Epistemic Status," *Grazer Philosophische Studien* 74: 1–26. Reprinted in C. Beyer and A. Burri (eds.), *Philosophical Knowledge: Its Possibility and Scope*. Amsterdam: Rodopi.

_____ (2008a). "Reliabilism," *The Stanford Encyclopedia of Philosophy (Summer 2008 Edition)*, Edward N. Zalta (ed.), http://plato.stanford.edu/archives/sum2008/entries/reliabilism/.

_____ (2008b). "The Social Epistemology of Blogging," in J. van den Hoven and J. Weckert (eds.), *Information Technology and Moral Philosophy*. Cambridge: Cambridge University Press.

_____ (forthcoming a). "Reliabilism," in M. Steup and E. Sosa (eds.), *Blackwell Companion to Epistemology*, 2nd edition

_____ (unpublished). "Internalism, Externalism, and the Architecture of Justification."

_____ and Cox, James (1996). "Speech, Truth, and the Free Market for Ideas," *Legal Theory* 2: 1–32.

_____ and Olsson, Erik J. (2009). "Reliabilism and the Value of Knowledge," in D. Pritchard, A. Millar and A. Haddock, eds., *Epistemic Value*. Oxford: Oxford University Press.

_____ and Pust, Joel. (1998). "Philosophical Theory and Intuitional Evidence," in M. DePaul and W. Ramsey (eds.), *Rethinking Intuition: The Psychology of Intuition and Its Role in Philosophical Inquiry*. Lanham, MD: Rowman and Littlefield.

_____ and Shaked, Moshe (1991). "An Economic Model of Scientific Activity and Truth Acquisition," *Philosophical Studies* 63: 31–55.

_____ and Whitcomb, Dennis, eds. (forthcoming). *Readings in Social Epistemology*. New York: Oxford University Press.

Grice, H. P. (1961). "The Causal Theory of Perception," *Proceedings of the Aristotelian Society*, vol. 35.

Kitcher, Philip (1990). "The Division of Cognitive Labor," *Journal of Philosophy* 87: 5–22.

_____ (1993). *The Advancement of Science*. Oxford: Oxford University Press.

_____ (2008). "Science, Religion, and Democracy," *Episteme, A Journal of Social Epistemology* 5: 5–18.

Koppl, Roger, Kurzban, Robert and Kobilinksy, Lawrence (2008). "Epistemics for Forensics," *Episteme, A Journal of Social Epistemology* 5: 141–159.

Kornblith, Hilary (2001). "Internalism and Externalism: A Brief Historical Introduction," in H. Kornblith (ed.), *Epistemology: Internalism and Externalism*. Malden, MA: Blackwell Publishers.

Kuhn, Thomas (1962). *The Structure of Scientific Revolutions*. Chicago: University of Chicago Press.

Laudan, Larry (2006). *Truth, Error, and Criminal Law: An Essay in Legal Epistemology*. Cambridge: Cambridge University Press.

List, Christian (2005). "Group Knowledge and Group Rationality: A Judgment Aggregation Perspective," *Episteme, A Journal of Social Epistemology* 2(1): 25–38.

_____ and Pettit, Philip (2002). "Aggregating Sets of Judgments: An Impossibility Result," *Economics and Philosophy* 18: 89–110.

_____ (forthcoming). *Group Agency: The Possibility, Design, and Status of Corporate Agents*.

Martin, C. B. and Deutscher, Max (1966), "Remembering," *Philosophical Review* 75: 161–196.

Pritchard, Duncan, ed. (forthcoming). *Social Epistemology*.

Quine, W. V. (1969). "Epistemology Naturalized," in *Ontological Relativity and Other Essays*. New York: Columbia University Press.

Reichenbach, Hans (1938). *Experience and Prediction*. Chicago: University of Chicago Press.

Rorty, Richard (1979). *Philosophy and the Mirror of Nature*. Princeton, NJ: Princeton University Press.

Siegel, Harvey (1997). *Rationality Redeemed? Further Diaglogues on an Educational Ideal*. New York: Routledge.

Sunstein, Cass R. (2003). *Why Societies Need Dissent*. Cambridge, MA: Harvard University Press.

_____ (2006). *Infotopia: How Many Minds Produce Knowledge*. New York: Oxford University Press.

Talbott, William and Goldman, Alvin (1998). "Games Lawyers Play: Legal Discovery and Social Epistemology," *Legal Theory* 4: 93–163.

Weinberg, Jonathan, Nichols, Shaun, and Stich, Stephen (2001). "Normativity and Epistemic Intuitions," *Philosophical Topics* 29: 429–460.

13
Alan Hájek

Professor of Philosophy

Philosophy Program

Research School of Social Sciences

Australian National University, Australia

Why were you initially drawn to epistemology (and what keeps you interested)?

If there's any truth to the old saw 'Show me the child, and I'll show you the man', then I suppose my philosophical infancy has a lot to answer for. Let me begin by explaining how I was initially drawn to philosophy.

I was always torn between the sciences and the humanities, but I finished up doing a science degree at Melbourne University, majoring in mathematics and statistics. I loved probability theory, but I wanted to know more about that 'P' that kept appearing in its equations and theorems. When I asked one of my professors about it he was unimpressed. He remarked, somewhat sneeringly, that some people regarded it as a *subjective* notion. It was clear to me that he did not encourage this line of enquiry. So I continued learning more theorems. I got the impression that all the low fruit had already been picked—it seemed that every significant result had either been proven already, or would be prohibitively difficult to prove. One day in the university café, I was poring over an article on stochastic monotonicity. Like Jules in *Pulp Fiction*, I had a moment of clarity: I realized my future lay elsewhere.

But where? Faced with this intellectual crisis, like a good Australian I decided to travel around the world, to 'find myself' on the road (as they used to say). The remarkable thing is that I did. My second moment of clarity occurred in London, Ontario, of all places. I was visiting a friend of mine, another science undergraduate from Melbourne Uni, who had seen the light first and was now studying philosophy at the University of Western Ontario. I looked at what he was studying, and I thought 'Wow! I wish I were doing that!' The penny dropped so loudly it could be heard several provinces away. I picked up the application form for their graduate program that day. Later that year they were kind enough to admit me despite my complete lack of training in philosophy. (All I knew about philosophy was the Monty Python *Philosophers Song*.) And before I knew it, I was a philosopher.

It turned out that Bill Harper also wanted to know more about that 'P' that kept appearing in the equations and theorems of probability theory, and he was my first philosophy mentor. I completed an MA at Western. I went on to do my PhD at Princeton, under the supervision of Bas van Fraassen and David Lewis, and the further influence of Dick Jeffrey and various terrific students. I wrote a dissertation on probabilities of conditionals and conditional probabilities. I imprinted on Bayesian epistemology, and I never looked back. I liked the idea that belief comes in degrees, and I was gripped by the Bayesian view that those degrees should conform to the probability calculus. (My training in probability theory wasn't wasted after all!) A formal theory searching for an interpretation met a notion of graded belief searching for a formal theory. A blissful marriage!

Or so it seemed to me at the time. More recently, I have questioned various aspects of Bayesian epistemology, and this is an ongoing line of research of mine now. Along the way I have also become fascinated by Moore's paradox. This brings me to the next question ...

What do you see as being your main contributions to epistemology?

Williamson (2000) is well known for advocating a 'knowledge first' epistemology. I am attracted to an 'uncertainty first' epistemology, with that uncertainty codified by probability in the Bayesian tradition of Ramsey, de Finetti, Jeffrey, and others. And much as Williamson takes the concept of knowledge to be unanalysable, so I take the concept of degrees of belief to be unanalysable. (I spell this out in more detail in part of my contribution to Eriksson and Hájek 2007.) But taking a concept to be primitive in this way does not preclude us from saying many illuminating things about it. For starters, the axioms of probability theory already say a lot about it, the theorems still more. The theory is wonderfully simple, yet extraordinarily powerful. Indeed, it achieves such a balance of simplicity and strength that, by analogy to Lewis's analysis of 'laws of nature'[1], I am tempted to say that probability theory codifies the laws of epistemology—or at least, the laws of 'uncertainty first' epistemology, where this uncertainty is rationally constrained.

A garden of philosophical delights awaits you once you embrace Bayesian epistemology. Old chestnuts in confirmation theory, such as the ravens paradox, the grue paradox, and the Quine-Duhem problem, suddenly come into relief and can be given a unified treatment. (See Hájek and Joyce 2008.) And unlike traditional epistemology, trafficking as it does in the all-or-nothing notions of knowledge and belief, Bayesian epistemology naturally underwrites *decision theory*. In the next section I will discuss how well Bayesianism serves various areas of philosophy.

And yet I have become something of a Trojan Horse. I come to Bayesianism as a friend, but I have misgivings about some of the most important arguments that degrees of belief – 'credences' – are rationally required to be probabilities. (See especially my 2009.)

Take, for example, the Dutch Book argument. We identify your credences with your betting rates, and then appeal to the Dutch Book theorem: if your credences violate probability theory, then there exists a set of bets, each acceptable according to your betting rates, which collectively guarantee your loss. This is often made vivid with the image of a bookie, who for some reason is supposed to be Dutch, buying or selling bets to you at prices that you find acceptable, and thereby draining you of your money. Thus, the argument concludes, your credences should obey probability theory.

But the argument faces a dilemma. Either we take this talk of 'guaranteed loss' literally, or not. The former, rather flat-footed interpretation of the argument, is easily rebutted: as various authors have pointed out, you can simply refuse the bets. As I would put the point, you can *mask* your disposition to accept the bets with a stronger disposition to do something else—e.g. to walk away when you see the Dutch guy coming, or to *mimic* having different betting dispositions. Surely Skyrms (1984, 1987) is right that we should not take the cautionary tale literally. He goes on to

---

[1] According to Lewis (1973), a law of nature is a theorem of the best systematization of the universe—the true theory that best balances simplicity and strength.

argue that it merely dramatizes a deeper defect: an *inconsistency* in your evaluations. (Compare Ramsey's 1990/1931 remark that probability theory provides a *logic* for partial belief.)

However, this interpretation of the Dutch Book argument *doesn't* seem right to me. For starters, if there is an inconsistency at all, it seems to be some sort of 'pragmatic' inconsistency—perhaps troubling all the same, but surely not on all fours with logical inconsistency. But it is also not clear that there need be even a pragmatic inconsistency. For the Dutch Book argument presupposes a *package principle* that requires one to value a set of bets at the sum of the values of the bets taken individually, or less specifically, to regard a set of bets as fair if one regards each bet individually as fair. The package principle seems especially problematic when there are interference effects between the bets in a package—e.g. the placement of one bet is correlated with the outcome of another—and when the package is infinite (see Arntzenius, Elga, and Hawthorne 2004). So the whole is not just the sum of the parts when it comes to betting packages. Moreover, McGee (1999) offers an "airtight" Dutch Book against any agent who has an unbounded utility function and who assigns positive probability to infinitely many possibilities, but it is hard to see how there is any inconsistency in that—or if this is some kind of 'pragmatic' inconsistency, then there doesn't seem to be anything irrational about it. And Briggs (forthcoming) shows how you are Dutch Bookable if you are unsure of your own credences, or if your credences are Moore paradoxical in a certain way. Neither seems to be a case of logical inconsistency, even in some extended sense. I have pursued these themes further in my 2005, 2008b, and 2009.

This gives me the smoothest segue that I can manage to a completely different strand of my work in epistemology: Moore's paradox (Hájek and Stoljar 2001, Chalmers and Hájek 2007, Hájek 2007, Williams and Hájek MS). G. E. Moore famously observed (1942) that it would be "absurd" to assert a sentence of the form 'p and I don't believe that p'—e.g., 'it is raining and I don't believe that it is raining'. Since then, a vast literature has appeared, attempting to explain just what this "absurdity" consists in. Here is my top-ten list of reasons why the paradox fascinates me (although I don't expect to see it on the *David Letterman Show* any time soon):

1. Moore sentences can obviously be true—e.g. it really might be raining, and yet I really don't believe that it is. They are thus not semantically inconsistent. Yet equally obviously,

there is typically something defective in asserting or believing them. In particular, it seems that the very act of asserting or believing them should somehow render them false. This suggests that there is another kind of inconsistency—call it *pragmatic* inconsistency.

2. In putting constraints on reasonable assertion, Moore's paradox has consequences for any theory of assertion.

3. In putting constraints on reasonable belief, Moore's paradox has consequences for any theory of belief.

4. The paradox beautifully brings out an important difference between what philosophers call 'first person' and 'third person' perspectives. Note that there is nothing defective about my asserting or believing, say, 'It is raining and Renée believes it is not raining'. It is only in Moore sentences about *oneself* that things go awry.

5. Moore sentences involve 'higher-order' thoughts—e.g. beliefs about one's own beliefs. Some philosophers (e.g. Rosenthal 2005) think that such thoughts are the basis of consciousness.

6. There is apparently something *irrational* about asserting or believing Moore sentences. They thus shed some light on the nature of rationality.

7. They provide instances of what Sorensen (1988) calls 'blindspots': sentences that can be true, but that cannot rationally be believed. It's remarkable that Moore sentences seem to involve *individual* blindspots, each involving exactly one person. For example, 'It is raining and I believe it is not raining' could be true, and it could rationally be believed by everyone *except me*. I am the only possible agent 'blind' to its truth.

8. Moore sentences are subtly implicated in other philosophical problems and paradoxes—e.g. the surprise exam paradox, according to Sorensen and others.

9. Moore's paradox provides philosophers with a new weapon in their philosophical arsenal: a new kind of *reductio ad absurdum*. In a usual reductio, some assumption is shown to lead to inconsistency. But it is also salutary if an assumption can be shown to lead to *pragmatic* inconsistency, à la

Moore's paradox. David Chalmers and I deployed this technique in our "Ramsey + Moore = God" (2007). We argued that the Ramsey test for the acceptability of an indicative conditional, as it is usually understood[2], leads to Moorean absurdity. It commits you to accepting all instances of conditionals of the form 'if p, then I believe that p', which commits you to accepting that you are omniscient, and all instances of the form 'if I believe that p, then p', which commits you to accepting that you are infallible—on pain of Moorean absurdity. Since Moorean absurdity is, well, *absurd*, as is the extreme hubris of attributing to yourself God-like epistemic powers, this is a reductio of the Ramsey test, so understood.

10. And yet certain philosophical positions may be able to embrace their own Moorean reductio. For example, eliminativists about beliefs (e.g. Churchland 1981, Stich 1983) argue that 'belief' is part of a suspect folk psychology, ultimately to be discarded by science. Thus, Churchland and Stich are committed to uttering sentences of the form: "it is raining and I don't believe it is raining (and neither do you, nor anybody else, for 'belief' is part of a suspect theory of the mental)". Now, Churchland and Stich would not be fazed by this gambit—nor by the putative reductio that 'they offer a philosophical position that they don't really *believe*!' The right thing for them to say, of course, is that their mental state regarding the rain, or their own position, is whatever the fully developed psychological theory postulates it to be. Still, their commitment to Moore sentences is genuine, as is the puzzlement that it may induce in many of the rest of us.

In my (2007) I canvas a series of philosophical positions that apparently have such Moorean commitments. In some cases, the commitments seem to be fatal to the positions; in others, the commitments seem not so troubling after all. Either way, the situation is interesting. And to the extent that the commitments are not so troubling, it seems that pragmatic inconsistency cannot be so readily assimilated after all to logical inconsistency, which *really is* troubling, Priest (1987) notwithstanding! (Compare my remarks above about the Ramsey/Skyrms interpretation of the Dutch Book argument.)

---

[2] The understanding of the test is: 'if p then q' is acceptable to a subject S iff, were S to accept p and consider q, S would accept q.

But let's return to probability theory and Bayesian epistemology, since I'm back at work on that. Recently I have been completing a book manuscript entitled *Arrows and Haloes: Probabilities, Conditionals, Desires and Beliefs*. I argue that two seemingly disparate debates are strikingly similar. The first concerns the thesis, associated with Stalnaker (1970) and Adams (1975), that probabilities of conditionals are conditional probabilities:

$$P(A \to B) = P(B|A) \qquad \text{(provided } P(A) > 0\text{)}$$

Here $A \to B$ should be interpreted as the conditional 'if A then B'. The second concerns the thesis, associated with certain anti-Humeans, that desires are beliefs (as it might be, my desire for Tilly to win is a belief that her winning would be good). The thesis was formulated by Lewis as follows, and then attacked by him:

$$V(A) = P(A^o) \qquad \text{(provided } P(A) > 0\text{)}$$

Here, V is expected value as computed by evidential decision theory, and A^o is naturally interpreted as 'A is good'.

Notice that both theses employ Bayesian resources. Indeed, Stalnaker and Adams specifically intended the 'P' in the first equation to be interpreted subjectively. Likewise, the 'P' in the second equation should obviously be interpreted subjectively: it is a 'desire as *belief*' thesis, after all. Each thesis, if true, would tell us something interesting about rational mental states. In the first case, a rational agent's attitude to conditionals is constrained by her conditional probabilities, which in turn constrain her updating dispositions. (Shades of the Ramsey test here.) In the second case, desire-like states appear to be reducible to belief-like states. In an inversion of Hume's famous dictum, the passions are the slave of reason.

Lewis (1976, 1986) famously offered 'triviality' results against these theses. We have yet another kind of reductio ad absurdum argument—the theses don't quite lead to contradiction, but they putatively lead to the unpalatable conclusion that the P's (and V's) that can sustain the equations are somehow radically impoverished, unworthy of your typical rational agent. Notice that I put this point a little cagily—for it seems that a rational agent *could* have a radically impoverished probability function. For example, the functions that sustain the first equation are trivial because they are at most four-valued. But an ideally rational agent *could* have such a function. Indeed, an ideally rational omniscient God presumably has a *two*valued function—he or she assigns probability 1 to the actual world, and 0 to all others! The point is that the equation is supposed to govern the credence functions of *all* rational agents, and rationality surely permits non-trivial functions. Various other authors since Lewis have piled on further triviality results against the equation; mine can be found in my (1989), (1994), (1996) and Hájek and Hall (1994). But as usual, there are ways of fighting back (e.g. van Fraassen 1976)—this is philosophy, after all.

A few years ago I noticed some structural parallels between the two theses, and between Lewis's triviality results against them, which I found striking. Then, to an extent that surprised me, I realized that one could mimic the moves and countermoves in one of the debates that had already been made in the other. I have found this to be illuminating about the debates themselves, and it has also provided a handy heuristic for generating new results. Watch out for my book (forthcoming) when it hits a bookstore near you—avoid the lines, avoid disappointment and order your copy early!

And so here I am, returning full circle to work I began in my PhD dissertation. Talk about regressing to one's (philosophical) childhood!

What do you think is the proper role of epistemology in relation to other areas of philosophy and other academic disciplines?

Picture philosophical topics like a big subway map. For me, probability is Grand Central Station. From there, I can get almost anywhere I want to go (well, maybe with a transfer or two). So I will answer a more specific version of this question: what I think is the proper role of *Bayesian* epistemology in relation to other areas of philosophy and other academic disciplines.

It's hard to know where to draw the line between the use of Bayesian methods, and Bayesian epistemology *per se*. If the methods count as part of the epistemology itself, then I might as well list every science in my list of other academic disciplines informed and shaped to some extent by the epistemology. But let me confine myself to some of the roles Bayesian epistemology plays in philosophy, where its employment is especially self-conscious and distinctive. Again, it makes its way into almost every major branch of philosophy. In epistemology, philosophy of mind, and cognitive science, subjective probability functions model states of opinion. Since subjective probabilities are found at the heart of decision theory (and to some extent, game theory), they have ramifications for ethics and political philosophy. Subjective probability appears again in the philosophy of science in the analysis of confirmation of theories, in statistical inference, and in the rational reconstruction of various episodes in the history of science; and in the philosophy of specific scientific theories, such as quantum mechanics, and evolutionary biology. Bayesian methodology can play a central role in metaphysics, the philosophy of logic, the philosophy of language, and even the philosophy of religion. Just to take the last case, I have written extensively on Pascal's Wager (1997, 2000, 2003, 2008c), and on Hume's miracles arguments (1995, 2008a) from a Bayesian perspective.

Now there's a philosophical Grand Central station for you!

What do you consider to be the most neglected topics and/or contributions in contemporary epistemology?

And yet traditional epistemology and Bayesian epistemology seem to be on completely separate tracks. Think of some of the time-honored debates in traditional epistemology: skepticism, Gettierology, reliabilism, internalism vs externalism, foundationalism vs coherentism. Think of some of the currently hot topics: contextualism, subject-sensitive invariantism, relativism, luminosity, 'knowledge how' (as opposed to 'knowledge that'), knowledge 'wh—' (who, where, when), ... Where are the counterpart debates in Bayesian epistemology? Going in the other direction, think of some of the time-honored debates in Bayesian epistemology: constraints on priors, updating rules, the extension of subjective probabilities to infinite spaces. And think of some currently hot topics: credences about chances (as codified in Lewis's Principal Principle, 1980), credences about one's future credences (as codified in van Fraassen's Reflection Principle, 1984), updating credences on 'centered' or 'indexical' propositions, ... Where are the counterpart debates in traditional epistemology? It's not much of an exaggeration to say: *wherever we have a debate in one of the epistemologies but not the other, we have a neglected topic.*

A topic that has received some attention, but that deserves more, is the relationship between subjective probability, and the staples of traditional epistemology—knowledge, belief, truth, justification, and maybe some kind of 'fourth condition' that yields knowledge when added to justified true belief. For example, there has been a recent resurgence of interest in versions of the so-called 'Lockean thesis' that belief (or perhaps rational belief) can be reduced to credence—e.g. belief is credence above some threshold, perhaps contextually determined. Jeffrey thought that belief had passed its use-by date some time ago: "[I am not] disturbed by the fact that our ordinary notion of *belief* is only vestigially present in the notion of degree of belief. I am inclined to think that Ramsey sucked the marrow out of the ordinary notion, and used it to nourish a more adequate view." (1970, 171-2). He is referring to Ramsey's decision-theoretic approach to credence—"belief *qua* basis of action", which is ultimately preference-based.

But credences, preferences, and actions are certainly separable in thought, and sometimes in practice. Imagine a Zen Buddhist monk who has credences but no preferences, or a chronic apathetic who has credences but no inclination to action. Moreover, credences explain other aspects of behavior besides those that are preference-related, and they explain much more than behavior. (See Christensen 2004 and Eriksson and Hájek 2007.) Offhand, I would have thought that belief's primary job description is belief *qua representing the way things are*; action is downstream, both causally and conceptually. Furthermore, the ordinary notion of belief plays a vital role in psychological explanations, which is not obviously played by credence, however high. For example, we may say that a small child is reaching in the box simply because she *believes* her toy is there; to attribute a high subjective probability to her seems to over-intellectualize her psychological state.

And what about knowledge, truth, justification, and the American way? For starters, subjective probability theory seems to offer nothing corresponding to the *factivity* of knowledge. The Bayesian similarly lacks a notion of 'justification'—or to the extent that she has one, it is too permissive. Any prior is a suitable starting point for a Bayesian odyssey—yet mere conformity to the probability calculus is scant justification. Now, the Bayesian will be quick to appeal to various *convergence theorems*. For example, Gaifman and Snir (1982) show essentially that for each suitably open-minded agent, there is a data set sufficiently rich to force her arbitrarily close to assigning probability 1 to the true member of a partition of hypotheses. And she is presumably justified in doing so, for it was her evidence that drove her there.

This is a striking theorem, but one should not overstate its epistemological significance (not that Gaifman and Snir do). It is 'glass half-full' theorems, but a simple alternation of the quantifiers turns it into a 'glass half-empty' theorem. For each data set, there is a suitably open-minded agent whose prior is sufficiently perverse to thwart such convergence. And strong assumptions underlie the innocent-sounding phrases "suitably open-minded agent" and "sufficiently rich data set". No data set, however rich, will drive a dogmatic agent anywhere at all. Worse, an agent with a wacky enough prior will be driven *away* from the truth. Consider someone who starts by giving low probability to being a brain in a vat, but whose prior regards all the evidence that she actually gets as confirming that she is. And we can always come up with rival hypotheses that no courses of evidence can discriminate between—think of the irresolvable conflict between an atheist and a creationist who sees God's handiwork in everything. Finally, I don't see how the convergence theorems help one iota in addressing simple skeptical challenges, such as *how do I know, right now, that I have a hand?*

As for the so-called 'fourth condition' on knowledge: various reliabilist and anti-luck epistemologists advocate versions of *safety* as a condition on knowledge—roughly, at the closest worlds in which a given agent believes p, p is true. Others advocate *sensitivity*—roughly, at the closest worlds in which p is false, the agent does not believe p. (And some advocate both.) But note well: the *closest* worlds. Here we find another disjuncture between traditional and Bayesian epistemology: nothing in the standard Bayesian apparatus reflects the notion of 'similarity' of worlds that has recently taken center-stage in the analysis of knowledge.

Bayesian epistemologists have become alive to such concerns. Indeed, a large part of what has come to be known as *formal epistemology* seeks to build bridges between traditional and Bayesian epistemology, and it is a movement that is building momentum. (I've tried to build a bridge—or perhaps a tiny platform—between the two epistemologies by offering a Bayesian analysis of 'agnosticism' in my 1998.) So I see hope that the long-neglected topics of connecting the traditional and the Bayesian concepts are now receiving their due attention. This makes me sanguine that there will eventually be a rapprochement between these approaches to epistemology.

What do you think the future of epistemology will (or should) hold?

Rapprochement.

References

Adams, Ernest (1975): *The Logic of Conditionals*, Dordrecht: Reidel.

Arntzenius, Frank, Adam Elga, and John Hawthorne (2004): "Bayesianism, Infinite Decisions, and Binding", *Mind* 113, 251–283.

Briggs, Rachael (forthcoming): "Distorted Reflection", *Philosophical Review*.

Chalmers, David and Hájek, Alan (2007): "Ramsey + Moore = God", *Analysis* 67 (294), April, 170–172.

Christensen, David (2004): *Putting Logic In Its Place*, New York: Oxford University Press.

Churchland, P. M. (1981): "Eliminative Materialism and the Propositional Attitudes", *The Journal of Philosophy* 78: 67–90.

Eriksson, Lina and Alan Hájek (2007): "What Are Degrees of Belief?", *Studia Logica* 86, July, (Formal Epistemology I), 185–215, ed. Branden Fitelson.

Gaifman, Haim and Marc Snir (1982): "Probabilities over Rich Languages, Testing, and Randomness", *Journal of Symbolic Logic* 47, 495–548.

Hájek, Alan (1989): "Probabilities of Conditionals—Revisited", *Journal of Philosophical Logic* 18, No. 4, 423–428.

Hájek, Alan (1994): "Triviality on the Cheap?", in *Probability and Conditionals*, ed. Ellery Eells and Brian Skyrms, Cambridge University Press, 113–140.

Hájek, Alan (1995): "In Defense of Hume's Balancing of Probabilities in the Miracles Argument", *Southwest Philosophy Review* 11, Number 1, (January), 111–118.

Hájek, Alan (1996): "The Fearless and Moderate Revision: Extending Lewis' Triviality Results", *Proceedings of the 9th Logica International Symposium*, Liblice, ed. T. Childers et al, 171-178, Filosophia, The Institute of Philosophy of the Academy of Sciences of the Czech Republic.

Hájek, Alan (1997): *"The Illogic of Pascal's Wager"*, *Proceedings of the 10th Logica International Symposium*, Liblice, ed. T. Childers et al, 239-249, Filosophia, The Institute of Philosophy of the Academy of Sciences of the Czech Republic.

Hájek, Alan (1998): "Agnosticism Meets Bayesianism", *Analysis* 58, No. 3, 199–206.

Hájek, Alan (2000): "Objecting Vaguely to Pascal's Wager", *Philosophical Studies* 98 (1), 1–16.

Hájek, Alan (2003): "Waging War On Pascal's Wager", *Philosophical Review* 113, January, 27–56. Reprinted in *The Philosopher's Annual* 2004, ed. Patrick Grim, www.philosophersannual.org.

Hájek, Alan (2005): "Scotching Dutch Books?", *Philosophical Perspectives* 19 (issue on Epistemology), ed. John Hawthorne, 139-151.

Hájek, Alan (2007): "My Philosophical Position Says 'p', and I Don't Believe 'p'", in *Moore's Paradox: New Essays on Belief, Rationality, and the First Person*, ed. Mitchell S. Green and John N. Williams, Oxford University Press.

Hájek, Alan (2008a): "Are Miracles Chimerical?", in *Oxford Studies in Philosophy of Religion*, ed. Jon Kvanvig, Oxford University Press.

Hájek, Alan (2008b): "Dutch Book Arguments", in *The Oxford Handbook of Rational and Social Choice*, ed. Paul Anand, Prasanta Pattanaik, and Clemens Puppe.

Hájek, Alan (2008c): "Pascal's Wager", *The Stanford Encyclopedia of Philosophy*, ed. Edward N. Zalta, http://plato.stanford.edu/entries/pascal-wager/

Hájek, Alan (2009): "Arguments For – Or Against – Probabilism?", forthcoming in *Degrees of Belief*, ed. Franz Huber and Christoph Schmidt-Petri, Springer.

Hájek, Alan (forthcoming): *Arrows and Haloes: Probabilities, Conditionals, Desires and Beliefs*, Oxford University Press.

Hájek, Alan and Daniel Stoljar (2001): "Crimmins, Gonzales, and Moore", *Analysis* 61, No. 3, 208–213.

Hájek, Alan and James M. Joyce (2008): "Confirmation", in the *Routledge Companion to the Philosophy of Science*, ed. Stathis Psillos and Martin Curd.

Hájek, Alan and Ned Hall (1994): "The Hypothesis of the Conditional Construal of Conditional Probability", in *Probability and Conditionals*, ed. Ellery Eells and Brian Skyrms, Cambridge University Press, 75–111.

Jeffrey, Richard (1970): "Dracula Meets Wolfman: Acceptance vs. Partial Belief", in Marshall Swain, ed., *Induction, Acceptance, and Rational Belief*, Dordrecht: Reidel.

Lewis, David (1973): *Counterfactuals*, Blackwell and Harvard University Press.

Lewis, David (1976): "Probabilities of Conditionals and Conditional Probabilities", *Philosophical Review* 85, 297–315.

Lewis, David (1980): "A Subjectivist's Guide to Objective Chance", in *Studies in Inductive Logic and Probability*, Vol II., University of California Press, 263–293.

Lewis, David (1986): "Probabilities of Conditionals and Conditional Probabilities II", *Philosophical Review* 95, 581–589.

Lewis, David (1988): "Desire as Belief", *Mind* 97, 323–332.

McGee, Vann (1999): "An Airtight Dutch Book", *Analysis* Vol. 59, No. 264, (1999), October, 257–65.

Moore. G. E. (1942): "A Reply to My Critics" in *The Philosophy of G. E. Moore*, ed. P. Schilpp, Evanston: Tudor, 535–677.

Priest, Graham (1987): *In Contradiction*, Dordrecht: M. Nijhoff.

Ramsey, F. P. (1990): "Truth and Probability", in *Philosophical Papers*, D. H. Mellor (ed.) Cambridge: University Press, Cambridge (first published in *Foundations of Mathematics and other Essays*, R. B. Braithwaite (ed.), London: Routledge & P. Kegan, 1931, 156–198; reprinted in *Studies in Subjective Probability*, H. E. Kyburg, Jr. and H. E. Smokler (eds.), 2nd ed., Huntington, NY: R. E. Krieger Publishing Company, 1980, 23–52.

Rosenthal, David (2005): *Consciousness and Mind*. Oxford: Oxford University Press.

Skyrms, Brian, *Pragmatics and Empiricism* (New Haven: Yale University, 1984).

Skyrms, Brian (1987): 'Coherence', in *Scientific Inquiry in Philosophical Perspective*, ed. N. Rescher, Pittsburgh: University of Pittsburgh Press, 225–42.

Stalnaker, Robert (1970): "Probability and Conditionals", *Philosophy of Science* 37, 64–80.

Sorensen, Roy (1988): *Blindspots*, Oxford: Oxford University Press.

Stich, Stephen (1983): *From Folk Psychology to Cognitive Science*, Cambridge, MA: MIT Press.

van Fraassen, Bas (1976): "Probabilities of Conditionals", in *Foundations of Probability Theory, Statistical Inference and Statistical Theories of Science*, ed. W. L. Harper and C. Hooker, Vol. I, Reidel, 261–301.

van Fraassen, Bas (1984): "Belief and the Will", *Journal of Philosophy* 81, 235–256.

Williams, John and Alan Hájek (MS): "'p, and I Have Absolutely No Justification For Believing that p': the Necessary Falsehood of Orthodox Bayesianism".

Williamson, Timothy (2000): *Knowledge and Its Limits*, Oxford: Oxford University Press.

I thank Elle Benjamin, Ralph Miles, and Declan Smithies for helpful feedback.

14
Joseph Y. Halpern

Professor
Department of Computer Science
Cornell University, USA

Why were you initially drawn to epistemology (and what keeps you interested)?

I was initially drawn to epistemology because I enjoyed looking at puzzles that involved epistemic reasoning. Perhaps my favorite is the *muddy children puzzle*, which is a variant of the well known "wise men" or "cheating wives" puzzles [Gamow and Stern 1985; Gardner 1984; Littlewood 1953]. The following version is taken almost verbatim from [Barwise 1981].

> Imagine n children playing together. The mother of these children has told them that if they get dirty there will be severe consequences. So, of course, each child wants to keep clean, but each would love to see the others get dirty. Now it happens during their play that some of the children, say k of them, get mud on their foreheads. Each can see the mud on others but not on his own forehead. So, of course, no one says a thing. Along comes the father, who says, "At least one of you has mud on your forehead," thus expressing a fact known to each of them before he spoke (if $k > 1$). The father then asks the following question, over and over: "Does any of you know whether you have mud on your own forehead?" Assuming that all the children are perceptive, intelligent, truthful, and that they answer simultaneously, what will happen?
>
> There is a "proof" that the first $k-1$ times he asks the question, they will all say "No," but then the kth time the children with muddy foreheads will all answer "Yes."

The "proof" is by induction on k. For $k = 1$ the result is obvious: the one child with a muddy forehead sees that no one else is muddy. Since he knows that there is at least one child with a muddy forehead, he concludes that he must be the one. Now suppose $k = 2$. So there are just two muddy children, a and b. Each answers "No" the first time, because of the mud on the other. But, when b says "No," a realizes that he must be muddy, for otherwise b would have known the mud was on his forehead and answered "Yes" the first time. Thus a answers "Yes" the second time. But b goes through the same reasoning. Now suppose $k = 3$; so there are three muddy children, a, b, c. Child a argues as follows. Assume that I do not have mud on my forehead. Then, by the $k = 2$ case, both b and c will answer "Yes" the second time. When they do not, he realizes that the assumption was false, that he is muddy, and so will answer "Yes" on the third question. Similarly for b and c.

The argument in the general case proceeds along identical lines.

Let us denote the fact "at least one child has a muddy forehead" by p. Suppose that in fact there are 5 muddy children. Then even before the father speaks, each child knows p. So it would seem that the father does not provide the children with any new information. This suggests that the father he should not need to tell them that p holds when $k > 1$. But this is false. In fact, it is not hard to show that if the father does not announce p, the muddy children are never able to conclude that their foreheads are muddy (see [Fagin, Halpern, Moses, and Vardi 1995] for details).

The key point here turns out to be that the father gives the children *common knowledge* of p. I found understanding the role of common knowledge, and how Kripke structures could be used to explain what was going on in this puzzle at so many levels – logical, psychological, and linguistic – absolutely fascinating.

While puzzles were perhaps what drew me into epistemology, it was the intimate connection between epistemology and other topics of arguably more practical concern, particularly distributed computing, AI, and game theory, that kept me interested. I found it wonderful how reasoning about the knowledge of agents in a system could give insight into so many problems in all these areas, from coordination to agreement to bargaining. But here too, it was thinking about puzzles that initially brought out the connection. Aumann's famous result that we can't agree to disagree [Aumann 1976] (somewhat more precisely, it cannot common knowledge among agents that have a common prior that they have different posteriors) brought out the importance of epistemic reasoning to game theory. But this leads to an obvious puzzle: how do agents still manage to trade stocks (which, after all, involves agreeing to disagree about the expected value of a stock, which is impossible if agents cannot have different posteriors). (Of course, an agent that needs to sell a stock to finance his child's university education may be willing to trade even if he agrees that the stock that he is selling will go up relative to the rest of the market, but there is still an issue as to how agents only interested in making a profit are able to trade.) This seemed to me a great area in which to do research.

As a computer scientist, even more influential was what is perhaps my second-favorite puzzle, the *coordinated attack problem*. This problem was originally introduced by Gray [1978] as an abstraction of database issues, and can be described informally as follows (the description is taken from [Halpern and Moses 1990]:

> Two divisions of an army, each commanded by a general, are camped on two hilltops overlooking a valley. In the valley awaits the enemy. It is clear that if both divisions attack the enemy simultaneously they will win the battle, while if only one division attacks it will be defeated. As a result, neither general will attack unless he is absolutely sure that the other will attack with him. In particular, a general will not attack if he receives no messages. The commanding general of the first division wishes to coordinate a simultaneous attack (at some time the next day). The generals can communicate only by means of messengers. Normally, it takes a messenger one hour to get from one encampment to the other. However, it is possible that he will get lost in the dark or, worse yet, be captured by the enemy. Fortunately, on this particular night, everything goes smoothly. How long will it take them to coordinate an attack?

Suppose that the messenger sent by General A makes it to General B with a message saying "Let's attack at dawn". Will general B attack? Of course not, since General A does not know he got the message, and thus may not attack. So General B sends the messenger back with an acknowledgement. Suppose that the messenger makes it. Will General A attack? No, because now General B does not know that General A got the message, so General B thinks General A may think that he (B) didn't get the original message, and thus not attack. So A sends the messenger back with an acknowledgement. But of course, this is not enough either.

What is going on here is that each time an acknowledgement is received, the level of knowledge increases by one. However, the generals never achieve common knowledge of the message. As Yoram Moses and I showed [Halpern and Moses 1990], common knowledge is required for coordinated attack (and, more generally, for coordination of all types). Moreover, in a system where communication is not guaranteed (roughly speaking, one where there is always a possibility that a message sent might not arrive), agents can never attain common knowledge of a fact that wasn't common knowledge to start with. It easily follows that coordinated attack is impossible in systems where communication is not guaranteed.

The fact that reasoning about knowledge could provide such insights was to me very exciting.

What do you see as being your main contributions to epistemology?

I started working on epistemic logic in 1983 or so, with Yoram Moses, who was then my Ph.D. student. (It's hard to believe that it was really 25 years ago!) I found much of the work in the philosophy literature in epistemology at the time quite frustrating. The focus seemed to be on finding the "right, true properties" of knowledge. The implicit picture seemed to be that we all, at heart, understood what "knowledge" was; it was the philosopher's job to explicate the notion clearly. So there would be debates about whether, for example, it was "really" the case that knowledge satisfied S4; was it really true that if you knew something, you knew that you knew it? Much of the debate was relatively informal. In some of the papers, it seemed that the definition of knowledge changed from paragraph to paragraph. (Perhaps fortunately, I've forgotten exactly which papers in this literature I found particularly annoying!) It seemed to me that there was no one "right, true" notion of knowledge. People use the word in many different ways. In any case, my interests were more pragmatic.[1] Although philosophers going back to Hintikka had argued that S5 was not the appropriate logic of knowledge (in particular, they argued that the negative introspection axiom—if you know something you know that you don't know it—was inappropriate), S5 seemed to me the most natural epistemic logic for distributed computing applications. Game theorists independently adopted S5 for their applications, with much the same motivation. While I was willing to back off from S5 for computational reasons (see below), using it gave a great deal of insight, so I was more than happy to adopt it.

The philosophy literature also focused on the single-agent case—when debating the "right, true properties" of knowledge, there's no need to consider multiple agents. (Although, to be fair, Lewis's seminal work on convention [Lewis 1969] introduced the notion of common knowledge and pointed out its importance to characterizing conventions.) Distributed systems are composed of many agents, so I was interested in the describing the knowledge of not just of one agent, but of groups of agents, and how that could change as a result of communication. Particularly important was what one agents knew about other agents' knowledge.

I see my biggest contribution as the work I did with Yoram Moses [Halpern and Moses 1990] showing how knowledge could be used to help understand and analyze distributed systems, and in defining a concrete model of knowledge in distributed systems (the so-called *runs-and-systems model*, which is developed further in [Halpern and Fagin 1989] and [Fagin, Halpern, Moses, and Vardi 1995]). "Possible worlds" and "accessibility relations" had a concrete meaning in this framework, one that computer scientists interested in designing systems could understand, even if they were not so concerned with the philosophical issues. This word introduced the vocabulary of epistemic logic to distributed computing, and emphasized the connection between common knowledge and important notions like agreement and coordination. This initial work was followed by a great deal of work that expanded on these themes, joint with Ron Fagin, Yoram Moses, Mark Tuttle, Moshe Vardi, Lenore Zuck, and others (largely summarized in [Fagin, Halpern, Moses, and Vardi 1995]).

---

[1] While it's true that my primary interests were and continue to be somewhat more pragmatic, I must confess that I actually have a recent paper that considers definitions of knowledge in terms of (true) belief [Halpern, Samet, and Segev 2008].

Distributed computing concerns also motivated a second line of work that is enjoying newfound life in game theory. Hintikka [1962] had already observed that the standard possible-worlds semantics of epistemic logic suffers from the *logical omniscience problem*: agents knew all tautologies and that agents knew the logical consequences of their knowledge. This clearly is not a particularly accurate description of people's knowledge. Ron Fagin and I [1988] suggested that one way of dealing with the problem was in terms of *awareness*. The idea is that there is a distinction between an agent's *implicit knowledge* and her *explicit knowledge*. Implicit knowledge is defined in the usual way, as truth in all worlds; to have explicit knowledge of a fact ϕ, you must implicitly know ϕ and be aware of it. What does it mean to be aware of ϕ? That depends. It could mean that there are basic concepts in ϕ that the agent is not aware of (for example, an agent who has never heard of astrology might not be aware that the moon is in the seventh house); this is the interpretation that seems to be the one that game theorists are now focusing on. However, it might also mean that the agent cannot compute the truth of ϕ. In any case, there has been a great deal of work on awareness recently, largely published in economics journals (see, for example, [Dekel, Lipman, and Rustichini 1998; Feinberg 2004; Halpern 2001a; Halpern and Rêgo 2006a; Halpern and Rêgo 2006b; Heifetz, Meier, and Schipper 2006; Heifetz, Meier, and Schipper 2007; Modica and Rustichini 1994; Modica and Rustichini 1999] but this is just the tip of the iceberg).

What do you think is the proper role of epistemology in relation to other areas of philosophy and other academic disciplines?

Since I'm not a philosopher by training or background, I can't comment on what the proper role of epistemology is in relation to other areas of philosophy. I feel somewhat more confident in commenting on the role of knowledge in computer science and economics. We make decisions on the basis of our knowledge and belief. Understanding the connection between knowledge, belief, and action plays a key role in both computer science and economics. This connection may involve counterfactual beliefs as well (see, for example, [Halpern 2001b; Halpern and Moses 2004]). I believe that epistemology can help elucidate these issues.

What do you consider to be the most neglected topics and/or contributions in contemporary epistemology?

I'm not sure what the most neglected topics or contributions in epistemology are (I've probably neglected them along with everyone else!), so let me change the question slightly to one that I think is more interesting: What are the most pressing issues in epistemology today? To me, perhaps the most pressing issue is that of getting a good model of knowledge that takes resource-bounded reasoners, and particularly the computation involved in computing what you know, into account. This is hardly a new topic, but I think the problem is far from solved. A "good" model is one what is easy to work with, mathematically well founded, and leads to new insights. In particular, I would hope that such a model would give insights into cryptographic notions like *zero knowledge proofs* [Goldwasser, Micali, and Rackoff 1989]), and be used to define solutions concepts that take computation into account in a serious way. I believe that the notion of awareness should help here, as will perhaps the notion of *algorithmic knowledge* [Fagin, Halpern, Moses and Vardi 1995]. However, much more remains to be done.

In addition, I would like to see more work using epistemic logic on analyzing and synthesizing programs from knowledge-based specifications. The *synthesis* problem in computer science is that of deriving a program, given a specification that the program should satisfy. In many cases, what the system is supposed to do is best expressed in terms of knowledge. This is particularly true for specifications involving security; for example, we may not want an adversary to *know* certain secret information. (See [Halpern and O'Neill 2002; Halpern and O'Neill] for some discussion of how security specifications can be expressed in terms of knowledge.) There has been some work on automatically synthesizing programs from the specifications that they must satisfy (see [Bickford, Constable, Halpern, and Petride 2005; Engelhardt, Meyden, and Moses 1998; Engelhardt, Meyden, and Moses 2001]), but I think that much more can and should be done.

The first topic I mentioned, finding a good computational notion of knowledge, should have some important philosophical implications. Among other things, it would give a notion of knowledge that does not suffer from the logical omniscience problem. To the extent that it can be used to help clarify important issues in distributed computing and game theory, it will also capture important features of human epistemic reasoning. The second topic is perhaps of more pragmatic rather than philosophical interest, but it would show the applicability of epistemic reasoning to an important class of problems.

What do you think the future of epistemology will (or should) hold?

I believe that the connections between epistemology, computer science, and game theory will continue to broaden and deepen. Issues of knowledge, belief, awareness (or lack of it), computation, and counterfactuals will play an increasingly important role in the future. Philosophers could have a significant impact here and, indeed, some already have. For example, Bob Stalnaker's recent work on game theory has been quite influential (see, for example, [Stalnaker 1996]); his early work on counterfactuals [Stalnaker 1968] has turned out to be quite relevant to game theory as well. However, having an influence will require understanding, not just the philosophical issues, but the concerns of computer scientists and economists.

References

Aumann, R. J. (1976). Agreeing to disagree. *Annals of Statistics* 4(6), 1236–1239.

Barwise, J. (1981). Scenes and other situations. *Journal of Philosophy* 78(7), 369–397.

Bickford, M., R. L. Constable, J. Y. Halpern, and S. Petride (2005). Knowledge-based synthesis of distributed systems using event structures. In *Proc. 11th Int. Conf. on Logic for Programming, Artificial Intelligence, and Reasoning (LPAR 2004)*, Lecture Notes in Computer Science, vol. 3452, pp. 449–465. Springer-Verlag.

Dekel, E., B. Lipman, and A. Rustichini (1998). Standard state-space models preclude unawareness. *Econometrica 66*, 159–173.

Engelhardt, K., R. van der Meyden, and Y. Moses (1998). A program refinement framework supporting reasoning about knowledge and time. In J. Tiuryn (Ed.), *Proc. Foundations of Software Science and Computation Structures (FOSSACS 2000)*, pp. 114–129. Berlin/New York: Springer-Verlag.

Engelhardt, K., R. van der Meyden, and Y. Moses (2001). A refinement theory that supports reasoning about knowledge and time for synchronous agents. In *Proc. International Conference on Logic for Programming, Artificial Intelligence, and Reasoning*, pp. 125–141. Berlin/New York: Springer-Verlag.

Fagin, R. and J. Y. Halpern (1988). Belief, awareness, and limited reasoning. *Artificial Intelligence 34*, 39–76.

Fagin, R., J. Y. Halpern, Y. Moses, and M. Y. Vardi (1995). *Reasoning About Knowledge*. Cambridge, Mass.: MIT Press. A slightly revised paperback version was published in 2003.

Feinberg, Y. (2004). Subjective reasoning—games with unawareness. Technical Report Resarch Paper Series #1875, Stanford Graduate School of Business.

Gamow, G. and M. Stern (1958). *Puzzle Math*. New York: Viking Press.

Gardner, M. (1984). *Puzzles From Other Worlds*. New York: Viking Press.

Goldwasser, S., S. Micali, and C. Rackoff (1989). The knowledge complexity of interactive proof systems. *SIAM Journal on Computing 18*(1), 186–208.

Gray, J. (1978). Notes on database operating systems. In R. Bayer, R. M. Graham, and G. Seegmuller (Eds.), *Operating Systems: An Advanced Course*, Lecture Notes in Computer Science, Volume 66. Berlin/New York: Springer-Verlag. Also appears as IBM Research Report RJ 2188, 1978.

Halpern, J. Y. (2001a). Alternative semantics for unawareness. *Games and Economic Behavior 37*, 321–339.

Halpern, J. Y. (2001b). Substantive rationality and backward induction. *Games and Economic Behavior 37*, 425–435.

Halpern, J. Y. and R. Fagin (1989). Modelling knowledge and action in distributed systems. *Distributed Computing 3*(4), 159–179. A preliminary version appeared in *Proc. 4th ACM Symposium on Principles of Distributed Computing*, 1985, with the title "A formal model of knowledge, action, and communication in distributed systems: preliminary report".

Halpern, J. Y. and Y. Moses (1990). Knowledge and common knowledge in a distributed environment. *Journal of the ACM 37*(3), 549–587. A preliminary version appeared in *Proc. 3rd ACM Symposium on Principles of Distributed Computing*, 1984.

Halpern, J. Y. and Y. Moses (2004). Using counterfactuals in knowledge-based programming. *Distributed Computing* 17(2), 91–106.

Halpern, J. Y. and K. O'Neill. Anonymity and information hiding in multiagent systems. *Journal and Computer Security* 13(3), 483–514.

Halpern, J. Y. and K. O'Neill (2002). Secrecy in multiagent systems. In *Proc. 15th IEEE Computer Security Foundations Workshop*, pp. 32–46. To appear, *ACM Transactions on Information and System Security*.

Halpern, J. Y. and L. C. Rêgo (2006a). Extensive games with possibly unaware players. In *Proc. Fifth International Joint Conference on Autonomous Agents and Multiagent Systems*, pp. 744–751. Full version available at arxiv.org/abs/0704.2014.

Halpern, J. Y. and L. C. Rêgo (2006b). Reasoning about knowledge of unawareness. In *Principles of Knowledge Representation and Reasoning: Proc. Tenth International Conference (KR '06)*, pp. 6–13. Full version available at arxiv.org/cs.LO/0603020.

Halpern, J. Y., D. Samet, and E. Segev (2008). On definability in multimodal logic II. Defining knowledge in terms of belief. Unpublished manuscript, available at www.cs.cornell.edu/home/halpern/papers.

Heifetz, A., M. Meier, and B. Schipper (2006). Interactive unawareness. *Journal of Economic Theory* 130, 78–94.

Heifetz, A., M. Meier, and B. Schipper (2007). Unawareness, beliefs and games. In *Theoretical Aspects of Rationality and Knowledge: Proc. Eleventh Conference (TARK 2007)*, pp. 183–192.

Hintikka, J. (1962). *Knowledge and Belief.* Ithaca, N.Y.: Cornell University Press.

Lewis, D. (1969). *Convention, A Philosophical Study.* Cambridge, Mass.: Harvard University Press.

Littlewood, J. E. (1953). *A Mathematician's Miscellany.* London: Methuen and Co.

Modica, S. and A. Rustichini (1994). Awareness and partitional information structures. *Theory and Decision* 37, 107–124.

Modica, S. and A. Rustichini (1999). Unawareness and partitional information structures. *Games and Economic Behavior* 27(2), 265–298.

Stalnaker, R. C. (1968). A semantic analysis of conditional logic. In N. Rescher (Ed.), *Studies in Logical Theory*, pp. 98–112. Oxford University Press.

Stalnaker, R. C. (1996). Knowledge, belief and counterfactual reasoning in games. *Economics and Philosophy 12*, 133–163.

15
Sven Ove Hansson

Professor and Head of Department
Department of Philosophy and the History of Technology
Royal Institute of Technology, Stockholm, Sweden

Why were you initially drawn to epistemology (and what keeps you interested)?

My road to epistemology, and to philosophy in general, was somewhat more indirect than that of many colleagues. My first university studies were in medicine, and I spent several years working with trade unions in occupational health issues. When I returned to the university in order to study philosophy, my experiences from public health controversies contributed much to my interest in epistemology. The history of public health is full of conflicts in which opinions have been divided on the possible dangers associated with an exposure.

Some of these controversies can be solved with the available scientific knowledge, but many of them are cases of genuine scientific uncertainty. In such cases experts trying honestly and competently to assess the risks may come to widely different conclusions. The decisions made in such cases will in practice depend on how the burden of proof is distributed. In most practical cases we consider it worse to treat a harmful exposure as harmless than a harmless exposure as harmful. Consequently, it has often been claimed that the onus of proof should fall to those who claim that a substance or a technology can be used with impunity, rather than to those who wish to restrict its use. This has been called the "reversed burden of proof". It certainly makes sense as a policy principle, but its application requires more philosophical sophistication than has usually been realized.

The major problem with the "reversed burden of proof" is that the moral values we wish to apply in our lives are not easily compatible with the epistemic conditions under which we live. In order to apply a reversed burden of proof, we would need some methodology to prove the harmlessness for instance of a chemical exposure. Unfortunately, no such methodology is available.[1] We have methods to establish some kinds of harmfulness beyond reasonable doubt, but if we do not obtain any indication of harm in such studies this is no proof that the exposure is harmless. (This applies not only to animal experiments but also to epidemiological studies. Effects as large as the death of 1 % of the exposed population can be missed even in large and well-conducted epidemiological studies.[2]) This is a case in which rather intricate epistemic issues have immediate practical importance. The fallacious inference from "No known hazard" or "No hazard detected in these studies" to "No hazard exists" has caused much death and suffering.

On the other hand, resources for public health measures are limited. It would not be feasible to forbid every exposure for which there is some weak evidence that it may be harmful. We need to prioritize, and we have to do so in the rather difficult epistemic situation that I just described. How to do this is an issue in practical epistemology and decision theory to which I have returned repeatedly.[3]

It does not take much reflection to realize that if we want to protect ourselves against possible dangers, then we will on many occasions have to act without full scientific evidence. If there are strong scientific indications that a volcano may erupt in the next few days, then decision-makers will expectedly evacuate its surroundings as soon as possible, rather than wait for full scientific evidence that an eruption will take place. Similarly, if we have relevant but insufficient scientific evidence that a chemical substance may be dangerous to our health, then we are well advised to take precautionary measures to avoid or reduce exposure, even if we do not have full scientific evidence that it will harm our health. In

---

[1] S.O. Hansson, "Can we reverse the burden of proof?", *Toxicology Letters* 90:223-228, 1997.

[2] S.O. Hansson, "Seven Myths of Risk", *Risk Management* 7(2):7-17, 2005, esp. pp. 14-16.

[3] S.O. Hansson, "Replacing the No Effect Level (NOEL) with Bounded Effect Levels (OBEL and LEBEL)", *Statistics in Medicine* 21:3071-3078, 2002. S.O. Hansson and C. Rudén "Priority-Setting in the REACH System", *Toxicological Sciences* 90(2): 304-308, 2006. A. Nordberg, C. Rudén, and S.O. Hansson "Towards more efficient testing strategies – analyzing the efficiency of toxicity data requirements in relation to the criteria for classification and labelling", *Regulatory Toxicology and Pharmacology* 50:412–419, 2008. S.O. Hansson, "Regulating BFRs - from science to policy", *Chemosphere*, in press.

other words, the criteria of full scientific evidence do not coincide with the criteria for practical action.

This might sound uncontroversial, but in debates on public health it is far from that. There are outspoken proponents of another view, namely the view that only well-established scientific fact should be used in decision-making. This has been advertised as the application of "sound science". Proponents of so-called "sound science" claim that the intrascientific burden of proof should be used also in practical decisions that are based on science. This means that an exposure should be treated as innocuous when there are indications but yet not full proof that it is harmful. In particular, "sound science" advocates have opposed regulation against passive smoking since the evidence of its harmful effects did not in their view amount to full scientific evidence.

Despite its name, "sound science" is of course not required or implied by science. It is not a scientific standpoint but a policy standpoint. Furthermore, it is quite an implausible policy standpoint. Few of us are prepared to follow it in our daily lives. For example, consider the issue whether the variety of bilberries that grows in western Sweden is toxic. As far as I know, there is some evidence that these berries may be toxic, but there is not full scientific evidence that this is so. If a child asks you whether she may eat some of these berries, would you answer: "We do not have full scientific evidence that they are harmful, so please go ahead and eat as many as you like"?

Not surprisingly, the strange principle of "sound science" has its origin in the public relations efforts of corporations promoting the sale of harmful consumer products, in particular tobacco.[4] (Tobacco companies kill about half of their customers.[5]) Furthermore, all "sound science" proposals that I am aware of have been targeted at specific, mostly environmental, decisions. Even those who apply it to environmental measures tend to honour other principles in other decision areas, such as security policies. Consider the American decision in 2003 to act as if Iraq had weapons of mass destruction. This decision was made by an administration that has followed the advice of "sound science" advocates in many issues concerning public health and the environment. But

---

[4] Chris Mooney, *The Republican War On Science*, Basic Books, New York 2005.

[5] P. Boyle, "Cancer, cigarette smoking and premature death in Europe: a review including the Recommendations of European Cancer Experts Consensus Meeting, Helsinki, October 1996", *Lung Cancer* 17(1):1-60, 1997.

of course, the Iraq decision was based on a much lower level of evidence than the full scientific proof required by "sound science" in environmental policies.

There may certainly be legitimate reasons to apply different epistemic criteria in different areas of public policy. Then, however, intellectually tenable arguments must be given for doing so. In environmental and public health policies we have at least the beginnings of a discussion and analysis of the epistemic criteria of public policy decisions. In most other areas we do not even have that.

It was practical issues like these that brought me to epistemology. I still work with them, but unfortunately I do not see many other epistemologists doing so. In my view, current epistemological discussions have too little connection with practical problems of knowledge and belief. There is nothing wrong in pondering how we can know that we exist, but we also need to pay some attention to how we can acquire the knowledge necessary to ensure our continued existence.

What do you see as being your main contributions to epistemology?

In answering this question I would like to turn to quite another area of epistemology, namely the traditional distinction between coherentism and foundationalism. I am dissatisfied with this distinction since I believe that it gives an incorrect picture of how a rational system for knowledge and belief can work.[6]

In order to investigate the interrelations between epistemic coherentism and foundationalism we need to clarify exactly what it means for a set of beliefs to have a coherentist, respectively foundationalist, structure. According to a classic formulation, coherentism means that "a body of knowledge is a free-floating raft every plank of which helps directly or indirectly to keep all the others in place, and no plank of which would retain its status with no help from the others." In contrast, foundationalism means that "every piece of knowledge stands at the apex of a pyramid that rests on stable and secure foundations whose stability and security

---

[6] S.O. Hansson, "The False Dichotomy Between Coherentism and Foundationalism", *Journal of Philosophy* 104(6):290-300, 2007. See also S.O. Hansson, "Coherence in Epistemology and Belief Revision", *Philosophical Studies* 128:93-108, 2006.

does not derive from the upper stories or sections."[7] Hence both coherentism and foundationalism concern a relation of support. Let us denote this support relation by S ("supports"). It can for instance be inferential, explanatory, justificatory, or probabilistic. It operates on some set E of beliefs. What properties must S have in order to make the belief system coherentist, respectively foundationalist?

The "raft" analogy might induce us to require that all beliefs in a coherent belief system have to support each other. We could then use $(\forall x)(\forall y)(xSy)$ as a criterion of coherentism. However, this is a much too strong condition. We have beliefs that are not directly related to each other. Hence, there is no reason why my belief that the female redback spider eats the male should directly support or be supported by my belief that Brutus stabbed Caesar. A much more plausible criterion of coherentism is $(\forall x)(\forall y)(xS^*y)$, according to which every belief must, directly or indirectly, support every other belief.[8] However, a good case can be made that it is still a too strong criterion. If the two beliefs just mentioned, about Brutus and about the redback spider, do indeed support each other indirectly then this must be a case of *very* indirect support. Arguably, the most credible connection between them derives from the fact that they both support and are supported by the same general beliefs such as those referring to the reliability of certain types of sources. If we find such indirect connections insufficient for the support relation, then we will have to look for weaker conditions of coherentism.

One quite plausible such condition is that every belief is supported by some other belief, $(\forall x)(\exists y)(ySx)$.[9] It can be combined with the requirement that every belief supports some other belief, $(\forall x)(\exists y)(xSy)$. But even this combination is not enough for a credible explication of coherentism. The major reason for this is that both these conditions can be satisfied in a belief system that consists of two or more compartments that are not connected by S. We would then have two or several rafts floating beside each other, rather than a single raft. Clearly, a definition of coheren-

---

[7] Ernest Sosa, "The Raft and the Pyramid: Coherence versus Foundations in the Theory of Knowledge," *Midwest Studies in Philosophy* 5: 3-25, 1980, p. 24

[8] S^* is the ancestral of S. Hence, aS^*b holds if and only if either aSb or there is a finite series of elements $x_1, ..., x_n$ such that aSx_1, $x_k S x_{k+1}$ for all $l \leq k < n$, and $x_n Sb$.

[9] For simplicity of notation I assume that S is irreflexive.

tism should include some condition that prohibits such a fragmentation of the belief system. The simplest criterion that achieves this is $(\exists x)(\forall y)(xS^*y)$. We can use the combination of the three conditions $(\forall x)(\exists y)(ySx)$, $(\forall x)(\exists y)(xSy)$, and $(\exists x)(\forall y)(ySx)$ as a criterion of coherence. This combination is implied by, but does not imply, $(\forall x)(\forall y)(xS^*y)$.

Next, let us look at foundationalism. According to the pyramid analogy, a foundationalist belief system should have a base that supports the other beliefs but is not supported by them. (However, there is no reason as far as I can see to require that elements of the base do not support each other.) This means that there must be a set $E\prime$ with $\varnothing \neq E\prime \subset E$, such that

$$(\forall y \in E\backslash E\prime)(\forall x \in E\prime)\neg(yS^*x)$$

and

$$(\forall y \in E\backslash E\prime)(\exists x \in E\prime)(xS^*y).$$

With this definition, the base will not in all cases be uniquely defined. However, it is easy to show that there is always an inclusion-minimal base.[10] It can be treated as the "canonical" base.

We can consider this condition, i.e. the existence of a base that supports the rest of the structure without being supported by it, as a defining condition for foundationalism. As I just mentioned, the combination of the three conditions, $(\forall x)(\exists y)(ySx)$, $(\forall x)(\exists y)(xSy)$, and $(\exists x)(\forall y)(xS^*y)$ can be used as a criterion of coherence. It turns out that that these conditions are compatible, or in other words: coherence and foundationalism, as defined in this way, are compatible properties. This can be proved by drawing a simple diagram (reproduced).

I believe that these simple insights have philosophical significance. Structures of support that satisfy both the criterion for coherentism and that for foundationalism may in some contexts be more plausible than structures that satisfy only one of these criteria. Instead of classifying support structures according to the traditional dichotomy between coherentism and foundationalism, we should investigate the many variations and nuances in actual structures of support. I have myself tried to do this in studies of belief revision using belief bases (sets not closed under logical consequence) rather than belief sets (sets closed under logical consequence) to represent states of belief. Belief bases have often

---

[10]See Observation 3 in my "The False Dichotomy Between Coherentism and Foundationalism", *Journal of Philosophy* 104(6):290-300, 2007.

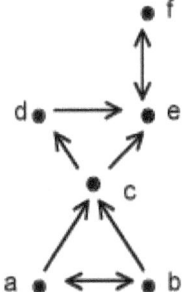

FIGURE 15.1. A belief structure exhibiting both coherentist and foundationalist features. The dots denote beliefs. An arrow from one belief to another signifies that the first belief supports the other. A double arrow denotes mutual support.

been taken to represent a foundationalist belief structure in the classical sense, but in my view this is misleading. In fact, the coherence of a belief system can be represented by (logical) support relations among elements of the base.[11]

What do you think is the proper role of epistemology in relation to other areas of philosophy and other academic disciplines?

Epistemology and the philosophy of science are closely related. In some respects they are different traditions treating the same issues. One important characteristic that they have in common is that they are both unabashedly normative. They are both concerned with how we can obtain reliable knowledge.

Common usage of the term "science" is partly descriptive, partly normative. When we recognize an activity as science this usually involves an acknowledgement that it has a positive role in our strivings for knowledge. On the other hand the concept of science has been formed through a historical process, and many contingencies influence what we call and do not call science. For philosophical purposes, it is mostly useful to disregard these contingencies and focus on the normative, epistemological aspect of the concept of science. Our focus should then be on the fundamental task

---

[11] S.O. Hansson, "Coherentist Contraction", *Journal of Philosophical Logic* 29:315-330, 2000.

of science, namely to develop gradually more and more reliable knowledge about the workings of nature, man, and human society. This is a joint undertaking by a community of interdependent knowledge disciplines that includes the natural and social sciences but also the humanities.[12] (The German word "Wissenschaft", has the advantage over the English "science" of having a much broader meaning and including also the humanities.)

In recent years, a form of vulgar relativism has gained influence in some segments of the social sciences, often using sceptical arguments from the philosophical tradition without attending to their proper scope and their epistemological implications.[13] This trend is represented by the "strong programme" in the sociology of science and by other scholars who take an "agnostic stance on what constitutes good science".[14] But studying science – or any other epistemic enterprise – while blindfolding oneself to the distinction between epistemic failure and epistemic success is about as debilitating as studying warfare without allowing any information about who lost or who won the battles and the wars.

Epistemology has an important task in clarifying the essential role that criteria of epistemic success have in any account of strivings for knowledge. A closely related task is to investigate the nature of scientific knowledge. We know from the efficiency of science in various technological applications that science is epistemically successful. (If science were just a social construction on par with astrology and dowsing, how come that science but not astrology can take us to the moon? And why was global warming discovered by scientists and not by dowsers?) But philosophy has not been able to account satisfactorily for the epistemic reliability of science. Kuhn observed that although his own and Popper's criteria for the demarcation of science are profoundly different, they lead to essentially the same standpoint in practical issues on what should be counted as science.[15] This convergence also applies to

---

[12] S.O. Hansson, "Values in Pure and Applied Science", *Foundations of Science* 12:257-268, 2007.

[13] Mario Bunge, "A Critical Examination of the New Sociology of Science Part 1" *Philosophy of the Social Sciences* 21:524-560(1991). Mario Bunge, "A Critical Examination of the New Sociology of Science Part 2" *Philosophy of the Social Sciences* 22:46-76 (1992).

[14] Brian Wynne, "Carving out Science (And Politics) in the Regulatory Jungle", *Social Studies of Science* 22:745-758, 1992. Quotation from p. 753.

[15] Thomas S Kuhn "Logic of Discovery or Psychology of Research?", pp. 798-819 in P.A. Schilpp, *The Philosophy of Karl Popper*, The Library of Living Philosophers, vol xiv, book ii. La Salle: Open Court, 1974. See p. 803.

other demarcation criteria.[16] Our choice between different theories of science do not seem to have much relevance for what we count as science. This is of course highly unsatisfactory. It seems to me that philosophical theories of science have not yet reached the epistemic core of scientific methodology.

What do you consider to be the most neglected topics and/or contributions in contemporary epistemology?

I have already mentioned a couple of neglected topics, but I would like to mention two more. The first of these is the role of uncontroversial values in science. This may sound a bit surprising as a topic, but let me explain.

The role of values in science was excellently clarified by Carl Hempel when he introduced the notion of epistemic values (or utilities as he first called them). He did this as part of a concession that the choice whether or not to accept a scientific hypothesis depends on values. However, he claimed that this should be "the value or disvalue which the different outcomes have from the point of view of pure scientific research rather than the practical advantages or disadvantages that might result from the application of an accepted hypothesis, according as the latter is true or false."[17] In other words, epistemic utilities should reflect truth, simplicity, explanatory power and other desiderata of scientific theories. According to the ethos of science, our assessment of scientific evidence should be influenced by epistemic values but not by non-epistemic values. It is part of every scientist's training to leave out non-epistemic values from her scientific deliberations as far as possible. This ideal is of course seldom if ever perfectly achieved. There has been much discussion about deviations from the ideal. However, this discussion has been almost entirely focused on deviations that involve controversial non-epistemic values. Possibly, the largest deviations from the ideal are driven by non-controversial values, i.e. values that are shared by virtually everyone or by everyone who takes part in a particular discourse.

Medical science provides good examples of this. When discussing analgesics, we take for granted that it is better if patients have

---

[16] S.O. Hansson, "Science and pseudo-science". Entry for the *Stanford Encyclopedia of Philosophy*, to be published.

[17] Carl G Hempel, "Inductive inconsistencies", *Synthese* 12:439-469, 1960. See p. 465.

less rather than more pain. There is no need to interrupt a discussion on this topic in order to point out that a statement that one analgesic is better than another depends on this value assumption. More generally speaking, the value assumption that health is better than disease permeates medical science, for instance in its criteria of evidence.

The influence of non-controversial values in science may seem innocuous, but it is nevertheless important to understand in order to understand the workings of science. It would seem better for this influence to be explicit rather than implicit. A further reason to investigate the role of uncontroversial values is that uncontroversialness is contestable and liable to change. Consensus views among economists about economic growth have been attacked by non-economists, and feminists have uncovered androcentric values that were uncontroversial in expert communities dominated by men.

The other issue that I would like to bring up is a problem in the dynamics of belief, namely the order-dependence of belief change. In belief revision theory, we study how rational agents change their beliefs in response to new information.[18] The standard model in belief change theory is an input-output model. The inputs are represented by sentences, and basically there are two types of sentential inputs: Sentences to be removed and sentences to be added. Given a belief state K, we can contract by some sentence p and obtain a new belief state $K \div p$ not containing p, or we can revise by some sentence q and obtain a new belief state K^*q that contains q. But of course we change our beliefs many times in our lives. Therefore, belief changes take place in the form of long series such as $K \div a^*b^*c \div d$ ...

It turns out that the outcome of a series of belief changes is highly dependent on the order in which we perform the changes. Hence, it makes a difference if we contract first by a and then by b, $K \div a \div b$, or the other way around, $K \div b \div a$. This is a recalcitrant feature of belief change models; it does not seem possible to construct a model in which contraction or revision is order-independent.[19] I believe that in this respect, belief change theory reflects the dynamics of actual human belief. It is for instance a

---

[18] S.O. Hansson, *A Textbook of Belief Dynamics. Theory Change and Database Updating*. Kluwer 1999. Sven Ove Hansson, "Specified Meet Contraction", *Erkenntnis* 69:31-54, 2008.

[19] S.O. Hansson, "Multiple and iterated contraction reduced to single-step, single-sentence contraction", in preparation.

common claim in folk psychology that first impressions determine our beliefs about a person.

But generally speaking the recalcitrance of order-dependence is an undesirable feature of our belief systems. In most cases it would seem more rational to treat the pieces of information that we receive on an equal footing, irrespective of the order in which they arrive. One way to achieve this would be to keep track of our previous belief changes in a particular subject-matter and (hypothetically) rescind them in order to deal with all the relevant information at one and the same time.

However, there is a limit to the usefulness of this strategy. We cannot revert to some sort of primordial belief state whenever we receive new information, in order to reconsider all previously received information together with the new one. Therefore it is in practice unavoidable that we often have to perform belief changes consecutively. This is one of the cognitive limitations on our ability to perform belief changes rationally, and it may well be one of the more important of these limitations.

All this applies not only to changes in individual beliefs but also to changes in the collective belief system of science, the corpus of scientific knowledge.[20] The order in which we receive information in some knowledge area, be it Persian history or neurochemistry, may influence the way in which we systematize our knowledge and construct our theories in that area. This, again, is an undesirable influence on the structure of science. We need to investigate the effects of order-dependence on science and to develop strategies to avoid its undesirable effects as far as possible. This is one of the areas in which I believe that formal epistemology, in this case particularly belief revision theory, can be practically relevant.

What do you think the future of epistemology will (or should) hold?

As I see it, epistemology is (or at least should be) primarily concerned with *human* belief and knowledge. This has at least two important implications.

First, it gives us reason to pay close attention to the effects of cognitive limitations on the formation of knowledge and belief. There is a tendency both in epistemology and in other disciplines

---

[20] On the corpus, see: S.O. Hansson, "Values in Pure and Applied Science", *Foundations of Science*, 12:257-268, 2007.

to discuss rationality in terms of how hypothetical beings with transfinite cognitive capacity would reason. If we are interested in *human* rationality it is more useful to focus on how agents with limited cognitive capacity can make rational use of that capacity. The best use of limited cognitive resources may require that one follows principles and processes that would not be useful for logically omniscient beings.[21] This, by the way, is yet another neglected topic in epistemology.

Secondly, human knowledge and belief are phenomena of the human brain. Therefore epistemology has important connections with the neurosciences and with psychology. However, there are surprisingly few references to these disciplines in the epistemological literature. Isolation from the empirical literature is of course not tenable in the long run.

Does this mean that epistemology should be "naturalized"? Yes, and perhaps even more thoroughly than what we usually mean by "naturalized". Perhaps epistemology should be "naturalized" in the same sense as physics has been. I see no reason why epistemology, conceived as the study of human knowledge and belief, should not develop into an independent discipline that may come to be seen as one of the natural (or behavioural) sciences.

---

[21] S.O. Hansson, "Levi's ideals", in Erik J Olsson, ed. *Knowledge and Inquiry. Essays on the Pragmatism of Isaac Levi.* Cambridge University Press, 2006, pp. 241-247.

16
Jaakko Hintikka

Professor

Boston University, USA

Why were you initially drawn to epistemology (and what keeps you interested)?

For the same reason as I was drawn to philosophy in the first place, in that for me epistemology has always been an integral part of the philosophical enterprise in general. My first philosophical inspiration came form Eine Kaila, and one of the first substantial books on philosophy was his *Inhimillinen tieto* (Human Knowledge).

What do you see as being your main contributions to epistemology?

Each of my major contributions relevant to epistemology has usually led me to new questions and then through to new insights. It is therefore impossible to rank them in isolation from each other. I took up G.H. von Wright's suggestive suggestions in his 1952 book *An Essay in Modal Logic* and articulated one of the first explicit treatments of epistemic logic in my 1962 book *Knowledge and Belief*. Alas, I came to realize that this logic was not yet really general. Only by bringing the notion of informational independence to bear on epistemic logic in 1999 could I make it to apply to all uses of our epistemic concepts. The role of informational independence is absolutely crucial for all epistemic logic. Even linguistically, it is not much of an exaggeration to say that the independence indicator *is* the wh-ingredient in direct and indirect questions.

I called the resulting logic "second generation epistemic logic". This term is perhaps misleading for what it is is the first truly general epistemic logic. Its significance is shown by the fact that it also made it possible to formulate for the first time a satisfactory theory of questions and answers, a theory that could among other things yield an analysis of the all-important question-answer relation and of the notion of the presupposition of a question.

This theory of questions and answers is throwing sharp new light to a number of central philosophical issues. Some of them are examined in my 2007 book *Socratic Epistemology*. For one such issue, induction turns out to involve not one, but two interrelated lines of inquiry. In experimental questions to nature particular observations yield in the limit a function-in-extension, as it were a curve on graph paper. The curve (function) does not constitute a full answer unless and until we have also identified the mathematical function that the curve represents.

An adequate logic of questions and answers made it possible for me to outline a general theory of epistemological inquiry as a questioning process. The idea goes back to the Socratic elenchus, but only now are we in a position to spell what Socrates' method amounts to.

The resulting interrogative approach ("inquiry as inquiry") constitutes in a genuine sense a "logic of inquiry". It disproves among other things the myth that "contexts of discovery" are not amenable to explicit logical and epistemological analysis.

The interrogative approach allows the application of strategic concepts to inquiry. Even though question-answer steps in inquiry are categorically different from deductive inferences, it turns out that optimal strategies of questioning (albeit only in context of pure knowledge-seeking) are essentially the same as optimal strategies of deduction. Sherlock Holmes was right: strategically speaking all discovery turns on "logic" and "deduction". This insight into the rule of logic in all inquiry is probably my neatest contribution to epistemology, even if it is not the most central one.

In knowledge-seeking inquiry, the same strategies have to serve both discovery and confirmation. Hence the conventional view on context of discovery vs. contexts of justification is mistaken in yet another respect. The "logic" of justification cannot be in the last strategic analysis be separated from the "logic" of discovery, and is bound to be more complicated.

Along a different line of thought I have made contributions to inductive logic and to the analysis of the concept to information (especially in the form of a distinction between surface information and depth information).

Furthermore, I have outlined a theory of explanation, including the first adequate analysis of "how possible" explanations. The future will show which of these contributions is going to be most consequential.

What do you think is the proper role of epistemology in relation to other areas of philosophy and other academic disciplines?

I would rather speak of a collaboration of epistemology with other kinds of academic enterprise than of a "role" of epistemology in relation to other disciplines. Such collaboration takes different forms in different directions.

In the direction of logic and mathematics, epistemology could profit greatly from sharper tools than those that most philosophers are employing. This is amply in evidence in what has already happened. Epistemic logic reached maturity only when the relatively new and sophisticated concept of informational independence was brought to bear on it, borrowed from the most abstract "mathematical" logic. The study of the concept of explanation was conducted for decades in a horse-and-buggy methodology of trying to capture different homemade examples under a verbally formulated generalization. It took the discovery of a new sharper interpolation theorem from general logic to spell out precisely in what sense even a logical deduction can provide an explanation for its conclusion. An account of "how possible" explanations turned out to be implicit in the well-known *tableau* method of general logic. Such examples can be easily multiplied.

As far as other parts of philosophy are concerned, I cannot see that there could – or should – be any boundary between epistemology and philosophy of science. Different sciences should not be used merely or even primarily as source material for philosophical reflection. In many sciences, there are foundational problems of great significance for the science in question that are genuinely epistemological and hence cry out for a joint effort to solve them. Epistemologists should have the courage (and the scientific education) to tackle them. For instance, theoretical linguists could use ideas from logic and epistemology. For instance, I have not seen any recent linguist acknowledge the fact that in any sufficiently rich language there are two different negations implicitly present.

At first sight, this interplay with science and the philosophy of science might not seem to affect some of the more traditional parts of epistemology, such as the philosophical theories of perception.

In my view, this is diametrically contrary to truth. Modern neuroscience (which I want to distinguish from what typically goes under the title "cognitive science") is already in a position to offer insights that are going to affect deeply epistemology. For one thing, neuroscience has already made it overwhelmingly clear that much maybe most of the cognitive processing of one's experience takes place under the surface of consciousness. Even such apparently simple experience as color perception turns out to be the product of complicated (and completely unconscious) processing in our central nervous system. This shows that phenomenological methods and appeals to conscious experience are much more limited in their scope than most traditional epistemologists realize. I expect that phenomenological epistemology will be gradually replaced by the kind of work that in David Marr's trichotomy of neuro-scientist's tasks takes place on what Marr calls the computational level. By this I mean (and I think Marr means) conceptual analyses of the tasks that our brain has to perform not trying to tell on this level how it performs them.

I have even tried to show (together with John Symons) what such an analysis might be in the case of the two systems of visual cognition. We were so bold as to surmise that such an analysis could in principle have influenced the actual formation in neuroscience.

What do you consider to be the most neglected topics and/or contributions in contemporary epistemology?

Whatever gross oversights I have become aware of, I have tried (or am trying) to correct. Among the relatively specific topics that at least relatively speaking deserve more attention there are the following:

1. It is an old idea that the success of induction is based on the regularity of the universe. But what precisely is this regularity? There are obviously many different kinds of regularity. Which of them does the old idea refer to? In the simple inductive situations that Carnap studied, the choice of his parameter lambda amounts to a relative regularity assumption. Can this parameter be generalized? Some work in this direction was done by Finnish inductive logicians in the sixties and seventies, but it should be continued. There are in fact extremely important connections between the choice of

priors in Bayesian inference and assumptions of regularity. They deserve careful examination.

2. Induction meant for Newton something quite different from what it meant for Hume, viz. extrapolation and interpolation of partial generalization, not inference from particulars to a generalization. This concept (whether or not you call it "induction") has not been given its due either systematically or historically. Historically, Newton's notion of induction is but a quantitative version of Aristotle's notion of *apagoge*.

3. In spite of the immense popularity of the notion of information, this notion is still in need of closer study. The term is being used in several different disciplines in what obviously are different meanings. Yet we do not have a sharp account of how these several meanings are related to each other or what they have in common—if anything. Likewise, the relation of the notion of information to other epistemological concepts, especially knowledge and belief, needs closer scrutiny. In particular, the precise roles of these concepts in knowledge-seeking (or is it information-seeking?) needs to be spelled out.

Or is the real neglect here a failure to realize that a logical theory of information already tacitly exists? All information amounts to the elimination of some alternative possibilities. A general theory of information therefore is a study of how different possibilities concerning reality expressible in language can be distinguished from each other (e.g. in a suitable logical language). Now the theory of distributive normal focus and constituents is precisely such a theory of information.

4. In contemporary theory of rational decision, an agent's decision is considered to be a result of his, her or its (if the decision-maker is a computer) utilities and beliefs (subjective probabilities). But in reality rational decision-makers ought to take into account also the way in which those beliefs are acquired. Conceiving them as subjective probabilities does not do so adequately. Hence a critical epistemological look at these decision theories might not be a bad idea.

What do you think the future of epistemology will (or should) hold?

I leave all actual predictions of the future of epistemology to historians and sociologists of science and learning. What the future of epistemology should be like in my considered judgment is shown by the direction of my own research: I am trying to bring about the right future

My main recommendation to epistemologists is a change of direction of their work (or at least of their emphasis). In recent and current epistemology, the main interest has been in the justification of knowledge claims. As was pointed out, questions of justification cannot be adequately studied in isolation from the process of knowledge acquisition. Such a change could among other things make epistemology more relevant to the methodology of science.

As a practical recommendation to the philosophical community I urge serious epistemologists and logicians to put their insights to use for the purpose of teaching reasoning and critical thinking and argumentation. This teaching constitutes the most important contribution that philosophy can make to general education. It can be enormously useful to students. Yet currently the teaching of reasoning and introductory logic deals largely with antiquated platitudes without any theoretical basis whatsoever. Epistemologists should take their educational mission more seriously. In my experience, attention to the educational function of epistemology can even inspire one's own research. In this direction, too, maybe Socrates is our best role model.

17

Wiebe van der Hoek

Professor and Head of Agent ART
Department of Computer Science
The University of Liverpool, UK

Why were you initially drawn to epistemology (and what keeps you interested)?

My connection with epistemology is through epistemic logic, endowing me with admittedly a particular and probably limited view on the subject as a whole. And indeed, my interest in epistemic logic arose from working in modal logic. The most popular and accepted epistemic logic, called S5, intrigued me because it is very simple and rich at the same time. When there is only one knower, the semantics of S5 is extremely simple and attractive, and reasoning in it is computationally not harder than in propositional logic.

When there are more than one knower, or agents, things become a little bit more complex, but also far more expressive and rich. And group notions of knowledge, like distributed knowledge and common knowledge are again on the one hand mathematically very elegant and clear, but conceptually quite involved. Up to today, I find it exciting to teach such notions to students: there are many 'paradoxes' and puzzles that are challenging to solve but, once solved, give the impression that one masters the subject better. (This in contrast to many puzzles and paradoxes in probability theory, of which I often have the feeling that once I 'solved' them, there is still something not explained, and one might easily convince me of another, contradicting solution again. This probably says more about me than probability theory, I realise.)

And, even when one has a language with notions of individual and group knowledge, there is far more to say. For instance one can add a notion of time, and reason about properties like *recall* and *learning*. And, again in many cases there is a price to pay for the added expressivity: logics about knowledge and time have high computational cost, and become in some cases undecidable. And again, it does not stop here, we may want to reason about knowledge and action, and the actions themselves may be intrinsically epistemic, like in Dynamic Epistemic Logic.

And enriching such logical systems is not an artificial exercise at all. In contemporary computational systems (like multi agent systems), information, and hence knowledge, is one of the main characteristics to be modeled. A simple (programming) instruction like 'If the flight is intercontinental, go to terminal A, if it is continental, to terminal B' of course involves an epistemic test, and when fed to an agent, in the ideal situation it comes with a recipe to gather the information needed (doing certain epistemic actions). Epistemic logic provides tools to work with, but also to understand the kind of reasoning that underpins iterated elimination of dominated strategies which lead to a Nash equilibrium in games: not only do I have to know that my opponent is rational, but also that he knows that I know that.

What I like about epistemic logic is its many faces with a constant constructive mood: many formalisms are proposed to tackle or even only model certain problems, and often the simplest are the most attractive, and make themselves available for other extensions.

What do you see as being your main contributions to epistemology?

My co-authored[1] book 'Epistemic Logic for Computer Science and AI' (1995) helped maybe make more researchers in the Sciences interested in a rather philosophically perceived subject (or even, in the case of Reasoning about Belief, a religiously perceived one, as I experienced personally during my PhD time at the Free University of Amsterdam, a University originally established in 1880 by orthodox protestants). My most recent co-authored book 'Dynamic Epistemic Logic' (2007) is a report on the state of the art in its area. This book will soon be overruled by many new results: there are far more logicians, philosophers, game theorists and computer scientists interested and active in this area now than 12 years ago.

---

[1] Almost all of my work was done with inspiring colleagues, to which I am much indebted. In order not to make this overview a numerous list and to treat my co-authors all the same (but not fairly) I decided to mention none of them here.

Between these two books, I contributed to the development of the modal logic for knowledge and belief. One line of research was on trying to combine well-known logics into one logic (KARO) for agency: this combined Knowledge, Actions, Results and Opportunities in one framework. In other work we studied the notion of 'only knowing'. One the one hand, we argued that if one really wants to reason about agents that know *nothing*, partial modal logic is a good starting point. On the other hand, we showed that by choosing an appropriate relation between models, one could generalize notions of 'single-agent only knowing' to the multi-agent case. Although the mathematics of those relations could get rather involved, the basic idea was simple: weak knowledge of an agent corresponds with allowing him 'big models'.

Work that I particularly liked was on Belief Revision in a non-monotonic context. In nonmonotonic logics, inferences are often allowed on the basis of some ignorance. We showed that in such a framework, the 'best' way to contract beliefs, i.e. to get rid of 'inconsistencies', was to *add* beliefs to the underlying base, namely beliefs that would block to make a specific inference based on ignorance. We were able to relate 'classical belief revision' as a limiting case of our postulates.

I have worked on logics for games as well, and currently we are studying to add a notion of knowledge to a logic called *Alternating-time Temporal Logic*. Other than its name suggest, ATL is a very attractive logic to reason about what groups of agents can enforce. Its semantics has a strong game theoretic flavour. When studying epistemics in this context, I am excited by the many problems and challenges triggered by the idea of mixing two well-understood formalisms (ATL and Epistemic Logic). This forces one to rethink the notions of uniform strategies, of memoryless strategies, of recall, and to distinguish between knowing *de re* to have a strategy from having this knowledge *de dicto*. And again, group notions become interesting: what does it mean for a group to have common knowledge that there is a Nash equilibrium when such an equilibrium is not unique: how do the agents synchronise and decide upon their strategy?

What do you think is the proper role of epistemology in relation to other areas of philosophy and other academic disciplines?

It looks like epistemology is a good example of an area where philosophers started to ask the very right and relevant questions, but which only came to full development when others (logicians and computer scientists) formalized specific (but in my view still rich enough, and interesting) kinds of it. And although the initial motivation for this formalisation seemed quite peculiar, i.e. to reason about communication protocols, this same formalisation is still the basis for logics of knowledge and belief useful in a much wider context. One can even say that this formalisation has inspired others to also formalise other 'mental' notions, like belief, desires and intentions. (Here, it is interesting to note that the same is not true for revision of such mental notions: although philosophers and logicians have been very active and successful in the theory of Belief Revision, there is, to the best of my knowledge, no well developed work on, say, Intention Revision.) At the moment, one sees a similar development in the area of ontologies: having its roots in philosophy, it is now making a very rapid development by theoreticians that work on description logic, and computer scientists that study the semantic web. It seems here is a general phenomenon: the widely posed questions posed by Philosophers are intellectually challenging and weed the ground for something nice to grow, but real progress is then made when some discipline attaches a specific interpretation to it, makes a number of strong assumptions, and demonstrates what kind of nice landscapes emerge when doing so. This need not be discouraging for the Philosopher: he should on the one hand point at the limited scope of the route taken, but also, ask questions when enjoying the scenery provided by the landscapes that are discovered!

The role of epistemology to computer science in general, and artificial intelligence in particular is maybe not a very clear one, but very important: systems make their decision based on the knowledge (or the lack of it) that they have in a particular situation, and such a decision may involve acquiring more information, or maybe giving it to others. This is true both in the case of systems that cooperate or compete: knowledge and information is a key asset.

What do you consider to be the most neglected topics and/or contributions in contemporary epistemology?

For applications in Computer Science and Artificial Intelligence, the assumptions underlying the standard notions of knowledge are very strong. All agents are considered the same, and they are assumed to have unlimited reasoning power, and are unboundedly rational. There seems to be a trade-off – I am not sure this is governed by some overall principle – between the mathematical elegance that one often encounters under the 'ideal and strong' assumptions about the agents one is modeling, and the more cumbersome and less straight-forward formalisations one often sees when for instance bounded rationality is taken serious.

Also, there is still a big gap between well-developed theoretical frameworks that represent knowledge on the one hand, and the way how information is represented in applications. Take for example the Agent Programming paradigm, where programs (agents) are specified and designed on a high level, referring to their Goals, Desires, Intentions and Beliefs. This is a big step forward compared to 'conventional' programs, but still, one rarely comes across agent programs in which the agent refers to a model that an other agent has about him (like in, 'If I believe that the other robot believes that I believe that he will replace the block, I better inform him that I really don't expect that of him and he can continue finishing his own task').

I like to mention here a very successful (in terms of attention, and as opposed to a neglected) topic in contemporary epistemology, i.e., that of Belief Revision. It would be interesting to understand how this topic keeps our academic minds busy for such a long time. The notions of expansion, contraction, and revision are conceptually very clear, and yet the Belief Revision community has been very active for over 20 years. The motivation of the first papers on Belief Revision were much less concrete than the motivation that the computer scientists had in looking at epistemic logic, but still Belief Revision kept being a very active area of research. One can say it has inspired Dynamic Epistemic Logic, which, in turn, has revived the interest in Belief Revision again. But if one looks at for instance implemented robot systems (systems that are prone to constant change of beliefs), I am afraid one finds very little of the ideas provided by the Belief Revision area.

What do you think the future of epistemology will (or should) hold?

I think epistemology has a key role to play in the further development of modern technology. We all know that contemporary technology generates huge amounts of data, like on the internet, monitoring and surveillance systems, and log-information of computer systems. A lot of this data never reaches the status of information, let alone knowledge. For the Semantic Web, many believe that the work on Ontologies will help bridge this gap. But one can imagine going much further than 'just' linking web pages on the level of words. In one specific context, or culture, even one word is interpreted different than in another. Also, in many cases the data is not even represented on the level of words. Distributed sensor networks are thought to have a main application in for instance surveillance systems, whether they are used in macro systems like satellites monitoring a widely stretched environment (to monitor climate change for example), or micro systems that guide the everyday life of elderly people (like monitoring whether they take their medicine, drink water regularly, or even whether they 'feel well'. But again, there is an overkill of data generated by those sensors, and very little knowledge.

This of course is also true for interacting Intelligent Systems. Two robots can exchange photographs from different perspective in a situation, but the question is what they do with it. Talking about the area of robotics, this is another area where 'well understood' epistemological phenomena like belief revision, belief merging, and reasoning about how the other reasons about me are in a very strong need to be trimmed down (or even be re-designed) for practical implementations. It looks to me that probabilistic, or maybe fuzzy formal approaches will be successful here.

Group notions of knowledge are relatively well understood in logic. Still, there seems to be something missing here. One can for instance refer to what a specific Institution knows ('Institution' as a semi-formalised organization). But this seems to be neither distributed knowledge, nor common knowledge, in the technical sense. It even becomes more interesting if one combines informational attitudes of groups with motivational attitudes. What does an institution want? Or what are the desires of a group of agents? And if we are going to determine a group preference on the basis of individual preferences, there is of course the issue of the individuals reasoning strategically and unwilling to make their preferences known. (Computational) Social Choice Theory is a very exciting area, with on the one hand many impossibility results, but on the other hand we are all the time making more and more (temporary) communities that often have to make quick decisions. And also here, it will be interesting to look across borders, like at cognitive science and at anthropology. Primates and other animals are well able to make group decisions and to reach agreement: there are for instance fish of different species that hunt their prey together, with each species and individual playing their own role.

18
Kevin T. Kelly
Professor
Carnegie Mellon University, USA

Five Questions[1]

Why were you initially drawn to epistemology (and what keeps you interested)?

I have always thought of myself as a philosopher whose primary interest is the truth-conduciveness of inductive inference and scientific method, a fundamental topic that falls between the cracks of epistemology, philosophy of science, statistics, and computer science. My interest was piqued already in college, when I first encountered Hume, Mill's methods, and logical positivism. In my graduate course work at the University of Pittsburgh, I learned in seminars by Carl Hempel and Clark Glymour about "confirmation", "Bayesian rationality", "justification", and "probability", but I was left to wonder how these ideas connect with truth. And instead of apologizing for failure to address such a fundamental question, the philosophy of science literature insulted me for even considering it! I read that Hume had already refuted the possibility of such an explanation; that I was confusing the pure study of justification with the psychological discovery of actual discovery processes; that I had lost sight of the fact that once a hypothesis is justified, the process leading to its discovery is irrelevant to that justification; that no explicit procedure can introduce hidden variables; and that to be justified in believing that a theory is true is merely to be justified in believing the theory, so there is no further question about truth. All of that struck me as desperately evasive, defeatist nonsense—and it still does (Kelly 1987, 2000a).

---

[1] This work was supported by National Science Foundation grant 0750681.

There was, after all, some solace in the philosophy of science literature. For example, Hans Reichenbach (1949) conceived of science not as an abstract relation of justification or confirmation, but as a method or process that converges to the truth in the limit and Bayesians had a more general argument for this kind of convergence. The usual objection to these ideas was a vague hope for more and the correct observation that in any event convergence in the long run is compatible with any theory choice whatever in the short run, so convergence cannot explain scientific practice (Salmon 1967). Also, the question of truth vs. method arose sharply in the then-raging debate over scientific realism. Realists, like Clark Glymour (1980), claimed that unified theories are better confirmed by the evidence, but could not connect confirmation with truth. Anti-realists, like Bas van Fraassen (1981), viewed explanation and theoretical simplicity as values extraneous to truth, making Ockham's razor an instance of the fallacy of wishful thinking. I knew from my historical studies with Larry Laudan and others that theoretical unification, of the sort embodied in Glymour's confirmation theory, was a major factor in the history of scientific theory choice, so I had to admit that it was awkward to dismiss it as wishful thinking irrelevant to truth. But I sympathized with the anti-realist demand to explain what the connection with truth was supposed to be.

I received some inspiration, as well, from the "naturalistic" movement that had emerged both in epistemology and in the philosophy of science. Here, there was no shrinking from truth-conduciveness as an aim, and there were also clear proposals for what truth-conduciveness amounts to—reliability and truth-tracking. But these concepts did not seem to apply to scientific knowledge. For when one accepts a precise scientific hypothesis, there is (notoriously) no bound on one's chance of error in doing so, because the hypothesis might be false in a subtle way that would still have eluded detection. Thus, tracking and reliabilist accounts of theory choice require either unrealistic background assumptions that beg the question against the problem of induction, or hidden, occult forces that make the tracking relation work (I call the latter view "woo-woo realism", where "woo-woo" is the sound that occult forces would make if there were any).

In view of my emerging interest in discovering true theories as opposed to merely confirming them, Clark Glymour recommended that I look at the literature on learning and discovery in artificial intelligence and even attend artificial intelligence classes at neighboring Carnegie Mellon. In place of philosophical defeatism, I encountered was a breathless faith that the complete automation of super-human discovery was around the corner—or even already at hand. But now I had qualms of my own. The practice was to write learning programs and to compare their run-times on some standard examples of learning problems that floated between research groups. But the point of learning and scientific procedure is to succeed over a wide range of possible truths: without some theory to control the trade-off of speed vs. scope, it was a matter of comparing apples with oranges.

I did not anticipate any new insight about the truth-conduciveness of scientific method from my courses in logic, computability, and incompleteness, since I already "knew" that these topics belong to the philosophy of logic and mathematics rather than to the logic of science and induction. Upon closer examination, however, I was inspired. An algorithm has to find the right answer to the problem it solves—the philosopher's routine, bait-and-switch swerve to "confirmation" or "rationality" does not arise. Also, it is clear what makes one algorithm a better truth-finder than another—it finds the right answer efficiently. Efficiency, of course, depends on the mathematical structure of the problem addressed: finding a formal needle in a formal haystack is hard, whereas telling a formal needle from a formal hayseed is easy. I began to hanker after a story like that for inductive inference. Then scientific method might also be justified, non-magically, but in virtue of truth-finding performance better than that of alternative methods.

Finally, from several nearly simultaneous sources,[2] I learned of something called "formal learning theory", which analyzes a stereotypical version of empirical theory choice using the concepts and techniques of the theory of computability. The basic idea (Cf. Osherson et al. 1999) is to relax the "halting" condition of standard computability theory so that one can consider methods—both ideal and computable—that can process an unending stream of external inputs for eternity. Then, in place of halting with the right answer, one can substitute efficient convergence to the true answer, where efficiency is measured in terms of costs like the number of changes of opinion prior to convergence, the number of errors prior to convergence, etc. One might describe it, in traditional terms, as a fusion of computability theory with

---

[2] Scott Weinstein, Clark Glymour, Ken Manders, and Bob Daley.

Reichenbach's convergent conception of inquiry (Kelly 1991).

Here was just the sort of thing I had vaguely been seeking. Like the theory of computability, formal learning theory was principled, a priori, mathematically precise, and focused squarely on the aim of truth-finding—the weasel-words "justification" and "confirmation" do not even arise. But by dropping the halting requirement on procedures and substituting various notions of convergence and efficiency, the approach eludes the usual argument for inductive skepticism. Furthermore, as in the theory of computability, the best sense in which one can solve an inference problem depends on, and reflects, the intrinsic complexity of the problem. Negative results (e.g., the classical argument for inductive skepticism) show that halting with the right answer is not possible and, hence, *justify* rather than *undermine* inductive inference. As icing on the cake, I discovered that the subject was (co-)invented by Hilary Putnam (1963), who was Reichenbach's student and that Putnam invented formal learning theory for the explicit purpose of refuting Rudolf Carnap's theory of confirmation!

But there were limitations. The formal learning theory of the time focused on a rather narrow conception of inquiry in which reality is a computable function or set and the scientist is a computer who has to learn how to compute that function or set. And, being based on convergence in the limit, it still implied no short-run constraints on which theory to choose *now* and, hence, no real insight into epistemic justification as confirmation theorists and traditional epistemologists conceive of it. Many of the results involved very detailed trade-offs between retractions, errors, and reliability that did not seem to connect in any natural way with real scientific practice. The challenge was to transform formal learning theory into a recognizable philosophy of science and induction grounded entirely in truth-finding performance. I undertook the challenge in my doctoral thesis *The Automated Discovery of Universal Theories*, and it has continued to inspire me since.

What do you see as being your main contributions to epistemology?

The Mathematical Structure of Learnability. Optimal truth-conduciveness has two crucial components: the capacity to find the truth in so-and-so sense (the positive component) and the fact that truths of that kind cannot be found in a better or more efficient sense (the negative component). An important question, then, is to characterize the best feasible sense in which the truth can be found in a given theory choice problem. In purely formal problems, the answer is well-known: algorithmic efficiency depends on the problem's computational complexity. In my thesis and in some papers with Clark Glymour, I originally followed the logical positivist tradition that located complexity in the syntactic forms of the theories under consideration (Kelly 1989, Kelly and Glymour 1989, 1990a, 1990b). However, that approach revealed repeating mathematical patterns beneath the logical syntax that seemed to be doing the real work, and I realized, very suddenly and distinctly in 1989 (during a magically golden evening in Roskilde, Denmark) that the underlying structure is *topology* (Kelly 1993, 1994, 2000, Kelly, Schulte, and Juhl 1997). This topological viewpoint is the core idea of my book *The Logic of Reliable Inquiry* (1996).[3]

Topology may sound completely out of place in epistemology—isn't it about twisting doughnuts into coffee cups? Yes, when the topology under consideration is taken over geometrical points, but when the points under consideration are possible worlds, the epistemologically central concepts of verifiability and refutability are *already* topological—there is nothing further to *impose*. To see why, let W be a set of possible worlds. Say that a proposition $P \subseteq W$ is verifiable just in case there exists an empirical procedure that reads data and then halts with "yes" if and only if P is true. Then the tautological hypothesis W is verifiable (say "yes" and halt no matter what); the contradictory hypothesis $\emptyset$ is verifiable (never halt with "yes"); given any finite collection $\mathcal{H}$ of verifiable hypotheses, verify their conjunction by halting with "yes" when each individual hypothesis' verifier halts with "yes"; and, finally, given an arbitrary collection $\mathcal{H}$ of verifiable hypotheses, verify their disjunction by halting with "yes" when the individual verifier for some hypothesis in $\mathcal{H}$ halts with "yes". Note that infinite conjunctions of verifiable propositions are not necessarily verifiable—"black at stage n" is verifiable but "black at every stage" is not—so the characteristic asymmetry between countable union and countable intersection in the definition of a topological space corresponds to the ancient problem of induction! It follows almost immediately that refutable propositions are closed

---

[3] I was assisted considerably by careful study of Peter Hinman's beautiful book *Recursion Theoretic Hierarchies* (1978), to which I was introduced in a seminar on truth by Jamie Tappenden. Much of the book's focus is on the delicate interplay between computability and topology.

sets, decidable propositions are both closed and open, propositions that one can converge to the truth about are countable disjunctions of closed propositions, that the problem of induction arises in hypothesis boundaries, and so on. Hence, the necessary and sufficient conditions for the usual methodological concepts of truth-conduciveness are topological! That insight places topology squarely in the center of epistemology and opens a floodgate of connections between topological results and epistemological issues, some of which are presented *The Logic of Reliable Inquiry*.

Ockham's Razor Derived from Truth-Conduciveness. The topological viewpoint developed in *The Logic of Reliable Inquiry* did not yet entail any short-run constraints on scientific method. In particular, they did not provide any special connection between simplicity and truth, so I could not yet explain Ockham's razor—a problem that had been on my mind for over a decade. It was particularly disappointing not to have much to say about my colleagues' procedures for causal inference (Spirtes et al. 2000), which rely heavily on a tacit appeal to Ockham's razor, since I had been involved closely in the early phases of that project (Glymour, Scheines, Spirtes, and Kelly 1987). But without knowing it, I did possess the main component of a new explanation. Long ago, Hilary Putnam (1963) invented the idea of n-trial predicates: formal properties that can be decided by a Turing machine that converges to the truth with at most n reversals of opinion prior to convergence to the truth and, subsequently, "mind-changes" have been a familiar measure of learning efficiency in the learning-theoretic literature. In *The Logic of Reliable Inquiry* I provided a topological characterization of the learning problems that can be solved with at most n mind-changes. Right after the book's publication, I noticed that achievement of the minimum retraction bound imposes severe constraints on which theory a convergent method can select at each stage. For example, suppose that you will see at most two marbles and the question is how many you will see. That problem can be solved with just two retractions: $(0, 1, 2)$. But if you start with the guess 2 before any marbles have been seen, nature can withhold marbles until you converge to 0, present a single marble followed by no more until you converge to 1, and then show the last marble after that, forcing you through the answers $(2, 0, 1, 2)$, which is worse. After hearing an artificial intelligence talk on the automated inference of conservation laws in particle physics (Valdez-Peres 1996), Oliver Schulte and I recognized that the selection of maximally restrictive conservation laws compatible with the observed reactions was an instance of this idea (think of each newly observed reaction as the appearance of a new marble). So are curve fitting (marbles are refutations of lower polynomial degrees) and my colleagues' various algorithms for inferring causal networks from correlational data (marbles are observed correlations) (Spirtes et al. 2000, Schulte 2007). Thus, we came to see a striking connection between judgments of empirical simplicity and the learning-theoretic concept of retractions forcible by nature from an arbitrary, convergent method (Schulte 1999a, 1999b, 2000). Putting this conception of empirical simplicity together with the efficiency argument, I showed,[4] for non-stochastic data, that:

1. **Ockham Efficiency Theorem:** The following statements are equivalent, for a given theory choice problem:

   (a) Convergent method M never selects a theory other than the simplest theory compatible with experience and never drops a theory, once selected, until that theory is no longer uniquely simplest compatible with experience.

   (b) For each n, convergent method M achieves the least achievable bound on retractions and the least achievable bound on errors over worlds of empirical complexity degree n.[5]

Most recently, the theorem has been extended to random methods (Kelly and Mayo-Wilson 2008). The current task is to extend the argument further to the inference of properly stochastic theories from random data.

No alternative approach has explained, without circularity, how Ockham's razor is more truth-conducive than other possible strategies for finding the true theory. Standard approaches either substitute some alternative aim or virtue (accurate prediction, testability, unity) for finding the true theory, fail to explain how Ockham's razor finds the truth better than alternative methods, or simply

---

[4] Cf.(Kelly 2000, 2004a, 2007a, 2007b, 2007d, 2007e, Kelly and Glymour 2004).

[5] In some published versions of the argument, errors are replaced by or augmented with the times at which the retractions occur. The statement in terms of errors is more intuitive and much easier to set up.

beg the question at the outset by assuming that the truth is probably simple. The evident difficulty, faced by all approaches, is to show how violating Ockham's razor by favoring a complex theory would hurt *even if the complex theory were true*. The retraction-minimization argument surmounts that obstacle because, in the worst case, the Ockham violator who starts out with answer 2 traverses path $(2, 0, 1, 2)$ en route to complex theory 2, whereas the Ockham method traverses the more direct path $(0, 1, 2)$. Of course, this does not imply that Ockham's razor points at or tracks the truth immediately, but one cannot show such a thing without begging the question or appealing to unknown, occult, truth-tracking forces. The problem at hand is to explain, without circles, why Ockham's razor is optimally truth-conducive, and that problem has been addressed (more on this below).

Relations of Ideas are Matters of Fact. It is clear already from Putnam's (1963) and E.M. Gold's (1967) early papers that learning theoretic arguments involve a deft interplay between purely empirical complexity (the problem of induction) and formal complexity (uncomputability). But since the usual learning-theoretic setup envisions theories as computable objects, Oliver Schulte and I thought it would be interesting to analyze the computable learnability of theories whose empirical predictions are not computably derivable. We proved a comprehensive series of results about this question (Kelly and Schulte 1995, 1997, Kelly 2004b, Leeds 1996). It is no surprise that being able to compute the predictions of a theory allows one to computably refute the theory (wait for the deduced predictions to disagree with experience). One might expect the converse as well—that computability of the theory's predictions is also necessary for the existence of a computable refutation method. But surprisingly, there do exist empirical hypotheses that are effectively refutable even though their predictions are, in a sense, infinitely uncomputable! That has two important consequences. First, the computable refuting method for such a hypothesis cannot possibly work by *first* deriving the predictions of the theory (even in the limit) and comparing them against the data. The only way to find the truth is to let the theorem prover see future empirical data to determine whether the theory was refuted *already*. This considerably amplifies Quine's thesis that logical conclusions are sensitive to future empirical data: for the sake of truth-conduciveness, sometimes they *should* be. Second, since Bayesian rationality literally demands that refutations be noticed right away, the computable refuting method just described cannot be Bayesian. There are computable Bayesians with respect to this question, but they can't even converge to the truth in the limit even though a computable method can succeed with just one retraction. That is a much stronger critique of ideal rationality than was Putnam's original argument against Carnap's confirmation theory.

The Learning Power of Belief Revision. Horacio Arló-Costa and Vincent F. Hendricks first introduced me to belief revision theory some time around 1996. Belief revision theory began as a bare set of axioms about how to update beliefs in the face of evidence contradicting some of them (Alchourron, Gardenfors, and Mackinson 1985, Spohn 1988, Darwiche and Pearl 1997). The methods satisfying these axioms start out with a kind of bookshelf on which to arrange possible worlds. Upon receiving new evidence E, push all the worlds that satisfy E to the left, all the worlds that fail to satisfy E to the right, saw the shelves in half, and jack up the right-hand side of the book-case by some distance, so that every world on the bottom shelf satisfies E. Keep doing this forever. Your belief at each stage is the proposition satisfied exactly by the worlds on the bottom-most shelf. Since refuted worlds are only jacked up, rather than being discarded altogether, there is the possibility for a world in which E is false to migrate back down to the bottom shelf again. In fact, it can be shown (Kelly, Schulte, and Hendricks 1995, Kelly 1998) that there are published belief revision methods that, for each initial ranking of worlds, either forget the past or fail to ever project the future. I called this new, rationally inspired malady *inductive amnesia*.

That was the sort of limitation I had anticipated. What I did not expect is that some of the proposed belief revision methods can learn very well—if their initial ranking of worlds is tweaked just right. I found the right kind of tweaking by computer simulations and then characterized it mathematically. That is news, because it is widely thought that there is nothing rational about one such ranking as opposed to another (they are supposed to be analogous to subjective Bayesian prior probabilities in that respect). It is also news because the right sort of ranking turns out to be the notion of simplicity employed later in my work on Ockham's razor! There is, therefore, the prospect that efficient convergence to the truth may explain features of belief revision theory as well as Ockham's razor.

Infinite Regresses of Methods. During a reception for the Center for Philosophy of Science around 1999, Robert Nola told me about his work on Larry Laudan's "Normative Naturalism". Laudan's idea (1984) was to justify empirical methods using other empirical methods, to justify these other methods by still other methods, etc. I thought I saw a new objection to the idea. Every empirical method requires some material background assumptions. If one could tell via method M_1 that the background assumptions for method M_2 were true, then one could chain M_1 and M_2 together to construct a method succeeding in the same sense as the original methods but requiring no background assumptions, which is absurd. When that happens, say that the regress (M_1, M_2) can be *collapsed*. This collapse, I thought, would show that there is no real advantage to regresses of methods, which would be a kind of learning-theoretic embarrassment for Laudan's program. When the paper was due I sat down to write out the easy argument and it failed. I constructed a counterexample and discovered, to may surprise, that not every regress of methods is collapsible, so such a regress can have a point. Then I wrote a pair of papers (Kelly 2000, 2007c) characterizing collapsibility of a variety of types of finite and infinite regresses of methods.

What do you think is the proper role of epistemology in relation to other areas of philosophy and other academic disciplines?

Quine's critique of analyticity and his accompanying metaphor of the web of belief signaled to many that epistemology must somehow collapse into empirical psychology. But that is an awkward fit to philosophical skills and interests—epistemology is supposed to have something to do with justification and, when it comes to actual cognitive causes, psychologists are already deft at finding experiments to discover them. Quine (1969) actually suggested something different and far more appealing: epistemology as *engineering*. Quine never really developed the idea—his book *Pursuit of Truth* (1992) does not contain a single interesting idea about how to design optimal procedures for finding the truth. But the learning theoretic approach, grounded in efficient convergnce to the truth, provides a solid example, with detailed results, of what epistemology-naturalized-as-engineering would be like. It defies the tired epistemological dichotomy between empirical naturalism and a priori internalism. It is naturalistic (learning procedures are discrete dynamical systems kicked by input data) but it is also normative (grounded in efficiency) and largely a priori (since the analysis of efficiency is mathematical). Finally, formal learning theory has an air of philosophical familiarity, since it is built of concepts and techniques familiar from the usual graduate philosophy course on computability and incompleteness.

The engineering viewpoint, if seriously pursued, is not so much a defeat for epistemology as an advance. The more traditional approach to normative philosophy is to consult a wide range of intuitions about what we ought to do in particular cases and to systematize them into an idealized, normative theory of what we ought to do by some sort of process vaguely referred to as "reflective equilibrium". The theory so obtained can be explanatory, in the sense of reducing a confusing array of normative judgments to a small set of principles and it is hard to deny that there is some cognitive reality lying behind such a theory. But that reality may, itself, be a purely psychological "is" incapable of entailing any of the diverse, intuitive "oughts" the theory is invoked to explain: an explanatory gap endemic to the process of mining intuitions for normative conclusions. The engineering approach is actually harder, in a sense: methodological intuitions—even very strong ones like Ockham's razor—must be held in suspicion as possibly arbitrary cognitive aberrations until vindicated by an explanation of their truth-conduciveness. But when such an explanation is found, the result is more satisfactory because the explanatory gap endemic to intuition-mining disappears.

What do you consider to be the most neglected topics and/or contributions in contemporary epistemology?

Some topics and tendencies would benefit from more neglect.

1. Philosophers are too quick to give up on truth and to substitute something else like confirmation or Bayesian rationality. The reason is pretty obvious: the Bayesian setup yields detailed recommendations about what and how to believe in every conceivable circumstance, as long as values are assumed for its many free parameters. I urge some restraint before taking that plunge. Stop to consider how intuitions might be explained in terms of optimal truth-conduciveness before plugging in parameters and turning the Bayesian crank.

2. Philosophers think of themselves as specialists at conceptual refinement. But in epistemology, only a very few concepts of truth-conduciveness are entertained, such as reliability, tracking, and convergence in the limit. The key to the Ockham efficiency theorem was to find a notion of truth-conduciveness properly between convergence in the limit and reliability or tracking. At least some of the effort spent on theories of rationality and confirmation might usefully be spent on the development of a wider range of possible, precise explications of "truth-conduciveness".

3. A recent, Orwellian strategy for connecting Bayesian credence with truth is simply to *define* "truth-conduciveness" as increased Bayesian credence (Klein and Warfield 1994). But old-speak already has a good word for what increases belief: *belief*-conduciveness or *rhetoric*. Although new-speak has all the epistemological advantages of theft over honest toil, honest toil yields rewards theft never can – e.g., edifying explanations – so I prefer old-speak.

4. If there is any excuse whatever for a surreptitious slide from rational credence to truth, it resides, presumably, in familiar argument that Bayesian updating converges to the truth as the evidence increases. Is that argument sufficient?

   (a) First of all, the convergence theorems in question do not guarantee convergence in the limit. What they say is that, for each hypothesis h, a rational agent must be certain (have credence 1) that she decides h in the limit (in the sense that her degree of belief in h goes to 0 or 1 depending on whether the hypothesis is true. Now it is easy to show that uncountably many measurable hypotheses are not decidable in the limit by *any* method, Bayesian or otherwise, unless extra, material background assumptions are granted. So what the Bayesian convergence theorems actually say is that, for every hypothesis h whatever (no matter how undecidable in the limit), rationality *compels* one to be certain of some background belief under which h is decidable in the limit. In other words, *pure* rationality commits one dogmatically to methodologically powerful *material* beliefs. That is more unsettling than reassuring (Kelly 1996).

(b) Moreover, the Bayesian convergence theorems do not imply that Bayesian updating is *necessary* for almost sure convergence in the limit. Given material assumptions sufficient to make an hypothesis decidable in the limit by Bayesian updating, uncountably many alternative methods would also converge to the truth in the limit. So again, the convergence theorems are more about the dogmatic consequences of rationality than about the peculiar learning power of Bayesian updating (Kelly 1996).

(c) Furthermore, the almost sure convergence theorems assume that degrees of belief are assumed to be countably additive (the probability of a countable disjunction of mutually incompatible events is the sum of the probabilities of the events). But countable additivity is tantamount to an outright denial of skepticism, since it entails that one's belief in a universal hypothesis being refuted after a sufficiently long wait is negligible. Expectably, almost sure convergence theorems fail when this powerful, anti-skeptical postulate is dropped (Kelly 1996, theorem 13.20). Dogma in, dogma out.

(d) Worse still, recall that for computable agents, there exist hypotheses that a Turing machine can converge to the truth about with just one retraction, for which no finitely additive computable Bayesian can even converge to the truth about in the limit, with arbitrarily many retractions. So far from being a one-size-fits-all recipe for convergence, Bayesian rationality can severely *restrict* the potential learning power of computable agents.

(e) Finally, some Bayesian explanations of method depend upon special prior probability assignments. For example, the Bayesian explanation of Ockham's razor is to impose a simplicity-biased prior probability and then to calculate that the posterior probability of the simpler theory is higher. That sort of argument evidently fails to establish truth-conduciveness unless the prior probabilities reflect cosmic chances. But they are actually just a Bayesian model of a cognitive bias whose truth-finding efficacy is hardly explained simply by presupposing it.

5. The riches of ideal Bayesian rationality can be embarrassing—logical omniscience being a case in point. There are perennial attempts to weaken the requirement of logical omniscience within Bayesian theory, but they are always necessarily grudging, because the ultimate solution is to give up on logico-algebraic idealizations (i.e., Bayesian rationality) altogether. Truth-conduciveness occasions no such problem; as discussed above, it argues against rational idealizations like consistency with the data when such requirements restrict the potential power of computable science.

6. Finally, the Ockham efficiency theorem raises an interesting, general question about the relationship between rhetoric and epistemology. Ockham's razor is already rhetorically powerful, but it is not clear why it *should* be. The Ockham efficiency theorem answers that question, but it does not make Ockham's razor any more convincing—perhaps it even raises new reflective doubts. To learn that Ockham's razor is reliable or tracks the truth in the short run would, perhaps, enhance its credibility, but such explanations are circular and, therefore, unsatisfactory. So the simplicity puzzle is grounded, in part, in a tacit hope or demand that epistemology also be rhetorical: i.e., that the explanation of epistemic justification that p convince us that p. But the two-for-one deal yields zero: no added rhetorical force and no explanation. Since scientific arguments have been persuading for centuries without any assistance from epistemology, a better division of labor is to focus on explaining scientific method and to leave the rhetoric to scientists, themselves.

What do you think the future of epistemology will (or should) hold?

There are two things, epistemology the noble subject and Epistemology the line-item in philosophy curricula and internet philosophy department ratings. In the former sense, epistemological questions will enjoy increasingly intense interest from increasing numbers of increasingly well-informed researchers from statistics, artificial intelligence, theoretical computer science, and cognitive psychology. Nowadays, computer scientists are doing epistemic logic, something I never expected to see. Artificial intelligence researchers still routinely use the term "knowledge" as though it were just belief, but it would not surprise me if artificial intelligence were to see an explosion of activity concerning the Gettier problem in a few years—the undergraduate computer scientists in my epistemology courses see the point immediately. The question is whether Epistemology's response to these encroachments will be creative engagement and competition, or retrenchment and successively narrower mission statements. Of course, I urge the former course and I have been trying to do my part.

References

Alchourròn, C., Gärdenfors, P., and Makinson, D. (1985) "On the logic of theory change: Partial meet contraction and revision functions", *Journal of Symbolic Logic* 50: 510–530.

Darwiche, A. and Pearl, J. (1997) "On the logic of iterated belief revision", *Artificial Intelligence* 89: 1–29.

Glymour, C. (1980). *Theory and Evidence*, Princeton University Press, 1980.

Glymour, C., Scheines, R., Spirtes, P. and Kelly, K.(1987) *Discovering Causal Structure: Artificial Intelligence, Philosophy of Science, and Statistical Modelling*, Orlando: Academic Press.

Hinman, P. (1987) *Recursion Theoretic Hierarchies*, New York: Springer.

Kelly, K. (1987) "The Logic of Discovery", *Philosophy of Science* 54: 435–452.

Kelly, K. (1989) "Induction from the General to the More General", *Proceedings of the Second Annual Workshop on Computational Learning Theory*, San Mateo, CA: Morgan Kaufmann, pp. 334–348.

Kelly, K. (1991) "Reichenbach, Induction, and Discovery", *Erkenntnis*, 35: 123–149.

Kelly, K. (1993) "Learning Theory and Descriptive Set Theory", *Logic and Computation*, 3:1, pp. 27–45.

Kelly, K. (1994) "Reliable Methods", in *Logic, Methodology and Philosophy of Science IX*, D. Prawitz, B. Skyrms, and D. Westerstahl, eds., Amsterdam: Elsevier, pp. 353–381.

Kelly, K. (1996) *The Logic of Reliable Inquiry*, New York: Oxford.

Kelly, K. (1998) "Iterated Belief Revision, Reliability, and Inductive Amnesia," *Erkenntnis*, 50: 1998 pp. 11–58.

Kelly, K. (2000a) "The Logic of Success", *British Journal for the Philosophy of Science*, 51: 639–666.

Kelly, K. (2000b) "Naturalism Logicized", in *After Popper, Kuhn and Feyerabend: Current Issues in Scientific Method'*, R. Nola and H. Sankey, eds, 34 Dordrecht: Kluwer, pp. 177–210.

Kelly, K. (2002) "Efficient Convergence Implies Ockham's Razor," *Proceedings of the 2002 International Workshop on Computational Models of Scientific Reasoning and Applications*, Las Vegas, USA, June 24–27.

Kelly, K. (2004a) "Justification as Truth-finding Efficiency: How Ockham's Razor Works," *Minds and Machines* 14: 485–505.

Kelly, K. (2004b) "Uncomputability: The Problem of Induction Internalized," *Theoretical Computer Science* 317: 227–249.

Kelly, K. (2007a) "A New Solution to the Puzzle of Simplicity", *Philosophy of Science* 74: 561–573.

Kelly, K. (2007b) "How Simplicity Helps You Find the Truth Without Pointing at it", in V. Harazinov, M. Friend, and N. Goethe, eds. *Philosophy of Mathematics and Induction*, Dordrecht: Springer.

Kelly, K. (2007c) "How to Do Things with an Infinite Regress", V. Harazinov, M. Friend, and N. Goethe, eds. *Philosophy of Mathematics and Induction*, Dordrecht: Springer.

Kelly, K. (2007d) "Ockham's Razor, Empirical Complexity, and Truth-finding Efficiency," *Theoretical Computer Science* 317: 227–249.

Kelly, K. (2007e) "Simplicity, Truth, and the Unending Game of Science", *Infinite Games: Foundations of the Formal Sciences V*, S. Bold, B. Löwe, T. Räsch, J. van Benthem eds, London: College Press, pp. 223–270.

Kelly, K. and Glymour, C. (1989) "Convergence to the Truth and Nothing but the Truth", *Philosophy of Science* 56: 185–220.

Kelly, K. and Glymour, C. (1990a) "Getting to the Truth Through Conceptual Revolutions", *Proceedings of the 1990 Biennial Meeting of the Philosophy of Science Association*, vol. one, Arthur Fine, Micky Forbes Linda Wessels, eds., East Lansing, Mich.: Philosophy of Science Association, 1990, pp. 89–96.

Kelly, K. and Glymour, C. (1990b) "Theory Discovery from Data with Mixed Quantifiers", *Journal of Philosophical Logic*, 19: 1–33.

Kelly, K. and Glymour, C. (2004) "Why Probability Does Not Capture the Logic of Scientific Justification", C. Hitchcock, ed., *Contemporary Debates in the Philosophy of Science*, Oxford: Blackwell, 2004 pp. 94–114.

Kelly, K. and Schulte, O. (1997) "Church's Thesis and Hume's Problem," in *Logic and Scientific Methods*, M. L. Dalla Chiara, et al., eds. Dordrecht: Kluwer. pp. 383–398.

Kelly, K. and Schulte, O. (1995) "The Computable Testability of Theories with Uncomputable Predictions", *Erkenntnis* 43: 29–66.

Kelly, K., Schulte, O. and Hendricks, V. (1997) "Reliable Belief Revision", in *Logic and Scientfic Methods*, M. L. Dalla Chiara, et al., eds. Dordrecht: Kluwer, 1997.

Kelly, K. Schulte, O., and Juhl, C. (1997) "Learning Theory and the Philosophy of Science", *Philosophy of Science* 64: 245–267.

Kelly, K. and Mayo-Wilson, C. (2008) "Ockham Efficiency Theorem for Empirical Methods Conceived as Empirically-Driven, Countable-State Stochastic Processes", manuscript.

Klein, P. and Warfield, T. A. (1994), "What Price Coherence?", Analysis, 54: 129–32.

Laudan, Larry (1984) *Science and Values*, Berkeley: University of California Press.

Leeds, S. (1996) "Review: Kevin T. Kelly, Oliver Schulte, The Computable Testability of Theories Making Uncomputable Predictions", *Journal of Symbolic Logic* 61: 1049-***.

Osherson, D., Stob, M., and Weinstein, S. (1999) *Systems that Learn*, 2nd. ed., Cambridge: M.I.T. Press.

Putnam, H. (1965) "Trial and Error Predicates and a Solution to a Problem of Mostowski", *Journal of Symbolic Logic*, 30: 49–57.

Putnam, H. (1963) "Degree of Confirmation and Inductive Logic", in *The Philosophy of Rudolf Carnap*, A. Schilpp, ed., LaSalle: Open Court.

Quine, W. (1969) "Epistemology Naturalized", in *Ontological Relativity and Other Essays*, New York: Columbia University Press.

Quine, W. (1992) *Pursuit of Truth*, Cambridge: Harvard University Press.

Reichenbach, H. (1949) *The Theory of Probability*, London: Cambridge University Press.

Salmon, W. (1967) *The Logic of Scientific Inference*, Pittsburgh: University of Pittsburgh Press.

Schulte, O. (1999a) "The Logic of Reliable and Efficient Inquiry," *The Journal of Philosophical Logic*, 28: 399–438.

Schulte, O. (1999b), "Means-Ends Epistemology," *The British Journal for the Philosophy of Science*, 50: 1–31.

Schulte, O. (2001) "Inferring Conservation Laws in Particle Physics: A Case Study in the Problem of Induction," *The British Journal for the Philosophy of Science*, 51: 771–806.

Schulte, O., Luo, W., and Greiner, R. (2007) "Mind Change Optimal Learning of Bayes Net Structure" in *20th Annual Conference on Learning Theory (COLT)*, San Diego.

Spohn, W (1988) "Ordinal conditional functions: a dynamic theory of epistemic states", in: W.L. Harper, B. Skyrms, eds., *Causation in Decision, Belief Change, and Statistics II*. Kluwer:Dordrecht pp. 105–134.

Spirtes, P., Glymour, C.N., and R. Scheines (2000) *Causation, Prediction, and Search*. Cambridge: M.I.T. Press.

Valdés-Pérez, R. (1996) "A New Theorem in Particle Physics Enabled by Machine Discovery", *Artificial Intelligence* 82: 331-339.

van Fraassen, B. (1981) *The Scientific Image*, Oxford: Clarendon Press.

19
Hilary Kornblith

Professor

University of Massachusetts, Amherst, USA

Why were you initially drawn to epistemology (and what keeps you interested)?

During my first semester in college, I took a philosophy of science course which consisted almost entirely of a reading of Locke's *Essay concerning Human Understanding*. I was immediately engaged by Locke's concerns. The idea that inquiry itself might be an object of intellectual investigation, and that an understanding of the very nature and limits of human knowledge might not only be possible, but might aid in the conduct of inquiry, was a revelation to me. Locke's engagement with the best available science of his time, and his attempt both to make sense of that science, and to use it to make sense of inquiry, captured my attention. I had no doubt that this was a worthwhile project, and I was fascinated by the ins and outs of Locke's work on it. I also wondered what such a project would look like if it were informed by the science of our time rather than that of Locke's. I knew very little about contemporary psychology, but I had the impression that the project might look quite different if, among other things, one were able to bring to bear a more up-to-date picture of the mind.

I read Descartes as well, and, as with Locke, I found that many of the concerns which motivated Descartes were ones which genuinely animated me. The concern to improve inquiry, and the focus, in the first *Meditation*, on the many and varied sources of error, were all of great interest to me. Unlike many others, I did not find the skeptical problem presented in the *Meditations* terribly absorbing. It certainly presented an intellectual puzzle, one I had no idea how to resolve, but unlike the problems about improving inquiry, it was a puzzle which failed to move me. When I took a course on contemporary epistemology and read a good deal of work which seemed motivated by a desire to solve the skeptical puzzle, I found much of it unsatisfying. To this day, I'm largely unmoved by worries about global skepticism; it is the more local worries about bias and error which I find engaging.

There are philosophers who see the wide range of different views on offer in philosophy, both in the past and at the present time, as a feature of the human condition. Philosophy, on this view, cannot make the kind of progress that science does on the questions it addresses; rather, it is an inevitable feature of philosophy, and of human beings, that we should be torn in different directions by the deep and abiding questions we attempt to address. This is not a view I share, and, if it were, then philosophy would not be the sort of discipline in which I could take an interest. Perhaps this makes me some sort of philosophical philistine. My own view of epistemology, and philosophy generally, is that it is a discipline in which we may make real progress. Questions in epistemology which were once addressed in a merely speculative way, and which were later addressed with the aid of fairly primitive scientific theories, both of ourselves and of the world around us, are now addressed with the aid of a far more sophisticated scientific understanding. It is in this way, I believe, that we may make real progress on the issues which concern us, and which, in many cases, concerned philosophers of the past as well. The current scientific understanding of the mind, imperfect as it is, provides us with a rich source of insight into epistemological issues, and it is the understanding which science affords which keeps me interested in epistemology.

What do you see as being your main contributions to epistemology?

I have tried throughout my career to show the ways in which work in the sciences, and especially the cognitive sciences, may shed important light on epistemological issues. In doing this, I have tried to advance a certain positive research program, while, at the same time, maintaining a dialogue with more traditionally minded epistemologists.

I have spent a good deal of time trying to undermine the appeal of internalist approaches to epistemological issues. The Cartesian tradition from which this sort of view stems has a great deal of intuitive appeal. We tend to think of the reflective individual as more intellectually responsible than one who is unreflective, and the idea that justified belief, and knowledge, require a certain sort of reflection on one's beliefs and their logical relations seems utterly commonsensical. Spelling out the details here is, of course, no mean feat, but the centrality of reflection to any account of justification and knowledge seems hard to deny. It is, however, exactly this big picture which I have been at pains to argue against. There is a good deal of experimental work on what it is that happens when individuals reflect on the status of their beliefs, and, by and large, it does not suggest that such reflection tends to play a constructive epistemic role. The ways in which our beliefs are formed are not transparent to reflection, and the picture we have of belief acquisition when we introspect is often extremely inaccurate. When we attempt to examine our beliefs by way of reflection, then, and put reflection in charge of the very important project of epistemic improvement, we set off on the wrong foot.

Indeed, as I see it, reflection on our beliefs is very often epiphenomenal with respect to the fixation of belief. We have the impression, when we reflect, that reflection on our beliefs plays a crucial role in determining what it is that we will believe. But much of the psychological literature suggests that this simply isn't true. I have devoted a good deal of effort to combating the picture of reflection which presents it as utterly central to responsible and effective cognition.

I have also devoted a good deal of effort to arguing against conceptual analysis as a profitable approach to epistemological issues, or, indeed, to any issues in philosophy. When we engage in conceptual analysis, we make explicit many of the commonsensical presuppositions which we bring to bear when we think about philosophical issues. While the traditional view holds that we thereby illuminate the subject matter of our thoughts – for example, thereby coming to understand what knowledge is, or what justification is, and so on – I have argued that conceptual analysis provides no such illumination. There is a robust phenomenon of, for example, human knowledge, and if that is what we are interested in, then we must study knowledge itself rather than our concept of it. We can no more achieve an understanding of knowledge by studying our pretheoretical concept of it than we can achieve an understanding of what aluminum is by studying our pretheoretical concept of it.

I have tried to show, in some detail, what epistemology might look like when it is entirely divorced from conceptual analysis and when the study of knowledge, for example, is made thoroughly empirical. In recent work, I have tried to show how work in cognitive ethology not only shows us something very interesting about the cognitive states of other species, but that it serves to show us something very important about knowledge in general.

In all of this work, I have tried to show how traditional philosophical problems may be illuminated by way of empirical work in the sciences.

What do you think is the proper role of epistemology in relation to other areas of philosophy and other academic disciplines?

I was very fortunate to go to graduate school in a small program, one where it simply wasn't possible to talk only with epistemologists. Graduate students were in constant dialogue with one another, and we all were inevitably exposed to many areas of philosophy which we would not otherwise have shown an interest in. This was, I believe, an extremely good thing. It is hard for me to imagine doing good work in epistemology without a real understanding of related issues in philosophy of science, philosophy of mind, philosophy of language, and metaphysics; an understanding of work in ethics doesn't hurt either since there is a rich body of work here on the relationship between normative and descriptive claims. A serious appreciation of the history of philosophy, to my mind, is crucial to understanding the philosophical enterprise.

As is clear from my comments above in answer to previous questions, an appreciation of related work in the sciences is also essential, on my view. The history of science, too, has many lessons to offer. It is in the sciences that we see the greatest intellectual achievement of the human species, and if we are to understand what knowledge is, then we cannot neglect this achievement, nor can we fail to examine the history and development of scientific understanding. An epistemology which is solely informed by an examination of everyday knowledge—cases of looking at medium-sized objects in good light at a close distance–together with our commonsense views of these matters misses out on much of the phenomenon of human knowledge, and many of the most important sources of correction to commonsense misconceptions about it.

What do you consider to be the most neglected topics and/or contributions in contemporary epistemology?

The great majority of work in contemporary epistemology which is devoted to questions about knowledge has focused on propositional knowledge; my own work is certainly no exception here. Other sorts of knowledge, and especially knowledge how, are likely to be worthy of extended treatment, treatment of a sort they have yet to receive. Quite recently, this has begun to be remedied as a result of a provocative piece by Stanley and Williamson arguing that knowledge how is just a species of knowledge that. I am quite skeptical of the Stanley and Williamson line, but I believe that one effect of their work is that knowledge how, and other sorts of knowledge as well, may begin to receive much needed additional attention.

This is only one example of the way in which the fairly narrow range of epistemic notions which receive a good deal of attention may well leave out important categories. Periodically someone will suggest, for example, that understanding is an important epistemic category which should receive a good deal more attention than it has. Nevertheless, even most of those who have made this suggestion have done relatively little to remedy the problem. It would certainly be interesting to see more work expanding the range of epistemic categories which receive serious attention from epistemologists.

I don't know whether any of this will, in the end, bear real fruit, but I do think that it would be a good thing for the field if the range of issues and categories which it explores were expanded.

What do you think the future of epistemology will (or should) hold?

It would, I believe, be foolhardy to try to predict very much about the future of the field. Epistemology, like other fields of intellectual endeavor, will certainly find new and promising directions to move in, ones which cannot now be foreseen; it will also, as it has in the past, have fads and fashions which prove, in retrospect, to involve intellectual dead ends. The course of true progress never did run smooth. The impetus for new work can come from suggestive work in the empirical sciences, work which sheds new light on problems that are already familiar, and it can also come from creative conceptual work with little direct connection to the sciences.

There are areas which I would very much like to see further explored. I believe that the role of reflection in human cognition is not currently well understood. Philosophers, I believe, have a tendency to overvalue reflection and overestimate its positive effects. At the same time, there can be no doubt that reflection does, at times, play a positive role in cognition, and that the ability to reflect is, if not uniquely human, then developed to an extent in humans which far outstrips what one sees in other animals. Understanding the role that reflection plays in cognition, and seeing it in a clear light, would be a major advance in epistemology.

Closely related to this is work on self-knowledge generally, and the relationship between self-knowledge and knowledge of the mental states of others. A good deal of work has been done in this area recently, and one may hope that there will continue to be interesting developments here.

Finally, there has also been a good deal of work recently on the methodology of epistemology, and of philosophy more generally. Continued work in this area would, to my mind, be a good thing. We have come, in recent years, to think more self-consciously about the methodology of the field in which we are all engaged, and this is likely, I believe, to pay substantial dividends.

20
Martin Kusch

Professor

University of Cambridge, UK

Why were you initially drawn to epistemology (and what keeps you interested)?

On my – perhaps unusually broad – understanding, epistemology is the systematic study of our cognitive achievements[1] and failures[2]. It includes a number of related projects; the most important ones are the following:

(a) rendering explicit our folk theory of cognitive achievements and failures; amongst other things, this folk theory specifies the conditions under which these achievements and failures are correctly attributed to others and ourselves;

(b) constructing a systematic-theoretical account of cognitive achievements and failures, often for the purpose of improving our cognition;

(c) investigating the developmental-psychological, historical and cultural variation in cognitive achievements and failures as well as the variation in how they are understood; and

(d) analyzing how our cognitive achievements and failures, as well as their interpretation and attribution, are influenced by, inseparable from, or identical with, various psychological, social and political phenomena.

---

[1] E.g. justified belief, knowledge, wisdom, or understanding.
[2] E.g. irrational belief, lack of knowledge, lack of wisdom, or misunderstanding.

The inclusion of projects (c) and (d) under the heading "epistemology" will likely be frowned upon by many philosophers. I expect even less sympathy for my further contention that epistemology is not an exclusively philosophical pursuit: cognitive science, developmental psychology, logic, linguistics, sociology of knowledge, history of science, political theory, studies of gender and race – to name just the most obvious candidates – are also contributing much to our understanding of cognitive achievement and its attribution. *Philosophical* epistemology is continuous with these other forms of epistemology. Finally, I also believe that epistemology is not just a subfield of *analytic* philosophy: thinkers conventionally classified as "Continental" have also made important inroads into epistemology (as I see it).

It is only against this broad conception of epistemology that I am able to explain how I first got drawn to epistemology and why my preoccupation with it has not lessened. My interest in epistemology was first triggered by work in the so-called "Continental Tradition" and by *historical* and *social-political* questions about *scientific* knowledge.

Being a native speaker of German, "naturally" I started off my philosophical career working on "incomprehensible thinkers beginning with the letter 'H'" (as the medievalist and philosopher, Calvin Normore, once put it so well): Hegel, Husserl, Heidegger and Habermas.[3] Hegel's critique of the Kantian project of epistemology as first philosophy, Husserl's heroic struggles with naturalism and relativism, Heidegger's criticism of Husserl's foundationalism, and Habermas' attempt to analyze (scientific) knowledge in terms of social interests – these were the topics that got me hooked on epistemology, and that have in good part shaped my research agenda to this day.

Even though my fascination with epistemological questions was first kindled by the great German thinkers, I soon became curious also about other traditions. This lead me to study the work of Michel Foucault, the French tradition of "epistémologie" (Gaston Bachelard, Georges Canguilhem), and the "Sociology of Scientific Knowledge" (especially David Bloor, Barry Barnes, Harry Collins, Simon Schaffer and Steve Shapin).[4] I struggle to disentangle the

---

[3] Kusch (1986, 1989).

[4] Kusch (1991). The sociological texts that have influenced me most are Barnes (1982, 2000), Bloor (1983, 1991, 1997), Collins (1991), Shapin and Schaffer (1985), Shapin (1991). Bloor and I were colleagues at the Science Studies Unit in Edinburgh from 1993 until 1996; Collins and I have co-

main epistemological lessons of these encounters. Here are the more prominent ones. First and foremost, the French philosopher-historians and the British sociologists taught me the value of the history of science as the "epistemologist's laboratory"; scientific reasoning is usually much better documented than other forms of cognition, and thus constitutes data that the epistemologist can ill afford to ignore. Second, the two traditions made me appreciate the "case-study method" as a way of addressing abstract (philosophical) questions: the detailed investigation of a historical episode can do important theoretical work as either a possibility proof or as a refutation of a general claim. Third, from the sociologists I learnt the value of using empirical methods, from interviewing scientists to observing their practices.[5] The epistemologist need not confine herself to historical sources or her own intuitions: she can also generate new data through experimental intervention. Fourth, Foucault, Bloor and Barnes impressed upon me the importance of a set of *social-theoretical* questions about knowledge (and other cognitive achievements): what is the role, in our social-communal life, of language games in which we classify cognitive achievements and failings? Why do we distinguish and rank cognitive achievements in one way rather than another – what is the social function of such distinctions and rankings? And why is it that our pre-theoretical intuitions about cognitive achievements are what they are?

The British tradition in the sociology of knowledge has a complicated and troubled relationship with analytic philosophy: on the one hand, it draws very heavily on the work of Wittgenstein (and some of his communitarian followers), on the other hand it tends to be dismissive of mainstream philosophy of natural and social science as well as of philosophical epistemology.[6] These two attitudes towards philosophy resonated rather differently with me. The first fitted perfectly with the philosophical training I had received in Finland: due to the influence of Georg Henrik von Wright and Jaakko Hintikka, Wittgenstein's work had a very central position in Finnish philosophy in the 1980s (when I studied there and did a PhD under Hintikka's supervision[7]). But the second attitude, the

---

authored a book (Collins and Kusch 1998); Schaffer and I have been colleagues since 1997. Our discussions have, and continue to be, central to much of what I do in epistemology.

[5] See Collins and Kusch (1998).
[6] Bloor (1983, 1997).
[7] Kusch (1989).

sociologists' hostility towards most other, non-Wittgensteinian, analytic philosophy, has never seemed reasonable to me. I have never been able to understand why so many of my friends in the sociology of knowledge are inclined to think that their work has made the efforts of most analytic philosophers somehow obsolete. The thought seems wrong on at least two counts: on the one hand, much work in analytic philosophy in general, or epistemology in particular, simply leaves untouched the sorts of claims advanced and defended by sociologists of knowledge. To pick a recent example almost at random, I am unable to find a single claim advanced in Timothy Williamson's *Knowledge and Its Limits*[8] that contradicts, say, ideas advanced by Barnes, Bloor or Collins. On the other hand, there is much work in Anglophone mainstream philosophical epistemology that provides either important challenges to, or interesting – though usually equivocal – support for the sorts of claims that sociologists of knowledge seek to advance. Work in the burgeoning fields of "social epistemology" (e.g. Tony Coady, Alvin Goldman) or "epistemic relativism" (e.g. Steven Stich) are obvious cases in point.[9]

Accordingly, in more recent years, I have increasingly become preoccupied with projects that bring together sociology of knowledge and analytic philosophy. My aim has been to defend – using the tools and techniques of "pure" philosophy – some of the "communitarian" ideas dear to sociologists of knowledge. Of course some of this work has brought me right back to Wittgenstein, or rather Saul Kripke's controversial communitarian interpretation[10]. But I have also learnt enormously from many analytic epistemologists: perhaps especially from Tony Coady, Edward Craig, Donald Davidson, Hillary Kornblith, Peter Lipton, Ernest Sosa, Bernard Williams, Michael Williams, and Timothy Williamson.[11]

What do you see as being your main contributions to epistemology?

My two main contributions to epistemology (broadly construed) come under the headings "sociology of philosophical knowledge"

---

[8] Williamson (2000).

[9] E.g. Coady (1992), Goldman (1999), Stich (1991).

[10] Kripke (1982).

[11] Coady (1991), Craig (1990), Davidson (1991), Kornblith (2002), Lipton (1991), Sosa (1991), B. Williams (2002), M. Williams (1991), Williamson (2000).

and "communitarian epistemology".

My contributions to the sociology of philosophical knowledge were triggered by the thought that the *history of philosophy* deserves to be written with the same kind of social-historical sensitivity which is now common in the *history of science*. Philosophers working on the history of their field usually refuse to pay much attention to the psychological, social or political factors that influenced or shaped the thinking and debates of the great philosophers of the past. All too often historians of philosophy insist that any approach heeding such factors must be committed to "reductionism" or "sociologism". They maintain that to take the history of philosophy seriously is to pay attention to the arguments – and to nothing else. Maybe it is due to my early fascination with the German philosophical tradition from Hegel to Habermas that I find this restriction to arguments and arguments alone both unhistorical and *unphilosophical*. If philosophy had an "essence", would not that essence have something to do with "reflection" and "self-awareness"? And must not this self-awareness include a serious appreciation of the historical contingency of the questions one asks and the vocabularies one employs? If philosophy is after conditions of possibility, surely the historical, social and political conditions of the possibility of philosophy itself must inevitably be a central philosophical concern.

Experience has taught me that few analytic philosophers agree with me on the above – even the German ones are skeptical! Nevertheless, I consider it one of my main achievements in epistemology to have defended and developed sociologies of philosophical knowledge in two monographs: *Psychologism* (1995) and *Psychological Knowledge* (1999). The first-mentioned book is a history of the dispute over the relationship between (experimental) psychology, epistemology and logic in German-speaking philosophy between, roughly, 1900 and 1930. I try to document the wide variety of positions on this relationship, not least in order to bring out that Frege and Husserl were not lone heroic proponents of anti-psychologism. And I seek to explain the eventual (though temporary) defeat of psychologism and naturalism in social-political terms. This is meant to convince the reader that there was nothing inevitable about the (temporary) triumph of anti-psychologism, nothing inevitable about the institutional separation of psychology from the rest of philosophy, and nothing inevitable about the self-image of philosophy as based on non-empirical methods of inquiry. *Psychological Knowledge* tries to do something similar for early-twentieth philosophical dispute in Germany over the nature of thought and the possibility of introspection. I argue that the distribution of positions was socially patterned: philosophers' stance on the nature of thought varied, amongst other things, according to their party-political and confessional commitments.

I introduced the title "communitarian epistemology" for a specific brand of social epistemology. When I first used the label, I thought of "communitarian epistemology" as the philosophical counterpart of the sociology of scientific knowledge, especially the relativistic "Strong Programme" advocated by Barnes and Bloor. Accordingly, my book *Knowledge by Agreement: The Programme of Communitarian Epistemology* (2002) tried to outline and defend – in what I hope are recognizably philosophical ways – four epistemological theses of "Strong Programme" vintage: that our epistemic dependence upon testimony runs too deep for us to be able to produce a non-circular general justification for our trust in others' words; that testimony is a generative source of knowledge insofar as it is always in part performative; that "knower" is a social status; and that a communitarian reading of Wittgenstein supports a strong form of epistemic relativism. I consider *Knowledge by Agreement* one of my two main contributions to epistemology even though I now find the book a little too quick and programmatic for my taste. I took too much for granted, and I related to some of the sociologists' views too uncritically. I have addressed some of these shortcomings in my work of the last six years. For instance, my book *A Skeptical Guide to Meaning and Rules: Defending Kripke's Wittgenstein* (2006) defends the communitarian reading of Wittgenstein and its consequences at much greater length than anything offered in *Knowledge by Agreement*. And my paper "Testimony and the Value of Knowledge" (2009) outlines a communitarian theory of epistemic value: at least *scientific* knowledge is valuable as a collective good.

What do you think is the proper role of epistemology in relation to other areas of philosophy and other academic disciplines?

In answer to the first question I outlined an understanding of epistemology according to which it is a broad *interdisciplinary* field of study rather than a narrow specialization *within* philosophy. Thus for me the proper role of philosophical epistemology in relation to other areas of philosophy, and to other academic disciplines, is – in good part – that of an interlocutor and collaborator.

Of course, this is not a radical proposal. Philosophical epistemologists recognize that linguistic data is often important for identifying our epistemic practices and intuitions. And few of them would disagree with the suggestion that often the proper collection and interpretation of such linguistic data calls for a linguist's training or expertise. Or consider the various links between philosophy and psychology. The work of developmental and cognitive psychologists has been an important inspiration and challenge for epistemologists since the early twentieth century. Psychologists' research into cognitive illusions has impacted not only on work in Bayesian epistemology but has reverberated through many other areas of epistemology as well. Some epistemologists have been influenced by psychologists even to the extent that they have begun conducting their own "epistemological experiments", for instance, on the cultural and socioeconomic variability of epistemic intuitions.[12] More generally, it is now widely accepted that philosophical work on the sources of knowledge – perception, reasoning, memory, testimony – has to take note of what psychologists of different specializations tell us about these processes. It should not come as surprise that I would widen the range of relevant work to include (at least) the sociology of knowledge. This is unlikely to trigger much opposition as long as we stick to various "pathologies of testimony" (lying, prejudice, gossip, etc.)[13], but it will be more controversial with respect to, say, perception and reasoning.

One particularly fruitful area of collaboration between epistemologists and social scientists seems to me to be the project of a "genealogy of epistemic concepts and practices" (as suggested and initially developed by Edward Craig and Bernard Williams[14]). Early chapters of genealogical narratives must inevitably be "imaginary" "just-so" stories: we have no written sources of any historical period prior to the "invention" of the concepts of "belief" or "knowledge" (or primitive forms thereof). But other, later, chapters can be "real genealogies", that is, genealogies based on the historical record. Historical record or not, both *imaginary and real* genealogies have much to learn from anthropology, developmental psychology, and the history and sociology of science. As Williams himself put it so well: "At a certain point philosophy needs to

---

[12] Weinberg, Nichols and Stich (2001).
[13] Coady (2006).
[14] Craig (1990), B. Williams (2002).

make way to history, or, as I prefer to say, to involve itself in it."[15] Hear, hear! Intriguingly enough, some leading historians of science have formed a new subfield that seems ideally suited to function as a historical counterpart to Craig's and Williams' philosophical "genealogy": the "historical epistemology" of Lorraine Daston, Peter Galison and Hans-Jörg Rheinberger.[16] Historians of science following this programme seek to show that key epistemological concepts – like evidence, objectivity or proof – have a contingent history; that nothing about these concepts is or was inevitable or permanent.

Of course further examples of areas of fruitful exchanges between philosophical epistemologists and natural and social scientists could easily be added to the short list provided over the past couple of paragraphs. But here it seems more important to briefly address the relationship between epistemology and other subfields of philosophy. Arguably, some of the most fruitful new avenues in epistemology have opened up whenever epistemologists had the courage to look beyond their own specialty and to recast their subject matter and their theoretical aims in the light of developments elsewhere in philosophy. My two favorite examples of this phenomenon are Hintikka's epistemic logic and Williamson's recent attempt to turn epistemology into a chapter in the philosophy of mind and in the metaphysics of mental states.[17]

Not *all* is well, however, in the relations between epistemology and other subfields of philosophy. Closest to home, it has always struck me as odd that so much of twentieth-century epistemology and philosophy of science have – especially in the Anglophone world – lead separate lives. My (untested) hypothesis is that, at least in the U.S., more epistemologists cite philosophy of religion as a second specialty than philosophy of science. I have no idea why this is so – I hope that a future sociology of philosophy in America will tell us. Be this as it may, I believe that epistemology and philosophy of science would benefit from a much closer interaction. (Certainly some of the finest work in philosophy of science in recent years has been done by people with a strong background in epistemology; the work of my late Cambridge colleague Peter Lipton is a case in point.[18])

---

[15] B. Williams (2002: 93).

[16] E.g. Daston and Galison (2007), Rheinberger (2007).

[17] Hintikka (1962), Williamson (2000).

[18] Lipton (1991). I have learnt much from my many discussions with Lipton over the past ten years.

As far as the future is concerned I place strong hopes on an increased interaction between epistemology, ethics and political philosophy. Feminist epistemology has of course always made much of this link. But the vast majority of epistemologists have paid little attention. There are indications that this is beginning to change. I am thinking here for instance of recent work in the epistemology of testimony where ethical and epistemological issues are closely intertwined. The same is true of the burgeoning field of "value-driven epistemology" where the best work is often deeply indebted to sophisticated approaches in moral value theory.[19] I also agree with Miranda Fricker's claim that any social epistemology worth its salt must be political: epistemic dependence upon others is inseparable from differentials of social power.[20] – Foucault was right.

What do you consider to be the most neglected topics and/or contributions in contemporary epistemology?

In answering this question it is natural for me to focus on topics I have already touched upon above. I shall mention three "neglected topics and/or contributions".

My introduction of the first topic naturally follows on from my answer to the last question, more precisely, from my plea for more interaction between epistemology and political theory. One important lacuna in this area could be entitled "applied epistemology": by this I mean a form a epistemology that seeks to be relevant to political decision-making in modern democratic societies. Applied epistemology might address questions like: How should we rationally decide between conflicting scientific expert advice when we ourselves are not competent in the relevant sciences? Who should sit at the table when it comes to deciding what kind of scientific research should be funded? Who should be involved when it comes to determining which technological risks are worth taking? And who should have a say when it comes to agreeing on rules for ethical conduct in science? What types of institutional arrangements maximize the possibility of a rational input into such decisions from non-experts? How are we to balance epistemic and ethical factors? Aside from Alvin Goldman and some of his students, few

---

[19] Kvanvig (2003).
[20] Fricker (2007).

epistemologists have had much to say on these pressing issues.[21] The mainstream in epistemology is happy to leave such questions to the sociologists and political scientists. This is deeply regrettable. Epistemologists should accept their share of responsibility for our modern political culture.

A second neglected topic is the already mentioned work by Craig and B. Williams on the genealogy of epistemic concepts. I am referring here to Craig's *Knowledge and the State of Nature: An Essay in Conceptual Synthesis* (1990), and Williams' *Truth and Truthfulness: An Essay in Genealogy* (2002). In my view Craig and Williams give us one of the most fruitful frameworks for understanding our epistemic practices – our practices of attributing cognitive achievements and failures to others and ourselves. Rather than engage in a-temporal conceptual analysis of our current key epistemic terms, Craig and Williams invite us to theorize about how and why social creatures like us might have ended up with the epistemic concepts of roughly their current shape. This method enables us to better understand the concepts we now have; it makes us appreciate that epistemic concepts and social relations are just two sides of the same coin; and it highlights some of the relations that exist between epistemic and other concepts, say between the concepts of knowledge and autonomy. A few authors have picked up the torch where Craig and Williams have left it but much interesting work remains to be done. (I have myself used Craig's and Williams' work to argue for a communitarian conception of epistemic value.)[22]

My third neglected topic is – surprise, surprise! – the sociology of knowledge. Perhaps it is to be expected that epistemologists working on Bayesianism or Gettier cases ignore what social scientists have to say about knowledge and other cognitive achievements. But it is strange that social epistemologists do not pay much attention either. The sociology of knowledge appears in their texts only as a whipping boy – be it because of its alleged relativism and "constructivism", or because of its alleged commitment to a non-factive use of "knowledge". This attitude of disinterest and hostility contrasts sharply with many epistemologists' keen eye for new developments in cognitive and social psychology. In

---

[21] Goldman (1999). In unpublished work, K. Kappel, E. Olsson and D. Pritchard call this field "Epistemology of Liberal Democracy". My own contribution to this area is Kusch (2007).

[22] Fricker (2007), Lane (1999), Kusch (2009).

my view, the different treatment of psychology and sociology – respect here, disrespect there – is simply not justified. To ignore the work of the sociology of knowledge is to disregard important theoretical options and challenges. Such options and challenges are, for example, that key epistemological terms functions as indicators, and as constitutive, of social status; that knowledge might be of collective rather than individual value; or that different epistemic cultures operate with very different criteria for knowledge or epistemic justification.

What do you think the future of epistemology will (or should) hold?

In my answers to previous questions I have pointed to some areas where I would like to see more work done. But these suggestions should be understood correctly: rather than have this proposed new work *replace* existing research programmes, I would prefer seeing it *complementing* the latter. In other words, I do not claim that the currently dominant lines of inquiry are doomed or worthless. On the contrary, the progress of (philosophical) epistemology over the past two decades has been stunning, and a number of new ideas and approaches have rightly attracted plenty of attention.

In light of my high appreciation of much recent work in philosophical epistemology it will not come as a surprise that I both predict and hope that many of the currently influential projects will continue to prosper. I am thinking here, for example, of the research programmes on contextualism, externalism, epistemic luck, epistemic value, the "knowledge first" approach, epistemic logic, Bayesian epistemology, a priori knowledge, social epistemology, justification ... and much else besides. Of course the future of epistemology will also hold many ideas and approaches that are impossible to foresee at this point.

As far as my own "future *in* epistemology" is concerned, I hope to continue my uneasy balancing act between philosophy and the sociology of knowledge, both in the form of a *sociology of philosophy*, and in the form of a *communitarian epistemology*. The project that will occupy me over the next few years will be a historical and philosophical study of epistemic relativism: I want to understand historically-sociologically how epistemic relativism became – during the nineteenth century – a central topic of philosophical reflection; and I want to reply to the best of anti-relativistic books published by distinguished philosophers/epistemologists over the past two decades (I am thinking here especially of the books by Simon Blackburn, Paul Boghossian, Susan Haack, and Thomas Nagel[23]). My wish for the future is that one day epistemic relativism will be discussed in the same dispassionate and sophisticated ways that already characterize our best literature on epistemic skepticism.

References

Barnes, B. (1982), *T. S. Kuhn and Social Science*, London: MacMillan.

Barnes, B. (2000), *Understanding Agency: Social Theory and Responsible Action*, London: Sage.

Blackburn, S. (2005), *Truth: A Guide for the Perplexed*, London: Penguin.

Bloor, D. (1983), *Wittgenstein: A Social Theory of Knowledge*, London: Macmillan.

Bloor, D. (1991), *Knowledge and Social Imagery*, Chicago: Chicago University Press.

Bloor, D. (1997), *Wittgenstein, Rules and Institutions*, London: Routledge.

Boghossian, P. (2006), *Fear of Knowledge: Against Relativism and Constructivism*, Oxford: Oxford University Press.

Coady, C. A. J. (1992), *Testimony: A Philosophical Study*, Oxford: Oxford University Press.

Coady, C. A. J. (2006), "Pathologies of Testimony", in J. Lackey and E. Sosa (eds.), *The Epistemology of Testimony*, Oxford: Oxford University Press, 253–271.

Collins, H. M. (1992), *Changing Order: Replication and Induction in Scientific Practice*, 2nd ed., Chicago: University of Chicago Press.

Collins, H. M. and M. Kusch (1998), *The Shape of Actions: What Humans and Machines Can Do*, Cambridge, Mass.: MIT Press.

Craig, E. (1990), *Knowledge and the State of Nature: An Essay in Conceptual Synthesis*, Oxford: Clarendon.

---

[23] Blackburn (2005), Boghossian (2006), Haack (1998), Nagel (1997).

Daston, L. and P. Galison (2007), *Objectivity*, New York: Zone Books.

Davidson, D. (1991), "Three Varieties of Knowledge", in A. Phillips Griffiths (ed.), *A. J. Ayer: Memorial Essays*, Royal Institute of Philosophy suppl. 30, Cambridge: Cambridge University Press, 153–55.

Fricker, M. (2007), *Epistemic Injustice: Power & the Ethics of Knowing*, Oxford: Oxford University Press.

Goldman, A. (1999), *Knowledge in a Social World*, Princeton and Oxford: Oxford University Press.

Haack, S. (1998), *Confessions of a Passionate Moderate*, Chicago: Chicago University Press.

Hintikka, J. (1962), *Knowledge and Belief: An Introduction to the Logic of the Two Notions*, Ithaca, N.Y.: Cornell University Press.

Kornblith, H. (2002), *Knowledge and Its Place in Nature*, Oxford: Oxford University Press.

Kripke, S. A. (1982), *Wittgenstein on Rules and Private Language*, Oxford: Blackwell.

Kusch, M. (1986), *Ymmartämisen haaste* (= *The Challenge of Understanding*, in Finnish), Oulu: Prometheus.

Kusch, M. (1989), *Language as Calculus vs. Language as Universal Medium: A Study in Husserl, Heidegger and Gadamer*, Dordrecht: Kluwer.

Kusch, M. (1991), *Foucault's Strata and Fields: An Investigation into Archeaological and Genealogical Science Studies*, Dordrecht: Kluwer.

Kusch, M. (1995), *Psychologism: A Case Study in the Sociology of Philosophical Knowledge*, London: Routledge.

Kusch, M. (1999), *Psychological Knowledge: A Social History and Philosophy*, London: Routledge.

Kusch, M. (2002), *Knowledge by Agreement: The Programme of Communitarian Epistemology*, Oxford: Oxford University Press.

Kusch, M. (2006), *A Sceptical Guide to Meaning and Rules: Defending Kripke's Wittgenstein*, Chesham: Acumen.

Kusch, M. (2007), "Towards a Political Philosophy of Risk: Experts and Publics in Deliberative Democracy", in T. Lewens (ed.), *Risk: Philosophical Perspectives*, London: Routledge, 131–155.

Kusch, M. (2009), "Testimony and the Value of Knowledge", forthcoming in a volume edited by D. Pritchard for Oxford University Press.

Kvanvig, J. (2003), *The Value of Knowledge and the Pursuit of Understanding*, Cambridge: Cambridge University Press.

Lane, M. (1999), "States of Nature, Epistemic and Political", *Proceedings of the Aristotelian Society* 99: 211–24.

Lipton, P. (1991), *Inference to the Best Explanation*, London: Routledge.

Nagel, T. (1997), *The Last Word*, Oxford: Oxford University Press.

Rheinberger, H.-J. (2007), *Historische Epistemologie*, Hamburg: Junius.

Shapin, S. (1994), *A Social History of Truth*, Chicago: University of Chicago Press.

Shapin S. and S. Schaffer (1985), *Leviathan and the Air-Pump*, Princeton, N.J.: Princeton University Press.

Sosa, E. (1991), *Knowledge in Perspective*, Cambridge: Cambridge University Press.

Stich, S. (1991), *The Fragmentation of Reason: Preface to a Pragmatic Theory of Cognitive Evaluation*, London: MIT Press.

Weinberg, J. M., S. Nichols, S. Stich (2001), "Normativity and Epistemic Intuitions", *Philosophical Topics*, Volume 29, 2001: pp. 429–460.

Williams, B. (2002), *Truth and Truthfulness: An Essay in Genealogy*, Princeton and Oxford: Oxford University Press.

Williams, M. (1991), *Unnatural Doubts*, Oxford: Blackwell.

Williamson, T. (2000), *Knowledge and Its Limits*, Oxford: Oxford University Press.

21
Jonathan L. Kvanvig
Distinguished Professor of Philosophy
Baylor University, USA

Why were you initially drawn to epistemology (and what keeps you interested)?

I came to epistemology through an interest in the concept of rationality, and especially through the attacks on the rationality of religious believers. My thoughts at the time focused on the disappointing quality of the arguments for and against religious belief, and I recall being astonished at the time that philosophers capable of such penetrating insight in other areas had nothing that seemed either penetrating or original. The defenders sounded too much like mere apologists for the faith, and the attackers arid and dull, with both sides often exuding a scent of intellectual dishonesty.

I now see in looking back that the driving consideration here was not the topic of religion itself but rather the way in which this area is especially illustrative when one is interested in the idea of cognitive dissonance or incoherence. This interest is quite common in epistemology, and can be displayed in many ways. An interest in counterexamples, for example, is an interest in incoherence between general and particular judgements. A love of ad hominem arguments is perhaps the lowest level of such an interest, even though such arguments have not been given their epistemic due, having been relegated too quickly to the heap of informal fallacies. A related way of seeing the philosophical landscape is in terms of what Alston has termed "epistemic imperialism," where standards for rationality imposed in one area undermine positions one wishes to hold in other areas. The logical endpoint of this kind of cognitive dissonance is arguments and positions that are self-refuting, and a interest in cognitive dissonance or incoherence displays itself in a predilection to look for difficulties of all these sorts. And an interest in self-refuting arguments and positions ties in quite naturally with a fascination with paradoxes. I never thought of my own motivations in this way at the time, but it is clear to me now that it was this collage of things that made the literature on the rationality of religious belief such a powerful source of interest in epistemology itself.

The ubiquity of cognitive dissonance and incoherence is still something that fascinates me. Not only its ubiquity, but its hiddenness. Among human capacities that are the most intriguing to me are the capacities for motivated ignorance, self-deception, and suppressed incoherence: we are not just unaware of a lot of things both about our environment and about ourselves, we seem to be motivated to be unaware, or to have an interest in being so. We catch a glimpse of this in paradoxes, but in more mundane ways as well. It is at least a partial truth that philosophy in general and epistemology in particular lives at the edge of the paradoxes, and the importance of achieving coherence and the variety of paths toward resolving tension and paradox in a system of thought and understanding still leaves me spellbound. In it is found my attraction to coherentism in epistemology as well as my reservations about it, since one of the lessons of the epistemic paradoxes is the fallibilistic necessity of learning how and why we must live with our own incoherencies.

It is this mystery of motivated lack of self-understanding and self-knowledge that keeps me interested in epistemology. Lots of epistemological theories work best when cognizers are assumed to be otherwise, where the contents of the mind are transparent to reflection, where degree of confidence is unmistakeable, where the precise nature of our experience of the world is foundational and never unrecoverable in spite of the various interpretive strategies, both conscious and unconscious, in which we engage. Such approaches strike me as the vestiges of untenable epistemology, remnants of a failure to see the lessons of fallibilism.

What do you see as being your main contributions to epistemology?

There are two aspects to what I consider my main contribution to epistemology. The fundamental aspect is meta-epistemological, a way of viewing the vast landscape of possible inquiry into the nature of successful cognition. The meta-epistemological perspective that I have advocated and practiced is that the most productive and interesting way to think about the subdiscipline is to approach it from a value-driven perspective. This way of thinking has come to be called "value-driven epistemology." It is my opinion that the contemporary interest in rationality, justification, and warrant arises quite naturally from such a perspective, and less naturally from competing perspectives (such as the perspective that insists that epistemology is the theory of knowledge and which tries to motivate an interest in these concepts in virtue of their connection to knowledge). We are interested in rationality, justification, and warrant because it is a matter of unsurpassed importance what we are to believe (or, for those who prefer degrees of belief or levels of confidence, what level or degree to adopt). Moreover, the answer we get must be, we might say, instructive. An uninstructive answer is one that fails to take into account our fallibility. If we weren't fallible, the appropriate answer would be "believe whatever you can," since following that advice would never lead one astray on the assumption of infallibilism. And if the answer didn't need to be instructive, an appropriate answer could be "believe the truth and eschew error." Value-driven epistemology, sensitive to our own fallibility and the need for instructive answers, will focus on answers that relativize to what seems true by our own lights, and the ordinary notions of rationality, justification, and warrant are well-suited for this task. They are well-suited for this task only when explicated by a substantive theory, but the natural fit between such concepts and the question of paramount intellectual importance, the question of what to believe, makes it easy to see why a value-driven perspective will devote considerable attention to these issues.

But value-driven epistemology doesn't only explain existing practice in epistemology, it also raises the possibility that epistemology suffers from improper focus and misplaced emphasis. I have argued that such is the case with respect to knowledge itself and the related concept of understanding. I have argued that knowledge doesn't have the unique value it would need to have to legitimately dominate the history of epistemology in the way it has, and that understanding deserves much greater attention than it has received.

This last point brings us to the secondary aspect of my contribution to the discipline, which is an an application of this value-driven approach. This application involves first a kind of skepticism about the value of knowledge and the centrality of knowledge to the general task of understanding the idea of successful or admirable cognition. Knowledge is better than true belief (from the perspective that abstracts from interests other than purely cognitive ones), but an interest in knowledge isn't what drives the cognitive machine nor is knowledge itself what sates the intellectual appetite upon achieving it. The lament by T.S. Eliot in the opening stanza of the choruses of "The Rock" is one with which I strongly resonate: "Where is the wisdom we have lost in knowledge? Where is the knowledge we have lost in information?" This sentiment strikes me as useful, though I would have preferred the second question to contain the concept of understanding rather than the concept of knowledge. We are awash in a sea of experience and reflection, trying to make sense of it all. Along the way, when things goes well, we latch onto some truths, and in some of these cases, the form such latching takes is knowledge. But such accomplishments can be isolated and episodic. What drives inquiry is not such accomplishments, but an interest in making sense of things. I prefer talking about this more fundamental inclination in terms of understanding, but it is a special kind of understanding, aimed not at the individual propositional level, but rather at the level of subject matter itself. What we are after is understanding of things themselves, not bits of knowledge.

In this way, my more recent work on the value of knowledge connects with my earlier interest in virtue epistemology, where I suggested that the role of the virtues in cognition will only be properly understood when one abandons what I termed Cartesian epistemology. One kind of break from Cartesian epistemology involves abandoning the atomistic, time-slice perspective of approaches to the nature of knowledge that have dominated post-Gettier epistemology. A turn toward the theory of understanding renounces the atomistic focus on individual propositions and emancipates this discipline fundamental to understanding the nature of the mind-world connection from a myopic focus on the theory of knowledge.

What do you think is the proper role of epistemology in relation to other areas of philosophy and other academic disciplines?

There is both a theoretical aspect and a practical aspect to this question. On the theoretical side, any kind of inquiry, whether in philosophy or outside of it, presupposes answers to fundamental epistemological questions. In this sense, epistemologists engage in inquiry concerning the foundations of nearly every other discipline. Much the same can be said of other areas of philosophy, and

I've always been struck by the way in which fundamental inquiry into any area of philosophy seems to lead inevitably to all the other areas. Epistemology is thus a piece of a larger puzzle, and there is no need for any hyperbolic talk about what is more central or more important or more foundational to our understanding of things. When one does ethics, one presupposes answers to epistemological issues, and when one does epistemology, one presupposes answers to metaphysical issues. The presuppositions come full circle, requiring that full understanding of any part requires full understanding of all parts. It is for this reason that the concept of understanding is much more central to the cognitive life than the history of epistemology would lead one to believe. That history, in my opinion, was hijacked by the skeptic, to the detriment of the discipline. Less defensive epistemology opens up many regions for exploration, and one of the most important and central is that of understanding itself.

On the more practical side, as with every discipline and subdiscipline, there remains the tension between insisting on respect for what we do without having to justify it in terms of other disciplines or subdisciplines and the demand for accountability in terms of some overall conception of the good life. Both at the personal and social levels, there is the question of what value there is in epistemological reflection and in the routing of resources in support of such reflection. It is pretty clear that epistemologists have done little to increase the gross domestic product, for example. But such a crassly pragmatic standard leaves out so much of the vast region of normative space that it hardly bears refutation. Though the questions here are not epistemological in nature, it is true that those best positioned to address them are practitioners of the discipline itself. On this point, a value-driven perspective on the discipline has decided advantages, since the connection between the topics and issues addressed and the pursuit of the good life is always in the forefront.

Unlike many other disciplines, however, philosophy is also intensely personal. It is not just a subject matter to be investigated, but a way of being as well. It is to live reflectively, to engage in self-examination and self-discovery in the process of sorting out how best to think and live. On this general question of normative space, my approach is Millian rather than Wittgensteinian. Wittgenstein in his late guise counseled finding a way to get the fly out of the bottle, to get oneself to a position of being able to let the questions of philosophy go. Mill, on the other hand, told us that the best way to determine which pleasures are qualitatively superior is to ask those who have experienced both. The lesson of the late Wittgenstein is that the empirical test must be done with the right controls in place, but any decent account of these controls will keep Wittgenstein himself from being a suitable test case. Here I side with Mill on the question of philosophical, and especially, epistemological, reflection. A life first capable of being a life of human flourishing, to which is added the ingredient of epistemological reflection and the development of the skills needed to reflect well about what and how to think, is a life that is richer and deeper than its alternative in ways hard to express. This point remains even when the grain of truth in Wittgenstein's counsel is acknowledged, the grain of truth that it is a good thing at times to lose one's reflective stance, wholly immersed in other loves, whether a fascinating personality, a McCarthy novel, or a peaty Scotch.

What do you consider to be the most neglected topics and/or contributions in contemporary epistemology?

Contemporary epistemology during the course of my career has seen a renewed interest in skepticism, abandoning the easy dismissals of it in the heyday of ordinary language philosophy. (It still astonishes me to find work from this era that elevates ordinary language to the status of a defensible Chisholmian principle: *if it is odd to say that p, then it is reasonable to believe that not-p.* As if we need a new operator, the odd-to-say operator, in our epistemic logic.) It has also seen a broadening of the scope of epistemological inquiry as new paradigms have arisen. Here I'm thinking of the empirically-minded work that is being done in a way that is motivated by reliabilist and naturalistic approaches to the discipline, as well as the interesting work being done through the rise of virtue and social epistemology. Since first beginning to work in epistemology, however, I have noticed the absence of connections between traditional epistemology and the work in confirmation theory being done by philosophers of science. It was clear to me early on that both camps were addressing, if not precisely the same questions and issues, at least ones that were substantially overlapping. It was perplexing to me that so little interaction occurred between the two groups. The historical answer is fairly clear: the work in confirmation theory traces primarily to Carnap and an underlying desire to make philosophy matter by making it mathematical, whereas traditional epistemology of the last 50 years has its primary influence in the work of G.E. Moore through Roderick Chisholm, and hence reaching back to C.I. Lewis as well. This lineage does not trace its roots to Logical Positivism in the way early confirmation theory does, and the result was independent historical development in spite of considerable overlap of issues and topics. Whatever the historical explanation, however, the fact remains that the overlap is extensive and the value of interaction high.

For example, my own work falls mainly within traditional epistemology, and yet the value-driven approach I counsel is probably best illustrated by formal approaches in confirmation theory. The ideal of such formal work, especially in Bayesian epistemology, is the handheld calculator: one wishes for a machine in which to input one's new evidence and which will then tell one what effect the new information should have on one's assessments. If anything in epistemology is a value-driven inquiry, trying to master the intricacies of confirmation in light of such an ideal surely counts.

It is here that tracing the significance of inquiry into the nature of justification, rationality, and warrant to a value-driven perspective on epistemology pays off. When these topics are addressed because of some supposed role they play in the theory of knowledge, connections to work in confirmation theory do not press on consciousness as easily as they do when they are addressed from a value-driven perspective. From a value-driven perspective, however, the failure of interaction is both theoretically puzzling and disappointing.

So, at the top of my list of neglected topics and contributions in contemporary epistemology is the overlap between formal and traditional epistemology. No matter which side of this division one falls on, the tendency is to pay too little attention and learn too little from the work being done on the other side. Comprehensive epistemologies will include assessments of where formalisms are appropriate and useful, and where they are out of place, in much the same way that traditional epistemologists have long focused on the place of deductive logic in the story of knowledge, rationality, and other central concepts in epistemology. There are many encouraging signs that the neglect noted is on the decline, not the least of which is the flourishing Formal Epistemology Workshop which is occurring annually, but it is fair to say that we are still at a very early stage in addressing the neglect in question.

As pointed out already, I also think that topics not obviously connected with the theory of knowledge have been neglected.

When one thinks of the discipline in terms of mind-world connections that are successful or count as accomplishments in a way that abstracts away from interests other than those that are purely intellectual or cognitive, there is some reason to think of knowledge as one item to be explored but certainly not the only one. Among the items neglected is understanding itself, but there are others as well. Some of the most important neglected items are intellectual virtues that seem unrelated to knowledge. My favorite examples here are the virtues of openmindedness and intellectual courage. There is both the question of how inquiry and investigation should be conducted, but there is also the question of what kind of inquirers we should aim to be and what it takes to achieve that aim. From a value-driven perspective, the attention paid to the virtues to this point has been a bit too driven by some desired connection to the theory of knowledge, to the neglect of the more general question of appropriate habits of the mind.

What do you think the future of epistemology will (or should) hold?

The danger is that of more and more "ordinary-language-on-logico-semantic-steroids" epistemology (to use Fritz Warfield's characterization of recent work on the contextualism/invariantism disputes at the characterized on Brian Weatherson's blog *Thoughts, Arguments, and Rants*). I expect the contextualism/invariantism dispute to continue well into the next decade, but my hope is that it will morph beyond more and more epicycles generated by eliciting intuitions at the level of semantic ascent. I believe that the dispute in question contains the seeds of a much more interesting issue, and it is the issue of pragmatic encroachment into the fundamental items of epistemological reflection, as determined from a value-driven approach to the discipline. The issue of pragmatic encroachment, a term I coined at the epistemology blog I administer, *Certain Doubts,* is the issue of whether and how and why pragmatic factors such as the practical cost of being mistaken affect whether one knows or understands or believes rationally or with justification. What is clear from the contextualism/invariantism debate is that ordinary language taken at face value favors pragmatic encroachment theories all over the epistemological landscape: the contextualisms of DeRose and Cohen, and the invariantisms of Hawthorne and Stanley are all developed to accommodate such a taking at face value. Though the arguments for and against pragmatic encroachment receive some attention in this literature, the issue so far is quite a distance from taking center stage. I believe, over the next decade or so, the issue of pragmatic encroachment itself will become the focus of discussion. Such a prediction is of course way beyond what anything approaching the knowledge norm of assertion would allow (i.e., don't say what you don't know to be true, and I certainly don't have anything approaching knowledge of what I just predicted), but such a turn in the direction of the literature would be all to the good, generating just the kind of corrective needed for approaches that are, in my opinion, a bit too facile at reading off epistemological conclusions from ordinary language responses.

I would also like to see greater focus on fundamental epistemology. Epistemology, at its core, is about the connection between mind and world, and what constitutes successful, useful, or appropriate connections between (aspects of) each. Understanding of any sort is subject to reflective ascent: we name advanced degrees using the name of our discipline because advanced understanding of anything involves the kind of reflection that is essentially philosophical. Satisfaction of our underlying curiosity requires a reflective ascent that turns reflection on itself: what is this understanding that we seek, and when do we have it? We grapple with the fundamental questions episodically, growing weary of their difficulty at times, and turning to spurs off the main track for diversion. The spurs are part of the totality of which understanding is sought, and are thus important. The danger is substituting the spurs for the main track. As I see it, the future of the discipline will resemble its past in this way. The cycle will continue to be one of frequent detours away from the central and deep questions of fundamental epistemology because of their difficulty and the perplexity that they engender, with the enduring temptation to spend more time on the sidetracks and confuse them with the main track. The little engine of epistemological inquiry will continue it's incessant "putt-putt-putt-ing" along tracks connected to the primary track of the understanding of the world and our place in it, and there is the hope, at least, that the story won't be dominated by the sidetracks. As I have argued above and elsewhere, the way to avoid spending too much time on the sidetracks is to engage in epistemological inquiry from a fundamentally value-driven perspective.

22
Isaac Levi
John Dewey Professor of Philosophy Emeritus
Columbia University, USA

I do not think I was ever drawn to epistemology as question 1 on the list of five questions presupposes. Most of the time I I was repelled by it. Thanks to teachers like Ernest Nagel and friends like Sidney Morgenbesser I did become interested in scientific methodology in the tradition of the great pragmatists. Consequently, I have discussed topics that somehow intersect with topics of concern to professional epistemologists. I shall try to provide a relevant response to the five questions by suggesting a philosophical task that ought to replace the traditional tasks of epistemology.

For many years, I have directed my attention to the question of justifying changes in points of view rather than justifying or explaining points of view. Focusing on how one ought to change one's beliefs rather than justifying these beliefs themselves argues for turning our backs on most of the central preoccupations of contemporary epistemology.

Pedigree epistemology should be abandoned. (Levi, 1980.) The tiresome "foundationalist" and "coherentist" programs for fending off the threats of skepticism or embracing them lead us nowhere. Students of the psychology and sociology of knowledge ought to focus their attention on problems of a clinical nature aimed at improving the performances of human inquirers and the institutions that support inquiry when such inquirers and institutions are called upon to fulfill doxastic, probabilistic and value commitments. Specifying truth conditions for knowledge attributions are at best expressions of the values those who propose such specifications think inquirers ought to be promoting and at worst a degenerate form of intuition mongering.

An account of changes of view and their justification presupposes some conception of points of view. On the view I favor, inquirer X's point of view at t is constituted by at least the following three salient commitments: (1) a state of full belief K, (2) a confirmational commitment and (3) a network of value commitments.

X's state of full belief K at time t is X's evidence and background information. It is embeddable in a network K of potential states of full belief to which the inquirer X can coherently move. I assume that K is a Boolean algebra. This means that X's state K at t has as consequences elements of a "filter" of the algebra. To say that X fully believes (is certain) that h is to assert that h is an element of that filter – i.e., is a consequence of K. K serves as X's standard for serious possibility in the sense that every element of K whose complement (negation) is a consequence of K should be judged impossible according to X and every other element of K should be be judged possible..

K thus sets up a space of possibilities over which credal probabilities conditional on potential states are definable. X is committed to judging some of these conditional probability functions to be permissible for use in assessing conditional expected utilities and others are impermissible. The set of permissible probabilities is X's credal state B relative to K.

Although the space of serious possibilities is uniquely determined by X's state of full belief or evidence K and the framework K of potential states or doxastic propositions in which it is embedded, X's credal state is not uniquely determined by these factors alone. B is determined by K and another component of X's point of view at t: X's *confirmational commitment* which may be represented as a function $C: K \to B$ from potential states of full belief in K to potential credal states in B. Justifying change in point of view is justifying changes in K, C or both.[1]

---

[1] I omit discussion as to whether rationality requires that commitments to full belief should be closed under logical consequence as I think. I also reject the probabilist claim that full belief can be fully characterized in terms of credal probability. I deny the strict Bayesian dogma that confirmational commitments should determine credal states representable by a single permissible (conditional) credal probability. Confirmational commitments should not be required to take as values intervals of probability – i.e., largest sets enveloped by intervals. They should be allowed to take as values any set of permissible conditional credal probabilities satisfying a convexity condition (Levi, 1980). Some authors (most notably Seidenfeld, Schervish and Kadane) take my view to be too restrictive. Another topic worth examining that will not be considered here is the relation between probability judgment and judgments of uncertainty or evidential support couched in non probabilistic terms.

Among the many details I am glossing over here are concerns over the constraints of synchronic rationality or rational coherence that states of full belief and confirmational commitments should satisfy.

Considering these questions presupposes a system K of potential states of full belief that I assume to be representable by a Boolean algebra. When studying some particular budget of inquiries, K should be as rich as is required to characterize the issues that are under investigation. The system required need not, therefore, capture all topics that should be accessible to inquirers under all conceivable circumstances but only those judged relevant to the problem or budget of problems under investigation—judgment that may be modified in inquiry itself. For this reason, I have tended to think of K as generated by a a minimal state of full belief LK and a *basic partition* U_{LK} of potential states where LK entails the truth of exactly one such state and each element of U_{LK} is consistent with LK. (Levi, 1991, 1996, 2004.) The potential states of full belief or "doxastic propositions" are representable by subsets of U_{LK} or the joins of members of such subsets. They are potential states of full belief and not to be confused with the sentences or other linguistic artifacts that may be used to express them. And they are not worlds in any sense congenial to modal realists. There is no fact of the matter as to how fine or coarse grained U_{LK} should be. Both may be modified in the ongoing coarse of inquiry in ways that meet modifications in the inquirer's demands for information or research program.

Questions pertaining to how to understand judgments of certainty and uncertainty should be characterized with reference to their relevance to how deliberations aimed at evaluating options in deliberate choice, to assessing programs for routine decision making and to the justification of change in view..

I take for granted that justifying changes in points of view whether these be changes in states of full belief or in confirmational commitment invoke practical argument. The challenge is to identify those changes that are options for the inquirer at the given time and to determine which of these are admissible for choice given the goals and values of the inquirer.

The justification should be based on the views of the inquirer X prior to making a change and not from the point of view of Y, whether Y be X at some other time, some other individual, some social institution or agent, or some deity or group of deities. And I take it that seeking such justification by appealing to "the facts" rather than some point of view concerning what are the facts is just another manifestation of an inappropriate lust for metaphysical mystery.

Inquirer X could be a person or some persona in a multiple personality or a social institution or agency. The account of justified change I propose is "individualistic" in that it does not invoke any appeal to an irreducibly social type of argumentation.

Many authors give a social dimension more weight than I do. "Putting forward a sentence as true or as information—that is, asserting it—has been glossed as putting it forward as fit to be a reason for other assertions, making it available as a premise from which others can be inferred." (Brandom, 1994, 170.). A social demand is always in force for a warrant or justification for the assertion and belief expressed by an act of asserting. Consequently, *all* beliefs, in the sense of doxastic commitments, require "entitlements". These entitlements may be "defaults" that license assertion until someone calls the default into question. This attitude stands in stark contrast to the view I favor according to which *no* beliefs in the sense of doxastic commitments require warrant or justification whether the warrant is sought by the inquirer or by some social agency. Commitments in Brandom's sense incur obligations to others. (Brandom, 1994, 176–8.) Commitments in my sense do not.

Agents making the assertion need not be concerned to change the views of others. The assertion may be intended solely as expression of X's commitment to full belief – a commitment X undertakes to fulfill by his performances. X does not require a license to take such commitments upon his or herself. By undertaking such commitments, X obligates him or herself to use X's commitments to full belief to draw inferences when occasion requires and the impediments to doing so are readily overcome. X is committed to judging all deductive consequences of h and X's other beliefs true, ruling out the logical possibility that $\sim h$ as a serious possibility, etc. X is not shouldering responsibility for the beliefs that Y should adopt. If X wishes to convince Y, X may need to marshall reasons that will convince Y to change Y's beliefs by becoming certain that h is true. Attempts at such justification are not attempts to justify X's changing X's doxastic commitments.

If Y dissents from X's view, Y's challenge may or may not provide a warrant for X to surrender X's belief. Y's reason is a good reason from Y's perspective but not necessarily from X's perspective. X may have contempt for Y's challenge.

Contemptuous or not, X can feign respect and pretend to come into suspense and still rationally remain convinced of the truth of h. When X is concerned to win Y's agreement, feigning an open mind is highly advisable. But X should not give up belief that h unless X has good reason to do so. Y's dissent might provide such good reason under some circumstances. But by no means always. Epistemologists ought to be concerned with identifying conditions under which a reasonable inquirer should open his or her mind to dissent and when not. (See Levi, 1997, ch.12.)

To be sure, in order to convince Y, X could contract X's state of full belief by giving up h. X would then be in a position to engage in joint inquiry with Y to settle their dispute from point of view that begs no questions for or against the truth of h. It is important that there be no conceptual impediments to doing so. However, X should open up X's mind in this way only if X has good reason for contraction given the two desiderata of acquiring valuable information and avoiding error. Recognition that Y disagrees with X is not sufficient warrant for such contraction. Indeed, even a desire to be in agreement with Y may not be warrant enough for an inquirer seeking error free information to do so. I am interested in justifying changes in belief where the inquirer respects the desiderata of avoiding error and acquiring valuable information.

According to my view (Levi, 1980, 1991), all changes in states of full belief that are legitimate are sequences of legitimate expansions and legitimate contractions.

Legitimate expansions fall into the following two broad categories:

1. *Routine expansion* where X is committed (precommitted) to a program for adding information to X's initial state of full belief that K in response to some source of information (source of sensory information, testimony of witnesses, opinions of others) before having the opportunity of finding out the information retailed by the source. X endorses the program either by nature, nurture or deliberate choice prior to having information as to what the testimony of the senses or the experts will be. Such programs are intended to yield new information satisfying the demands of the inquiry with low risk of error.

Strictly speaking routine expansions are not justifications of changes in states of full belief. However, when the reliability of a program for routine expansion is legitimately challenged, the program becomes a legitimate target for critical review.

2. *Deliberate Expansion* (inductive expansion) of the initial state of full belief by weighing the merits of a range of rival expansions qualifying as potential answers to some question under investigation with an eye to choosing one that will best promote the goals of the inquirer given the evidence or information contained in the initial state of full belief. The first version of my proposal for modeling deliberate or inductive expansion is based on ideas presented in Levi, 1967a and then modified in Levi 1967b. Further discussion ensued in Levi, 1979, 1980, 1991, 1998 and 2004.

The core idea is that the inquirer ought to choose between rival potential expansions of the initial state of full belief K in a manner that maximizes expected epistemic utility where expected epistemic utility is a weighted average of the credal probability of avoiding error and acquiring valuable new information satisfying the demands of the inquiry.

When credal probability or the value of new information is indeterminate, the decision criterion cannot recommend expected utility maximization. In Levi, 1974, 1980 and 1986 I proposed an account of rational choice designed to cope with such indeterminacy. According to the proposal, rational agent X should restrict choice to feasible options that are *E-admissible* – i.e., are optimal according to some permissible probability-utility pairs belonging to the cross product of a set of permissible credal probability functions and a set of permissible utilities. Further secondary criteria may then be invoked to choose between the E-admissible options. In the case of inductive expansion, the permissible utilities should be weighted averages of permissible trade-offs of the value of avoiding error and valuable information.

Trade offs between avoiding error and amassing valuable information are reflected in an index off boldness. I have shown how to reconstruct Shackle's measures of potential surprise and degrees of belief utilizing this index. The result is a measure of degree of belief that can be used in a rule recommending the "acceptance" of a proposition into an expanded state of full belief if its degree of belief relative to the prior state of full belief is high enough. Thus, Shackle-type measures become satisficing measures of degree of belief as L.J. Cohen (1977) also insisted in defending his 'Baconian probabilities'.

Contractions also fall into two categories:

1. *Contraction from inadvertent expansion into inconsistency.* Such inadvertent expansion into inconsistency can happen in routine expansion where observation or the testimony of experts contradicts the initial state of full belief. In this kind of situation, the issue of whether to contract is settled. The inquirer needs to settle on what to remove in order to achieve consistency. Roughly speaking, the retreat from inconsistency should be to one of the following three states: (i) to the point of view prior to routine expansion, (ii) to the AGM revision of the initial point of view that accommodates the information delivered by the routine expansion or (iii) to suspense between (i) and (ii). The decision between these three depends on the informational values of these options. (Levi 1980a, 1991, 2003 and Olsson, 2003.)

2. *Deliberate Contraction in order to give a hearing to a hypothesis that has great informational value but is initially judged to be impossible.* (Levi, 1980a, 1991.) In this case, the problem is to decide whether to contract or not. What proposition should be removed, however, is clear. It is the negation of the hypothesis that is to be given a hearing.

Once it is settled that X needs to move to a state of full belief that is a contraction K_h^- of K by removing h, the problem of how to contract remains to be tackled. In contrast to the AGM view, I favor considering the entire range of potential contractions from K removing h including both partial meet contractions and withdrawals that are recognized by the basic partition U_{LK}. The inquirer should choose in a manner defended in my last book (Levi, 2004) where loss of damped informational value is minimized. How to contract is thus rationalized from decision theoretical principles and an account of the goals of contraction just as inductive expansion is. The rationalization recommends contractions from a class independently studied by Rott and Pagnucco (1999) who offer a rationalization of a quite different kind.

The two types of expansion and two types of contraction included here are types of change in doxastic commitment.

According to my view, all changes in states of full belief that are legitimate are decomposable into sequences of warranted expansions and warranted contractions of the four kinds listed above.

This claim has an immediate relevance to the scope of applicability of theories of belief change such as AGM theory.

AGM revision is a transformation of an initial deductively closed set K to another deductively closed set K_h^* where the main interest is in the case where K entails $\sim h$. An interesting context of application arises when the inquirer adds $\sim h$ to K where K entails h and then transforms to $K^*{}_h$.

On the view I favor, no X who fully believes that h should ever deliberately expand X's state of full belief by adding $\sim h$. That maneuver defies the inquirer's commitment to avoiding error in making changes in X's full beliefs.

X may, however, expand into inconsistency in routine expansion where X inadvertently expands by responding to input (the testimony of experts or the senses) by adding h. That is where the first kind of contraction comes into play. When retreating from $K_\perp$, X has a choice between variants of three alternatives: X may throw out h and revert to K, throw out $\sim h$ and shift to the AGM revisiom $K^*{}_h$ of K or suspend judgment between the two. The considerations recommending one or the other choice involve appeal to the value of the information assigned the end state in each case. Sometimes but not always AGM revision will be recommended.[2]

This is one type of case where issues about values (in this case cognitive values) play a central role in evaluating changes in state of full belief. The program for epistemology I propose does not explore changes in the value commitments that characterize the cognitive goals. I have suggested the kinds of epistemic values I think appropriate for inquiry. Even so, I think such change is often appropriate, feasible and an important topic for philosophical reflection.

When justifying changes in full belief (or justifying programs for acquiring beliefs in response to external signals), the goals and values should be cognitive or theoretic ones distinct from moral, political, aesthetic or other practical goals that may, indeed, conflict with them on occasion. The specific goals and values are diverse. I advocate the view that, in spite of the diversity, the common features of goals should be avoidance of error and the acquisition of valuable information. In inquiry, agents may have many other goals and promote other value commitments. And these may conflict with their cognitive goals. These conflicts when they are ur-

---

[2] In my opinion, this application does not justify the central role that revision plays in AGM theory. There is another application of AGM theory – in the context of suppositional reasoning – where supposition can be "counterfactual" or "belief contravening" and revision can play a more prominent role.

gent can be the occasion of the kind of moral struggle or inquiry that concerned John Dewey.

According to the classical Bayesian view of probability judgment endorsed by authors like Bayes, Laplace, Broad, Johnson, Jeffreys and the early Carnap, rational agents are committed to rules for deriving states of credal probability judgment from states of full belief. Such rules are representable as functions $C: K \to B$ from potential states of full belief in K to potential states of credal probability judgment in B. These rules have been called various things in the literature. I call them *confirmational commitments* (Levi, 1980),

Classical Bayesians impose certain conditions on candidate confirmational commitments:

Confirmational consistency: If K is consistent, $C(K)$ is a nonempty set of conditional probability functions – the permissible probability functions according to K. Otherwise $C(K)$ is empty.

Confirmational Coherence: Every permissible probability $p_K(x/y)$ according to $C(K)$ is defined where K is consistent, for every y in K consistent with K and every x in K. For fixed K and y, $p_K(x/y)$ is finitely additive probability over the quotient algebra of potential states in K under equivalence given K $\wedge y$. In addition, for every $y \wedge z$ consistent with K, $p_K(x \wedge z/y) = p_K(x/y \wedge z)p_K(z/y)$.

Confirmational Conditionalization: Let K$^+$e be the expansion of consistent K by adding e consistent with K to K. $C(K_e^+)$ is obtained from $C(K)$ by replacing every permissible $p_K(x/y \wedge e)$ in $C(K)$ by $p_{K+e}(x/y)$ in $C(K_e^+)$.[3]

Strict Bayesians insist that $C(K)$ should be a singleton. (*Confirmational Uniqueness.*) In that case, confirmational commitments are numerically determinate. The authors listed above all appear to have endorsed strict Bayesianism. In addition, they all were looking for a standard confirmational commitment satisfying confirmational consistency, coherence and conditionalization as well uniqueness where the standard would be sanctioned by a prob-

---

[3] I also favor a principle of direct inference as a constraint on confirmational commitments. Such a principle presupposes that claims about statistical probability or objective chance are important in inquiry and intelligible. Like Ernest Nagel, I am in favor of recognizing both the intelligibility of statistical probability and belief or credal probability. I was provoked to take the position I did in Levi (1980) in dissenting reaction to the pioneering work of H.E.Kyburg (1961) from which I learnt so much.

ability logic that would restrict the set of coherent probability functions to a singleton rather than mandate uniqueness by fiat.

Skepticism concerning the prospects for the success this program led authors like Ramsey, de Finetti and Savage to abandon necessarianism. The subjectivists or personalists acknowledged that there are principles of probability logic as prescriptions specifying necessary conditions for rational probability judgment. They disagreed with classical authors concerning the strength of these principles. But like the classical advocates of the use of logical probability, they endorsed confirmational uniqueness. This led them to embrace the following peculiar position.

Personalists or subjectivists deny the cogency of logical or necessarian confirmational commitment CIL according to which $CIL(K)$ is the set of all conditional credal probability functions p_K permissible according to probability logic given the state of full belief K. If CIL were so conceived, it could not satisfy confirmational uniqueness. Since personalists at least tacitly endorse confirmational uniqueness, they were constrained to withhold from CIL the status of a confirmational commitment.

I cannot survey all forms of dissent from confirmational uniqueness here. I advertise my preferred way of representing credal states: to wit, by sets of conditional credal probability functions that satisfy a condition of confirmational convexity.

I have argued elsewhere (for example, Levi,,1980) that such representations are of importance if one thinks as I do that confirmational commitments, like states of full belief, are modifiable and that changes in confirmational commitment should call for justification just as changes in state of full belief do.

Necessarians, of course, sought to endorse logical confirmational commitments. They thus tended to favor endowing confirmational commitments with whatever incorrigibility conceptually supported confirmational commitments might have. Subjectivists have, curiously enough, by default, tended to embrace such incorrigibility as well or, if not, to think of changes in confirmational commitment as not requiring justification.

If one recognizes that confirmational commitments are revisable in ways that call for justification, one should allow for confirmational commitments that represent suspense between other confirmational commitments. It is this circumstance that has motivated my interest in indeterminate probability and the representation of credal states by convex sets of probability functions. Space does not permit delving into this matter more elaborately. But I wish to emphasize two points.

In contrast to the personalists, it seems to me that *CIL* should be recognized as the logical confirmational commitment. It is the weakest potential confirmational commitment an inquirer could entertain. Precisely for that reason *CIL* should not be mandated as a standard confirmational commitment. Rational inquirers should be allowed to endorse extra logical confirmational commitments. And this should also obligate them to be in a position to change them when there is good reason to do so.

The second point I wish to emphasize is that inquirers may change confirmational commitments without changing states of full belief. They may also change states of full belief without changing confirmational commitments. In this sense, probability and full belief are *separable*.

Efforts to reduce, analyse or explicate full belief in terms of credal probability are inadvisable if the seperability of probability (or confirmational commitment) and full belief is endorsed.

For example, the proposal suggested by H. Arló Costa (2001) to exploit B.van Fraassen's belief cores to derive a distinction between propositions that carry probability that are full beliefs and those that are 'expectations' from a primitive conditional probability function implies that changes in credal state and full belief come in a single package.

Adopting the suggestion is inadvisable if one is interested in accounts of justified changes in probability. The single package approach implies that the state of full belief and credal state cannot be severed as the separability condition requires. We should not rule out as incoherent the idea of states of full belief changing independently of confirmational commitments. Accounts of how changes in states of full belief and how changes in confirmational commitments are to be justified may then be explored separately. If there are dependencies in the way changes in one impact on changes in the other as the single package approach favored by the probabilists contend, these should emerge from such investigations and not be postulated at the outset in a manner that preempts serious discussion.

According to Samuelson (1961, p.61), the "method of comparative statics" is "the investigation of changes in a system from one position of equilibrium to another without regard to the transitional process involved in the adjustment." This kind of investigation has been conducted in thermodynamics in the discussing "reversible processes" and in economic theorizing. Two kind of changes are recognized: changes in equilibrium state and changes involved when the system is not in equilibrium. Comparative statics focuses on the first kind of change.

The proposed accounts of when and how states of full belief (states of probability judgment, probability judgment, etc) ought to be modified in inquiry recognizes two kinds of changes just as the method of comparative statics does. Instead of focusing on changes in equilibrium state, attention is directed to changes in states of *commitment*. Instead of investigating transitional processes involved in moves to and a way from equilibrium, changes in *performance* that bring the inquirer closer to or further away from fulfilling such commitments should be considered.

Comparative statics in economics is advertised to be a positive science studying, describing, predicting and explaining economic phenomena. I am interested in *prescribing* how changes in states of commitment to full belief, probability judgment and value judgment ought to be made. This frankly normative inquiry presupposes a conception of what a state of commitment to full belief (state of doxastic commitment), state of commitment to credal probability judgments (credal state and confirmational commitment) and state of value commitment should be and how they should interact to prescribe how an agent facing a choice ought to choose among options. So this interest is doubly normative. Prescriptions for changes in rational commitment are prescriptions of changes in state that are normative analogues of the equilibrium states of comparative statics. Prescriptions for changes in performance are recommendations for changes in word and deed that improve the agent's efforts to satisfy commitments. (See Levi, 1991, ch.2 and 1997, ch.s 1 and 3.)

In predicaments that do not tax their computational capacities and their wills to think carefully, the performances of flesh and blood agents may satisfy their commitments. It is clear, however, that agents are not logically omniscient and, indeed, lack the capacity to make accurate determinations of what would fulfill their commitments.

There is a widespread temptation to conclude that the standards of rationality should be modified so that flesh and blood agents would be capable in a more extensive variety of situations to conform to these standards. I disagree. We should not respond to recognition of our infirmities by "dumbing down" the standards of rationality constitutive of our commitments. Sometimes we can identify new technologies that will enhance the capacities of flesh and blood to overcome some of limitations. If we were to lower the standards, there might not be the rational incentive to improve our performance.

Psychological inquiry into human reasoning ought to be oriented to clinical studies aimed at improving human capacity to fulfill the commitments of inquirers. In any case, the study of how agents ought to modify their attitudes of full belief, probability judgment, value judgment and admissibility of options in decision problems is an investigation of how such agents ought to change their *commitments*. How agents should change their *performances* depends on what the commitments and the minimal constraints of rationality are as well as our best judgments as to what their capacities for reasoning well are. There should be no serious objection to such studies if they take into account the standards of rationality that are to be fulfilled.[4]

In any case, studies of changes in beliefs and other attitudes recommended by clinical studies ought not to be confused with studies of the conditions under which changes in commitments to full belief, probability judgment, value judgment and judgments as to what is to be chosen are warranted. The kind of epistemology in which I am interested is concerned with justification of changes in commitments to full belief and to probability judgment and with the norms of rational full belief and probability judgment that characterize the minimal requirements that commitments to full belief and probability judgment should satisfy.

In Levi, 1967, I was not clear as to what I meant by "belief" or "acceptance as true". I did insist that such belief is not equivalent to high probability or even probability 1. Nonetheless, I also paid some sort of lipservice to the fashionable fallibilism that claimed that believing that h while acknowledging that it might be false is somehow coherent. Moving from Case Western Reserve University to Columbia University in 1970 witnessed some important changes in my thinking. I realized that I had been confusing corrigibilism

---

[4]I do not understand what a "purely descriptive" and value neutral investigation of the propositional attitudes could be. The fits of doxastic conviction, oral and written expressions of belief are attempts to fulfill doxastic commitments and are thus value laden as are the dispositions to such manifestations. To abstract away from the evaluative aspects of such performances is also to abstract away from their intentionality. A purely descriptive and value neutral investigation of these performances is not an investigation of these performances as successful or unsuccessful attempts at fulfillments of doxastic commitments. Intentionality has been stripped away.

with what I later called "epistemological fallibilism".

Epistemological fallibilism is the thesis that from X's current point of view, X's full beliefs might be false. Corrigibilism insists that X can and should acknowledge that X's current full beliefs might be subject justifiably to modification in future inquiry. Peirce's fallibilism encompassed both epistemological fallibilism as I understand it and corrigibilism. I continue to embrace the latter but not the former.

I first advanced this view in "Truth, Fallibility and the Growth of Knowledge".[5] I discussed the issue in other papers published in the 1970's that culminated in *The Enterprise of Knowledge* of 1980. Following what I continue to think is a novel insight of Charles Peirce, I deny that rational and reflective agents ought to be in a position ideally to justify their current beliefs. The demand for justification is legitimate only when directed at *changes* in belief. That is to say, justification is appropriate for giving up beliefs already held (contraction) and for adding new beliefs to the old stock (expansion). My disagreement with Peirce is connected with my rejection of Peirce's (and Popper's) *Messianic Realism* in favor of a *secular realism* (or myopic realism). (Levi, 1980, 1991).

References

Arló Costa, H.(2001), "Bayesian Epistemology and Epistemic Conditionals: On the Status of the Export-Import Laws," *The Journal of Philosophy*, Vol. 98, pp. 555–593

Brandom, R.B.(1994), *Making it Explicit*, Cambridge, Mass.: Harvard University Press.

Cohen, L.J. (1977), *The Probable and the Provable*, Oxford: Clarendon Press.

deFinetti, B. (1974), *Theory of Probability*, New York: Wiley, two volumes.

Kyburg, H.E. (1961), *Probability and the Logic of Rational Belief*, Middletown, Conn.: Wesleyan University Press.

Levi, I. (1967), *Gambling with Truth*.New York: Knopf reprinted in paper by MIT Press in 1973.

---

[5] A first draft was written in 1970 even though it was not published until 1983 and subsequently reprinted in Levi, 1984, ch.8.

Levi, I. (1984), *Decisions and Revisions*, Cambridge: Cambridge U. Press.

Levi, I. (1991), *The Fixation of Belief and Its Undoing*, Cambridge: Cambridge U. Press.

Levi, I. (1996). *For the Sake of the Argument*, Cambridge: Cambridge U. Press.

Levi, I. (1997), *The Covenant of Reason*, Cambridge: Cambridge U. Press.

Levi, I (2003), "Contracting from Epistemic Hell is Routine," *Synthese* 135, 141–64.

Levi, I. (2004), *Mild Contraction*, Oxford: Oxford U. Press.

Olsson, E. (2003), "Avoiding Epistemic Hell: Levi on Pragmatism and Inconsistency," *Synthese*135, 119–40.

Rott,H. and Pagnucco, M. (1999), "Severe Withdrawal and Recovery," *Journal of Philosophical Logic* 28, 501–47.

Samuelson, P.A.(1961), *Foundations of Economic Analysis*, Cambridge, Mass.: Harvard University Press.

23
Rohit Parikh

Distinguished Professor
Brooklyn College and CUNY Graduate Center, USA

Why were you initially drawn to epistemology (and what keeps you interested)?

I was drawn initially to *epistemic logic* rather than to epistemology as such. My interests have broadened to include epistemology itself, but logic still occupies an important role. I became involved with epistemic logic because I had been working in dynamic logic for a while, and epistemic logic, typically a modal logic, seemed rather like dynamic logic, but simpler. An event which might have been decisive is when (in the early 80's) Albert Meyer asked me to referee a paper in epistemic logic.

What do you see as being your main contributions to epistemology?

I have thought about axiomatization, *all I know* situations [20], the semantics of messages (jointly with Ramanujam) [25], applications to consensus in economics (jointly with Krasucki) [19], applications of epistemic logic to topology (jointly with Moss) [24], the problem of logical omniscience [17, 21, 23], and the problem of knowledge based obligation (with Cogan and Pacuit) [16].

What do you think is the proper role of epistemology in relation to other areas of philosophy and other academic disciplines?

Surely epistemology is crucial. Of course a great deal of it has been done in philosophy in response to skepticism, dealing with issues like our knowledge of an external world, of other minds, or mathematical knowledge. More recently, much has been done in response to the Gettier puzzle [9]. But I think the importance of knowledge in the structure of society has still to be fully appreciated. The following quote from F. Hayek is prescient.

> The peculiar character of the problem of a rational economic order is determined precisely by the fact that the knowledge of the circumstances of which we must make use never exists in concentrated or integrated form, but solely as the dispersed bits of incomplete and frequently contradictory knowledge which all the separate individuals possess. The economic problem of society is thus not merely a problem of how to allocate "given" resources – if "given' is taken to mean given to a single mind which deliberately solves the problem set by these "data." It is rather a problem of how to secure the best use of resources known to any of the members of society, for ends whose relative importance only these individuals know. Or, to put it briefly, it is a problem of the utilization of knowledge not given to anyone in its totality.

Here Hayek is drawing attention to the fact that apart from goods and services, the usual 'assets' of society, knowledge is of crucial importance, and implicit in his suggestion is the importance of the transfer of knowledge. Hayek seems not to have noticed the logical implications of the fact that the various agents in society might not actually want the same things. Arrow's theorem [2] had not appeared at that time.

In [16], Pacuit, Cogan and I investigate the role of knowledge in creating deontic obligations. An example is a physician who has the obligation to treat a sick person, but *only* if she knows he is sick. By contrast, a hospital with a sick patient also has an additional obligation to *remain aware* of the patient's condition. If the patient has a heart attack, the hospital does not have the excuse which a private physician would have had, to say "We did not know he was having a heart attack."

This is just one of many examples. The role of knowledge in social procedures [22] is ubiquitous.

What do you consider to be the most neglected topics and/or contributions in contemporary epistemology?

There are several points here. For one, everyone agrees that even though *true belief* does not imply knowledge, it is a *necessary condition* for it . But we have not thought enough about belief, and concentrated on *when* a true belief becomes knowledge. But since belief is a precondition for knowledge, pursuing epistemology implies studying belief.

There are, to my mind, three approaches to belief. One is *Cartesian*, which draws on a picture of an agent seeing some cloud of possible worlds, and whatever is common to these worlds is what is believed by the agent. It is this picture which is behind most semantic approaches, like Kripke structures for instance, to epistemic logic. But this picture has several defects. One is that it makes it impossible to understand why our mathematical knowledge is not perfect, since mathematical facts are true in all these worlds. Secondly, when the number of possible worlds is large, then it is difficult to see how one can run through all of them in one's mind. And finally, it is impossible on this picture to understand why we might know ϕ and know $\phi \to \psi$ but not know ψ.

A second model is a 'stored sentences' model, which looks rather syntactic. In this model one stores representations in one's brain of propositions one believes. These representations might be sentences in 'mentalese' [8] or perhaps in the form of some sort of maps.

A third approach which I favor is to relate belief to behavior, including linguistic behavior, which owes much to Ramsey and Savage, [30, 31]. When we ask someone, "Well, what do you think?", we are prompting linguistic behavior. But sometimes we just watch what someone does. Someone dashing out into the street clearly has the belief that no car is coming, even though that person has not said anything. Thus we have a direct route to belief via behavior, and nothing forces logical omniscience in such a case. We ask a mathematician, "Do you know if Goldbach's conjecture is true?" and he says, "I have no idea", so we conclude that the person lacks the belief that Goldbach's conjecture is true (or false). Perhaps a person's belief manifesting behavior is buttressed by some kind of 'store' of sentences in Mentalese (though I doubt that), or perhaps there is a computer inside their heads. We don't need to care since we already have access to the behaviour.

There is of course the tricky issue of those beliefs which may not be correlated with any actual behaviour, like my belief that Elizabeth I was a well educated queen. It is not clear how that belief changes my life. By contrast, if I believe it is raining I will take an umbrella. The second belief affects my actions, and it is not clear how the first does. But at least I will *say* or *would say if asked*, that Elizabeth I was well educated. So the belief about her can be traced to linguistic behavior which is connected in turn with other beliefs; and some of these other beliefs may well have connections with how I act in real life.

An advantage of a behavior based account of belief (and hence of knowledge) is that it also allows us to deal with belief and knowledge in animals and young children. Animals and young children don't talk (very much – see, however, [26]) but they do act, and while being rightly cautious about anthropomophising, we still find it useful to ascribe beliefs or knowledge to them. [28] give accounts of a large amount of intelligence in animals, and while such intelligence does not usually approach human standards, it can be substantial in certain cases.[1]

What do you think the future of epistemology will (or should) hold?

I want to draw attention to three issues.

1. **Knowledge in society**
2. **Animal cognition**
3. **Conversation and cognition**

Knowledge in society

I think the most important aspect of this is the knowledge that we have, or lack, about other people's knowledge. In other words, many person epistemology should now occupy center stage. This is already happening to a fair extent, and I expect that the pace will pick up. There are many aspects to social epistemology. There

---

[1] The following amusing interchange occurs in *Our Town* by Thornton Wilder.
Dr Gibbs: *How's your knee Joe?*.
Joe Crowell, Jr: *Fine Doc, I never think about it at all. Only, like you said, it always tells me when it's going to rain.*
Dr. Gibbs (a little later): *Knee ever make a mistake?*
Joe Crowell Jr: *No, sir.*
Of course it would be ridiculous to ascribe 'knowledge' to knees, Joe notwithstanding, but knees can clearly be *transmitters* of knowledge, and with the higher primates like our cousins the chimps and bonobos, it is hard to avoid ascribing some knowledge to them.

are the issues about Theory of Mind (or lack of such a theory), which appear in the work of Wimmer and Perner [38] or in the work of the Premacks [28]. What Wimmer and Perner show is that young children of age up to about four do not have a sense that other people see the world differently. Thus they tend to assume that someone who was out of a room still knows things which happened in the room, simply because they themselves know it. So we could say that such young children do not have a theory of *other minds* (TOM). Even as adults, many of us do not pay sufficient attention to what others know or don't know. But such knowledge is crucial. Here is a relevant quote from Umberto Eco.

> Not long ago, if you wanted to seize political power in a country, you had merely to control the army and the police. Today it is only in the most backward countries that fascist generals, in carrying out a coup d'etat, still use tanks. If a country has reached a high level of industrialization, the whole scene changes. The day after the fall of Khruschev, the editors of Pravda, Izvestiia, the heads of the radio and television were replaced; the army wasn't called out. Today, a country belongs to the person who controls communications.
>
> **Umberto Eco**
> *Towards a Semiological Guerrilla Warfare*, (1967)

Animal Cognition

We are now pretty far from Descartes' belief that animals are mere automata. While Hume disagreed with this view, Davidson [5] has endorsed a weaker version of Descartes' belief; he claims that animals cannot have propositional attitudes because they lack the background knowledge which is needed to individuate propositions. Thus a dog cannot have a belief that cats are awful because dogs don't really know what cats are, e.g., that they are mammals. Much recent research [33, 36, 26, 28] has tended to somewhat ameliorate Davidson's harsh judgment. Needless to say, the fact that Darwin [6] was impressed by the intelligent behaviour even of earthworms carries a great deal of clout, given his authority. We now believe that animals plan, that they can learn, and that they even have weak versions of 'other minds'.

Conversation and cognition

There are important issues about the transfer of information. The media, and now the Web have made a lot of social knowledge possible which did not exist a hundred (or even twenty) years ago. And finally, there is the issue of Cheap Talk [4, 35], where, when examining what others have said, we ask, "How do they stand to gain or lose by what they have just said?" Grice's work and the notion of implicature immediately go back to the consideration of *why* someone said what they said. For instance if I say, *Some of the girls came to the seminar*, I have implicated but not said that not all of the girls came to the seminar. If all had come, then along with the Gricean maxim [10] of supplying the most relevant information, I should have made the stronger assertion.

Now Grice assumes a co-operative attitude in communication. But as the current political campaign makes vivid, full co-operation rarely exists when much is at stake. All three major candidates, Clinton, McCain, Obama, have resorted to vague or misleading statements in order to garner votes. Thus people may speak vaguely on purpose, or they may even say something which is true, but carries with it a Gricean implicature which is actually false. A Gricean example would be where your car is out of petrol and I tell you that there is a petrol station around the corner, knowing full well that it isn't open, I have used a true statement to deceive you, perhaps because I want you to be delayed to where you are going. Such issues live at the border of what has been epistemology so far, but surely they will become more prominent as time passes.

All in all, it is a thrilling area to work in.

23.1 REFERENCES

[1] Artemov, S., and E. Nogina, "On epistemic logics with justifications", *Theoretical Aspects of Rationality and Knowledge*, ed. Ron Meyden, University of Singapore press, (2005), 279-294.

[2] Arrow, Kenneth J (1951, 1963). *Social Choice and Individual Values*, New York: John Wiley and Sons.

[3] Aumann, R., "Agreeing to disagree", *Annals of Statistics*, **4** (1976) 1236-1239.

[4] Vincent Crawford and Joel Sobel, "Strategic information transmission", in *Econometrica*, **50** (1982) 1431-1451.

[5] D. Davidson, "Thought and Talk", in *Mind and Language*, Edited by S. Guttenplan, Oxford University Press 1975.

[6] Charles Darwin, *The Formation of Vegetable Mould through the Action of Worms with Observations on their Habits*, John Murray, London, 1881; Faber and Faber, London, 1945

[7] Fagin, R., Halpern, J., Moses, Y. and Vardi, M., *Reasoning about knowledge*, M.I.T. Press, 1995.

[8] J. Fodor, *The Modularity of Mind*, MIT press (1983)

[9] E. Gettier, "Is justified true belief knowledge?", *Analysis*, **23** (1963), 121-123.

[10] Paul Grice, *Studies in the Way of Words*, Harvard U. Press (1989).

[11] Hayek, F.A., "The use of knowledge in society", *The American Economic Review*, **35** (1945) 519-530.

[12] Levinson, Stephen C. *Pragmatics*, Cambridge, England: Cambridge University press (1983).

[13] R. Marcus, "Some revisionary proposals about belief and believing," *Philosophy and Phenomenological Research*, **50** (1990) 133-153.

[14] R. Marcus, "The anti-naturalism of some language centere accounts of belief," *Dialectica*, **49** (1995) 112-129.

[15] Ruth Millikan, "Styles of Rationality", in *Rationality in Animals*, ed. M. Nudds and S. Hurley, Oxford 2006, pp. 117-126.

[16] Eric Pacuit, Rohit Parikh and Eva Cogan, "The logic of knowledge based obligation", in *Synthese*, **149** (2006) 311-341.

[17] R. Parikh, "Knowledge and the Problem of Logical Omniscience" *ISMIS- 87* (International Symp. on Methodology for IntelligentSystems), North Holland (1987) 432-439.

[18] R. Parikh, "Finite and Infinite Dialogues", in the *Proceedings of a Workshop on Logic from Computer Science*, Ed. Moschovakis, MSRI publications, Springer 1991 481-498.

[19] R. Parikh and P. Krasucki, "Communication, Consensus and Knowledge", *J. Economic Theory* **52** (1990) pp. 178-189.

[20] R. Parikh, "Monotonic and Non-monotonic Logics of Knowledge", in *Fundamenta Informatica*, special issue, *Logics for Artificial Intelligence* vol XV (1991) pp. 255-274.

[21] R. Parikh, "Logical omniscience", in *Logic and Computational Complexity*, Ed. Leivant, Springer Lecture Notes in Computer Science no. 960, (1995) 22-29.

[22] R. Parikh, "Social Software", *Synthese*, **132**, Sep 2002, 187-211.

[23] R. Parikh, "Sentences, Belief and Logical Omniscience, or What does Deduction tell us?", to appear in *Review of Symbolic Logic* (2008)

[24] Rohit Parikh, Larry Moss and Chris Steinsvold, "Topology and Epistemic Logic", to appear in *Logic of Space*, edited by Johan van Benthem et al, 2007.

[25] R. Parikh, and R. Ramanujam, A Knowledge based Semantics of Messages, in *J. Logic, Language and Information*, **12**, (2003) 453-467.

[26] Irene Pepperberg, "Talking with Alex: Logic and Speech in Parrots; Exploring Intelligence," *Scientific American Mind*, August 2004.

[27] *Meno*, by Plato, translation by Benjamin Jovett. Available online at http://classics.mit.edu//Plato/meno.html

[28] David and Ann Premack, *Original Intelligence*, McGraw Hill 2003.

[29] Ramsey, F. P., "Facts and propositions", in *Philosophical Papers*, edited by D.H. Mellor, Cambridge U. Press 1990, 34-51.

[30] Ramsey, F.P., 'Truth and probability', in *The Foundations of Mathematics*, Routledge and Kegan Paul (1931), 156-198.

[31] L. J. Savage, *The Foundations of Statistics*, Wiley 1954.

[32] Schwitzgebel, Eric, "Belief", *The Stanford Encyclopedia of Philosophy
(Fall 2006 Edition)*, Edward N. Zalta (ed.), URL = http://plato.stanford.edu/archives/fall2006/entries/belief/.

[33] J. Searle, "Animal Minds", in *Philosophical Naturalism, Midwest Studies in Philosophy*, editors French and Wettstein, XIX (1994) 206-219.

[34] Stalnaker, R., *Context and Content*, Oxford University Press, 1999.

[35] R. Stalnaker, "Saying and meaning, cheap talk and credibility", in *Game Theory and Pragmatics*, eds. Benz, Jaeger, Rooij, Macmillan 2006, 83-100.

[36] Frans de Waal, *Our Inner Ape*, Penguin 2005.

[37] Whyte, J.T., "Success semantics", *Analysis*, **50** (1990), 149-157.

[38] H. Wimmer and J. Perner, "Beliefs about beliefs: representation and constraining function of wrong beliefs in young children's understanding of deception", *Cognition*, **13** (1983) 103-128.

[39] Wittgenstein, L., *Philosophical Investigations*, MacMillan, 1958.

24
John L. Pollock

Regents' Professor and Philosophy
and Research Professor of Cognitive Science
University of Arizona, USA

Why were you initially drawn to epistemology (and what keeps you interested)?

As a high school student, I rediscovered Hume's problem of induction on my own. For a while, I was horrified. I thought, "We cannot know anything!" After a couple of weeks I calmed down and reasoned that there had to be something wrong with my thinking, and that led me quickly to the realization that good reasons need not be deductive, and to the discovery of defeasible reasoning. From there it was a short jump to a more general interest in how rational cognition works.

I am interested in rational cognition in general. Epistemology is one constituent of rational cognition, practical cognition (rational decision making) another. Much of the work on rational cognition begins with the supposition that only ideal agents can be truly rational. Real agents have limited powers of reasoning and limited memory capacity. It is often supposed that such resource-bounded agents can only approximate rationality, and that as philosophers we should confine our attention to ideal agents. If one wishes, one can of course define "rationality" in this way, but this has never been what interested me. We come to philosophy wondering what *we* should believe, what *we* should do, and how *we* should go about deciding these matters. These are questions about ourselves, with all of our cognitive limitations. For example, it is often claimed that ideal agents, with unlimited cognitive powers, should believe all of the logical consequences of their beliefs. But we, as real resource-bounded agents, cannot do that, so that is not something we *should* do. What I want to know is how I, as a real agent, should go about deciding what to believe and what to do. Thus my topic is *real rationality* as opposed to *ideal rationality*. In the realm of practical decision making, I have explored this distinction at great length in my recent book (2006). Here I will focus on its implications for epistemology.

For many years epistemology was derailed by the Gettier problem. That distracted philosophers from what I regard as the more interesting questions of how specific kinds of epistemic cognition work. How does perception apprise us of the state of our surroundings? How do induction and abduction lead to the discovery of general truths? How is it possible to know the mental states of others? These were once among the central problems of epistemology, but most of the energy that would otherwise have been directed at these problems was drained off by the Gettier problem. The Gettier problem is just an interesting puzzle, and solving it is unlikely to throw much light on how rational cognition works.

What do you see as being your main contributions to epistemology?

Defeasible Reasoning

My most important contribution to epistemology was to be one of the discoverers of defeasible reasoning and its central role in rational cognition. Today's younger epistemologists find it incredible that anyone ever thought that all good reasoning had to be deductive, even though that was an almost universally shared opinion prior to the 1960's. I first wrote about defeasible reasoning in an appendix to my PhD dissertation, in 1965, and my first paper on the topic was my (1967). A few other philosophers, most notably Stephen Toulmin (1950), Roderick Chisholm (1966) and Nicholas Rescher (1967), were also starting to think about defeasible reasoning at that time. Insofar as my early views were infuenced by other philosophers, the main influence was probably Wittgenstein's remarks about criteria in *Philosophical Investigations* (1953)

Initially, epistemologists writing about defeasible reasoning used the concept as a tool for the analysis of specific kinds of epistemic cognition (and as a tool for attempts to solve the Gettier problem). They did not give too much thought to precisely how defeasible reasoning works from a logical point of view. More than others, I investigated some of the logical details because that was necessary for understanding how the reasoning was used in specific epistemological problems. In 1978, I produced what was probably the world's first formal semantics for defeasible reasoning. However, I did not publish it until (Pollock 1986, 1987) because I doubted that other philosophers would be interested in the question. I did not realize then that there was a developing interest among artificial intelligence researchers in the same question.

Direct Realism and Non-Doxastic Theories

My initial application of defeasible reasoning was to perceptual knowledge, where I argued (1967, 1968, 1971, 1974) for the then-radical thesis that "x looks red to me" gives me a defeasible reasoning for believing "x is red", where this reason does not derive from anything else more fundamental, and most importantly, not from a definition of (logically necessary and sufficient conditions for) "red".

Historically, most epistemological theories were *doxastic theories*, in the sense that they endorsed the *doxastic assumption*. That is the assumption that the justifiability of a cognizer's belief is a function exclusively of what beliefs he or she holds. Perceptual beliefs – the first beliefs formed on the basis of perception – are by their very nature not obtained by inference from previously held beliefs. But on a doxastic theory, the justification of a belief cannot depend on anything other than the cognizer's beliefs. Thus perceptual beliefs must be *self-justified* in the sense that they are justified (at least defeasibly) by the mere fact that the cognizer holds them.

Historical foundations theories tried to make this plausible by taking perceptual beliefs to be about the cognizer's perceptual experience. The trouble is, perceptual beliefs, as the first beliefs the agent forms on the basis of perception, are not generally about appearances. It is rare to have any beliefs at all about how things look to you. You normally just form beliefs about ordinary physical objects. You look at your dinner table and judge perceptually that your cat is sitting on the table licking the dirty plates. It never occurs to you to form a belief like, "It appears to me that there is a fuzzy brown blob atop an oval surface and a strangely shaped pink object next to it is moving in the vicinity of another smaller oval shape". You do not have the latter belief (although you could form it with a shift of attention), and the belief about the cat cannot be self-justified because the very same belief can be held for non-perceptual reasons or for inadequate reasons. Still, such beliefs can be justified by perception. What is it about my perceptual experience that justifies me in believing, for example, that the cat is licking the plates? It seems clear that the belief is justified by *the fact that* it looks to me that way. In general, there are various states of affairs P for which visual experience gives us direct evidence. Let us say that the relevant visual experience is that of *being appeared to as if P*. Then *direct realism* is the following principle:

> For appropriate P's, if S believes P on the basis of being appeared to as if P, S is defeasibly justified in doing so.

Direct realism is "direct" in the sense that our beliefs about our physical surroundings are the first beliefs produced by cognition in response to perceptual input, and they are not inferred from lower-level beliefs about the perceptual input itself. But, according to direct realism, these beliefs are not self-justified either. Their justification depends upon having the appropriate perceptual experiences. Thus the doxastic assumption is false.

Direct realism has had occasional supporters in the history of philosophy, perhaps most notably Peter John Olivi in the 13th century and Thomas Reid in the 18th century. But the theory was largely ignored by contemporary epistemologists until I resurrected it (1971, 1974, 1986) on the basis of the preceding argument.

Procedural Justification

Non-doxastic theories of epistemic justification cry out for an explanation of how beliefs can be justified by non-beliefs, i.e., by perceptual states. Investigating this question led me to what I regard as a fundamental insight that profoundly changed my perspective on epistemology. Thirty years ago, a philosopher could write a paper on epistemology, making free and frequent use of the term "epistemic justification", without further explanation and confident that his audience would understand him. That is no longer a reasonable way to proceed. It has become increasingly apparent that there is more than one important concept that might reasonably be called "epistemic justification", and it seems clear that these different concepts have often been confused with one another in the epistemological literature. The literature on the Gettier problem has highlighted one concept, dear to the hearts of many epistemologists, which is something like "what turns true belief into knowledge". The reliabilist literature, for example, might best be read as pertaining to some such concept as this. But there is at least one other important concept that pertains to "the directing of one's own cognition". This is an essentially first person concept. In my book *Contemporary Theories of Knowledge* (Pollock 1986, Pollock and Cruz 2000), I proposed that this concept could be understood as descriptive of our procedural knowledge for "how to cognize". That part of epistemology that is more concerned with the procedural aspects of rationality than with the analysis of "S knows that P" can, I urged, be viewed as pursuing a competence theory of cognition, in the same way that theories of grammar in Linguistics are competence theories of language. On this view, the normative language employed in the formulation of both theories of grammar and epistemological theories is a reflection, in part, of the competence/performance distinction that can be drawn in connection with any procedural knowledge. More recently (Pollock 2008), I have come to realize that the normativity also reflects the fact that the competence theory of cognition is actually embedded in the performance theory of human cognition. Human cognition is organized so that when we violate the norms of the competence theory, and realize that we have done so, we are moved to attempt to correct our cognition and bring it into conformance with the norms. This is a purely descriptive fact about human cognition, and amounts to saying that we treat the norms of competent cognition normatively (not just that we *should* treat them that way).

This leads to a shift of perspective. We can think of epistemology as being part of the enterprise of designing a rational cognizer. That is the traditional task of artificial intelligence, and epistemology provides part of the analysis of rationality driving the design. What I will call *procedural epistemology* is directed at how to build the system of cognition. My interest can then be described as one in procedural epistemology. I want to know how the rules of epistemic cognition should be formulated in order for cognition to conform to our pre-analytic judgments of rationality.

The OSCAR Project

Procedural epistemology is a theory about how something works—rational epistemic cognition. It became clear to me quite early that the standard methodology of armchair philosophy is not well suited to getting such theories right. Armchair epistemology can go a long way to getting us started in constructing theories of procedural epistemology, but human beings are quite limited in the complexity of examples they can construct and evaluate from the armchair. Rules of cognition must be applicable to cases of arbitrary complexity, and my experience has revealed many cases in which rules that appear to work in simple cases produce absurd results in some complex cases. Part of the difficulty is that it can be hard to tell what a theory even implies about a sufficiently complex case. A philosopher may think that it has one implication, and deem that correct, when in fact the subtle complexities of the case yield a different and unacceptable implication. I became convinced that the only way to avoid this problem is to mechanize the production of test cases and the application of epistemological theories to them. To do that we must build a system that models proposed accounts of cognition, so that we can see what the system really does in complex cases. The best way to do that is with a computer model, and the resulting system becomes an AI system. Given a precise implementation of a procedural epistemological theory, we can apply it automatically to complex cases and see what it does, and then evaluate whether that is what it rationally should do. (See Pollock (1998) for an extended example dealing with perceptual, temporal, and causal reasoning.) It is noteworthy that such systems almost always misbehave initially in complex cases. We can then investigate why we got the unexpected result, and modify the cognitive system being modeled to try to get it to produce more congenial results.

Thus the OSCAR Project was born in 1985. OSCAR is an AI system that seeks to model various aspects of human rational cognition. OSCAR has been generously supported by the National Science Foundation for a number of years. In its current state, OSCAR is a general architecture for rational cognition based on a system of defeasible reasoning and natural deduction, and implements rules for many specific kinds of cognition including perceptual reasoning, temporal reasoning, causal reasoning, and various kinds of probabilistic reasoning (Pollock 2008c). OSCAR performs both epistemic cognition and rational decision making, the latter driven by systems of decision-theoretic planning that are currently under development (Pollock 2006a).

The core of OSCAR is a system of defeasible reasoning. This system has changed in important ways over the years in response to failures revealed by actually running the system and applying it to interesting examples. The early system of my (1986, 1987) proved inadequate for dealing with "self-defeating arguments"—

arguments that support defeaters for some of their own steps. Such arguments are produced with surprising frequency in the course of reasoning about matters that would not naturally be expected to produce self-defeating arguments. In my (1994, 1995) I produced a new semantics that seemed to get most of the problematic cases right. More recently, however, I have become convinced that the new semantics is not quite right either, and I proposed a newer semantics (Pollock 2002). I am still working on modification to that semantics, and it has not yet been implemented in OSCAR.

Epistemology and Probability

I have long been interested in the role of probability in epistemology. Most probabilists working in epistemology are Bayesians who think that all of epistemology is reducible to subjective probability and the probability calculus. I have repeatedly argued (e.g., in my 2006a) that the logical structure of probabilities does not mimic that of epistemic justification. For example, it follows from the probability calculus that all necessary truths have probability 1, but clearly we are not automatically justified in believing necessary truths. For most of them we only become justified as a result of giving an argument, but giving an argument cannot affect their probabilities. They had probability 1 all along — we just did not know that they did. So their having probability 1 did not make us justified in believing them.

Bayesians sometimes reply that they are only interested in ideal agents, unconstrained by the realistic limits on memory and reasoning ability that plague real agents. But my interest is in real agents. I want to know how I should solve cognitive problems, not how a mythical ideal agent should do it. So I do not think Bayesians have much to tell us about epistemology.

Still, probabilities are important. Most of our general knowledge of the world is probabilistic. These cannot be subjective probabilities, so I have spent a lot of time trying to make sense of objective and partly objective probabilities (Pollock 1990, 2006). At the time subjective probabilities were becoming popular, objective probabilities were being roundly criticized because their defenders were unable to define them (state necessary and sufficient conditions) in terms of philosophically simpler notions. But that was in the middle of the twentieth century when people still thought that most concepts had definitions and good philosophical analyses consisted of giving definitions. If we learned anything from the 1960's and 1970's, it is that this is a bad theory of philosophical analysis. Few if any philosophically interesting concepts have definitions. You cannot define "person" in terms of behavior, "red" in terms of "looks red", or concepts like "time" or "physical object" in terms of anything. Concepts just do not work that way. The best way to clarify such concepts philosophically is instead by constructing precise theories of how to use them in reasoning. Thus direct realism clarifies concepts like "red" by explaining how to reason defeasibly about the colors of things on the basis of perception.

Although nobody believes any more that concepts are somehow illegitimate or philosophically confused if we cannot define them, objective probability was tarred with that brush and somehow the smear has stuck in many minds. This is a completely illegitimate charge. We should no more expect "probability" to have a definition than "red" or "person". To clarify the concept of objective probability, we need an epistemological theory of how to reason about probabilities, and that has been the goal of my work.

There is a nowadays often overlooked distinction between *generic probabilities*, which relate properties, and *singular probabilities*, which attach to propositions. For example, on the basis of statistical evidence the medical community may estimate that the probability of an adult male of Slavic descent being lactose intolerant is .6. This is not about any particular adult male—it relates the *property* of being an adult male of Slavic descent to the *property* of being lactose intolerant. A doctor may go on to inquire about the probability that Boris, a particular Slavic male, is lactose intolerant. This is a singular probability, about the proposition that Boris is lactose intolerant, and that need not be the same as the generic probability because we may have other relevant information about Boris. Historically, theories of objective probability have tended to be theories of generic probability, and then theories of "direct inference" were proposed for how to infer the values of singular probabilities from knowledge of collections of relevant generic probabilities (Reichenbach 1949, Kyburg 1974, Pollock 1990, Bacchus 1990, Halpern 1990, Bacchus et al 1996).

I regard one of my most important accomplishments to be the theory of nomic probability (Pollock 1990). Nomic probabilities are generic probabilities glossed informally by taking $prob(Fx/Gx)$ to be a measure of the proportion of physically possible G's that would be F's. I showed that if we make a small number of seemingly obvious assumptions about the proportion function used in this formulation, all of which are trivial theorems of set theory for proportions among finite sets, we can generate a very rich calculus of nomic probabilities. This is coupled with a single pair of epistemological principles, *the statistical syllogism* and *subproperty defeat*, formulated as follows:

Statistical Syllogism:

If F is projectible with respect to G and $r > 0.5$, then $\ulcorner Gc \& prob(Fx/Gx) \geq r \urcorner$ is a defeasible reason for $\ulcorner Fc \urcorner$, the strength of the reason being a monotonic increasing function of r.

Subproperty Defeat for the Statistical Syllogism:

If H is projectible with respect to G, then

$$\ulcorner Hc \& prob(Fx/Gx \& Hx) < prob(Fx/Gx) \urcorner$$

is an undercutting defeater for the inference by the statistical syllogism from

$$\ulcorner Gc \& prob(Fx/Gx) \geq r \urcorner$$

to $\ulcorner Fc \urcorner$.

In my (1990) I was able to show that from this parsimonious set of assumptions we can derive a rich theory of probabilistic reasoning including a theory of direct inference and principles of statistical induction.

However, the theory of my (1990) left some important issues unresolved. One of the most important is that although direct inference is occasionally useful, very often we know too much to be able to use it. Suppose the generic probability of a person with Boris' symptoms being lactose intolerant is .6. Suppose we have two seemingly unrelated diagnostic tests for a disease, and Boris tests positive on both tests. We know that the probability of a person with his symptoms having the disease if he tests positive on the first test is .7, and the probability if he tests positive on the second test is .75. What should we conclude about the *joint probability* of his having the disease if he tests positive on both tests? The probability calculus gives us no guidance here. It is consistent with the probability calculus for the joint probability to be anything from 0 to 1. Nor does direct inference help. Direct inference gives us one reason for thinking that the probability of Boris having the disease is .7, and it gives us a different reason for drawing the conflicting conclusion that the probability is .75. It gives us no way to combine the information. Intuitively, it seems that the probability of his having the disease should be higher if he tests positive on both tests. But how can we justify this?

In my (2008a, 2008b), employing the same assumptions about the proportion function ρ, I proved the following very fundamental theorem about both proportions among finite sets and generic probabilities:

Expectable Probabilities Principle:

Let $U, X_1, ..., X_n$ be a set of variables ranging over sets, and consider a finite set LC of linear constraints on proportions between Boolean compounds of those variables. Then for any pair of Boolean compounds P, Q of $U, X_1, ..., X_n$ there is a real number r between 0 and 1 such that for every $\varepsilon, \delta > 0$, there is an N such that if U is finite and $\#U > N$, then

$$\rho\left(\rho(P,Q) \approx_\delta r \;/\; LC \;\&\; X_1, ..., X_n \subseteq U\right) \geq 1 - \varepsilon.$$

For any properties $X_1, ..., X_n$, if P and Q are the corresponding compound properties, it is defeasibly reasonable to expect that $prob(P/Q) = r$.

Furthermore, there is an algorithm for computing r. Applying this to the preceding problem, let us define:

$$Y(r, s \mid a) = \frac{rs(1-a)}{a(1-r-s) + rs}$$

I then proved:

Y-Principle:

Given background information U, if B, C include (i.e., nomically imply) U, $prob(A/B) = r$, $prob(A/C) = s$, and $prob(A/U) = a$, then it is defeasibly reasonable to expect that $prob(A/B\&C) = Y(r, s \mid a)$.

The Y-principle makes knowledge of generic probabilities useful in ways it was never previously useful. It tells us how to combine different probabilities that would lead to conflicting direct inferences and still arrive at a univocal value. Consider Boris again, who has symptoms suggesting a particular disease, and tests positive on two independent tests for the disease. Suppose again that the probability of a person with those symptoms having the disease is .6. Suppose the probability of such a person having the disease if they test positive on the first test is .7, and the probability of their having the disease if they test positive on the second test is .75. What is the probability of their having the disease if they test positive on both tests? We can infer defeasibly that it is $Y(.7,.75:.6) = .875$. We can then apply direct inference to conclude that the probability of Boris' having the disease is .875. This is a result that we could not have gotten from the probability calculus alone or from direct inference alone. Similar reasoning will have significant practical applications in many realms.

The Y-principle is just the tip of the iceberg. The expectable probabilities principle justifies an immense number of often previously unknown principles for reasoning defeasibly about probability, and promises to make probability practically useful in ways it was never previously useful because no one has known how to make reasonable defeasible estimates for probabilities whose values are uncomputable in the probability calculus. We can now solve analytically many problems that could previously only be solved using Monte Carlo methods.

What do you think is the proper role of epistemology in relation to other areas of philosophy and other academic disciplines?

Procedural epistemology is about how rational cognition works, and as I have urged, it makes up a large part of a purely psychological theory of how human cognition works in general. Not all cognition is rational, but you cannot understand cognition in general without understanding the central role rational cognition plays in it and the way in which general cognition tries to move human cognizers in the direction of rationality. As such, procedural epistemology is a subtheory of a psychological theory of human cognition. However, this does not mean that it is best studied by psychologists employing currently available psychological methodology. That methodology is well-suited for studying human epistemological performance, but as I urged above, the theory of rational cognition is a theory of cognitive competence, not a theory of cognitive performance (just as linguistic theories of grammar purport to be competence theories, while psycholinguistic theories are performance theories). At this time psychologists do not have good tools for studying competence theories experimentally. You cannot do it just by seeing how subjects handle epistemic problems at a surface level, because what is sought is how they would handle the problems given adequate time to fully deliberate, often with considerable help from their peers who can often point out errors in their reasoning that the subjects will ultimately recognize as errors. Take the Wason selection task (Wason 1966). Subjects are presented with four cards. One card shows a red face, one a black face, one a nine, and one a ten. The hypothesis is that all cards with one red face have an even number on the other side. Subjects are asked which cards they must turn over to determine whether that is true. Overwhelmingly, most subjects judge that they must turn over the red card and the ten. But the right answer is the red card and the nine. To confirm the hypothesis, they must verify that the nine is not red. Knowing whether the ten is red is irrelevant. Although people almost invariably get this wrong the first time, they also have no trouble seeing what the right answer is when it is explained to them. So a performance theory will describe them as turning over the red card and the ten, but a competence theory will have them turn over the red card and the nine. It is the latter kind of theory that procedural epistemology seeks, but an avenue to it through contemporary experimental psychology is obscure. This seems to be an error that is pervasive in much of the currently popular philosophical work on experimental epistemology.

If procedural epistemology is at heart a psychological theory about important aspects of human cognition, but it cannot be studied using standardly available psychological methodology, how can it be studied? Armchair epistemologists propound thought experiments, use their "philosophical intuitions" to judge whether certain reasoning would be rationally correct, and then search for general theories to accommodate their judgments. I agree that that is the right way to start, providing you are careful to rely only on very firm intuitions. The explanation for why this works is that the human cognitive architecture makes it possible for us to cognize irrationally (see my 2008 for a lengthy discussion of this), but also provides an important feedback mechanism for recognizing divergences from our built-in epistemic norms and a built-in conative disposition to correct our cognitive performance when we find ourselves making cognitive mistakes. The output of this feedback mechanism is our philosophical intuitions. Similar feedback mechanisms are ubiquitous in procedural knowledge. When linguists appeal to their linguistic intuitions to judge that certain utterances are ungrammatical, they are employing a similar feedback mechanism (Pollock 1986, 2008, Pollock and Cruz 2000). The philosophical intuitions thus produced are about single cases. We have no direct intuitive access to our built-in epistemic norms themselves. So our task becomes a standard problem in scientific reasoning to discover a general account of rational cognition that accommodates and explains our singular judgments.

Armchair epistemologists stop here. This is where I diverge from them in an important way. The complexity of the examples we can consider from the armchair is very limited . To test armchair-generated theories on real-world problems, we must mechanize the process by building a model that implements the theory. The result is an AI system, and once we have the implementation we can apply it automatically to complex problems and see how the resulting system reasons its way through the problems. 25 years of experience doing this in the OSCAR Project reveals two facts that philosophers find startling but scientists who build models in other disciplines will find commonplace. First, our armchair theories are never formulated precisely enough to be implemented. They tend to have huge holes in them that we do not notice until we try to implement them, but this has the consequence that the theories do not actually have any implications about interesting cases. So the implementation forces us to be much more careful in the formulation of our theories. The second observation is that once made precise, our initial theories never do what we expect them to do. In other words, they are wrong. No computer programmer will find this surprising. Basically, what we are trying to do is write a computer program for how to cognize, and nobody ever writes complex bug-free computer programs on a single pass. Once the simple programming bugs themselves are fixed, what remain are bugs in theory, and there will be lots of them that can only be found by running the resulting system and seeing what it does. Thus armchair epistemology is an appropriate starting point for procedural epistemology, but it can only be the starting point. To complete the theory in a credible way, a partial merger of philosophy and artificial intelligence is essential.

What do you consider to be the most neglected topics and/or contributions in contemporary epistemology?

Before the Gettier problem took the epistemological world by storm, much work was done on topics like perceptual knowledge, temporal reasoning, causal reasoning, knowledge of other minds, induction, inference to the best explanation, etc. These are topics that make up the core of procedural epistemology. I think it is time to deem the Gettier problem as what it is — an interesting puzzle, but not the central question of a mature discipline — and turn our attention back to the hard and more far-reaching issues of procedural epistemology.

What do you think the future of epistemology will (or should) hold?

I believe the future will hold a partial merger of epistemology with both psychology and artificial intelligence. That will never replace an appeal to philosophical intuitions. They will probably always provide the starting point for the construction of epistemological theories. But it is important to rely only upon very clear intuitions. When Nelson Goodman (1955) provided his "grue" counterexample to the Nicod principle, no one could doubt that he was right. The philosophical intuition was absolutely clear. But most philosophical intuitions are less clear. I welcome the development of psychological tools that will help clarify vague philosophical intuitions. This must be accompanied by a better understanding of how to investigate competence theories experimentally. When we have that, experimental epistemology will come of age. But even then, this provides only the single case data for theory construction. Constructing general epistemological theories to accommodate the single case data is a matter of scientific theory formation, and the resulting theories will be too complex to be tested just by looking at simple cases. They must be implemented and tested on real-world problems, and that requires a partial merger with artificial intelligence.

References

Bacchus, Fahiem

1990 "Representing and Reasoning with Probabilistic Knowledge", MIT Press.

Bacchus, Fahiem, Adam J. Grove, Joseph Y. Halpern, Daphne Koller

1996 "From statistical knowledge bases to degrees of belief", *Artificial Intelligence* **87**, 75–143.

Chisholm, Roderick

1966 *Theory of Knowledge*. Englewood Cliffs, NJ: Prentice-Hall.

Halpern, J. Y.

1990 "An analysis of first-order logics of probability", *Artificial Intelligence* **46**, 311–350.

Kyburg, Henry, Jr.

1974 *The Logical Foundations of Statistical Inference*. Dordrecht: Reidel.

Pollock, John

1967 "Criteria and our Knowledge of the Material World", *The Philosophical Review*, **76**, 28–60.

1968 What is an epistemological problem? *American Philosophical Quarterly* 5: 183–90.

1971 "Perceptual Knowledge", *Philosophical Review*, **80**, 287–319.

1974 *Knowledge and Justification*, Princeton University Press.

1986 *Contemporary Theories of Knowledge*, Rowman and Littlefield.

1987 "Defeasible reasoning", *Cognitive Science* **11**, 481–518.

1987a "Epistemic Norms", *Synthese* **71**, 61-96.

1990 Nomic Probability and the Foundations of Induction, Oxford University Press.

1994 "Justification and defeat", *Artificial Intelligence* 67: 377–408.

1995 *Cognitive Carpentry*, MIT Press.

1998 "Perceiving and reasoning about a changing world", *Computational Intelligence.* **14**, 498–562.

2002 "Defeasible reasoning with variable degrees of justification", *Artificial Intelligence* **133**, 233–282.

2006 *Thinking about Acting: Logical Foundations for Rational Decision Making*, New York: Oxford University Press.

2008 "Irrationality and cognition", in *Epistemology: New Philosophical Essays*, ed. Quentin Smith, New York: Oxford University Press.

2008a "Probable probabilities", http://oscarhome.soc-sci.arizona.edu/ftp/PAPERS/Probable Probabilities.pdf.

2008b "Reasoning defeasibly about probabilities", in Michael O'Rourke and Joseph Cambell (eds.), *Knowledge and Skepticism*, Cambridge, MA: MIT Press.

2008c "OSCAR: A Cognitive Architecture for Intelligent Agents", in *A Roadmap for Human-Level Intelligence*, eds. W. Duch and J. G. Taylor, Springer.Pollock, John

Pollock, John, and Joseph Cruz

1999 *Contemporary Theories of Knowledge*, 2nd edition, Lanham, Maryland: Rowman and Littlefield.

Reichenbach, Hans

1949 *A Theory of Probability.* Berkeley: University of California Press. (Original German edition 1935)

Rescher, Nicholas

1976 *Plausible Reasoning.* Amsterdam: Van Gorcum.

Toulmin, Stephen

1950 *An Examination of the Place of Reason in Ethics*, Chicago: University of Chicago Press.

Wason, P.

1966 "Reasoning". In B. Foss (ed.), *New Horizons in Psychology.* Harmondsworth, England: Penguin.

Wittgenstein, Ludwig

1953 *Philosophical Investigations.* Translated by G.E.M. Anscombe. New York: Macmillan.

25
Krister Segerberg

Professor Emeritus

Uppsala University, Sweden

A Conversation about Epistemic Logic

Dramatis personæ: SANDERSON *(the Professor's teaching assistant)*; JOHN *and* PHOEBE *(philosophy students)*; SEBASTIAN *and* CHARLOTTA LINNÉA *(the Professor's grand-children aged seven and four, respectively). The scene is the Professor's office, moderately untidy. On one wall a small blackboard. Three people in the room: Sanderson, Sebastian and Charlotta Linnéa. They have been waiting for John and Phoebe, who suddenly enter the room.*

JOHN. Hi, we have come from the student newspaper to interview the Professor. I am John the journalist.

PHOEBE. And I am Phoebe the photographer.

SANDERSON. Hi, and welcome. I am Thomas Anderson but my friends call me Sanderson. I am the Professor's T.A. and B.S. B.S. meaning baby sitter. Meet Sebastian and Charlotta Linnéa, the Professor's grand-children.

PHOEBE. *(Smiling at the children.)* Hi!

CHARLOTTA LINNÉA. I am not a baby!

SANDERSON. Of course not. I am sorry the Professor is late, but we are here to answer your questions.

JOHN. And the children?

SANDERSON. Actually, the Professor suggested to begin with them.

JOHN. I know the Professor is eccentric, but this is ridiculous. What do children know?

CHARLOTTA LINNÉA. *(Proudly, not waiting for an invitation to speak.)* I know how old I am.

PHOEBE. *(Friendly.)* And how old is that?

> *Charlotta Linnéa silently displays one hand: fingers spread out, thumb hidden.*

JOHN. *(Not so friendly.)* And just how much is that?

CHARLOTTA LINNÉA. *(Again displays her hand.)*

JOHN. So you don't know?

CHARLOTTA LINNÉA. Four, silly!

JOHN. So you *know* you are four, do you?

CHARLOTTA LINNÉA. *(Nods importantly.)*

JOHN. And how do you know?

CHARLOTTA LINNÉA. *(Counts on her fingers.)* One, two, three, four.

PHOEBE. *(Supportive.)* There you are! She really knows that she is four. Very clever!

JOHN. No, I don't think so. She has been told she is four and just repeats that. Counting to four does not mean you know what four is. I am not even sure that what she did was counting—a parrot could be taught to do what she did.

CHARLOTTA LINNÉA. *(Indignant.)* I am not a parrot!

JOHN. So how much is five plus seven?

PHOEBE. *(Trying to be helpful.)* That is too difficult for a little girl. Let's ask Sebastian instead. How old are you, Sebastian?

SEBASTIAN. Seven. And I can count to one thousand.

PHOEBE. You are older than your sister.

SEBASTIAN. Three years older.

JOHN. How do you know?

SEBASTIAN. Seven minus four is three.

JOHN. You *know* that?

SEBASTIAN. I can show you. But I need some coins.

At the request of Phoebe, John produces seven coins— as it happens, four nickels and three quarters. Sebastian begins by counting them.

SEBASTIAN. One—two—three—four—five—six—seven.

Sebastian then counts the nickels, handing each back to John as he is counting.

SEBASTIAN. One—two—three—four.

Sebastian finally counts the remaining coins—the quarters.

SEBASTIAN. One—two—three. So the answer is three.

Sebastian pockets the three coins.

JOHN. Hey, that is my money!

SEBASTIAN. But it is just three quarters!

CHARLOTTA LINNÉA. He is mean!

JOHN. This is getting tiresome. Give me back my money!

PHOEBE. (*Gently, as if to herself.*) "May I *please* have my money back!"

Sebastian returns the money.

SEBASTIAN. I'd settle for one quarter.

SANDERSON. Children: Why don't you go and do your home-work in the library. After that we will all go to Starbucks.

SEBASTIAN. But weren't we supposed to tell them about knowledge? That is what Grandpa said.

SANDERSON. But you have! Thanks, and see you later!

SEBASTIAN. I'd rather go to McDonald's.

CHARLOTTA LINNÉA. He's mean! I am not a parrot.

The children depart.

*

SANDERSON. So where were we? You wanted to know about epistemic logic?

JOHN. Yes, we are running a series in the campus newspaper about what's hot in various disciplines.

SANDERSON. And you were told that epistemic logic is "hot"?

JOHN. Right. So now we'd like to know, what has knowledge got to do with epistemic logic?

PHOEBE. Or, rather, what has epistemic logic got to do with knowledge?

SANDERSON. O.K., so let us start by saying that there are lots of important concepts involved here: not only knowledge but also belief, information, values, and action, to mention some. They are all intertwined.

PHOEBE. Aren't "belief" and "information" two words for the same thing?

SANDERSON. No, information is something you get and which you have to evaluate: whether to accept it or not. It may lead to belief, even knowledge. Or it may not. Now, what the Old Fog always stresses is that there are several dimensions to modelling knowledge: presentation, representation and commitment.

JOHN. What on earth is that supposed to mean?

PHOEBE. Who is the Old Fog?

SANDERSON. The Old Fog is the Professor. When we really want an answer, he always says that he hasn't got the foggiest idea. He is a dear, Old Foggie, but not always easy to understand. Please don't tell the children that we call him that! He is a logician, you know. Or a kind of logician. Model theorist. For him, models is everything. They represent something. They pack information. They help you see things. But just having a model is not enough, you must also know what to do with it. To be useful, models must be applied. Like maps.

JOHN. Maps?

SANDERSON. Maps. Remember what Ramsey is supposed to have said ...

PHOEBE. (*Enthusiastically.*) Oh, I know that!

JOHN. Ramsey?

PHOEBE. "Beliefs are maps we steer by." It's beautiful!

SANDERSON. And true in a very deep sense. You want to go from point A to point B. You get a map, or you get a description of how to get from A to B. Instructions or perhaps a set of rules. Whatever the form of the information, you hope that it correctly represents the features of the world that are of interest to you. In this case, to get from A to B.

PHOEBE. So maps are examples of models?

SANDERSON. Yes. I only wish there were a better term. "Model" is already used in so many contexts. "Map" would be misleading—too special. To get something neutral, how about "m.a.p."?

JOHN. I hate acronyms.

PHOEBE. What would "m.a.p." stand for?

SANDERSON. Well, for m read "multiple-use" or "multi-purpose" or something like that. For a, try "auxiliary" or "action-guiding". And for p, read "presentation". M.a.p. One m.a.p., many m.a.p.s. Not pretty, but at least a neutral term.

JOHN. For what?

SANDERSON. To cover all the concepts mentioned above: model, map, algorithm, set of rules, set of instructions, what not. I want to leave it vague.

JOHN. In other words, "m.a.p." is an ugly term for we don't know what.

SANDERSON. Sure, if you want to put it that way.

PHOEBE. May we have some examples?

JOHN. No, wait, I cannot stand "m.a.p.". If you don't like "model", how about "muddle"?

PHOEBE. Look, this is silly. Let us just stick with "model" and agree to remember that the term can cover lots of different things. The term would be clarified if we could have some examples?

SANDERSON. I am willing to compromise: *model, O.K.? You can pronounce that "star model", if you want. But perhaps best to let the star be silent. Like a nonstandard model. It is actually a nice term. Thanks for your input!

JOHN. (*Without enthusiasm.*) You are welcome.

PHOEBE. I take it that a model in the ordinary sense would also – or could also – be a *model. But what other examples are there?

SANDERSON. All right. Here is a map of New Zealand. A lot of symbols and a number of names. That is what I called a presentation: just an abstract structure, really. But there is a way to read it. For example, this dot represents Auckland, this dot Wellington, this line is the main road between them. That would be the representation.

JOHN. The re-presentation, as Heidegger would say.

SANDERSON. Let us keep Heidegger out of this, shall we?

PHOEBE. And commitment?

SANDERSON. You would not want to use the map if you didn't think it was true to the facts. Say you have several maps to choose between and that they differ in important ways. Then you have to make a choice. In my jargon: to make a commitment.

PHOEBE. Which then can be the basis for further action. Like motoring from Auckland to Wellington.

JOHN. (*Scornfully.*) "Motoring"!

PHOEBE. Isn't that what they say in New Zealand?

JOHN. I'm not sure they ever did. Today they certainly don't.

SANDERSON. What the children did can be seen in the same light. Lotta-Linnéa has a procedure of ticking off her fingers; at the same time she associates them with numbers; and then she assures you that this is the way to get an answer to your question. Similarly, Seb arranges his coins and performs an operation on them. Then he places an interpretation on what he has done. And finally, he gives you his answer. So in both cases we can use *models to represent what happened.

PHOEBE. Let us see if I got this. There are several parts to your modelling. One is an abstract structure of one sort or another that you call the *presentation*; one is an interpretation of the presentation which you call the *representation*. Then there is an *agent* and a relationship between agent and presentation-cum-representation you called the *commitment*. A bit complicated, but with a little good will I think one can accept that.

JOHN. It certainly requires more good will than I have.

SANDERSON. Let me add two things. One is that the representation really contains two elements: a *language* appropriate for the presentation, and an *interpretation* of that language over the presentation.

PHOEBE. Which means that if we want to think in terms of the usual jargon we can think of a *model as a triple $\langle \mathcal{P}, \mathcal{L}, \mathcal{I} \rangle$, where $\mathcal{P}, \mathcal{L}$ and $\mathcal{I}$ are, respectively, the presentation, the language and the interpretation. But that still leaves out the commitment part.

JOHN. I should have warned you that Phoebe is a philosophy major. She is good at talking like that. Me you can disregard, I'm majoring in English.

SANDERSON. I see. Well, it is all right if you want to analyse the *model as you do. The way you put it, we are reminded of the models that logicians use. For some purposes that might be too demanding. Too exact. Up to a point it is fine. But there may be differences. For example, the presentation $\mathcal{P}$ may be vague, and the language $\mathcal{L}$ may be very restricted, perhaps just a fragment of a language.

But even more important – this is the second thing I wanted to add – it must be clear that the commitment part is a totally different kind of thing. It belongs to pragmatics, if you know what I mean. The commitment, like the agent, is outside the *model. Let me draw you a picture.

> *Goes to the blackboard. First draws a circle with the label $\mathfrak{M}$ attached to it. Then draws a little man outside the circle and a dotted line connecting him and the circle.*

JOHN. Great piece of art. What is it supposed to mean?

SANDERSON. The little man is the agent. It could be you, if you wish. (*Writes "John" under the little man.*) The dotted line represents your commitment to $\mathfrak{M}$. And $\mathfrak{M}$ is simply the *-model that represents the content to which you are committing yourself. The important thing is that you are literally outside the *model. The commitment is outside $\mathfrak{M}$—it belongs to pragmatics.

PHOEBE. So this figure illustrates "John knows that p", say. But suppose that I know that John knows p and I want to illustrate that. Then I need another circle?

SANDERSON. Yes.

Draws a big circle around all of the old figure on the blackboard and places a little woman under it with the name "Phoebe" attached.

PHOEBE. And then I should think of a new, more inclusive language appropriate for the more inclusive presentation. That is, I really need a bigger *model, $\mathfrak{M}'$ say.

SANDERSON. Correct. (*Attaches the label "$\mathfrak{M}'$" to the second circle.*) And notice that you are committing yourself to $\mathfrak{M}'$ but not to $\mathfrak{M}$.

PHOEBE. Although I could commit myself to $\mathfrak{M}$ as well, if I wanted to?

SANDERSON. Of course, but it would be an extra. And if I go on to say that Phoebe knows that John knows that p, then in effect I am adding yet another circle.

Draws a third circle around everything, attaching the label $\mathfrak{M}''$ to it, and under it draws a little man with the label "Sanderson" attached to it.

PHOEBE. I understand. But then it occurs to me the relationship between agent and *model can be of different kinds. This is something I had wanted to ask you about anyway. Surely there can be different kinds of relationships between agent and *model? Endorsement? Leaning towards? Liking? In short, having some kind of attitude?

JOHN. Like a propositional attitude? Isn't that a term you philosophers use?

SANDERSON. Actually I have thought of the relationship as the result of some action. Commitment and endorsements are actions, you know. But perhaps it is enough to have an attitude. I shall have to think about it. But thanks for the suggestion!

JOHN. Now what has all this got to do with knowledge?

SANDERSON. O.K., what does it mean to say that you know something? According to the idea that I have in mind it means that if you say something is true, then it need not be true but it has to be true in the *model that is implicit—the one to which you are committed.

JOHN. On your map the cities are red, the country is green, and the roads are black. So that is what you are committed to? New Zealand is green?

PHOEBE. That's silly, John!

SANDERSON. Well, you know, New Zealand *is* green! Seriously, there is an important point here: we are only allowed to view the presentation through the lens of the representation. That is why the language of the *model is important.

JOHN. The *language, perhaps. You see, I am with you!

SANDERSON. And that language – the *language, if you wish – is usually quite restricted. In the case of maps, if colours are not just merely decorative, one needs a code to interpret them.

PHOEBE. O.K., let me try to express this more formally, Would it be right to put this idea in the following way: a knows that p if and only if there is a *model $\mathfrak{M}$ such that

- a is committed to $\mathfrak{M}$,

    there is a formula ϕ of the language of $\mathfrak{M}$—the *language, to use John's term—such that $p = [[\phi]]_{\mathfrak{M}}$,

- $\mathfrak{M} \vDash \phi$.

SANDERSON. Here I suppose that $p = [[\phi]]_{\mathfrak{M}}$ means that what p means is expressed in $\mathfrak{M}$ by ϕ? And that $\mathfrak{M} \vDash \phi$ means that ϕ is true in $\mathfrak{M}$?

PHOEBE. Right. And if you replace "a is committed to $\mathfrak{M}$" by "a endorses $\mathfrak{M}$" or "a supports $\mathfrak{M}$" you get belief rather than knowledge?

SANDERSON. If we suppose that commitment is stronger than endorsement and support. Commitment should be maximal in some sense.

JOHN. Like you would be willing to bet your life on it?

SANDERSON. No, I don't want to get into betting ratios and all that. In fact, I am not sure knowledge should be seen as the limiting case of belief. Beliefs are easily formed. For the most part they are revisable. Some have hardened into knowledge. That is how I see knowledge: belief that is no longer revisable. Or, rather, belief that a rational agent would not think of revising.

JOHN. (*Ironically.*) Unless he really, really had to.

PHOEBE. Are you telling us that there is no real knowledge?

SANDERSON. What do you mean, "real knowledge"?

PHOEBE. Well, you know, real knowledge. Knowledge that must be right. Knowledge that will never need to be revised. Knowledge that cannot be revised. At least not by a reasonable person.

SANDERSON. So what is a reasonable person?

PHOEBE. Well, a rational person.

JOHN. So what about mathematical knowledge?

SANDERSON. (*On the defensive.*) Mathematical knowledge?

*

JOHN. Yes, mathematical knowledge. Most of us think that there is something special about mathematical knowledge: it is true—necessarily true. It is certain—absolutely certain. Is that just prejudice?

SANDERSON. Mathematical knowledge is a difficult one. But let us begin with prejudice, which is an interesting concept in its own right. Interesting also to epistemologists. Notice how you say "just prejudice"? The word "prejudice" has a bad ring to it. Many are prejudiced towards prejudice. But actually I think we need prejudice. In many situations there is not time to check everything, so you fall back on stock beliefs that you hold. And most of the time they serve you well. The fact that prejudice sometimes leads you astray is true, but it is a price you may have to pay.

PHOEBE. Non-monotonic logic? Tweety is a bird, and all that?

SANDERSON. Right. Prejudice is often like a set of default rules that you have. Jumping to a conclusion saves time. Even if you sometimes jump to the wrong conclusion, in general that is a price worth paying.

JOHN. You already said that.

SANDERSON. Forgive me, but you are here to interview me about what epistemic logic has done for knowledge, and I think of non-monotonic logic – some kinds, at least – as kinds of epistemic logic.

And Reiter's default logic is one of the most important. It does tell you something about knowledge. Or at least rational belief.

JOHN. Fine. Now tell me about mathematical knowledge.

SANDERSON. I agree that mathematical knowledge is a special case. Can we come back to that?

*

JOHN. O.K., let us go back to your theory of muddles. It smacks of relativism. Are you a relativist?

SANDERSON. In one sense, yes. Knowledge claims, like existence claims, are relative to a *model.

JOHN. I hate relativism. Does Santa Claus exist?

SANDERSON. No.

JOHN. But aren't there muddles in which he exists?

SANDERSON. Yes. But he does not exist in any *model that I am willing to endorse.

JOHN. Wouldn't your theory have made it difficult for Descartes to get started? "I think in a star muddle to which I am committed, therefore I am." It does not roll well off the tongue.

PHOEBE. Perhaps it sounds better in Latin.

JOHN. But what if you commit yourself to one muddle in which it is true that p and also commit yourself to another muddle in which it is false that p?

SANDERSON. Well, then I am contradicting myself.

JOHN. Worse than that: according to your own theory you know that p and also you know that not-p.

PHOEBE. I was going to ask about that. It is not a problem for your theory if it allows an agent to believe both p and not-p (although it may be a problem for the agent!). But to know both p and not-p does not sound right.

JOHN. Provided you agree that knowledge implies truth. Which I thought every epistemic logician would do, however crazy.

PHOEBE. In other words, do you really deny the validity of the T-schema?

JOHN. Excuse me, but what it the T-schema?

PHOEBE. The T-schema is the corner stone of epistemic logic, in symbols $\mathbf{K}\phi \to \phi$. In English: if you know that ϕ, then it is true that ϕ.

JOHN. You call that English?

SANDERSON. Let us see how I can explain this. In order to discuss formal logic, you need *models of a certain kind. In particular, the chosen *language must contain the operators you wish to study. You can certainly find *models that validate the T-schema, just as you can find *models that don't. In either case you may commit to the *model in question. But no-one, not even you, can think about this without going to a bigger *model that sort of engulfs the original *model. Moreover, depending on your conception of knowledge, you commit to the bigger *model only if the agent's attitude in the smaller *model is the right one. So to speak.

PHOEBE. Could you go over that again?

JOHN. Yeah, I couldn't follow him either.

SANDERSON. First we have a *model, $\mathfrak{M}$ say, with respect to which some statement p is true (meaning that $\mathfrak{M} \models \phi$, for some formula ϕ in the language of $\mathfrak{M}$ corresponding to the informal p). Then we want to bring knowledge into the picture. This means introducing an agent, a say, who has a certain attitude towards $\mathfrak{M}$. Now that we are considering a and his relšation to $\mathfrak{M}$ we have in fact introduced yet another *model, containing (representations of) a and $\mathfrak{M}$. Call this new *model $\mathfrak{M}'$. We will obviously be making a number of assumptions. For example, in a simple case we will assume that the language of $\mathfrak{M}$ is included in the language of $\mathfrak{M}'$, and we will take it that $\mathfrak{M}$ and $\mathfrak{M}'$ agree on what is common to the two languages. Most important in this context, if you are taking a Cartesian view of knowledge ...

JOHN. (*Interrupting.*) What is Cartesian knowledge?

SANDERSON. Knowledge that is indubitable and absolutely certain. As I was saying, if you are taking a Cartesian view of knowledge, then you must assume that the agent in $\mathfrak{M}'$ will not accept anything that can be said in the common language that is not true in $\mathfrak{M}$.

JOHN. What if $\mathfrak{M}$ got it wrong, then we would still say the agent knew everything in $\mathfrak{M}$? Including the falsehoods?

SANDERSON. We would say that he "knew" them. That he thought he knew them.

PHOEBE. So if I understand you, the validity of the T-schema is built into your modelling. That is, when it is valid in a *model it is because you have built the model in such a way as to validate it.

JOHN. I may not be as smart as Phoebe, but is seems to me that in stead of talking about the commitment of the agent you should be talking about, say, the *relation between agent and muddle. You decide what the relation is and then you, the analyst, evaluate it. You decide whether the agent knows something or not.

SANDERSON. You, the analyst, draw the picture. Every time it is the little man outside all the circles that draws the entire diagram.

PHOEBE. Or woman.

SANDERSON. The important thing is that the analyst is always on the outside.

JOHN. The pot of gold at the end of the rainbow!

SANDERSON. Let me just say, before moving on to networks of *models, that there are many topics to discuss in connexion with even a single *model. As far as I am concerned, the most difficult of them is getting knowing-how into the picture.

JOHN. To get know-how into the picture?

SANDERSON. Not know-how: knowing-how. There is a difference between knowing-that and knowing-how: knowing that something is the case, and knowing how to do something. The Germans have different words for this: the *wissen-können* stuff, you know.

PHOEBE. Knowing-that and knowing-how? That's interesting. How about knowing-who, knowing-when, knowing-why? Perhaps there are other concepts like that?

SANDERSON. I think the idea is that if you can handle knowing-that and knowing-how, you should be able to take care of the others as well. Anyway, as I have said before, knowledge and belief are very closely connected with action. So here we are leaving out a big chunk.

JOHN. Good, we have not got all day. Was there anything else?

*

SANDERSON. If we are interested in epistemic agents, if I may call them that, then the concept of a *model is only a beginning. Here is how I see our agenda:

§1 Defining '*model'.

§2 Defining 'network of *models'.

§3 Studying how networks of *models change over time.

The first point, §1, we have already dealt with. Of course there are numerous other things to discuss but, as John points out, time is limited. Let us move on to §2: networks.

An agent has a lot of representations of those aspects of the world that are of interest to him. You may think of this as a craftsman having lots of tools. The *models we have talked may be interrelated. I can think of three basic relationships, although there may be others: subsumption, refinement, and allotropy. Again, maps provide an excellent example. If you cut out a piece of a bigger map, you may be said to have a *submap* of the larger map.

PHOEBE. So it makes sense to talk about "sub-*models", even though the term is awkward. Perhaps "*submodels" is better. The *model $\mathfrak{M}$ we just talked about is a *submodel of the bigger *model $\mathfrak{M}'$.

SANDERSON. Sometimes a map of a country will contain maps of the bigger cities of that country which appear like filled cirles or something on the main map; those smaller maps may be said to be *(partial) refinements* of the big map. Finally, you may map out different aspects of one and the same object. For example, you may have lots of different maps of the same city: a subway map, a street map, a geological map, and so on. In this case we use the term *allotropy*: those maps are all allotropes.

JOHN. "Allotropy" is a term chemists use for the property of a substance to exist in more than one form.

SANDERSON. That is right. Anyway, to make a long story short, in order to represent an agent's knowledge along these lines, we should think of a big network of *models interrelated in the ways mentioned. And perhaps others!

PHOEBE. Perhaps we should also be thinking of what the agent can do with these *models. Perhaps this is another place where the distinction between *wissen* and *können* comes in. At a higher level this time.

*

JOHN. Speaking of time, I'm not sure I can stay much longer.

PHOEBE. Speaking of time, shouldn't we talk also about change? Wasn't that §3 on your agenda?

SANDERSON. Of course, change is important. If we want to model the knowledge of an agent, we must consider change. A network of *models can only give the epistemic state of an agent at a particular time. But the epistemic state may change at any time. There are changes of at least two kinds: change due to new information and change due to introspection.

JOHN. It is obvious that we process new information almost all the time. But introspection?

SANDERSON. Introspection also goes on almost all the time. We reflect about what we know or believe. We see new connexions. We discover contradictions. We continue to work on *models we have already accepted.

PHOEBE. Trying to clean up, as it were.

SANDERSON. Suppose you review your current network of *models. Suddenly you realize that there is an implicit contradiction in the network. Obviously you try to revise it to get rid of the inconsistency. Or suddenly you see a connexion between two or more *models that sort of fuse into one. Or you add a new *model that is somehow inspired by the old one.

PHOEBE. Like set theoretical union?

SANDERSON. Union is one example, but union is more than union, if you know what I mean.

JOHN. Union is more than union?

SANDERSON. Yes: there may be something creative about the new *model that goes beyond the old ones. The new *model may be greater than the sum of the old ones. Call it "fusion". It has to do with getting an insight! Realizing something you knew without knowing you knew!

JOHN. You know, I sort of like this. I know without knowing, and the fusion is greater than the fuses. Confusion is greater than Confus-ius. It has a nice rhythm to it.

SANDERSON. Confus-ius? Do you mean Confucius? I don't understand.

PHOEBE. Don't pay any attention to John, Mr Anderson, he is just being silly. What I would like to know is this: Isn't change due to new information what is studied in the theory of belief revision?

SANDERSON. Yes, that has mushroomed into a big industry. But I think there is still room for more work. Personally, I am particularly interested in the concept of metaphor. Did you ever notice that new information can come in the form of a metaphor?

PHOEBE. I am sure metaphor has other uses than conveying information.

SANDERSON. No doubt, but conveying information is one of them. And when successful, it can be a very economic way of communication. Metaphor is of course intimately connected with change. Here knowledge change and language change go hand in hand.

PHOEBE. Could you be more precise?

SANDERSON. Successful metaphors function as a kind of inference rules. Suppose a poet says, "Oh, the pain when bud bursts into flower!".

JOHN. That is not even a sentence.

SANDERSON. That's right. Not a declarative one, at any rate.

JOHN. And it does not convey new knowledge. In fact, it is false: flowers don't feel anything.

SANDERSON. I suppose not. But in certain situations or contexts even a metaphor like that one may give you new knowledge—or perhaps we should call it insight or information. I can suggest a number of possible contexts in which the poet's outburst can make you draw an inference.

PHOEBE. Non-monotonic inference?

SANDERSON. Of course. An inference rule that you apply only if you want to. At your own risk and only if you want to. Take the phrase I quoted about the pain when buds burst into flowers. Here are some very simple examples.

First context: we are discussing teenagers and their problems. One possible inference is that it is painful to be a teenager. Which may be news to some. Another possible inference is that it is painful to have to deal with teenagers. Which also may be news to some.

Second context: we are discussing the economic situation today and the phenomenon of merger—smaller companies merging with or being swallowed up by bigger ones. One possible inference: that for some, economic growth can be painful.

Third context: ...

PHOEBE. (*Interrupting.*) But that is not generating new knowledge, it is rather focussing on features we already know. It makes knowledge we already have more vivid. It makes you see things, if you know what I mean.

SANDERSON. Metaphor certainly has that function as well. But I insist that metaphor can be a quick and effective method of transmitting information.

PHOEBE. But not reliable. A metaphor provides a form, you fill it with meaning.

JOHN. Now, there's a metaphor! I wonder what it means?

SANDERSON. But isn't it the same with inference rules?

PHOEBE. This is too vague for me. Shouldn't you work out a theory to back you up?

SANDERSON. I entirely agree. It would be nice if I could. Only I don't yet know how to do it. We need a topology for the space of (some class of) *models. Each metaphor inducing its own topology, you know. A metaphorical statement is usually either nonsensical or blatantly false in the *model with respect to which you are trying to evaluate it. So you need another *model to make sense. And that *model must be relevant to your concerns—as close to your current *model as possible.

PHOEBE. That is why you want topology, to express nearness?

SANDERSON. Right. But there are all sorts of problems. For example, metaphors are often incomplete in the sense that they can be cashed out in different ways. And there is in the class of metaphors a relation of subdivision or refinement that makes communication stimulating but also treacherous: the sender may have one subdivision in mind, while the receiver may seize upon another.

PHOEBE. But people have written tons about this. Do we really need epistemic logic here?

SANDERSON. Well, the theory of metaphor may not need epistemic logic, but for me as an epistemic logician it would be interesting to see whether some of the most important features of metaphor could not be analysed within the theory of belief revision. I think it would be possible.

JOHN. Why am I suddenly reminded of Dr Johnson's dancing dogs?

PHOEBE. John, that's not nice!

JOHN. (*Unperturbed.*) So what about mathematical knowledge?

SANDERSON. I wish the Professor were here to answer that one ...

JOHN. The Professor! The Old Fog! This is like waiting for Godot. I am leaving.

*

PHOEBE. (*Politely.*) I am afraid we have already stayed too long.

JOHN. We certainly have! At least I have. I thought we would be learning something about epistemic logic. But your muddles don't seem to have anything to do with anything.

PHOEBE. Don't think I haven't enjoyed our conversation. But at the same time I have to agree with John that I had expected something different. I understand that there is a lot of really important work going on in contemporary epistemic logic. The TARK conferences! The Amsterdam school! You might have told us about that.

SANDERSON. But you are philosophers! Much of what is going on in epistemic logic today might is really epistemic engineering.

JOHN AND PHOEBE. Epistemic engineering!

PHOEBE. That sounds patronizing.

JOHN. Disrespectful, I would say.

SANDERSON. No, no, I don't want to be appear either patronizing or lacking in respect. Engineering is very important. For example, it was engineering that put men on the moon, one of the most astounding feats of our time. Without the engineers we would never have got there. But just as we need philosophy of science to understand what scientists do, so we need philosophy of epistemic logic to understand what those clever people in epistemic logic do. What what they do has to do with knowledge. I mean, philosophy of soccer is not the same as soccer.

JOHN. Great! We sure need philosophy of soccer. Like we need philosophy of muddles.

PHOEBE. It is actually an interesting idea: in order to understand soccer it is not enough to play it. Not necessary, of course, but perhaps not sufficient either. Perhaps Mr Anderson is right.

JOHN. Understand soccer!

SANDERSON. I think there must something more to the philosophy of epistemic logic that just building those very technical models. That is all I am trying to say, really. (*With some emotion.*) That is what my muddled and ridiculed efforts were aimed at.

JOHN. (*Unperturbed.*) You mean "*modelled" efforts, don't you. The star silent, of course.

SANDERSON. No, I really mean "muddled". I am trying to work all this out, but as you can tell I find it difficult.

PHOEBE. I think I know what you mean. Game theory, for example. It has an important rôle in the analysis of rationality.

SANDERSON. Essential.

PHOEBE. O.K., game theory has an essential rôle in the analysis of rationality. It helps us define a kind of rationality. Or one kind of rationality. But mathematical analysis of abstract games is not the same as philosophical understanding of rationality.

SANDERSON. The theory of games is a beautiful creation. And of course I agree that game theory contributes to our understanding of rationality. In the same way I would hold that epistemic logic contributes to our understanding of knowledge and belief. I only wish I could understand more exactly how!

JOHN. I thought that was what you were supposed to tell us. That's why we came!

SANDERSON. Well, believe me or not, I have done my best. By the way, in epistemic logic I include doxastic logic.

PHOEBE. You might as well regard epistemic logic as a special case of doxastic logic.

SANDERSON. That is actually what I do, but I have common linguistic usage against me.

*

JOHN. So let's see what we have. (*Gets out a notebook and starts writing.*) You think there is a need for epistemic logic in order to analyse knowledge,

SANDERSON. Yes, I think epistemic logic has a rôle to play.

JOHN. Furthermore, you think that current epistemic logic must widen its purview, notably by paying more attention to the agent.

SANDERSON. And why knowledge is important to him.

PHOEBE. Or her.

SANDERSON. Something like that. The pragmatic aspect.

JOHN. You think that what is going on today is just epistemic engineering.

SANDERSON. That is not what I said. Epistemic engineering, as I called it, is very important. And I will tell you this: if my programme—vague and feckless as it may be ...

JOHN. What does "feckless" mean?

SANDERSON. In this context, how about "futile". If my programme were to be successful, then it, too, might develop into epistemic engineering. If it were useful, that is. If not useful, it would simply develop into another branch of mathematics.

JOHN. Not so fast, I am trying to take notes. "If not useful, it would become just mathematics."

SANDERSON. Not "just mathematics": just "mathematics". You see, there is a general pattern in abstract thinking. Ideas worth anything, if they have a minimum of structure, eventually they will be formalized. Formalisms, once born, live lives of their own. Mature formalizations grow into new disciplines. Eventually they may ossify—that happens. In rare cases they may even, in a sense, die.

JOHN. Wow! Quite a speech. So all formal philosophy ends in ossification and death?

SANDERSON. Again, that is not what I said. At least it is not what I meant to say. Perhaps all I want to say is, if you push formal philosophy too far, it ceases to be philosophy. But that isn't necessarily a bad thing. Think of the ugly duckling!

JOHN. Philosophy as the ugly duckling. Brilliant!

SANDERSON. I have a feeling you aren't really trying to understand what I am trying to say. But then I realize I am not very good at expressing what I think. I am as bad as the Professor.

JOHN. Not to worry. I am beginning to think I might be able to use some of this, after all.

*

Enter the children, Charlotta Linnéa carrying a drawing.

PHOEBE. Oh, a drawing. How nice!

CHARLOTTA LINNÉA. (*Walks up to John.*) For you!

PHOEBE. What is it? May I see? What a beautiful bird! Oh, I get it! (*Laughs.*) It is a parrot! And it has a little beard, just like John!

JOHN. (*Not amused.*) I'm out of here. Good-bye!

SANDERSON. Wait a second, what about mathematical knowledge? If you wish I could try to say something.

JOHN. Some other time! (*Prepares to leave.*)

CHARLOTTA LINNÉA. (*Importantly.*) I have a question. For you!

She points at John, clearly enjoying being the centre of attention.

CHARLOTTA LINNÉA. Why is water wet?

JOHN. I haven't got the foggiest idea.

SEBASTIAN. (*Surprised.*) That's what Grandpa always says!

John leaves.

CHARLOTTA LINNÉA. (*With evident satisfaction.*) *I* knew the answer to *my* question.

PHOEBE. (*To Charlotta Linnéa.*) I know you did! (*To Sanderson.*) I apologize for John, Mr Anderson. He is really much nicer than you might think. But Philosophy isn't his thing, you know.

SANDERSON. So I gathered. I'm not sure I want to read his article.

PHOEBE. It's clear John did not understand you. And perhaps didn't want to. But I promise to keep an eye on the article before it is published. Now, I wonder if what you are trying to say is something like this.

Knowledge and belief are philosophically central concepts. Epistemic logic has an important rôle to play in coming to a philosophical understanding of them.

SANDERSON. Indispensable.

PHOEBE. Indispensable. Nevertheless, being able to process claims to knowledge or belief isn't all there is to the philosophy of knowledge and belief. (*Pause.*) But that is obvious, isn't it?

SANDERSON. (*With some bitterness.*) That's the problem with philosophy (my problem, at least): what I don't understand is beyond my comprehension, what I understand is trivial.

PHOEBE. (*Laughing.*) You are too young to be a cynic, Mr Anderson!

SEBASTIAN. I am hungry. Let us go to McDonald's.

SANDERSON. O.K., I can take you to Starbucks.

CHARLOTTA LINNÉA. (*Points at Phoebe.*) She can come, too. She is nice!

PHOEBE. Thank you, I'd love to come. Then perhaps I can get a picture of you and your brother?

CHARLOTTA LINNÉA. And Sanderson.

PHOEBE. And Sanderson!

THE END

26
Ernest Sosa

Professor of Philosophy

Rutgers – The State University of New Jersey, USA

Why were you initially drawn to epistemology (and what keeps you interested)?

Several bits of luck first drew me to epistemology. Although at work on my dissertation while holding my first job in philosophy, I had not yet committed to any long-term research program, nor even to a subfield. I had come to philosophy late, in the summer between my junior and senior years as an undergraduate at the University of Miami, when I first encountered interesting philosophical texts, especially the writings of Bertrand Russell. These I found by accident, while browsing in a bookstore. My senior year then consisted of twelve philosophy courses, after which I went for graduate work to the University of Pittsburgh, the only place where I applied. As a college senior I had been too naïve, too busy with my twelve courses, and with no philosophy record to support my application. I got into Pitt because when I applied it was still a lowly program. (By contrast, my six fellow graduating seniors at the wonderful Miami department all won multi-year fellowships at excellent graduate programs.) Already as I traveled on my bus trip from Miami to Pittsburgh at the end of that summer, however, the Pitt department was beginning its meteoric rise from its then lowly status to the lofty heights that it soon reached, and has since then remarkably retained. During my one undergraduate philosophy year I had no course in epistemology, nor did I have any in my two years of graduate work at Pitt. Only in my first year of teaching, at the University of Western Ontario, did I come across a question in epistemology that gripped me immediately, and that would never afterwards release its grip. The question was that of the nature of knowledge, which I had encountered already by reading the *Theaetetus* in a Plato course. It had not then aroused my interest, however, not as it would in the form given to it by Ed Gettier in his celebrated note. I came across Gettier's paper while leafing through the pages of *Analysis* at the Western Ontario library. The first few sentences went by swiftly, as I stood next to the periodicals shelf, but I was soon struggling with the counterexamples, testing in my head successive revisions of the JTB analysis. The problem was not to be solved standing by those shelves, however, and I was soon settled into a comfortable library seat for some extended thought. Eventually I had a solution to propose and it was, I believe, the second published attempt to solve the Gettier problem, appearing in the 1964 *Analysis* volume.

Having sent my paper off, I awaited on tenterhooks the Editor's eventually favorable response, but another bit of excellent news preceded that: I was granted a two-year postdoctoral fellowship at Brown University. Upon arrival at Brown, with my Pitt diploma in my bags, I immediately came under the spell of someone with a philosophical style and persona the likes of which I had never come across: Roderick Chisholm, then at the height of his creativity. I soon joined several excellent graduate students, and some young faculty, including Jaegwon Kim, in auditing Chisholm's seminar every semester. I still had taken no course in epistemology, but of course had been thinking about epistemology in my solitary struggle with the Gettier problem. Chisholm's seminars were my first formal introduction to epistemology. He did not by then teach the subject often, as his teaching had switched to metaphysics. But he was still at work in the field, and to my delight would regularly invite me to discuss his ideas with him. At that point we still did not have individual computers, so our conversations were either through regular mail, or in person, or most often by telephone. That did not prove much of an obstacle: we discussed philosophy frequently, epistemology in particular, sometimes daily, as he worked on the first edition of his great epistemology text, *Theory of Knowledge*, published in 1966.

That is how I was initially drawn to the field. What keeps me interested is that the questions are so hard to answer with any permanent satisfaction. So it is my stubborn desire for satisfying answers that keeps me trying. Combined with that stubbornness is an optimism that my eventually preferred approach, "virtue epistemology," and "virtue perspectivism" more specifically, is headed in the right direction.

What do you see as being your main contributions to epistemology?

I propose that we understand human knowledge in terms of virtue epistemology. I say that knowledge is a kind of performance, to be evaluated in the distinctive terms of performance normativity. Performances generally have an aim, and attain success if and only if they reach their aim. The aim can be reached by luck, however, in which case that performance falls short of one that attains its aim not just through luck but through competence. Such performance I call "apt." An apt performance is one whose success is sufficiently attributable to the relevant competence exercised by the performer. Beliefs and judgments I view as performances of a certain sort, cognitive performances. So our three sorts of positive assessment can be applied to this special case. Thus, a belief can attain its aim, by being true. A belief can also manifest the believer's epistemic competence. In this case it is not only true, or accurate, but also competent, or adroit. A belief can be both accurate and adroit, however, while still falling short in a third important respect: it can fail to be *apt*, that is to say, accurate because adroit. These are main ideas of the sort of virtue epistemology that I advocate. They must be supplemented, however, and I am actively engaged in doing so, with several recent publications – including *A Virtue Epistemology* (OUP, 2007) – and others forthcoming, some of these in press.

One main set of issues has dominated epistemological reflection through the centuries: the Pyrrhonian problematic. These issues figure prominently among the ancients as the problem of the diallelus. They recur as the problem of the Cartesian Circle. And most recently they are highlighted by Chisholm in his repeated attacks on the "problem of the criterion." It seems to me that the best approach to this hoary problematic involves a distinction between two levels of knowledge, the animal and the reflective. In a forthcoming book, *Reflective Knowledge* (OUP, in press), I develop this approach, and argue for its superiority over main proposals advanced in the history of our discipline, including several in recent decades.

What do you think is the proper role of epistemology in relation to other areas of philosophy and other academic disciplines?

Epistemology in my view has its own autonomy and integrity,

and does not *depend* on interdisciplinary relations. All the same, it must not resist or avoid such relations. On the contrary, epistemology is enriched through cross-fertilizing relations to other subfields of our discipline and to nearby areas in other disciplines altogether. In recent years and decades, epistemology has benefited from its relations to philosophy of mind, cognitive science, and philosophy of language. In earlier decades it had already interacted fruitfully with metaphysics, as in the controversies concerning the ontology of perception in the first half of the twentieth century. Metaethics and moral epistemology are also relevant here, as is the epistemology of the a priori sciences. Finally, the epistemology of philosophy itself is drawing intense attention in recent years.

What do you consider to be the most neglected topics and/or contributions in contemporary epistemology?

Issues of epistemic agency form a fascinating cluster of topics that might reward closer, more sustained attention. Here I include the nature of reasons and reasoning, including deductive reasoning. Issues of wisdom and its relation to knowledge might also reward attention at this stage in the history of our subdiscipline. More generally, the epistemology of the humanities might be worth deeper study, and here I would include a study of how we form judgments competently in areas where scientific knowledge and objectivity seem out of human reach. The recent interest in the epistemology of disagreement may eventually bring such issues into starker relief, as we struggle with how best to accommodate the evident fact of persistent disagreement among apparent intellectual peers. Because such disagreement seems of a different and much more troubling order in the humanities, the problem of sustained reasonable judgment in such domains is especially problematic. I would not claim that this territory contains gold, but I do think it bears prospecting.

What do you think the future of epistemology will (or should) hold?

I have no idea. In fact, I anticipate no dramatic shift. If I did, I would explore this issue more vigorously. The main, fundamental questions that most interest me are those that interested Plato in his *Theaetetus* and Descartes in his *Meditations*, and some of interest to Aristotle in his *Nicomachean Ethics*, to mention only some highlights in the history of our discipline. The span of options presented by the issues taken up in those great works are among those we still debate today. I expect that they are ones we'll still debate tomorrow.

27
Wolfgang Spohn

Professor for Philosophy
and Philosophy of Science
University of Konstanz, Germany

Why were you initially drawn to epistemology (and what keeps you interested)?

I have the honor to be invited to this series for a second time. The first time, in its very first volume on Formal Philosophy, I told how I became determined to study philosophy when I was 16. So, let me add another bit of autobiography.

It is common for adolescents to approach philosophy via practical philosophy. One wants to know what is good and bad, right and wrong, one seeks guidance. I was no different. I recall having written a very idiosyncratic tractatus on the logic of volition (in retrospect a strange thing to do after the high school diploma). This interest continued till the present day, as is reflected in my master thesis on dyadic or conditional deontic logic (containing a correctness and completeness proof of an axiomatization of that logic discovered simultaneously with David Lewis' *Counterfactuals* (1973), but published only as Spohn (1975), my first publication), in my dissertation (1976/78) on decision theory, and in my ongoing work on decision and game theory and practical rationality in general.

How, though, could I not get interested in epistemology, with Wolfgang Stegmüller being my teacher and Rudolf Carnap being my philosophical hero at that time? I had the great luck of being employed by Stegmüller at a research project on de Finetti's philosophy of probability when I was 21. There, I just learned so much about that philosophy and the accompanying mathematics (and was even paid for it). Since then I keep claiming that probability theory is as important to philosophy as logic, a message not well respected by our curricula.

Another point I recall to have been important was that I concluded from my master thesis that the volitional or deontic side needs to be complemented by the doxastic or cognitive side; the former cannot be pursued independently of the latter; and the really interesting issue is the interplay of the theoretical and the practical attitudes. This interplay could apparently not be stated on a qualitative level. This is how I came to study decision theory in my dissertation (1976/78). Since decision theory is deeply entangled with issues of causation, I got ever more entangled, too, and finally wrote my Habilitationsschrift (1983) about causation. Thus, I moved more and more to epistemology. Or rather, my interest in theoretical philosophy in general became the dominating one which also covers philosophy of science, philosophy of language and mind and ontology and metaphysics.

What keeps me interested? Even the basics of many epistemological issues are in an unsatisfactory state. There are simply so many things left to do (see also below).

What do you see as being your main contributions to epistemology?

Ranking theory, of course. I remember the day in April 1982 when I finally knew how to do it; in retrospect I am surprised how difficult it was to come up with so simple a structure. It then formed a cornerstone of my Habilitationsschrift (1983) about causation. There, my aim was to reunite the theory of causation that seemed to have fallen apart into a deterministic and a probabilistic branch, with little communalities and communication in between. I felt that the probabilistic branch was much more advanced, roughly because of its much more sophisticated treatment of relevance relations provided by probability theory that found no counterpart whatsoever on the deterministic side. Ranking theory was designed to achieve the very same in the deterministic realm. Since then I keep claiming that there is a theory of causation that works exactly the same way for the deterministic and the probabilistic domain. This is a claim I still deeply believe in, though it has not been widely perceived. One reason may have been that the resulting theory of causation looked so dissuasively subjective; but that would be a misperception. The other reason certainly was that the theory of deterministic causation was dominated by the counterfactual approach and that the philosophers working within that approach did not take much notice of ranking theory, perhaps also because of my bad publication policy. I am confident this will change.

Well, what is ranking theory? This is certainly not the place for an introduction; I refer to my first English publication on the topic, Spohn (1988), and to the survey article Spohn (forthcoming a). One noteworthy fact is that initially I had given it a silly name, "the theory of ordinal conditional functions", and that I happily accepted the advice of Judea Pearl and Moises Goldszmidt in the early 90's to call it by the present name. The other noteworthy fact is that it is a theory of belief (or disbelief), in fact, as I claim, the only adequate, fully dynamic theory of belief (that is, contrary to appearances, *not* provided by belief revision theory, as I realized after a long struggle finally giving birth to ranking theory). *Could there be anything more central to epistemology?* (As long as one does not speak of knowledge; for some remarks on the theory of belief and the theory of knowledge see below.)

There is the beautiful book *The Probable and the Provable* by Cohen (1977) (which I did not know at that time) which expounded a far-reaching parallel or dualism between, well, the probable and the provable (not in the logical or mathematical, but rather in the juridical sense), between what he called Pascalian and Baconian probability in Cohen (1980). I like the latter terms very much. Of course, "Baconian probability" is a euphemism. There never was a theory of Baconian probability; Pascalian, genuine probability is centuries ahead. Alternatives, something like a formal theory, started only with Shackle (1949), and I feel that ranking theory finally established Baconian probability as a full, independent, and most fruitful theory. (It did so, I think, by transcending the predecessors by a hitherto unexplained notion of *conditional ranks* on which all the dynamic theorizing depends.)

I said that ranking theory is *the* theory of belief (or disbelief), and I mentioned causation as one important application. This may be reason enough to value this theory. What makes me really fond of it is its far-reaching parallel to probability theory that carried a 25 years long and nowhere exhausted research program. I knew about the parallel from the outset (see my remarks above about causation). So, the obvious move was to translate important and beautiful facts about probability into ranking theory. This looks like an automatic procedure, a simple working program. In some way this is true, although one must always reckon with mathematical niceties. The fact, however, that even surprised me was that the translation always resulted into something meaningful and important, something providing new insights into long-standing issues in philosophy of science and epistemology. Indeed, sometimes it was the other around. I thought about the issue, found a way of treating it with ranking theoretic means, and then noticed that this treatment parallels something well known from probability theory. If this is true, my enthusiasm is so as well.

What I have just indicated raises the deep question of the relation between probability and ranking theory, again an issue which I cannot discuss here and for which I have no conclusive response. There is a formal unification (cf. Spohn (forthcoming a), sect. 3.1) the substantial sense of which still escapes me. Therefore, my attitude has always been what I call methodological separatism that may not be satisfying, but is, I think, the best we can do. The simple fact is: belief and probability do not easily mesh, and no one has a good idea how they do. (Well, Isaac Levi is closest to such ideas, but I have doubts about his program; cf. Spohn (2006).) However, despite apparently unbridgeable gaps the parallel works, as indicated, in a most fruitful way. Of course, there are characteristic differences as well. On the negative side we find that decision theory, or practical reasoning in general, is a probabilistic affair. The best ranking theoretic analogue I know of is Giang, Shenoy (2000), but I am still unsure whether it makes more than formal sense. Secondly, we there find statistics, of course. However, on that score the difference is not so large as it may seem; there are quite a number of phenomena in science that are better treated in a ranking theoretic than in a statistical way; and the relation between statistics and ranking theory may be closer than expected (cf. Hild, to appear). On the positive side we find that ranking theory is a theory of belief, a notion probabilistically inexplicable (as the lottery paradox shows), that is related to truth in a way in which subjective probabilities are not and is thus connectible to all of traditional epistemology in a straightforward way. I do not say that probability and ranking theory are on a par. How could they after probability theory alone fills libraries? But if we find that probability theory has a little sister that can do many things equally well and some things even better than the big sister, this would be more than a surprise.

This is, by far, enough of self-advertising. Let me rush on.

What do you think is the proper role of epistemology in relation to other areas of philosophy and other academic disciplines?

First to philosophy! A preliminary rough grip on the history of philosophy divides the philosophical eras according to their leading discipline of theoretical philosophy; ethics never changed its importance. In ancient times metaphysics and ontology formed the *prima philosophia*; this is still true of the medieval times. In the 17th century, with the Enlightenment, epistemology took the leading role. And in the beginning of the 20th century we experienced the linguistic turn; philosophy had to first look at meanings and to start with philosophy of language. This era lasted for a surprisingly short time. (Well, perhaps not surprisingly; the number of philosophers grew exponentially, and so the length of philosophical eras might be expected to diminish exponentially.) I date its end with Kripke's *Naming and Necessity* and his rearrangement of modalities, others may date it with Rawls' *Theory of Justice* and his return from metaethics to material ethics; there is no sharp transition, anyway. (But let me hasten to add how glad I feel to have grown up in the era of philosophy of language; it had to teach so many invaluable lessons.)

And today? There is no longer any primacy of one discipline over the others; that would be presumptuous. Epistemology is just one central discipline of theoretical philosophy; metaphysics and ontology, philosophy of language and philosophy of mind are others; logic is a presupposition of all of them; and still others I find less central. However, I have a picture how the central disciplines relate:

Philosophy of mind falls into two parts. On the one hand, there is the mind-body problem. I tend to subsume it under ontology; after all, the main stances towards it, various forms of dualism and monism, are all ontological positions. On the other hand, there is the problem of intentionality; this is perhaps the most common label. It concerns the representational capacities of the mind, the nature of contents, the status of meanings; and it is the one justifying speaking of the philosophy of mind *and* language. So, in this extended sense we are left with ontology, epistemology, and philosophy of language. And the picture I have in mind relates theses three fields:

In my view, their relation is founded by two-dimensional semantics. This is a line of research deeply suggested by Saul Kripke and Hilary Putnam, definitely started by David Kaplan and Robert

Stalnaker, with discontinuous progress and presently with devoted disciples (like David Chalmers) in a largely skeptical or ignorant environment; its shape is not too good, and not too bad. I am one of its determinate defenders, too. Intensions, "senses", had a determinately epistemological character from Frege onwards. With Kripke and his predecessors like Ruth Barcan Marcus and Dagfinn Føllesdal intentions took on an ontological character. Two-dimensional semantics started with the insight that there are two different notions of an intension (of a linguistic expression). And it proposed to integrate these two notions into one scheme. Thus, the meaning of a linguistic expression became two-dimensional; its extension became doubly dependent, dependent on an ontological and on an epistemological dimension, on two dimensions of possibility, ontological and epistemological possibility. How precisely this double dependence should be construed is deeply contested. Still, I firmly believe into the truth of the basic scheme. It provides a fundamental connection between ontology, epistemology, and the theory of meaning. Whether it entails a primacy among these fields is not really of importance. My view is that one needs to develop ontology and epistemology and to pursue the consequences for the philosophy of language via the two-dimensional scheme. (For more on my picture, see Spohn (forthcoming b), introduction and chapters 14 and 16.)

Did I forget about metaphysics? It is not so clear what "metaphysics" presently denotes. Sometimes, it is taken as tantamount to ontology; and then it is part of the scheme indicated. Sometimes, it is taken to go beyond ontology in various ways. I shall comment on some of these ways below.

What is the relation of epistemology to other academic disciplines? This is, in a way, by far the more important issue; it addresses long-standing jealousies and misunderstandings between philosophy and the sciences. The basic issue is: who is first, the hen or the egg, philosophy or the sciences? Sciences seek knowledge; but then epistemology must first tell what that is and how to do it. Or the acquisition of knowledge is one of the many processes in the world that need to be studied by science. This opposition was paradigmatically exposed in Quine's famous essay *Epistemology Naturalized* and dissolved in favor of the naturalistic attitude.

The traditional version of this issue or opposition is this: Science makes knowledge claims, and they have to be justified. To some extent, this justification may refer to other knowledge claims; ultimately, though, this must be avoided, on pain of circularity. It is epistemology which is the judge of those claims, and it must be so on an a priori basis; otherwise, we would fall back into circularity. Very well. But then one looks at the poverty of centuries of aprioristic epistemology and thinks, as Quine did, how weird this conception is. No wonder how *in* naturalized epistemology presently is.

As I said, however, this is a big misunderstanding. Of course, naturalized epistemology is most valuable. We need to study how cognition actually works. This is not an inquiry confined to psychology and neurophysiology. It needs to be, and actually is, carried out on all human levels; it has not only an individual, but also a social and indeed a huge historical dimension. And many are working at it, from the biochemist to the historian of ideas. Philosophy always contributed to it. How else, for instance, can it be understood when Hume is widely admired and extensively quoted even in not so old teaching books of cognitive psychology as the founder of associationist psychology? In fact, naturalized epistemology had not been invented by Quine. For instance, the famous Austrian biologist and ethologist Konrad Lorenz has proposed an evolutionary reinterpretation of Kant long before (see Lorenz 1941).

We may grant all this. This is not to grant, however, that aprioristic epistemology would be meaningless or fruitless or superfluous. On the contrary, it is of the same importance as naturalized epistemology. It only needs to be properly understood.

There is a deep philosophical dispute how apriority is to be adequately explained. I can certainly not engage into it here. Let me only state my favorite explication: A feature of a doxastic state is *unrevisably a priori* if and only if all doxastic states capable of having it necessarily have it. (This is accompanied by a twin notion: A feature of a doxastic state is *defeasibly a priori* iff all initial doxastic states have it – where all depends on explaining initiality. But let us not pursue the twin notion.) So, in general it is such features that are a priori. That a proposition is believed in a doxastic state is a possible feature of the state. Hence, more specifically, a proposition is a priori iff it is necessarily believed in all doxastic states grasping it. (Note, by the way, how much better ranking theoretically conceived doxastic states are able to substantiate this definition than probabilistically conceived.)

It seems that this cannot be taken literally. People believe all kinds of nonsense and do not believe the most obvious things. So, hardly anything survives as a priori. However, this is not how the explication is to be read. It only refers to all *rational* doxastic states that conform to the principles epistemic rationality. Not that this would be clear. But it shifts the discussion to its proper place. There is not only naturalized epistemology, there is also *normative* epistemology that tells us what we should rationally believe or, more generally, how our doxastic states should rationally be. *The normativity is the source of the apriority.* Of course, the content of the norms of rationality is disputed and thus also the extension of apriority. How could it be otherwise? However, it is a legitimate dispute, and it is one about apriority.

Indeed, no one can doubt the legitimacy of normative epistemology. All scientists should welcome it since they are great practitioners of normative epistemology. All life long we face the question: what should we believe? Usually, this is a matter of course, but in complex epistemic situations some explicit guidance is most helpful. Such situations particularly obtain in the sciences. Each discipline has an elaborated methodology how to epistemically proceed; and methodology is normative through and through.

There is a lot of truth in the slogan: methodology follows content. Therefore scientists tend to become nervous when confronted with general principles by philosophers; they feel intruded into their domain of competence. However, the slogan cannot be the whole truth; there must be a rule how methodology follows content, and that rule cannot depend on content in turn. In other words, there must be a priori epistemic norms; epistemologists try to find out which they are; and of course they have to relate their findings with scientific practice, if only hypothetically, not apodictically. Normative theorizing is no less difficult than empirical research. Unlike cognitive science it is not an interdisciplinary enterprise, though; with the exception of statisticians philosophers are left alone, perhaps because empirical scientists hardly dare talking of normativity.

My basic point should be clear by now. There is no opposition whatsoever between aprioristic and naturalized epistemology. On the contrary, they necessarily and easily coexist. The reason is that epistemology is subject to both perspectives, the empirical and the normative, and that the a priori principles or features derive from the normative perspective. As things stand, the empirical perspective is mainly pursued in the cognitive sciences (although philosophers also engage in something like experimental philosophy), and the normative perspective is mainly pursued by philosophers. This is how epistemologists and scientists remain bound to inform each other.

What do you consider to be the most neglected topics and/or contributions in contemporary epistemology?

In my first contribution to this series I already made some general remarks about the well- and malfunctioning of historic memory in philosophy. In general, my complaints are little. In particular, I am not aware of any badly neglected topics or contributions in epistemology. I have three concerns, however:

The *first* concern is about the relation between the normative and the empirical perspective on epistemology I just spoke about. I find that normative epistemologists are too defensive about their mission, maybe because they are not trendy and to some extent marginalized, maybe because they have too weak a notion of their own potential. I am convinced that the normative perspective is much richer then it presently shows and that big progress concerning content and systematization lies ahead of us. In any case, I always perceived ranking theory as a decidedly normative enterprise, and I try to offer some new views from the normative perspective.

On the other hand, I find naturalized epistemology and cognitive science too dismissive about the normative perspective. I know we live in the era of neuroscience. The public is all too prone to believe in its benefits, and neuroscience skillfully exploits this favorable situation; this is not blameworthy. However, its representatives have adopted a style of exaggeration and a level of promise (at least in their public statements) that I find quite annoying; these promises won't come true. Moreover, I am alienated by the atheoretical, if not antitheoretical attitude to be found there. This cannot work; cognitive scientists should recognize all the theoretical work that is around, even if they cannot directly use it.

More to the point: It should be clear that the empirical perspective on epistemology cannot be completed without the normative perspective. Rationality is normative, in the first place. However, it is also an empirical ideal. What is going on empirically can ultimately not be understood without reference to this ideal that is provided only by the normative perspective. This is my basic reason why cognitive science should respect normative epistemology even in its own interest and why normative epistemologists should be more offensive.

My *second* concern is that I perceive a great schism in epistemology, namely between traditional and formal epistemology, (although this is almost as crooked an opposition as that between analytic and continental philosophy) or between a theory of knowledge and a theory of belief. These are obviously two different distinctions that must not be confused. Still, the factual overlap between them is large. This is indeed the crux.

Epistemology centers around two fundamental notions, knowledge and belief. Of course, they are related, the starting point being the "justified true belief" analysis of knowledge, even if it is to be rejected or amended. To some extent, though, they can be studied independently. Under the heading "belief" one must attend to degrees of belief, something foreign to knowledge discussions, and to the relations to perceptual input and behavioral output, etc. Under the heading "knowledge" one tends to focus on such topics as justification, on the relation between belief and truth, and perhaps on apriority (because what is a priori is always supposed to be knowledge), etc. This is legitimate.

What worries me is the fact that these studies are pursued in almost disjoint communities cultivating different philosophical styles and languages, different references to the history of philosophy, different attitudes to formal methods, and so on. I see little understanding and even less communication between the communities. This is definitely to the detriment of epistemology. If I have to take side, I would count myself among the "belief theorists", and when I read texts from the "knowledge camp" I often find them despairing and hopeless. Still, I see the urgent need to bring and keep the communities together. Ranking theory may be seen as my contribution to do this. In any case, the issue is worth of our joint efforts.

My *third* and final concern is the relation between ontology / metaphysics and epistemology. For me, this topic is the most confusing, the deepest, and the most pressing, the climax of theoretical philosophy we must reach. Theoretical philosophy during Enlightenment is characterized by a thorough-going epistemologization of ontology/metaphysics – I mentioned already that epistemology then became the prime discipline – and Kant's transcendental idealism brought this process to perfection. This was most insightful, and a terrible mistake at the same time, that started long before Kant, of course. The mistake held philosophy in its grip for a long time. For me it was vanquished only with Kripke's rearrangement of modalities and his reestablishment of genuine metaphysical necessity and with Putnam's proclamation of realism. What the insights to be preserved have been is, however, not so clear. Putnam soon started vacillating and invented various forms of soft realism. Sellars' and Strawson's great efforts to familiarize analytic philosophy with Kant did not have resounding success, it seems to me. Brandom's similar efforts with respect to German idealism are still too fresh. And so on.

These are all efforts to come to terms with the relation of ontology / metaphysics and epistemology, on the presupposition that there is no simple answer saying either there is no relation at all or there is a uni-directional relation (as metaphysical realism or idealism would have it). There are quite a number of further attempts beyond those just mentioned. To call all of them idiosyncratic is not meant pejoratively. It only means that they go different ways in a most uncertain terrain and are difficult to compare and assess. As I say, though, this issue is our ultimate task as epistemologists we must never lose sight of. We must prove worthy of our problems.

What do you think the future of epistemology will (or should) hold?

Let me be brief. As I had noticed with embarrassment, I had produced the longest contribution to the first volume of this series. I do not want to repeat this.

The future of mankind may be dark, but the future of epistemology is definitely bright. As long as mankind exists, it will be deeply engaged in epistemology; this is our reflective nature and our fate. Even on shorter terms, I can only foresee epistemology prospering. And it would prosper even more, if epistemologists would take my three concerns above to their heart.

References

Cohen, L. Jonathan (1977), *The Probable and the Provable*, Oxford University Press, Oxford.

Cohen, L. Jonathan (1980), "Some Historical Remarks on the Baconian Conception of Probability", *Journal of the History of Ideas* 41, 219–231.

Giang, Phan Hong, Prakash P. Shenoy (2000), "A Qualitative Linear Utility Theory for Spohn's Theory of Epistemic Beliefs", in: C. Boutilier, M. Goldszmidt (eds.), *Uncertainity in Artificial Intelligence, Vol. 16,* Morgan Kaufmann, San Francisco, pp. 220–229.

Hild, Matthias, *Introduction to Induction. On the First Principles of Reasoning*, to appear.

Lewis, David (1973), *Counterfactuals*, Blackwell, Oxford.

Lorenz, Konrad, "Kants Lehre vom Apriorischen im Lichte gegenwärtiger Biologie", in *Blätter für Deutsche Philosophie* 15, 1941, pp.94–125.

Shackle, George L.S. (1949), *Expectation in Economics*, Cambridge University Press, Cambridge.

Spohn, Wolfgang (1975), "An Analysis of Hansson's Dyadic Deontic Logic", *Journal of Philosophical Logic* 4, 237–252.

Spohn, Wolfgang (1976/78), *Grundlagen der Entscheidungstheorie*, Ph.D. Thesis, University of Munich 1976, published: Scriptor, Kronberg/Ts. 1978, out of print, pdf-version at:
http://www.uni-konstanz.de/FuF/Philo/Philosophie/
philosophie/files/ge.buch.gesamt.pdf.

Spohn, Wolfgang (1983), *Eine Theorie der Kausalität*, unpublished Habilitationsschrift, University of Munich, pdf-version at:
http://www.uni-konstanz.de/FuF/Philo/Philosophie/philosophie/
files/habilitation.pdf

Spohn, Wolfgang (1988), "Ordinal Conditional Functions. A Dynamic Theory of Epistemic States", in: W.L. Harper, B. Skyrms (eds.), *Causation in Decision, Belief Change, and Statistics*, vol. II, Kluwer, Dordrecht, pp. 105–134.

Spohn, Wolfgang (2006), "Isaac Levi's Potentially Surprising Epistemological Picture", in: E. Olsson (ed.), *Knowledge and Inquiry. Essays on the Pragmatism of Isaac Levi*, Cambridge University Press, Cambridge, pp. 125–142.

Spohn, Wolfgang (forthcoming *a*), "A Survey of Ranking Theory", in: F. Huber, C. Schmidt-Petri (eds.), *Degrees of Belief. An Anthology*, Springer, Dordrecht.

Spohn, Wolfgang (forthcoming *b*), *Causation, Coherence, and Concepts. A Collection of Essays*, Springer, Dordrecht.

28
Timothy Williamson

Wykeham Professor of Logic
University of Oxford, UK

Why were you initially drawn to epistemology (and what keeps you interested)?

My early interests in philosophy were more logical in nature than epistemological. I studied philosophy (and mathematics) as an undergraduate and graduate student at Oxford from 1973 to 1980. In that environment, epistemology was widely regarded as secondary in importance to philosophy of language. The usual sceptical problems must be what pull many epistemologists into the subject; I found them intelligible but not inspiring. J.L. Austin's *Sense and Sensibilia* impressed me, as much for its style and wit as for its good sense, but it does not present epistemology as an exciting area for investigation. The post-Gettier industry of fiddling with analyses of 'S knows that P' had been going long enough already to look unpromising.

An epistemological problem that did intrigue me at that time was the way in which bad intellectual judgment can be a trap from which someone cannot escape, because they misjudge all the escape routes on offer. Such bad judgment need not involve any formal fallacy. It seemed to be a factor in various unending philosophical debates, but at the time I had no idea how to develop the point. As far as my work goes, the point finally surfaced in my recent book *The Philosophy of Philosophy* (2007), in the emphasis on skill rather than entry-level competence in applying concepts as what matters for armchair knowledge, and in the critique of the assumption that evidence in philosophy must be philosophically neutral.

My doctoral thesis was on the concept of approximation to the truth, a problem raised by Karl Popper. He thought it overoptimistic to aim for strictly true theories in science: a more reasonable aim is that our theories should approximate better and better to the truth; in his terminology, that they should have increasing verisimilitude. A more formal account of verisimilitude seemed needed to give substance to this idea. I quickly proved that Popper's own attempts to provide one did not work, only to discover that David Miller had already published the results. Much of the subsequent debate on verisimilitude replayed issues about the over-sensitivity of formal definitions to the initial choice of language that had plagued Carnap's programme of formally defining probabilities. The account in my thesis was less formal; I abandoned it not long afterwards because it depended on a form of extreme foundationalism I found increasingly implausible. The only publication to come out of it was an article on the logic of similarity. Although the motivation for my project was partly epistemological, the central challenge was not. What it means for one theory to be a better approximation to the truth than another is a non-epistemic matter. The question still strikes me as under-explored, perhaps because the discussion of it then was conducted in rather narrow terms, with too much concern about measurement.

In the 1980s I became interested in formal issues raised by Michael Dummett's anti-realism and other forms of neo-verificationism. My first published article (in *Analysis*, 1982) was on the so-called paradox of knowability, Frederick Fitch's proof that if all truths are knowable then (absurdly) all truths are known (Fitch credited the proof to an anonymous referee, who was identified long after I wrote as Alonzo Church). I showed that the proof ran into a problem with intuitionistic logic, which Michael Dummett – one of my D.Phil supervisors – had proposed as the appropriate logic for the anti-realist view on which all truths are knowable. Although I have never had a shred of sympathy for anti-realism, I felt that Dummett's version could not be dismissed quite so quickly. That paper was dashed off on the spur of the moment and not intended to be part of a larger project, but it drew me into further debates on the 'paradox' of knowability. I also used modal logic to explore various neo-verificationist principles, reinterpreting the necessity operator as a verifiability operator, usually with a classical background logic. For example, what follows from the hypothesis that sentences with the same verification conditions and the same falsification conditions have the same truth conditions? My overall motivation was to defend a fully realist, non-epistemic conception of truth, as wholly independent of what anyone could verify or falsify, even in principle: to make epistemology mind its own business. Nevertheless, these inquiries made me think about epistemological issues. For example, some proofs depended on the principle that if one can verify something then one can verify that one can verify it, which resembles the 'KK' principle that if one knows something then one knows that one knows it; the rejection of that principle later became a cornerstone of my epistemology.

Since my first year as an undergraduate, I had been fascinated by the non-transitivity of indiscriminability, where one thing is indiscriminable from a second and the second from a third even though the first is discriminable from the third, as evidenced in long sorites series whose endpoints are easily discriminable from each other but no member is discriminable from its immediate neighbours (in the relevant respect by the relevant means). In writing my first book, *Identity and Discrimination* (1990), I came to the conclusion that discrimination is fundamentally an epistemological matter, of *knowing* things to be distinct. That enabled me to use epistemic logic to analyse the logic of indiscriminability. For example, one can predict the non-transitivity of indiscriminability on quite general grounds (recent claims to the contrary depend on a misuse of the word 'indiscriminable' to mean 'same in appearance'). Late in the writing of that book, I came on the idea that knowing requires a margin for error, that to know something one must be safe from error in relevantly similar cases. It turns out to be closely related to the non-transitivity of indiscriminability and to the failure of the 'KK' principle, which in the standard 'possible worlds' semantics for epistemic logic corresponds to the non-transitivity of the relation of relative epistemic possibility between worlds. Generalizing the argument for the failure of the KK principle took me to the anti-luminosity argument at the heart of *Knowledge and its Limits* (2000).

My realization that the margin for error principle can explain our ignorance of the whereabouts of the sharp boundary of a concept led me to the epistemicist account of vagueness. All these arguments involved limits on knowledge, and so flowed naturally from my concern with anti-realism. Indeed, one reason for writing *Vagueness* (1994) was the widespread assumption that if anti-realism is right about anything, it is right about vagueness—given which, by arguing that anti-realism is wrong about vagueness, I was in effect arguing that it is wrong about everything.

That discrimination is to be understood in terms of knowledge rather than belief was also an early clue to the 'knowledge first' epistemology of *Knowledge and its Limits*. I remember Jonathan

Bennett giving a paper on the problem of deciding to believe at the half-centenary *Analysis* conference in 1990. In the discussion, I idly suggested that one might take the difficulty of deciding to *know* that something obtains as a starting-point from which to explain the difficulty of deciding to *believe* that it obtains. Bennett replied with his usual vigour that he had been philosophizing happily for thirty years without appealing to the concept of knowledge and advised me to do the same. The thought came to me 'That's where you make your big mistake'. I realized that he was simply being more articulate and self-conscious than others about what was then (and to a lesser extent still is) a very common methodological presupposition.

In general, I don't first get interested in philosophical problems and then look for something to say about them. I find that I have something to say about them first, and then get interested in them as I develop it. Once I'm interested, new subtleties keep emerging so that there is no danger of losing interest.

But it's not accidental that I have spent so much time on epistemology. Its special flavour derives from its concern with subjective perspectives on an objective world of which they are part. What could be more philosophical than that?

What do you see as being your main contributions to epistemology?

In my answer to the previous question I already gave some indication of what I was doing in epistemology up to *Knowledge and its Limits*. I'll step back and try to explain in more general terms what I hope to have achieved in that book.

Arguably the most important movement in epistemology over the past fifty years has been externalism, which emphasizes the epistemic role of factors more or less opaque to the subject, such as causal relations to the environment. However, this movement was not as thoroughgoing as it seemed. It inherited the assumption that one must explain knowledge in terms of belief and other factors rather than *vice versa*. From an externalist perspective, why privilege belief over knowledge? Belief is a more 'internal' state than knowledge, since one can have the same belief about the external environment whether it is true or false, whereas whatever one knows is true, and introspection is more reliable about whether one believes than about whether one knows. It's almost as though economists studying the nature of money realized that its social role is very important, but still took for granted that a theory of money must start with its 'internal' physical constitution, which genuine currency shares with counterfeits. Knowledge corresponds to genuine currency, belief to what genuine currency and counterfeits have in common. Knowledge is what we get when cognition goes well. When it goes badly we may still get belief, but failure is best understood as a deviation from success. 'Knowledge first' epistemology is success-oriented. That is the strategy of *Knowledge and its Limits*, which reverses the traditional order of explanation to explain belief, justification, evidence and assertibility in terms of knowledge. Indeed, I argued, internalism has no starting-point: the mind contains no inner core of 'luminous' states transparent to the subject, such as beliefs or phenomenal appearances. The anti-luminosity argument also undermines anti-realism, since arguments for anti-realism presuppose that there are epistemically privileged linguistic or mental states, such as assertibility or belief.

Soon after *Knowledge and its Limits*, Jason Stanley and I published 'Knowing How' (*Journal of Philosophy*, 2001), in which we argued that, contrary to received opinion, all knowing how is knowing that. We weren't the first to make the point, but we did provide arguments too detailed to be ignored. We touched a sore spot, for the paper has provoked dozens of replies. Its methodology has been particularly controversial, since it uses a semantic analysis of English sentences like 'Richard knows how to swim' to reach the conclusion that if Richard knows how to swim then something is such that Richard knows that it is a way to swim, which is not about the English language at all. Critics have suspected that our arguments must involve a use-mention confusion. But there is no mystery. Semantic analysis can show that the sentence 'Richard knows how to swim' is true if and only if something is such that Richard knows that it is a way to swim. By the disquotational property of truth, 'Richard knows how to swim' is true if and only if Richard knows how to swim. These two biconditional premises logically entail the biconditional conclusion that Richard knows how to swim if and only if something is such that Richard knows that it is a way to swim.

More recently I have extended the theory in *Knowledge and its Limits* by investigating the relation between knowledge and probability more deeply. I also developed some criticisms of the popular idea that the application of the word 'know' depends on the conversational context.

In my latest book, *The Philosophy of Philosophy*, I develop an account that vindicates and demystifies the sort of armchair knowledge that philosophy can attain, while leaving room for new methods to be added to the philosopher's repertoire. Armchair knowledge cannot be explained as somehow linguistic or conceptual in nature, I argue. Rather, the skills we acquire in applying concepts online, most obviously in perception, we can also apply offline, in imagination, when evaluating everyday counterfactual conditionals about what *would* obtain if things were somehow different. Doing philosophical thought experiments is in effect just a special case of evaluating counterfactuals. This account turns out to disrupt the traditional distinction between *a priori* and *a posteriori* knowledge. In spirit, *The Philosophy of Philosophy* is an application of *Knowledge and its Limits* to the epistemology of philosophy. In particular, I argue that current self-images of analytic philosophy distort its epistemology by a typical internalist move: they psychologize its data, thereby making the data almost irrelevant to the subject matter of much philosophy as realists conceive it: a largely mind-independent world. An externalist approach does more justice to contemporary philosophy.

What do you think is the proper role of epistemology in relation to other areas of philosophy and other academic disciplines?

It has become a commonplace that epistemology cannot be expected to play the foundational role in which Descartes cast it, as first philosophy. If all other inquiries must be postponed until after we have completed our inquiry into inquiry itself, they will never get started. Indeed, epistemological inquiry should be sensitive to the results of other sorts of inquiry, such as psychology. It is not credible that the epistemology of perception has nothing to learn from the psychology of perception. To give a less obvious example, in *The Philosophy of Philosophy* I use results from the psychology of reasoning to undermine some popular accounts of the epistemology of reasoning. Epistemology also learns from other areas of philosophy: 'Knowing How' draws on philosophy of language.

Some contemporary philosophers go to the opposite, anti-Cartesian extreme, with a gung-ho insistence that metaphysics is prior to epistemology. On their picture, the subject-matter of metaphysics – the most general and necessary nature of the world, whatever any knowers it contains happen to know about it – is more fundamental than the subject-matter of epistemology. Although I like the realism of that picture, it doesn't have the methodological consequences those philosophers suppose. They haven't thoroughly learned the lesson they themselves teach. They rightly insist, against various forms of idealism and anti-realism, that being is prior in the order of being to knowing, and that the order of knowing is not the order of being. But then they should not conclude that being is prior in the order of knowing to knowing. When we start philosophical inquiry we must use the knowledge we already have, not much of which concerns metaphysical fundamentals. It's more ordinary than that, and some of it concerns our own knowledge and ignorance. When we know, we do not always know that we know, but we sometimes do. I know that I know that I'm typing. If some metaphysical theory T entails that I don't know that I'm typing, then I'm perfectly entitled to reply: "I know that I'm typing; if T is true I don't know that I'm typing; therefore T isn't true". For the argument is valid and I know the truth of its premises. Of course, it's wrong to argue for metaphysical conclusions from epistemological premises believed only on the basis of wishful thinking. But that is because they are believed only on the basis of wishful thinking, not because they are epistemological. It's equally wrong to argue for epistemological conclusions from metaphysical premises believed only on the basis of wishful thinking. Other areas of philosophy and other academic disciplines can learn from epistemology, just as it can learn from them.

Thus moral philosophy must learn from epistemology because our understanding of the nature of morality depends on whether we think that there can be moral knowledge. We seem to know that rape is wrong, but many philosophers argue from the depth and breadth of moral disagreement between individuals or societies that moral knowledge is some sort of illusion. In addressing the issue, we must do moral epistemology. Unfortunately, moral epistemology is too often done in isolation from recent general epistemology, and lacks depth as a result.

Formal epistemology provides examples in which academic disciplines outside philosophy have learnt from epistemology. Jaakko Hintikka founded modern epistemic logic with *Knowledge and Belief* (1962), which is clearly a work of epistemology. It turned out to provide a suitable setting for the analysis of common knowledge and related phenomena concerning the sharing of information between individuals or even parts of a computer. Consequently, epistemic logic has had major applications in both computer science and theoretical economics.

Academic disciplines typically and properly involve some level of epistemological self-reflection. Their methodology evolves over time; such changes raise questions about the comparative trustworthiness of new and old methods in producing knowledge. Such questions become epistemological when they attain a sufficient level of generality. Of course, they are usually best resolved by the practitioners of that discipline, but even they need to use broadly epistemological concepts and assumptions in discussing the questions. Epistemology should play some role in making appropriate concepts and assumptions available. If not, the practitioners may unreflectively rely on those from some obsolescent philosophy, such as logical positivism.

One reason for the intractability of the 'science wars' may have been that many on both sides had an impoverished conception of the range of epistemological options. Epistemologists could have played a more active role than they actually did in making available alternatives that did justice to the concerns of at least the more reasonable of those on each side. Bizarre though it may seem to analytic philosophers, many academics in the humanities and social sciences assume that 'true' implies 'certain'; that assumption converts a cautiously fallibilist scepticism about certainty into a crassly relativist scepticism about truth. If some elementary epistemology can help clarify that fundamental confusion, why shouldn't more sophisticated epistemology help clarify subtler confusions?

What do you consider to be the most neglected topics and/or contributions in contemporary epistemology?

Of course, the *most* neglected topics and contributions are probably ones I'm neglecting too, and so will fail to mention. Moreover, neglected topics and contributions are often neglected for good reasons. Nevertheless, I will stress a type of work too little done. The reason for this comparative neglect may be that the work requires unusual combinations of skills, combinations the philosophical community could realistically try to make more usual in the future.

The best hope for progress in epistemology lies in the use of methods that have not been part of its stock in trade for centuries. Close to my heart, of course, are the methods of formal epistemology, especially epistemic logic and probability theory. The methods of experimental psychology also promise to shake up comfortable assumptions about the structure of belief-forming processes. The semantics of natural languages can reveal that the underlying logical form of epistemic constructions is not what it appeared to be on the surface, thereby forcing us to reassess the validity or invalidity of arguments in which those constructions occur.

Lots of such work is being done; I'm confident that it will be done at an increasing rate in the future. Its neglect is not what concerns me. Nor do I see much danger that traditional epistemology will be neglected. What I fear is neglect of the need for bridges between these different areas of epistemology, so that no area learns enough from the others.

The case of formal epistemology is a worrying instance. Crudely put: for historical reasons, probabilistic epistemology has been dominated by remnants of traditions – operationalism, subjective Bayesianism, logical positivism – that tend to confine normative epistemology to matters of formal rationality, thereby restricting discussion to an epistemologically naïve level. Although the need for a more epistemologically sophisticated approach is increasingly recognized, there is still a severe shortage (not total absence) of work that combines a feel for mathematical probability with a feel for normative epistemology. As a result, more traditional epistemologists find probabilistic epistemology easier to dismiss and harder to learn from than they should: it really does have much to teach us all. Similarly, epistemic logic has tended to be done by logicians impatient with the legitimate concerns of less formal epistemologists about the strong axioms standardly assumed (logical omniscience, positive introspection, negative introspection). Again, the result has often been that neither side manages to learn as much as they should from the other.

The new vogue for experimental philosophy may be going the same way. The experimentalists tend to despise the traditional armchair methods of philosophy, because they are not based on experiment; consequently, the experimentalists are liable to commit logical blunders in attempting to apply experimental results to traditional philosophical questions, making it too easy for the traditionalists to shrug off those results. Yet again, neither side learns enough from the other. Physicists divide into experimentalists and theoreticians; the health of the discipline depends on keeping lines of communication sufficiently open between them.

One can understand how such divisions arise in philosophy, as elsewhere. A new method emerges, in some respects more scientific than the old ones; using it demands specialised technical skills. Those who master and apply the new method form their own intellectual community; they tend to look down on work that relies on the old methods. Suspicious of the old methods, they become less proficient in using them. Those who rely on the old methods may feel some fear and envy of the new method, but reassure themselves by noting its practitioners' lack of proficiency with the old methods. Upshot: those who use the old methods don't learn enough from the new method, those who do use it don't learn enough from the old methods. For progress comes from the skilful combination of *all* the methods, old and new. These negative effects are amplified in the next generation, some trained exclusively by one side, some trained exclusively by the other.

Bridges are also neglected between epistemology and philosophy of science. In consequence, neither side properly explores the way in which science provides enormous amounts of *knowledge*, in the most strict and literal sense. For philosophers of science tend to neglect the question of knowledge and epistemologists tend to neglect the case of science.

When no single individual combines all the requisite skills, cooperation is needed between several individuals who combine them collectively, which in turn demands an appreciation on all sides that they have something significant to learn from the others.

What do you think the future of epistemology will (or should) hold?

Epistemology will change slowly. Much of it will continue to be done in the traditional way. The new methods I've mentioned will gradually become more influential, but not dominant. Armchair theorizing will always play a central role, while making more use of explicitly articulated argumentation, mathematical models and findings from linguistics, psychology and other disciplines. If done well, it will raise epistemology to a higher level of intellectual discipline. If done badly, it will sink into crude scientism.

Many epistemologists still work with more or less sophisticated or disguised variations on an early modern theme: the mind starts with data that fall short of facts about the external world and thereby manage to have epistemic privileges denied to those facts: in short, luminous facts. These days the luminous facts often appear in the guise of facts about what people believe, but they occupy the same epistemological niche, falling short of facts about the subject matter of those beliefs and being assigned epistemic privileges denied the latter. That bad picture is often presented as how we find our mental world to be, but is really just how it is believed on prior philosophical grounds the mental world *must* be. The picture has had profoundly distorting effects on philosophy over the past few centuries, even if it was a stage we had to go through. It will undoubtedly be influential for decades to come. Nevertheless, I trust that – however slowly and painfully – philosophy will learn to live without it. That would be truly liberating for epistemology. Of course, the philosophers for whom the early modern picture holds the greatest attraction may be the ones most likely to go into epistemology, which is perhaps why I didn't start as an epistemologist. Nevertheless, epistemology without that picture has its own less cosy attractions, not only in epistemic logic, which is why I became an epistemologist in the end.

29
Linda Zagzebski

George Lynn Cross Research Professor
of Philosophy
University of Oklahoma, USA

Why were you initially drawn to epistemology (and what keeps you interested)?

I was not initially drawn to epistemology as such. When I joined the Society of Christian Philosophers in the mid-eighties, I began working in philosophy of religion and discovered that religious epistemology dominated the field. I went to lots of conferences and listened to paper after paper on the justification of religious belief or the possibility of religious knowledge. Since good religious epistemologists are good epistemologists, I was immersed in the major epistemological issues of the day: internalism vs. externalism, foundationalism vs. coherentism, reliabilism for and against, the many ways we can understand justification, and the seemingly impossible task of finding a counter-example-free definition of knowledge. I found much of it very boring and I thought that there must be a better way. Why not step back and look at the larger framework? Where does the concept of knowledge come from? Where does the more recent and problematic concept of justification come from?

It occurred to me that the concept of a justified belief has the same function in epistemic evaluation as the concept of a right act in moral evaluation. A right act makes no sense outside a network of ethical concepts that constitute its theoretical background, and I think the same thing can be said for a justified belief. Without attention to its theoretical framework, it is no wonder the concept of justification was a jumble. So I set out to investigate theoretical constructions in normative epistemology and noticed that they were either consciously or unconsciously borrowed from ethics. The main rivals were forms of reliabilism and deontological epistemology. The former was modeled on consequentialism, the latter on deontological ethics. (There were also epistemological versions of non-cognitivism and conventionalism). Since I preferred virtue theory in ethics, I wondered what would happen if we adapted a true virtue ethics to the purposes of epistemology. I had not written any epistemology before, but I decided to write a book.

The book I wrote was *Virtues of the Mind* (Cambridge University Press, 1996). In that book I proposed that we make the concept of intellectual virtue the focus of normative epistemology, and that we treat it as part of a general theory of virtue. Unfortunately, at that time there was virtually no work on intellectual virtue except for the Aristotelian concept of *phronesis*. What was needed, I thought, was a virtue theory rich enough to include intellectual virtues like open-mindedness, intellectual fairness, intellectual courage, carefulness, and thoroughness within the same theory as moral virtues. I outlined such a theory and argued that a virtue model is the best hope for addressing a number of difficulties within the field of epistemology.

First, there was the impasse over the nature of justification. If a justified belief is the counterpart of a right act, then since virtue ethics treats a right act as derivative from the deeper concept of a moral virtue, I thought that an epistemology modeled on virtue ethics would lead to a number of concepts of belief evaluation that would derive from the deeper concept of an intellectual virtue, and which could be used to disambiguate justification. The consequence of this approach is that justification becomes less important than it has been in recent epistemology, but I think that is the way it should be. A focus on intellectual character permits us to discuss good and bad believings, but it allows us to talk about much else besides. Among other advantages, it helps us overcome the neglect of the social dimension of epistemic states, and it has the potential to overcome the neglect of the values of understanding and wisdom.

In any case, I hoped that epistemologists would pay closer attention to ethics, whether or not they accepted the theory I proposed, and in the years since *V of the M*, I have continued to be fascinated with the many ways moral philosophy applies to the epistemic realm. We see these connections in the rarified issues of meta-ethics as well as in very concrete narratives displaying the causal links between moral and intellectual dispositions. Most meta-ethical issues have counterparts in epistemology. Moral realists and anti-realists dispute over the status of moral goodness or rightness. Is it a real property? Is it mind-dependent or independent? Similarly, there is the dispute over the status of epistemic justifiedness and other evaluative epistemic properties. Are they real properties, and if so, of what? There is a similar parallel in the dispute over the relationship between evaluative properties and natural properties. Are they distinct and independent, or does the former supervene on or reduce to the latter? No doubt there are also meta-ethical parallels that have not yet been noticed. For instance, I have argued that the Ideal Observer theory has a promising counterpart in epistemology.

There are many other parallels between ethics and epistemology that are as illuminating for their differences as for their similarities: moral and epistemic luck, skepticism in ethics and in epistemology, norms for practical and theoretical reasoning, and the place of motive and choice in acts and beliefs.

I find it interesting that the most important concept in epistemology does not have a counterpart in ethics: the concept of knowledge. But even here, attention to ethics can be helpful in identifying what kind of value knowledge has (intrinsic/ extrinsic, as a means/as an end), and in linking knowledge to related issues such as the attempt to eliminate luck from both moral and epistemic evaluation. Generally, when the parallel is clearly something about value or norms, the treatment of the topic in ethics is ahead of the treatment in epistemology, and the latter can benefit from the former. In some cases, the influence goes in the other direction. For instance, skepticism is an epistemological topic *par excellence*, and nobody could talk about moral skepticism without referring heavily to the epistemological literature. And I think that the internalism/ externalism distinction in epistemology is better articulated than the parallel distinction in ethics.

All of these issues are really exciting, and for me it ultimately comes down to a conviction that epistemology directly bears on the kind of life we want to live. An epistemically valuable life is part of a life that is valuable full stop.

What do you see as being your main contributions to epistemology?

My contributions are in the area my colleague, Wayne Riggs, calls "the value turn" in epistemology: a turn to normative or evaluative dimensions of epistemic states. My work in virtue epistemology is in that category, as is my work on what I call "the value problem," or the problem of what makes knowledge better than true belief. I am also one of the philosophers who has made a plea for a return to the values of understanding, insight, and wisdom, which received much more attention in former eras. I have not yet written much on these latter issues, but I am heartened to see that they are getting attention from others.

My work in virtue epistemology and virtue theory has attracted attention in fields outside philosophy, and I have consulted with researchers and research groups in psychology, education, philosophy of mathematics, and cognitive and social neuroscience. This work is not a direct contribution to epistemology, but it links epistemology with research in other fields.

What do you think is the proper role of epistemology in relation to other areas of philosophy and other academic disciplines?

This is an interesting question, particularly if we look at the place of epistemology within philosophy in different eras of its history. Plato talked about knowledge (*episteme*) as part of his investigation of the nature of the Forms and the steps towards achieving an ideal life. It is impossible to separate his epistemology from his metaphysics, and it is possible to separate his epistemology from his ethics only at the price of severe distortion. I have heard philosophers say that they cannot find Aristotle's epistemology at all, but of course, it is there; it's just not treated separately from his logic and his treatment of the human soul. For most of the classical and medieval period, an account of human cognitive and epistemic activity was secondary to something else– an account of human nature and the place of human beings in the world, whereas epistemology became First Philosophy in the work of Descartes, according to the standard reading of the history of philosophy. However, making the conscious subject primary is not the same as making epistemology primary. Epistemology is not necessarily a discipline that takes the first person perspective. In fact, it is common these days to take the third person perspective. With the third person approach to philosophical problems, it is not necessary or even natural to start with epistemological questions. And with the first person approach, epistemological questions (e.g. What can I know?) are only a subset of the questions one would ask. Self-consciousness leads as quickly to moral questions as to questions about knowledge, and among the latter questions, self-knowledge is at least as important from the first person perspective as knowledge of an external world—the usual subject matter of epistemology.

So whether our perspective is first personal or the third personal, I do not see that epistemology would naturally come first. But it might. The issue of the natural or logical order of the fields of philosophy is a meta-philosophical question about which I have no well thought out position. I suspect that metaphysics, including the metaphysics of value, has at least as good a claim to being First Philosophy as epistemology does, but I am not going to try to defend that. I think that whatever field of philosophy we start with is the one that ends up being the most elaborate, subtle, complex, and the most interesting—not because it is intrinsically the most interesting, but just because we treat it that way. For much of philosophical history metaphysics was the most interesting. Then for a while it was epistemology. For a while in the twentieth century it was philosophy of language. Now philosophy of mind is attracting a lot of attention. But ethics never goes away, and I think it worthwhile to recognize how many issues in philosophy have normative dimensions (What we should do) or evaluative dimensions (What is good or bad). I think it is important to look at those dimensions of epistemic states not only because they are there and we shouldn't ignore what's there, but because there are options in approaching epistemic value and epistemic norms, and the options we choose affect the way other parts of our epistemology come out.

How does epistemology relate to other academic disciplines? I suppose it is evident that differences in the objects of knowledge can lead to differences in the appropriate method for knowing them. Methods of scientific knowledge differ from methods of historical knowledge or moral knowledge or religious knowledge, and it is no doubt the business of each practice to determine the methods for acquiring knowledge within the field. A more interesting question is whether there are any variations in the state of knowledge itself from one field to another. Plato argued that *episteme* is connected with the mastery of a skill or *techne*.[1] One does not have *episteme* of an astronomical fact unless one has mastered

---

[1] See Gail Fine, "Knowledge and Belief in Republic v-vii," in Stephen Hetherson, editor, *Epistemology (Companions to Ancient Thought* I), Cambridge University Press, 1990.

the *techne* of astronomy, nor does one have knowledge in Plato's sense in any field unless one is able to understand the relationship between the immediate object of knowledge and numerous other facts that would enable one to answer questions about it with proficiency and authority. I find Plato's idea very plausible. It does not matter whether his notion of *episteme* exactly coincides with our notion of knowledge.In any case, he has identified an epistemic state that is highly desirable, and it is a state that requires the mastery of a *techne*. That suggests to me that virtually every human practice is relevant to epistemology in the sense that if you want to know what *episteme* is within that practice, you would refer to the masters of the practice. Knowledge of propositional objects within a given practice is a relation between those people—the masters of the practice, and those propositions. To find out details, we examine those people—how they answer questions about the proposition, how they relate it to other propositions, and so on. Epistemologists may find interesting similarities and differences among the masters of different *technai*. So one way other fields are relevant to epistemology is that we have models of people who really know something within a human practice and we can investigate them. Maybe we will find out that they have certain intellectual virtues in common, but we might also find out that they differ from each other in interesting ways.

What do you consider to be the most neglected topics and/or contributions in contemporary epistemology?

In the past I have argued that we need to give more attention to "high grade" knowledge, as well as the related states of understanding and wisdom. As I mentioned above, I wish I had gone farther in that direction in my own work, and I am glad to see that some philosophers are taking up those topics. But more would be better.

Another interesting topic is self-knowledge. This topic is not neglected, but it is neglected within epistemology, no doubt because it is enormously hard to design a research program that includes self-knowledge along with knowledge of an external world and other persons.

Another important topic is one I mentioned briefly at the end of my answer to the first question: the relationship between epistemic values and happiness. The kind of beliefs and other epistemic states we want to have are a part of the kind of life we want to live. How are epistemic values related to the other values of a good life, where a good life can mean either an admirable life or a desirable life? It is very hard to answer this question without first figuring out what makes a value epistemic. I've never heard an answer to that question that I found plausible.

Another under-explored topic is emotion as a source of belief and knowledge. I think that emotions have cognitive components, although I would not go as far as some philosophers and claim that emotions are judgments or have judgmental components. Even so, emotions are closely connected to epistemic states and often form the basis for belief states. I would like to see more work on the connection between emotion and belief and between emotion and understanding.

Most of the above questions are already getting attention, but there is at least one that is off the map entirely. I remember many years ago Ken Kemp said to me that the model for my work on intellectual virtue is that of inquiry. The virtues of the inquirer form the basis for my theory– what we do before we find out the truth. In contrast, the model of contemplation was more important to Aristotle and Aquinas– what we do after we find out the truth. I have thought of that comment from time to time, and I think that Ken was probably right, but I don't know what to make of it. Maybe somebody else does.

The final topic I want to mention is one that will be the focus of my work in the immediate future: epistemic autonomy and authority. One of the most important topics in modern philosophy is the relationship between authority and autonomy. This is widely addressed in political and moral philosophy, but hardly at all in epistemology. There are many notions of autonomy used by ethicists, but epistemologists think of epistemic autonomy (when they think of it at all) as something like epistemic independence. There does not seem to be an analogue of Kantian autonomy for epistemic states, and while the ideal of self-sufficiency applies to the epistemic realm, there is little, if any, defense of its value. A related issue is epistemic authority, which seems to operate in different ways in different epistemic communities. For instance, there are obvious differences between authority in scientific communities and authority in religious communities. Many philosophers are skeptical that there are moral authorities and maintain that no moral belief should be taken on the word of another, but it is not clear why they think so. I think, then, that epistemic autonomy is an important topic for investigation.

What do you think the future of epistemology will (or should) hold?

I'm not very good at predicting the future. Sometimes all it takes is one important book to turn the field in a new direction, and if so, we wouldn't know it until it happens. I have mentioned many new issues and many potential new issues, but I don't know which ones will capture the imaginations of philosophers. I think that in addition to the issues arising from epistemic value, social epistemology is an important future area of work, judging from the popularity of new work on testimony and reasonable disagreement. I also look forward to finding out what the future will bring in religious epistemology. For decades, religious epistemology was dominated by arguments for and against Reformed epistemology, but there are many new directions that religious epistemology can take. The recent work on reasonable disagreement, epistemic trust, and testimony have obvious applications to religious epistemology. I hope that my future project on epistemic autonomy and authority will also have interesting applications to religious epistemology.

About the Editors

Vincent F. Hendricks is University Professor of Formal Philosophy at Roskilde University and Elite Researcher of the Danish State. He is the author of many books, among them *Mainstream and Formal Epistemology* (Cambridge University Press, 2007) *Thought$_2$Talk* (Automatic Press / VIP, 2007), *The Convergence of Scientific Knowledge* (Springer, 2001). Editor-in-Chief of *Synthese* and *Synthese Library* he is also the founder of ΦLOG— *The Network for Philosophical Logic and Its Applications.*

Duncan Pritchard occupies the Chair in Epistemology at the University of Edinburgh. He has published widely, including two books, *Epistemic Luck* (Oxford Univeristy Press, 2005) and *What is this Thing Called Knowledge?* (Routledge, 2006).

About Epistemology: 5 Questions

Epistemology: 5 Questions is a collection of short interviews based on 5 questions presented to some of the most influential and prominent scholars in epistemology. We hear their views on epistemology with particular emphasis on the intersection between mainstream and formal approaches to the field, the aim, scope, the future direction of epistemology and how their work fits in these respects.

In your hands, you have a terrific collection of interviews about epistemology by some of the leading contemporary epistemologists. An impressive array of insight, charm, and iconoclastic comments by some of the people who changed the field forever. A must read!

—**Otávio Bueno**, University of Miami

Vincent F. Hendricks and Duncan Pritchard have done the epistemology community a big favor: they have elicited revealing personal histories and comments on the state of the field from a variety of the field's leading researchers. The result is a book that will entertain and enlighten in equal parts. It is both a snapshot of various influential research trajectories as they stand at the present time, and a collection of tantalizing suggestions for new avenues of research. I recommend it especially to those thinking about the connections between what Hendricks has elsewhere called "mainstream and formal epistemology".

—**Sanford Goldberg**, Northwestern University

Think of knowledge as a primitive concept, the dynamics of belief, reliable inquiry, social judgment. Think of traditional epistemology, formal epistemology, scientific epistemology. Think of philosophy crossing with computer science, logic, psychology, sociology. Think of some of the main figures in these fields. Think of a lot of fun. Don't think twice: It's *Epistemology: 5 Questions*.

—**Hannes Leitgeb,** University of Bristol

Vincent F. Hendricks and Duncan Pritchard have produced a remarkable volume: the list of 29 interviewees reads like a "who's who" of leading contemporary epistemologists, and by carrying out interviews structured around 5 leading questions, the editors have produced a collection that anyone interested in recent and contemporary debates in epistemology will find both useful and entertaining.

—**Alexander Miller**, University of Birmingham

Index

a posteriori, 328
a priori, 70, 107, 125, 201, 317, 328
abduction, 268
acceptance, 88, 246, 253
action, 8, 69, 187
Adriaans, P., 45
agency, 32, 187, 308
agent, 43, 159, 267
    interaction, 31, 36, 158, 159
    interaction, virtual, 32
    multi-, 186, 187
    programming, 189
    resource-bounded, 267
    single, 159, 185, 187
    super-, 31, 34
agreement, 159
Alchourrón, C., 1
Alston, W., 123, 231
analyticity, 200
Anderson, E., 130
anthropology, 190, 223
anti-luminosity, 325, 327
anti-psychologism, 45
anti-realism, 325
apagoge, 183
apt performance, 307
argument, 42
Aristotle, 34, 183, 309, 336, 338
Arló-Costa, H., 1, 199, 251
Armstrong, D.M., 123
Arnauld, A., 92
Arrow's theorem, 47, 258

Artemov, S., 11
artificial intelligence, 1, 15, 34, 156, 188, 192, 204, 272, 280
assertibility, 327
Aucher, G., 30
Aumann, R., 6, 32, 157
Austin, J.L., 103, 323
awareness, 160
axiomatization, 1, 257, 311

Bachelard, G., 218
Balbiani, P., 32
Baltag, A., 21
Barcan formula, 5
Barcan Marcus, R., 7, 316
Barnes, B., 218
Baron, J., 6
Bayesian networks, 48, 52
Bayesianism, 2, 6, 48, 88, 120, 141, 191, 192, 198, 201, 202, 223, 226, 249, 331
    convergence theorems, 148, 202
Beisbart, C., 49, 59
belief, 13, 29, 40, 51, 88, 147, 160, 171, 177, 188, 213, 223, 253, 269, 307, 320, 326
    change, 1, 2
    contraction, 3, 246
    degree of, 140, 246
    deliberate expansion, 246
    full, 242
    justified, 335

liberal contraction, 3
perceptual, 269
revision, 1, 3, 30, 42, 171, 187, 188, 199
revision AGM, 1, 199, 247
routine expansion, 245
web of, 200
Bennett, J., 325
Benthem, J. van, 30, 32, 39
Berkeley, G., 105
Blackburn, S., 228
blindsight, 79
Bloor, D., 218
BMS approach, 28
Boghossian, P., 228
BonJour, L., 65, 123
botany, 34
Bovens, L., 47
brain-in-a-vat, 22, 84
Brandom, R., 244, 321
Bratman, M., 88
Brown University, 108, 306
Buber, M., 35
Buffier, C., 92

Caltech, 10
Canguilhem, G., 218
Cantor, G., 24
Carnap, R., 182, 194, 236, 311, 324
Carnegie Mellon University, 8, 118, 193
Carson, R., 71
Cartesian circle, 307
Case Western Reserve University, 253
category theory, 29
causal inference, 196
Certain Doubts, 238
certainty, 243
Chalmers, D., 144, 316
change of view, 241

Chisholm, R., 39, 108, 121, 237, 268, 306
Church, A., 324
Churchland, P., 144
closure, 13, 72, 81, 259
Coady, T., 83, 220
Code, L., 63
cognition, 261, 262, 267, 271, 277
animal, 261
cognitive achievement, 217
cognitive economy, 3
cognitive science, 35, 45, 79, 92, 182, 190, 212, 218, 319
Cohen, L.J., 246, 313
Cohen, S., 238
coherentism, 170, 241
Collins, H., 218
Columbia University, 2, 5, 8, 121, 253
commitment, 70, 144, 222, 241, 244, 289
confirmational, 242, 249
salient, 242
value, 242
communication, 29, 35, 36
communism, 25
compatibilism, 89
complexity, 11, 46, 198
computability, 15, 119, 193, 194, 201
computation, 35, 42, 162
computational resource, 35
computer science, 6, 9, 15, 34, 43, 160, 162, 188, 191, 204, 330
synthesis problem, 161
Comte, A., 92
conceptual analysis, 122, 202, 213, 226
conditional, 2, 5, 6, 145

counterfactual, 42, 162
   independence, 48, 52
Condorcet jury theorem, 54, 130
confirmation, 6, 191–194, 201
confirmation theory, 192, 199, 236, 237
consensus, 257
consequentialism, 110, 336
conservation laws, 196
constructivism
   Russian, 11
contestation, 69
contextualism, 81, 92, 227, 238
convergence, 192, 194, 202
conversation, 262
coordinated attack problem, 157
coordination, 159
Cournot, A., 92
Cox, J., 131
Craig, E., 220, 226
credence, 48, 141, 148, 202
cryptography, 15
Curry-Howard isomorphism, 12
curve fitting, 197

Daston, L., 224
Davidson, D., 87, 220
de Finetti, B., 3, 311
deceit, 29
decision theory, 6, 7, 183, 243, 311
defeasibility theory, 30
defeatism, 193
deliberation, 69
democracy, 27, 130
DeRose, K., 238
Descartes, R., 22, 99, 105, 109, 211, 308, 338
desire, 188
dialectics, 23
Dietrich, F., 50

discovery, 121, 180, 191, 193, 268, 280
discursive dilemma, 55
distributed computing, 156, 159
distributed sensor network, 190
distributed system, 159
Ditmarsch, H. van, 30, 32
domain theory, 35
Dretske, F., 30, 40, 43, 79, 96, 123
Duhem-Quine problem, 49
Dummett, M., 87, 324
Dutch Book, 50, 141, 142

Ebert, T., 49
ecological thinking, 71
economics, 1, 6, 34, 35, 131, 160, 252, 257, 330
education, 131
efficiency, 119, 193
Eliade, M., 24
Eliot, T.S., 234
Ellsberg, D., 5
Elster, J., 47
Engel, P., 87
engineering, 200
Enlightenment, 315
episteme, 338
epistemic
   action model, 28
   authority, 341
   autonomy, 341
   evaluation, 335
   event, 31, 35
   event model, 28
   justice, 77
   luck, 227, 337
   norm, 31
   practice, 71
   program, 28
   relativism, 128
   responsibility, 65

state, 29
subjectivity, 70
value, 227, 233, 340
violence, 77
virtue, 66, 336, 337
voting procedure, 31
vulnerability, 77
epistemology, 36, 72, 162, 181, 191, 217, 308, 315, 328
  a prioristic, 315
  armchair, 271, 279
  Bayesian, 1, 3, 52, 53, 140, 145–147, 204, 223, 226, 237, 249, 273
  communitarian, 221
  defensive, 1
  deontological, 336
  "Erlangen Program", 30
  Erlangen program, 37
  experimental, 92, 126, 223, 278, 280
  feminist, 225
  formal, 2, 6, 8, 9, 13, 28, 46, 133, 237, 319, 330
  fundamental, 239
  historical, 224
  interactive, 6
  'knowledge first', 140
  mainstream, 8, 9, 13, 29, 34, 91, 120, 130, 147, 214, 237, 319
  meta-, 89
  naturalized, 8, 70, 122, 124, 317
  naturalized-as-engineering, 200
  normative, 88, 91, 318, 319
  pedigree, 241
  philosophical, 218
  procedural, 271, 277
  religious, 335
  social, 92, 127, 130, 225
  'value turn in', 337
  value-driven, 233
  virtue, 89, 133, 306
Estlund, D., 130
ethics, 73, 89, 214, 235, 336
  meta-, 89
evidence, 35, 39, 43, 60, 80, 199, 327
  legal, 129
  variety of, 54
evidentialism, 89
existentialism, 64
experiment, 8, 49, 80, 92, 125, 131, 180, 200, 213, 219, 223, 278, 331
  scientific, 83
  thought, 22, 278, 328
explanation, 180
externalism, 80, 82, 108, 123, 227, 326, 335
extinction, 79

Fagin, R., 13, 156, 159
Feyerabend, P., 79
first philosophy, 87, 218, 328, 339
Fitch paradox, 32, 42, 324
Fitch, F., 324
Fitting, M., 13
Fogelin, R.J., 95
Føllesdal, D., 316
formal learning theory, 6, 46, 119, 192, 193, 201
formalization, 28, 31, 188, 302
Foucault, M., 87, 218
foundationalism, 170, 241
Free University of Amsterdam, 186
Frege, G., 316
Fricker, M., 77, 225
Friedman, M., 118

Fries, J.F., 92
Fumerton, R., 105

Galison, P., 224
game theory, 7, 8, 32, 35, 37, 42, 156, 159, 162, 186, 311
Gärdenfors, P., 6
Gärdernfors, P., 1
Geach, P., 40
genealogy, 226
geography, 34
Gerbrandy, J., 30
German idealism, 321
Gettier problem, 40, 96, 121, 205, 226, 234, 258, 268, 280, 306, 323
Gettier, E., 306
Gigerenzer, G., 4, 6
Gilbert , M., 49
Ginet, C., 122
Glass, D., 53
Glymour, C., 117, 191
Gödel, K., 11
Gödel's incompleteness theorem, 11
Gold, E.M., 198
Goldman, A.I., 105, 225
Goldszmidt,M., 313
Goodman, N., 280
Grice, H.P., 121

Haack, S., 228
Habermas, J., 218
Hájek, A., 139
Halpern, J.Y., 13, 155
halting, 193
Hanson, N.R., 79
happiness, 340
Hardin, R., 69
Harper, W., 1
Hartmann, S., 49, 53
Hawthorne, J., 48, 52, 238

Hayek, F., 258
Hegel, G.W.F., 92, 218
Heidegger, M., 218
Helzner, J., 5
Hempel, C., 175, 191
Hendricks, V.F., 16, 199
Herzig, T., 32
Heyting, A., 11
Hinman, P., 195
Hintikka, J., 7, 9, 13, 40, 159, 179, 219, 224, 329
history of science, 218, 221
Hoek, W.v. der, 185
Hoshi, H., 32
Hume, D., 145, 183, 191, 267
Hurley, S., 47, 51
Hurwicz, L., 47
Husserl, E., 218

ideology, 21
ignorance, 29
illusion, 29
indiscriminability, 325
individualism, 69
induction, 2, 182, 191, 195, 246, 267, 268, 280
  backward, 32
  enumerative, 113
  problem of, 192
  statistical, 275
inductive amnesia, 199
inference, 29, 33, 91, 119, 147, 180, 183
inference to best explanation, 280
information, 16, 29, 35, 40, 41, 54, 79, 80, 183, 186, 298
  secret, 161
  theory, 46
information science, 131
inquiry, 180, 194, 211, 235, 241, 329

philosophical, 329
institution, 190
intension, 316
intention, 188
interaction, 35
   multi-agent, 43
internalism, 101, 114, 123, 201, 335
introspection, 29, 42, 126
   negative, 159, 331
   positive, 331, *see also* KK principle
intuition, 8, 102, 125, 201, 223, 278, 280
intuitionism, 42
invariantism, 238

Jackson, F., 109
Jeffrey, R., 1, 88, 140
journalism, 131
justification, 12, 14, 43, 80, 89, 105, 107, 121, 147, 180, 184, 191, 192, 194, 227, 233, 244, 269, 273, 327, 335, 336
   coherence theory, 58
   procedural, 270

Kadane, J., 242
Kahneman, D., 6
Kant, I., 34, 92, 317
Kaplan, D., 315
KARO, 187
Kelly, K.T., 191
Kemp, K., 341
Kim, J., 306
Kitcher, P., 130
KK principle, 325
Klein, F., 29
Klein, P., 30
knowability, 32, 324

knowledge, 13, 28, 30, 39, 41, 88, 130, 147, 158, 160, 177, 187, 213, 223, 260, 286, 307, 326, 337, 339
   -seeking, 183
   a posteriori, 328
   a priori, 227, 328
   acquisition, 184
   algorithmic, 161
   and democracy, 130
   armchair, 328
   Cartesian, 294
   causal theory, 121, 123
   change, 42
   commitment, 286
   common, 6, 29, 32, 99, 156, 185, 187
   de dicto, 187
   de re, 187
   distributed, 185
   empirical, 105
   everyday, 214
   explicit, 160
   group, 31, 190
   'high grade', 340
   how, 215
   implicit, 92, 160
   justified true belief, 14, 90, 96, 306, 320
   limit, 325
   logic of, 5
   mathematical, 292
   modal, 158
   no-relevant-alternatives, 123
   of other minds, 280
   perceptual, 122, 280
   philosophical, 221
   presentation, 286
   procedural, 279
   propositional, 215

reasoning about, 156
representation, 286
scientific, 90, 192
self-, 216, 340
sociology of, 174, 218, 222, 226, 241
sources, 69
that, 215
Kolmogorov, A.N., 3, 11
Kooi, B., 30
Koppl, R., 131
Kornblith, H., 124, 211, 220
Koster, M., 50
Kripke, S., 7, 13, 220, 315, 320
Kuhn, T., 79, 127, 174
Kvanvig, J., 231

language, 63
    evaluative, 95
Laudan, L., 129, 192, 200
law, 15
learnability, 32, 194, 198
learning, 29, 31, 35, 40, 42, 185, 193
learning efficiency, 196
Leeds, S., 48
Lehrer, K., 30, 88
Lehrer, T., 120
Levi, I., 1, 2, 9, 88, 241
Lewis, C.I., 113, 237
Lewis, D., 2, 6, 100, 140, 147, 311
Libertarian paradox, 51
Lindner, I., 50
linguistic relativism, 63
linguistics, 43, 63, 218
Lipton, P., 220
List, C., 131
Lloyd, G., 67
Locke, J., 211
logic, 25, 40, 44, 46, 218

alternating-time temporal, 187
categorical, 41
description, 188
doxastic, 179, 283
dynamic epistemic, 28, 30, 31, 42, 186
epistemic, 4, 12, 41, 158, 179, 185, 204, 224, 257, 283, 329, 331
first-order, 5, 12, 36
intuitionistic, 12, 324
justification, 12, 36
linear, 35
mathematical, 11, 26, 181
modal, 11, 12, 41, 158, 185, 257
    normal, 7
    S4, 12, 41, 158
    S5, 12, 159, 185
non-monotonic, 5, 187
of games, 42, 187
of induction, 193
of inquiry, 180
of knowledge, 159
of proofs, 12
philosophical, 6
philosophy of, 193
provability, 11
second generation epistemic, 179
temporal, 35
logical dynamics, 42
logical omniscience, 2, 4, 7, 13, 42, 160, 204, 257, 331
London School of Economics, 8
Lorenz, K., 317
Lorenzen, P., 40
Lottery paradox, 3, 5, 52

Macmurray, J., 64

Magid, C., 119
Makinson, D., 1
Margalit, E.U., 91
margin for error principle, 325
Markov, A.A., 11
Marr, D., 182
Martinez, M., 41
materialism, 24
mathematics, 15, 24, 27, 181, 193
Matrix, 22
meaning, 100
medicine, 167
Melbourne University, 139
memory, 42, 92, 267
Meno, 117
menu dependence, 4
Messing, K., 75
metaphysics, 7, 90, 93, 111, 214, 312, 316, 328, 338, 339
method, 119, 147, 192
    scientific, 59, 191, 196
methodology, 125, 181, 184, 191, 241, 271, 277, 318
Meyer, A., 257
Mihalache,D., 32
Mill, J.S., 92, 113, 191, 235
Miller, D., 324
modality, 7
    deontic, 95
    epistemic, 95
Montague, R., 5, 7
Moore, G.E., 237
Moore's paradox, 51, 142
morality, 110
Morgenbesser, S., 2, 241
Moscow University, 11
Moses, Y., 158, 159
Moss, L., 28
muddy children puzzle, 155

Nagel, E., 121, 241
Nagel, T., 228
Nash equilibrium, 186
naturalism, 122, 125, 178, 192, 200, 221, 236
    normative, 200
negotiation, 69, 70
neurophysiology, 317
neuroscience, 182
Newton, I., 183
Nicod principle, 280
Nola, R., 200
non-monotonicity, 2, 5
Normore, C., 218
Nozick, R., 5, 30, 40, 43

obligation, 258
observation, 29, 35, 36
observational equivalence, 35
occult force, 192
Ockham's razor, 192, 196, 198, 201
Oddie, G., 48
Olivi, P.J., 270
Olsson, E.J., 48, 52
operationalism, 331
opportunity, 187
OSCAR Project, 272
Osherson, D., 6

Pacuit, E., 5
Parikh, R., 3, 5, 35, 257
Pascal's wager, 147
Peacocke, C., 83
Pearl, J., 48, 313
Pedersen, P., 4
Peirce, C.S., 92, 254
perception, 79, 80, 111
perspective
    first person, 143, 271, 338
    third person, 143, 338
persuasion, 29
Pettit, P., 49, 131

phenomenology, 64
philosophy, 202, 212, 315
   analytic, 218
   armchair, 271, 328
   Continental, 64, 218
   experimental, 8, 126, 318, 331
   history of, 221
   moral, 51, 72, 329
   of action, 90
   of information, 44
   of language, 87, 90, 214, 312
   of logic, 311
   of mind, 79, 82, 214, 312
   of probability, 311
   of science, 44, 90, 109, 191, 214, 312
phronesis, 336
physics, 196
Plato, 24, 34, 308, 338
plausibility, 28
political science, 35
political theory, 130, 225
Pollock, J.L., 9, 267
Popkin, R., 96
Popper, K., 174, 323
positivism, 191, 195, 237, 331
possible worlds, 28, 29, 102, 159, 195, 199, 259
PPM, 50
pragmatism, 89, 241
prediction, 198
Preface paradox, 52
preference, 32, 44, 51
presumption, 91
Princeton University, 121
Principal principle, 147
priority update, 30
privacy, 29
probability, 28, 48, 311, 313, 324
   Baconian, 313
   conditional, 3, 145
   generic, 274
   nomic, 274
   prior, 203
   singular, 274
   subjective, 88, 147, 273
probability theory, 2, 3, 46, 139, 140, 145, 249, 273, 331
process, 35, 42
process algebra, 35
product, 42
product update, 29, 30
proof, 12, 42, 161
propositional attitude, 290
provability, 11, 313
psychologism, 221
psychology, 35, 45, 241, 317
   cognitive, 204
   developmental, 218, 223
   experimental, 331
   mathematical, 1
public announcement, 28
publicity, 28
Pulp Fiction, 139
Putnam, H., 83, 194, 196, 198, 315

Quine, W.V., 8, 70, 105, 122, 200, 317

Rabinowicz, W., 49, 55
radical interpretation, 87
Ramsey test, 42
Ramsey, F.P., 6
ranking theory, 312
rational choice theory, 47
rationality, 4, 7, 9, 32, 35, 110, 178, 193, 199, 233, 267, 318, 319
   bounded, 2, 4, 7
   paradoxes, 5

Rawls, J., 315
realism, 192
   direct, 269, 270
   messianic, 254
   modal , 7
   myopic, 254
   woo-woo, 192
reality, 22
reasoning, 16, 90, 161, 219, 267
   causal, 280
   counterfactual, 32
   defeasible, 268, 272
   probabilistic, 275
   temporal, 280
recall, 185
reductionism, 221
reflective equilibrium, 201
refutability, 195
Reichenbach, H., 192, 194
Reid, T., 270
relativism, 228
relevant alternatives, 81, 122
reliabilism, 123, 192, 236, 336
   process, 123
reliability, 54, 123, 192, 202
Rescher, N., 268
result, 187
Rheinberger, H.-J., 224
Riggs, W., 337
Romania, 21
Rorty, R., 128
Roskilde University, 195
Ross, S., 48
Rouse, J., 76
Rubinstein, A., 59
runs-and-systems model, 159
Russell, B., 64, 305
Ryle, G., 40

safety, 30
Samuelson, L., 251
Sapir-Whorf hypothesis, 63

Sartre, J.-P., 43
Schaffer, S., 218
Schervish, M., 242
Schulte, O., 196
science, 117, 169, 181, 191, 192
scientific practice, 192
scientific socialism, 23
Scott, D., 5, 7
security, 161
Seidenfeld, T., 242
Sellars, W., 321
semantic web, 189
semantics, 63, 187, 257
   game, 35
   Kripke, 13, 29
   neighborhood, 4, 7
   possible world, 4, 7, 41, 159, 325
   two-dimensional, 315
Sen, A., 4, 8
Shaked, M., 131
Shapin, S., 218
Sherlock Holmes, 180
Simon, H., 4, 7
simplicity, 192, 196
simulation, 8
situation theory, 41
skepticism, 44, 58, 64, 81, 89, 99, 110, 125, 235, 250, 337
   inductive, 194
   Pyrrhonian, 307
Skyrms, B., 141
Slangen, H., 39
Sleeping Beauty, 50, 59, 120
Smets, S., 30
Snyder, J., 50
social choice theory, 31, 43, 190
social software, 35, 260

Society of Christian Philosophers, 335
sociologism, 221
sociology, 35
Socrates, 184
Solecki, S., 28
Sosa, E., 108, 220, 305
split brains, 79
Spohn, W., 9, 30, 48, 311
Stalnaker, R., 2, 32, 88, 162, 315
Stanley, J., 215, 238, 327
statement, 42
  evaluative, 95
statistics, 191
Stegmüller, W., 311
Stich, S., 144
Strawson, P.F., 321
subjectivity, 35, 66, 69, 73
Sunstein, C., 130
Swampman, 44
Symons, J., 182

T-schema, 293
TARK, 41
techne, 339
theory choice, 192, 193
Thomason, R., 2
topology, 195, 257
Toulmin, S., 268
tracking, 45, 81
Tragedy of the Commons, 50
transcendental idealism, 320
truth, 21, 22, 27, 147, 191, 192, 196, 200, 201, 323, 324
  -conduciveness, 191, 194, 202
  -finding, 194
  -tracking, 192, 202
  occult, 198
  maker, 111
Turing machine, 36, 196

Tuttle, M., 159

UC Irvine, 8
uncertainty, 243
unilateral neglect, 79
University of Amsterdam, 45
University of Colorado, 47
University of Konstanz, 50
University of Konstanz , 48
University of Miami, 305
University of Michigan, 121
University of Minnesota, 47
University of Oklahoma, 48
University of Oslo, 47
University of Pittsburgh, 10, 191, 305
University of Western Ontario, 140, 305

vagueness, 325
value theory, 110, 225
values in science, 175
van Fraassen, B., 1, 3, 88, 140, 192, 251
Vardi, M., 156, 159
verifiability, 195
verificationism, 42, 324
verisimilitude, 324
visual cognition, 182
von Wright, G.H., 179, 219

Warfield, F., 238
warrant, 233, 244
Whewell, W., 92
Williams, B., 220, 226
Williams, M., 220
Williamson, T., 9, 30, 215, 220, 224, 323
Wissenschaft, 174
Wittgenstein, L., 64, 99, 103, 219, 235, 268

Zagzebski, L., 335

zoology, 34
Zuck, L., 159
Zvesper, J., 32

www.ingramcontent.com/pod-product-compliance
Lightning Source LLC
Chambersburg PA
CBHW032000220426
43664CB00005B/81